W9-CAA-895

Welcome to Scandinavia & Northern Europe

Effortlessly chic cities, many with charming historic centres, contrast with soul-stirring coastal scenery, remote wildernesses and cutting-edge urban design. Inspiring food and a full menu of seasons make Northern Europe a premium cruise destination.

Stolid northern stereotypes dissolve in the region's vibrant capitals. Crest-of-the-wave design can be seen in many, backed by outstanding modern architecture, excellent museums and galleries, imaginative solutions for 21st-century urban living, internationally acclaimed restaurants and a night-life that fizzes along despite sometimes-hefty beer prices.

A palpable sense of history is present throughout: the Vikings dominated these seas, the Hanseatic trading cartel put port cities on the map in medieval times, while the seismic impact of 20th-century events left deep scars throughout.

You'll rarely come across the word 'ecotourism' in northern Europe, but those values have long been an important part of life here. Generally, green, sustainable solutions are a way of living, rather than a gimmick to attract visitors. Scandinavia, in particular, will likely be significantly affected by climate change and big efforts to reduce emissions are being made across the region. Travelling here, you'll be struck by the excellent levels of environ-mental protection, the sensible 'why don't we do that back home' impact-reducing strategies and the forward thinking so much in evidence. It makes for pleasurably enlightening travel.

soul-stirring coastal scenery, remote wildernesses and cutting-edge urban design

Bergen, Norway (p126)

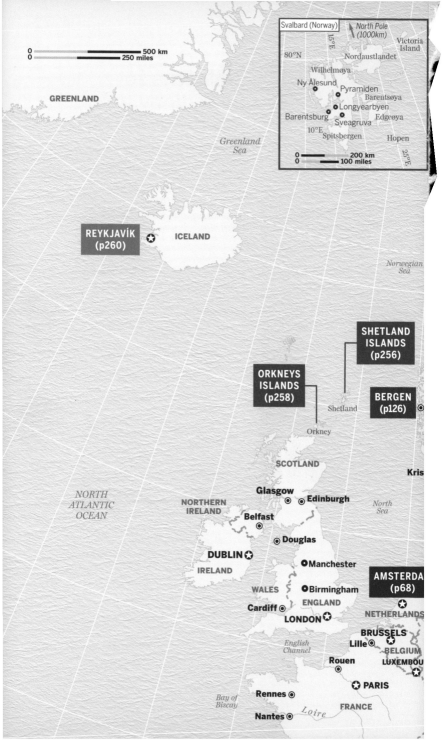

0 ————————— 500 km
0 ———— 250 miles

GREENLAND

Svalbard (Norway)

North Pole
(1000km)

80°N   Nordaustlandet   Victoria
                                            Island

Ny Ålesund   Pyramiden
                  •   Barentsøya
              Longyearbyen
Barentsburg   •   Edgeøya
              Sveagruva
10°E
      Spitsbergen   Hopen

0 ————— 200 km
0 ———— 100 miles

Greenland
Sea

Norwegian
Sea

REYKJAVÍK
(p260)   ICELAND

SHETLAND
ISLANDS
(p256)

ORKNEYS
ISLANDS
(p258)

BERGEN
(p126)

Shetland

Orkney

NORTH
ATLANTIC
OCEAN

SCOTLAND   Kris

Glasgow
      Edinburgh   *North*
NORTHERN   *Sea*
IRELAND
Belfast

Douglas

DUBLIN

IRELAND   Manchester

WALES   Birmingham
Cardiff   ENGLAND   **AMSTERDA**
LONDON   **(p68)**

                              NETHERLANDS

                        BRUSSELS
English   Lille
Channel   BELGIUM
            Rouen   **LUXEMBOU**

Bay of   Rennes   **PARIS**
Biscay
        Nantes   *Loire*   FRANCE

In Focus

Survival Guide

Geirangerfjord (p135), Norway
TRPHOTOS/SHUTTERSTOCK ©

Plan Your Trip
Scandinavia & Northern Europe's Top 12

MICHAEL BROOKS/ALAMY ©

Berlin

Edgy and innovative; a great European city

Berlin's glamour and grit are bound to mesmerise anyone keen on exploring its vibrant culture, edgy architecture, fabulous food, intense parties and palpable history. Since the Wall's demise in 1989, the German capital has become sophisticated, retaining its indie spirit and penchant for creative improvisation. Visit major historical sights – the Reichstag, Brandenburger Tor and Checkpoint Charlie – then feast on a smorgasbord of culture in myriad museums. Above from left: East Side Gallery (p39); Brandenburger Tor (p48)

MEUNIERD/SHUTTERSTOCK ©

YURY DMITRIENKO/SHUTTERSTOCK ©

Amsterdam

World-class art and sublime canalscapes

The Dutch capital is one of Europe's most vibrant cities, luring visitors with its top-notch art, urban vitality and watery geography. Amsterdam made its fortune in maritime trade, and its Canal Ring was constructed during the city's Golden Age. Stroll alongside the canals and check out the narrow, gabled houses and thousands of houseboats; relax on a canal-side *café* (pub) terrace; or, better still, go for a ride. Top: Van Gogh Museum (p72); Bottom: Herengracht canal (p88)

2

MECHIKA/ALAMY ©

Copenhagen

Trailblazing city in numerous ways

While this 850-year-old town retains its historic good looks (copper spires, cobbled squares and pastel-coloured gables), the focus is on innovation. Denmark's capital has a thriving design scene, a futuristic metro, and clean, green developments. Its streets are awash with effortlessly hip shops, cafes and bars; world-class museums and art collections; brave new architecture; and 15 Michelin-starred restaurants. Dining room at Geranium (p107)

3

Oslo

Elegant art city on the rise

Oslo is aiming to become nothing less than a world-renowned centre of art and culture. It's already bursting at the seams with superb museums, art galleries and a glacier-white opera house (pictured right) that could make even Sydney jealous, but in the past couple of years it has achieved a striking rebirth of its waterfront district complete with daring architecture, a grade-A modern-art gallery, new restaurants and even a beach. This is a city on the rise. Inside the Oslo Opera House (p119)

Bergen

Stunningly beautiful Norwegian waterside city

Set amid a picturesque and very Norwegian coastal landscape of fjords and mountains, Bergen is one of Europe's most beautiful cities. A celebrated history of seafaring trade has bequeathed to the city the stunning waterfront district of Bryggen, an archaic tangle of wooden buildings. A signpost to a history at once prosperous and tumultuous, the titled and colourful wooden buildings now shelter the artisan boutiques and traditional restaurants for which the city is increasingly famous.

KIEV.VICTOR/SHUTTERSTOCK ©

Stockholm

Stately, handsome monarch of the Baltic

Sweden's capital calls itself 'beauty on water', and it certainly doesn't disappoint: its many glittering waterways reflect slanted northern light onto spice-hued buildings, and the crooked cobblestone streets of Gamla Stan are magic to wander. Besides its aesthetic virtues, Stockholm also has wonderful museums, first-class dining and great shopping. Its clean and efficient public transport, and multilingual locals, make it a cinch to navigate.

GRISHA BRUEV/SHUTTERSTOCK ©

Helsinki

Architecture and design-driven archipelago capital

It's fitting that harbourside Helsinki, capital of a country with such a watery geography, melds so graciously into the Baltic; half the city seems to be liquid. It's a quirky, innovative place with legendary design shops, striking contemporary architecture and a humming music scene. On the other hand, its older charms are also lovable; savour the spacious elegance of its centenarian cafes and the careful preservation of Finnish heritage in its numerous museums.

7

St Petersburg
Imperial splendour; magnificent art and culture

This grand Baltic city is quite a sight. Grand imperial palaces line the embankments of the Neva River, its tributaries and canals. Restoration has been painstaking – and the results are breathtaking. Little can prepare most visitors for the scale and quality of the exhibits at the State Hermitage Museum, an almost unrivalled history of Western art, while the famed Mariinsky Theatre offers the ultimate in classical ballet and operatic experiences. Interior of St Isaac's Cathedral (p195)

ZHUKOV OLEG./SHUTTERSTOCK ©

GRISHA BRUEV/
SHUTTERSTOCK ©

9

Tallinn

Enticingly atmospheric medieval jewel

There was a time when sturdy walls and turreted towers enclosed most of Europe's cities, but wartime bombing and the advent of the car put paid to most of them. Tallinn's Old Town is a magical window into that bygone world. Rambling lanes lined with medieval dwellings open onto squares once covered in the filth of everyday commerce but now lined with cafes and altogether less gory markets selling souvenirs and handicrafts. From right: Katariina Käik (p219); Traditional knitwear

Reykjavík
Small but perfectly formed island capital

Though petite, Reykjavík boasts all the treats you'd expect of a European capital. With kilometres of nothing but nature all around, it's Iceland's confirmed repository of all things cultural. Striking modern architecture and excellent museums mean there's plenty to see, and the fabulous local cafe-bar culture is invigorating. There's also great shopping, from sleek, fish-skin purses to knitted *lopapeysur* (Icelandic woollen sweaters) and nature-inspired jewellery.

Top: Colourful houses; Above left: Hallgrímskirkja (p271); Above right: Knitted jumpers

Rīga

A treasure trove of art nouveau

Ask Rīgans where to find the city's world-famous art-nouveau architecture, and the answer is always 'Look up!' More than 750 buildings in Latvia's capital – more than any European city – boast this flamboyant, haunting style. Spend an afternoon photographing the imaginative facades in the Quiet Centre to find an ethereal, almost eerie melange of screaming demons, enraptured deities, overgrown flora and bizarre geometrical patterns.

11

Gdańsk

Classic Hanseatic mercantile port

Colossal red-brick churches peer over slender merchants' townhouses, wedged ornately between palaces that line wide, ancient thoroughfares and crooked medieval lanes. A cosmopolitan residue of art and artefact, from a rich maritime and trading past, fills whole museums; tourists from around the world compete with amber stalls and street performers for cobblestone space. Once part of the Hanseatic League, now it's in a league of its own.

12

Plan Your Trip
Need to Know

When to Go

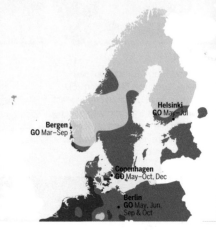

Warm to hot summers, cold winters
Mild year round
Mild summers, cold to very cold winters
Polar climate

Reykjavik
GO Jun–Aug

Helsinki
GO May–Jul

Bergen
GO Mar–Sep

Copenhagen
GO May–Oct, Dec

Berlin
GO May, Jun,
Sep & Oct

High Season (Jun–Aug)

o All attractions are open but can be very busy.

o Boat tours and other outdoor activities running.

o Long days; numerous festivals.

Shoulder (Apr, May, Sep & Oct)

o Expect chilly nights, and even snow in northern Scandinavia.

o Far less crowding at popular destinations like fjords.

o Less queuing at major attractions; some close or reduce their hours.

Low Season (Nov–Mar)

o Outside cities, some attractions are closed.

o Winter activities possible in Scandinavia.

o Short, cool or cold days.

Currency

Denmark: Danish krone (kr; DKK)
Germany, Netherlands, Finland, Estonia & Latvia: euro (€; EUR)
Iceland: Icelandic króna (kr; ISK)
Norway: Norwegian krone (kr; NOK)
Poland: złoty (zł)
Russia: rouble (R)
Scotland: pounds sterling (£)
Sweden: Swedish krona (kr; SEK)

Languages

Danish, Dutch, Estonian, Finnish, German, Icelandic, Latvian, Norwegian, Polish, Russian and Swedish. English is widely spoken.

Visas

Visas not needed for most nationalities for stays up to three months in most countries. Most visitors require visas for Russia, but this is waived for cruise passengers on organised tours.

Money

ATMs widely available, including in cruise terminals. Credit cards mostly accepted.

Costs for a Day in Port
Budget: Less than €80
- Bike hire for day: €10–25
- Lunch specials: €10–18
- Daily public transport pass: €4–8

Midrange: €80–150
- Group walking tour: €15–30
- Two-course meal for two with wine: €100–150
- Museum entry: €5–15

Top end: More than €150
- Private day tour: €200–400
- Upmarket degustation menu for two with wine: €200–400
- Taxi across town: €20–40

Pre-departure Checklist
- Make reservations for top restaurants way ahead of time.
- Book pre- and post-cruise accommodation.
- Check for reciprocal health cover and, if not available, arrange travel insurance.
- Obtain a Russian visa if you're planning independent exploration of St Petersburg.

What to Wear
Northern Europeans have mastered the art of dressing casually without looking scruffy, but you'll fit in no matter what you choose to wear. The St Petersburg entertainment and dining scenes are a bit dressier.

For winter visits you'll need decent thermal underwear, waterproof boots and top layer, woolly hat, gloves and a neck warmer.

What to wear in the sauna: nothing! Locals never wear swimsuits there.

Time Zones
- Iceland: Western European Time (GMT/UTC plus zero hours)
- Denmark, Germany, Netherlands, Norway, Poland and Sweden: Central European Time (GMT/UTC plus one hour)
- Finland, Estonia, Latvia and Russia (St Petersburg): Eastern European Time (GMT/UTC plus two hours)
All but Iceland and Russia use summer time from late March to late October.

Wi-fi Access
- Wireless (wi-fi) hot spots are rife. Numerous cafes and bars, and most tourist offices and libraries, offer the service for free. A number of towns and cities in the region have free public wi-fi across the centre.
- Data is cheap. Buy a local SIM card, pop it in an unlocked phone, laptop or USB modem, and away you go. Deals may mean you pay as little as €15 to €20 for a month's unlimited access in EU countries.
- Internet cafes are increasingly uncommon, but libraries provide free or very cheap internet service.

Getting Around the Port
- Shuttle services are often provided from cruise terminals to city centres, but these may be expensive and/or oblige you to take an associated tour. Most cruise terminals have effective public transport access too.
- The region's cities generally have efficient, integrated public transport networks with buses, trains and trams operating.
- Bike hire is a good way of getting around, with an excellent network of cycle lanes in most of the region's cities. Bike share schemes are common.
- Taxis are easily hired but are quite expensive in Nordic countries. Ride-sharing is available in some cities but banned in others.

For more on **transport**, see p312

Plan Your Trip
Hot Spots for...

MEUNIERD/SHUTTERSTOCK ©

Art

The cities of Northern Europe are treasure troves of local and international art, from venerable masterpieces to contemporary installations.

St Petersburg (p180)
The stupendous array of art assembled by the Russian royals is the world's largest collection of paintings.

The Hermitage (p184)
Perhaps the world's premier gallery.

Amsterdam (p68)
Admire the Rembrandts, Vermeers and van Goghs in Amsterdam's gallery district.

Van Gogh Museum (p72)
Grand collection of one of the world's best-loved artists.

Oslo (p110)
Oslo's art scene flies under the radar but is one of Europe's best, with a great range of galleries.

Astrup Fearnley Museet (p119)
Late-20th-century art surrounded by a sculpture park.

EVIKKA/SHUTTERSTOCK ©

Architecture & Design

From opulent royal palaces to avant-garde contemporary creations, striking buildings and innovative modern design are found right across the region.

Copenhagen (p90)
An eclectic assemblage of striking historic and modern buildings combine with shopping opportunities.

Designmuseum Danmark (p96) Crash course in Danish design.

Helsinki (p162)
The Finnish capital has long been enlivening its centre with striking contemporary buildings.

Musiikkitalo (p178)
Concert hall as crisp as a gin-and-tonic on a glacier.

Rīga (p222)
A menagerie of gargoyles, praying goddesses and twisting vines inhabits the city's art-nouveau architecture.

Alberta Iela (p228)
The Latvian capital's most striking Jugendstil street.

Scenery

The Baltic coast's waterways and islands are marvellously scenic. In the North Atlantic, Norway's epic beauty and Iceland's volcano-wrought majesty are never forgotten.

B-HIDE THE SCENE/SHUTTERSTOCK ©

Reykjavík (p260)
Iceland's capital is gateway to some easily accessed examples of the island's savage grandeur.

Golden Circle (p268)
Geological phenomena on this cracking daytrip.

Bergen (p126)
Picturesque Bergen is Norway's prettiest city and within easy reach of some of awe-inspiring fjords.

Geirangerfjord (p135)
Fjordland's poster child is heart-stoppingly beautiful.

Stockholm (p144)
The gentle watery beauty of the archipelago provides a spectacular setting for Sweden's capital.

Fjäderholmarna (p156)
A boat tour here is a great archipelago taster.

History

Awesome Stone Age monuments, the Hanseatic League and the seismic events of the 20th century: Northern Europe is full of reminders of the distant and recent past.

MICHAL BEDNAREK/SHUTTERSTOCK ©

Orkney Islands (p258)
Stunning neolithic remnants on this archipelago continue to revolutionise understanding of the period.

Skara Brae (p258)
Astonishingly well-preserved 5000-year-old village.

Berlin (p34)
Such a major focus of so much of 20th-century world history, from the Holocaust to the Cold War.

Holocaust Memorial (p48)
Sobering stones commemorate six million murdered souls.

Gdańsk (p238)
Reconstructed Hanseatic merchants' quarter contrasts with reminders of WWII and the Cold War.

Żuraw (p249)
Medieval masterpiece symbolising Gdańsk's past.

Plan Your Trip
Month by Month

GINGER POLINA BUBLIK/SHUTTERSTOCK ©

February

There's enough light now for it to be prime winter sports season in northern Scandinavia.

✗ Þorrablót, Iceland

Held all across the country, nominally in honour of the god Thor, this midwinter festival's centrepiece is a feast for the fearless that includes delicacies such as fermented shark.

☆ Berlin Film Festival

Stars, directors and critics sashay down the red carpet for two weeks of screenings and glamour parties at the Berlinale (www.berlinale.de), one of Europe's most prestigious celluloid festivals.

March

As the hours of light dramatically increase and temperatures begin to rise, the first rumours of spring appear in the south while there's still hefty snow cover further north.

⚐ Sled Trips

Whizzing across the snow pulled by a team of huskies or reindeer is a pretty spectacular way to see the northern wildernesses. Add snowmobiling or skiing to the mix and it's a top time to be at high latitude. Many winter cruises have options for doing this in northern Norway.

April

Easter is celebrated in a traditional fashion across the region. Spring is well underway in Denmark and other southern parts, but there's still solid snow in the north.

☆ Jazzkaar, Tallinn

Late April sees jazz greats from around the world converge on Estonia's picturesque capital (www.jazzkaar.ee).

✿ King's Day (Koningsdag), Amsterdam

The biggest – and possibly the best – street party in Europe celebrates the monarch on 27 April (26 April if the 27th is a Sunday).

STEVE PHOTOGRAPHY/SHUTTERSTOCK ©

In Amsterdam, expect plenty of uproarious boozing, live music and merriment, plus a giant free market.

May

A transitional month up north, with snow beginning to disappear and signs of life emerging after the long winter. Down south, spring is in full flow. A rewarding time to visit the southern capitals.

☆ Bergen International Festival, Norway

One of the biggest events on Norway's cultural calendar, this two-week festival (www.fib.no), in late May, showcases dance, music and folklore presentations, some international, some traditional local culture.

☆ Reykjavík Arts Festival, Iceland

Running for two weeks from late May to June in even-numbered years, this wide-ranging festival (www.listahatid.is) sees Iceland's capital taken over by theatre performances, films, lectures and music.

★ Best Events

King's Day, Amsterdam, April

Bergen International Festival, May

White Nights, St Petersburg, June-July

Aurora watching, November

Christmas, December

June

Midsummer is celebrated with gusto in Scandinavia, but it's typically a family event. The cities partly shut down so this is not always the best time to visit.

⚜ Old Town Days, Tallinn

This week-long Estonian festival (www.vanalinnapaevad.ee) in early June features dancing, concerts, costumed performers and plenty of medieval merrymaking in the heart of Tallinn's stunning historic centre.

From left: Aurora borealis; King's Day celebrations

☆ Stockholm Jazz Festival, Sweden

Held on the island of Skeppsholmen in the centre of Stockholm, this well-known jazz fest (stockholmjazz.se) brings artists from all over, including big international names.

✵ Midsummer, Denmark, Norway, Sweden, Finland

The year's biggest event in continental Nordic Europe sees fun family feasts, joyous celebrations of the summer, heady bonfires and copious drinking, often at normally peaceful lakeside summer cottages. On the weekend that falls between 19 and 26 June.

☆ White Nights, St Petersburg

As days lengthen, Russia's cultural capital, St Petersburg, hosts a huge party (until late July), including a jam-packed itinerary of shows at the Mariinsky Theatre & Concert Hall (p199).

July

Peak season sees long days and sunshine. Scandinavia is at its most vibrant, with many festivals and activities and a celebratory feel.

☆ Copenhagen Jazz Festival, Denmark

The year's biggest entertainment event over 10 days in early July. The festival (http://jazz.dk) features Danish and international jazz, blues and fusion music, at more than 500 indoor and outdoor concerts.

August

Decent weather across most of the region. Many Scandinavians are back at work, but other Europeans are on holidays. A great time for cruising, though some stops will be very busy.

✕ Copenhagen Cooking & Food Festival, Denmark

Scandinavia's largest food festival (www. copenhagencooking.com) focuses on the gourmet. It's a busy event that lets you see presentations from top chefs, go on food-oriented tours of the city and taste produce.

✵ Dominican Fair, Gdańsk

Gdańsk's biggest bash (www.jarmark dominika.pl) since 1260. Launched by Dominican monks as a feast day, the fun has spread to streets around the Main Town.

October

Snow is already beginning to carpet the region's north. It's generally a quiet time, as locals face the realities of yet another long winter approaching.

⌂ Hem & Villa, Stockholm, Sweden

Held across Sweden's two largest cities, Stockholm and Gothenburg, this major interior design fair (www.hemochvilla.se) highlights upcoming trends. You'll be years ahead of your Ikea-going friends.

November

The clocks change in late October; there's no denying winter. November's bad for winter activities as there's little light and not enough snow. It can be good for seeing the aurora borealis.

❅ Aurora Watching

Whether you are blessed with seeing the aurora borealis is largely a matter of luck, but the further north you are, the better the chances. Dark, cloudless nights, patience and a viewing spot away from lights are other key factors.

December

The Christmas period is celebrated enthusiastically across the region, with cinnamon, mulled drinks, romantic lights and festive traditions.

✵ Christmas

Whether visiting Santa and his reindeer in Lapland, admiring the magic of Copenhagen's Tivoli at night or sampling home-baked delicacies at a Berlin market, Christmas is a heart-warming time to be here.

Plan Your Trip
Get Inspired

Read

Njál's Saga (Anonymous; 13th century) Gloriously entertaining story of a bloody family feud in Iceland.

Kalevala (Elias Lönnrot; 1849) Finland's national epic is a wonderful world of everything from sorcerer-shamans to saunas and home-brewing tips.

The Diary of Anne Frank (Anne Frank; 1947) Moving account of a young girl's life hiding from the Nazis.

The Girl with the Dragon Tattoo (Stieg Larsson; 2005) The first book of the Swedish noir trilogy that captivated the world.

Berlin Alexanderplatz (Alfred Döblin; 1929) Berlin in the 1920s.

Watch

Wild Strawberries (1957) Ingmar Bergman's sensitivity comes to the fore in this masterpiece.

The Man without a Past (2002) Quirky Finnish brilliance from Aki Kaurismäki.

Dancer in the Dark (2000) Provocative director Lars von Trier and musician Björk combine in this melodramatic but masterful film.

The Bridge (2011) This excellent series takes place between Sweden and Denmark.

Downfall (Oliver Hirschbiegel; 2004) The final days of Adolf Hitler, holed up in his Berlin bunker.

Listen

Máttaráhku Askái (Ulla Pirttijärvi; 2002) Haunting title track from the yoik-inspired Sámi artist.

Leningrad (http://leningrad.top) Punk rock, Latino, polka and Tom Waits with a strong brass section.

Ghost Love Score (Nightwish; 2004) Epic track from Finland's symphonic metal masters.

Cocoon (Björk; 2001) Among the Icelander's most intimate songs.

In the Hall of the Mountain King (Edvard Grieg; 1875) Brilliant soundtrack to *Peer Gynt's* troll scene.

Best of ABBA (ABBA; 1975) It's impossible to pick a favourite.

Above: Sculptures of Kalevala heroes in Helsinki, Finland

Plan Your Trip
Local Life

Activities

Walking around Northern Europe's historic cities is a great way to experience them and blow off some shipboard cobwebs at the same time. Cycling is also a top option. These can be done either as self-guided explorations or as part of a tour.

Even though you've just stepped off a ship, boat tours can be great ways to explore the often-complex watery geography of the Northern European port cities and the Norwegian fjords.

Up north, on winter cruises, snowy experiences like husky-sledding are popular, as are wildlife-watching excursions year-round.

Shopping

There are excellent shopping options across the region. Design shopping, whether classic Scandinavian brands or quirky avant-garde innovation, is an essential activity in Copenhagen, Berlin, Stockholm and Helsinki.

Local handcrafts are appealing throughout, while amber is a popular product in Poland and the Baltic states.

Eating

Northern European cooking, once viewed as meatballs, herring and little else, has wowed the world in recent years with New Nordic cuisine, a culinary revolution that centred on Copenhagen. While the crest of that wave has now passed, the 'foraging' ethos it championed has made a permanent mark here and worldwide. Its focus is on showcasing local produce prepared using traditional techniques, contemporary experimentation and clean, natural flavours.

The region's cafe culture is a highlight, but there often isn't much coffee snobbery; the black gold is just knocked back in serious quantity. A cake or pastry accompaniment is usual.

Tipping isn't expected in Scandinavia but 5% to 10% is customary in restaurants in the other countries.

KEONGDAGREATS/SHUTTERSTOCK ©

Drinking & Nightlife

Beer is popular right across the region, with microbreweries thriving alongside the traditional staples.

Wine is widely drunk with meals, though restaurants in the Nordic countries charge a hefty supplement for it. Wine and stronger alcohol can only be bought in state alcohol stores in Sweden, Norway, Iceland and Finland.

Most nations have their own favourite shot as a post-meal digestif or a way to rev up the night. Upmarket cocktail bars are also abundant.

Depending on the country, pubs and bars may have table service. Rounding up the bill or tipping up to 10% is normal in this case; tipping when buying drinks across the bar is not, except in Germany where about 5% is standard. Table service

may run you a tab or expect you to pay for each drinks order as it comes.

★ Best for Performing Arts

Mariinsky Theatre (p204), St Petersburg

Berliner Philharmonie (p65), Berlin

Musiikkitalo (p178), Helsinki

Concertgebouw (p88), Amsterdam

Oslo Opera House (p119), Oslo

Harpa (p271), Reykjavík

Entertainment

Several of the cities have architecturally and culturally significant arts venues, with classical music, ballet and opera very strong and a particular highlight of St Petersburg.

From left: Herring appetiser; Reykjavík's Harpa (p271), Iceland

Plan Your Trip
Choose Your Cruise

VICTOR MASCHEK/SHUTTERSTOCK ©

Matching your expectations, budget and travel style to the right cruise is the most important decision of the trip, so it pays to think carefully about what's important to you. There's a very wide range of trips, from floating cities with thousands of passengers to smaller, more intimate ships.

Budget

Think about how much you want to spend. Would you prefer a cheaper cabin on a longer trip to a more luxurious one on a shorter one? Are all-inclusive trips going to save you money? Remember to factor onshore time into your calculations, as well as onboard services like wi-fi, which is often quite expensive, and compulsory gratuities for staff.

Size

The megaships are geared for various budgets, so the important decision is how many people you want to sail with. On large ships, you can have over 5000 fellow passengers and the greatest range of shipboard diversions, from live shows to active options. Small ships, while sometimes exclusive and luxurious, are not always so, and often lack the most family-friendly amenities. They are, however, able to stop at smaller places that can't cater for the larger vessels.

Demographics

How a cruise is marketed gives a good idea of what type of experience you can expect. Different cruise lines, and even ships within cruise lines, tend to appeal to different groups. Some ships have quite a party reputation; others are known for their bridge games, expert lectures and golden oldie songs in the lounges. Also consider

whether you're looking for a family- or singles-oriented cruise.

Seasons

The vast majority of Scandinavian and Baltic cruises operate from May to September. The high summer – late June to August – is prime time, when warm weather, long days and wide scope for onshore activities make it the busiest cruise season. Some winter cruises also operate; the snowy scenery is picturesque, but you'll have fewer daylight hours in which to appreciate it. Key attractions of a cruise at this time are onshore activities like husky-sledding, and the chance to see the aurora borealis.

Itinerary

Where do you want to go? If you stick to the Baltic, you'll essentially be getting a series of enticing city visits perhaps interspersed with some islands like Bornholm, Gotland or the Åland archipelago. Add in a Norwe-

gian leg and you'll be getting wild coastal scenery plus bird and marine wildlife into the bargain. Further afield, the seabirds and cetaceans multiply at places like the Faroe Islands, Shetland Islands and magnificent Iceland, while remote Arctic destinations like Svalbard and Greenland offer walruses, polar bears and more along with wild, epic scenery.

> ★ **Best Online Resources**
> Avid Cruiser (www.avidcruiser.com)
> Cruise Critic (www.cruisecritic.com)
> Cruise Line (www.cruiseline.com)
> Cruise Reviews (www.cruisereviews.com)

Above: Cruise ship in Norway

STEVE HEAP/SHUTTERSTOCK ©

Cabin Types

Some modern ships offer only exterior cabins with balcony, but typically you'll have a choice. It's worth looking at a map of the ship before you choose, as you may want to prioritise being near the pool, the bar, the lifts or a play area.

Interior cabins are generally compact, with little or no natural light, though some have interior windows. They are the cheapest category and will suit those who plan to spend most of their time in public areas.

Sea-view cabins offer a porthole or window but no exterior access. They are typically as compact as interior rooms or more so.

Balcony cabins give you some access to the outside. Balconies are often quite small but will have space for a couple of chairs and small table at least. This is generally the first category in which spending significant time in your room is appealing.

Suites are a significant upgrade in size and usually separate the sleeping and sitting areas.

Some ships have a few single cabins, but these get snapped up fast. Solo travellers will usually have to pay a hefty single supplement at best, or pay the full rate for a double cabin at worst.

Cruise Lines

Carnival Cruise Lines (www.carnival.com) The largest cruise company in the world, with more than 100 vessels across several subsidiary brands.

Celebrity Cruises (www.celebritycruises.com) An important brand of Royal Caribbean, this has huge ships that offer a more upscale experience, and itineraries that go right to the top of Norway.

Costa Cruises (www.costacruise.com) Owned by Carnival, Costa is aimed at European travellers: bigger spas, smaller cabins and better coffee. Ships are huge.

Cunard Line (www.cunard.com) Owned by Carnival, Cunard operates the huge *Queen Elizabeth*, *Queen Mary II* and *Queen Victoria*. The focus is on 'classic luxury' and the ships have limited Northern Europe sailings.

Fred Olsen (www.fredolsencruises.com) Operating principally from the UK, this Norwegian-owned company runs several North Sea and Baltic itineraries.

Holland America (www.hollandamerica.com) Owned by Carnival, Holland America offers a traditional cruising experience, generally for older passengers. Wide variety of Baltic and Scandinavian options.

Hurtigruten (www.hurtigruten.com) Famous daily ferry that runs the length of the Norwegian coast; also runs cruises.

MSC Cruises (www.msccruises.com) Italian-inflected cruising on large, luxurious ships.

Norwegian Cruise Line (www.ncl.com) Offers 'freestyle cruising' on large ships, which means that dress codes are relaxed and dining options more flexible than on other lines. Lots of 'extra-fee' dining choices.

Princess Cruises (www.princess.com) Owned by Carnival, Princess has large ships offering a wide range of Northern Europe itineraries. It offers a slightly older crowd a range of pampering activities onboard.

Royal Caribbean (www.royalcaribbean.com) This giant operator specialises in megaship cruising, with several carrying over 5000 passengers. It's family-friendly and aimed at the middle of the market, with a casual vibe.

Silversea (www.silversea.com) Luxury small-boat cruises. Some ships are Arctic-equipped and head right up to Svalbard and Greenland, with a focus on nature-watching and active onshore options.

Viking Cruises (www.vikingcruises.com) Luxurious trips on smaller ships with Baltic and Scandinavian expertise.

From left: Cruise ship docked in Norway; Two ships in port at Tallinn (p206), Estonia

Sustainable Cruising

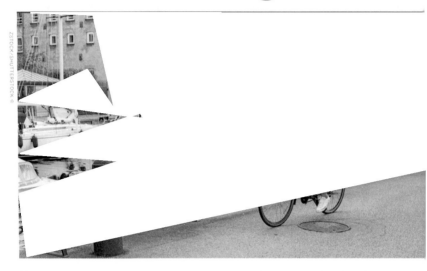

From air and water pollution to the swamping of popular destinations by hordes of tourists, travelling on cruise ships isn't without significant impacts – choose your cruise line carefully.

Environmental Issues

Although all travel comes with an environmental cost, by their very size, cruise ships have an outsized effect. Among the main issues:

Air pollution According to UK-based Climate Care, a carbon-offsetting company, cruise ships emit more carbon per passenger than airplanes – nearly twice as much – and that's not including the flights that most passengers take to get to their point of departure. Most ships burn low-grade bunker fuel, which contains more sulphur and particulates than higher-quality fuel. Some operators are more conscious of their emissions than others.

Water pollution Cruise ships generate enormous amounts of sewage, solid waste and grey water. A ban on sewage dumping in the Baltic is being phased in and several ports in the region encourage ships to pump out their waste for treatment on land.

Cultural impact Although cruise lines generate money for their ports of call, thousands of people arriving at once can change the character of a town and seem overwhelming to locals and noncruising travellers.

What You Can Do

If you're planning a cruise, it's worth doing some research. Email the cruise lines and ask them about their environmental policies: wastewater treatment, recycling initiatives and whether they use alternative energy sources. Knowing that customers care about these things has an impact.

There are also organisations that review lines and ships on their environmental records:

Friends of the Earth (https://foe.org/cruise-report-card) Letter grades given to cruise lines and ships for environmental and human health impacts.

World Travel Awards (www.worldtravelawards.com) Annual awards for the 'World's Leading Green Cruise Line'.

Consume Less

When you get off the ship, you can do your part and make a difference. Here are a few pointers for minimising your impact on the environment.

Skip bottled water If the water is safe to drink, use it to fill containers so you can skip bottled water.

Ride the bus or tram Most cities in the region have excellent public transport networks.

Hire a bike There's an excellent network of cycle paths and easy hiring in many of the cities you will visit.

Say no to plastic Try to carry your own bag for anything you buy. Straws are also best avoided because they float around for years.

★ Best for Sustainability

Copenhagen aims to become the world's first carbon neutral capital by 2025.

Finland has a legally binding target for an 80% reduction in emissions by 2050.

Oslo is reducing private cars in the city centre by creating new bike lanes, pedestrianising streets and improving the public transport system.

Be Ecosmart

Don't litter Almost everything discarded on land makes its way to the sea, where it can wreak havoc on marine life.

Don't drop rubbish over the rails of the ship When leaning on the rails looking over the sea, make sure to keep a firm grip on your garbage so that it doesn't end up hurting any of the marine life that calls that glistening water home.

From left: Cycling in Copenhagen (p90), Denmark; Tram in Oslo (p110), Norway

Plan Your Trip
Family Time Ashore

POPOVA VALERIYA/SHUTTERSTOCK ©

Most of the region is child friendly, with domestic tourism largely dictated by children's needs. It is prime family holiday territory, especially in the summer high season when theme parks, amusement parks, zoos and child-friendly beaches are just part of the story. Many museums have interactive elements specifically for the young and may have a dedicated children's section with toys, games and dress-up clothes.

Practicalities

○ Children are usually entitled to substantial discounts on admission fees and public transport.

○ Baby food, infant formula, soy and cow's milk, disposable nappies (diapers) etc are widely available in supermarkets.

○ Tour companies will normally have children's safety seats available, but reserving these in advance is essential.

○ Cycle hire is a great way to explore the region's cities and give children both agency and energy burn-off.

○ High chairs are standard in many restaurants but numbers may be limited.

○ Restaurants will often have children's menu options, and there are lots of chain eateries aimed at families.

○ Food markets are great places to put a picnic together.

○ Breastfeeding in public is common and often officially encouraged.

○ Many public toilets have baby-changing facilities.

○ Attractions like theme parks and water-parks are often cheaper if you book online, especially for discounted family tickets. Access to rides and ticket prices are often determined by height, so it's useful to have this measurement handy when booking.

FAG/SHUTTERSTOCK ©

○ Check local tourist offices – all cities and regions have places where kids are king, from huge indoor swim centres to play centres and petting farms.

○ For general suggestions on how to make a family trip easier, pick up a copy of Lonely Planet's *Travel with Children*.

★ **Best Stops for Children**

Amsterdam (p68)

Copenhagen (p90)

Helsinki (p162)

Stockholm (p144)

Berlin (p34)

City Delights

Amsterdam One of Europe's most kid-friendly cities, with an atmosphere that's cheerfully accommodating to children. In fact, most areas – except the Red Light District, of course – are fair game.

Bergen Numerous child-oriented attractions, while nearby there are boat trips on fjords and water-based activities.

Berlin Deutsches Technikmuseum is a shrine to technology – one of many family highlights.

Copenhagen Capital attractions include fun-park-meets-fairy-tale Tivoli, the swimming polar bears at the zoo and the insanely colourful fish of Den Blå Planet.

Helsinki Many attractions, with trams, boats, zoo, Suomenlinna fortress, Linnanmäki amusement park and Serena water park at Espoo. Most museums and galleries have child-friendly exhibits.

Oslo Abundant green parklands and an array of museums, many with an interactive component, mean there's plenty for children.

Stockholm Museums, a petting zoo and an amusement park make this city a delight for kids.

From left: Norsk Folkemuseum (p115), Oslo, Norway; Families on a ride at Linnanmäki amusement park in Helsinki, Finland

Fernsehturm (p54)

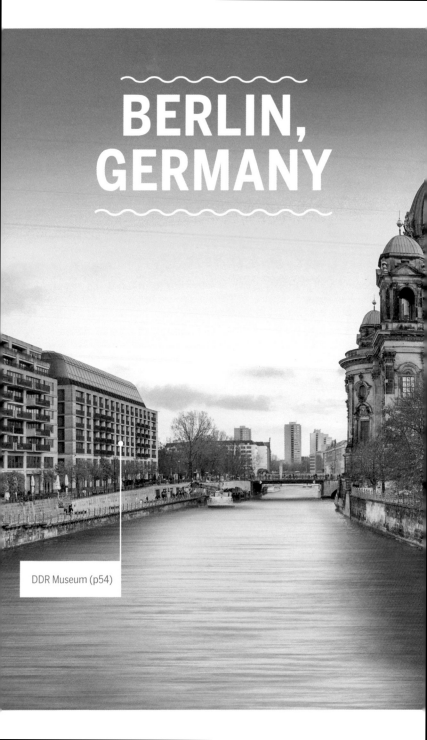

BERLIN, GERMANY

DDR Museum (p54)

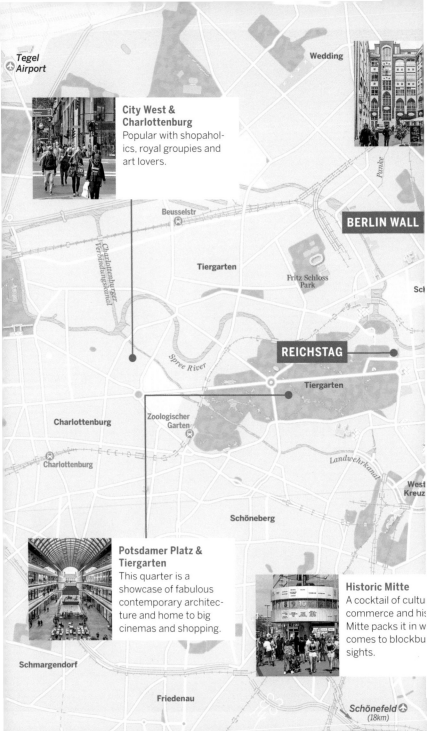

Tegel
Airport

Wedding

City West & Charlottenburg
Popular with shopaholics, royal groupies and art lovers.

Beusselstr

BERLIN WALL

Tiergarten

Fritz Schloss Park

Sch

Charlottenburger Verbindungskanal

REICHSTAG

Spree River

Tiergarten

Panke

Charlottenburg

Zoologischer Garten

Charlottenburg

Landwehrkanal

Schöneberg

West Kreuz

Potsdamer Platz & Tiergarten
This quarter is a showcase of fabulous contemporary architecture and home to big cinemas and shopping.

Schmargendorf

Historic Mitte
A cocktail of cultu commerce and his Mitte packs it in w comes to blockbu sights.

Friedenau

Schönefeld
(18km)

The view from Berliner Dom (p54)

Arriving in Berlin

Tegel Airport TXL express bus to Alexanderplatz (40 minutes) and bus X9 for City West (eg Kurfürstendamm, 20 minutes), €2.70; taxi €25.

Schönefeld Airport Airport-Express trains (RB14 or RE7) to central Berlin twice hourly (€3.40, 30 minutes); taxi €40 to Alexanderplatz.

Hauptbahnhof Main train station in the city centre; served by all public transport.

Cruise Port Cruise ships dock in Warnemünde, over three hours to Berlin by train. There are connections roughly every two hours (€40 to €50).

Fast Facts

Currency Euro (€)

Language German. English widely spoken.

Free wi-fi Free public wi-fi across large areas of the centre.

Tourist information Visit Berlin (www.visitberlin.de) has branches at the airports, the main train station, the Brandenburg Gate, the TV Tower and on Kurfürstendamm.

Transport The U-Bahn underground train and bike rental are great ways to get around.

The Berlin Wall

For 28 years the Berlin Wall was the most potent symbol of the Cold War. Surprisingly very few of its reinforced concrete slabs remain in today's reunited Berlin.

Great For...

☑ **Don't Miss**

The open-air mural collection of the East Side Gallery.

Construction

Shortly after midnight on 13 August 1961 East German soldiers and police began rolling out miles of barbed wire that would soon be replaced with prefab concrete slabs. The wall was a desperate measure taken by the German Democratic Republic (GDR) government to stop the sustained brain and brawn drain it had experienced since its 1949 founding. Around 3.6 million people had already left for the West, putting the GDR on the verge of economic and political collapse.

Demise

The Wall's demise in 1989 came as unexpectedly as its construction. Once again the GDR was losing its people in droves, this time via Hungary, which had opened its borders with Austria. Something had to give. It did on 9 November 1989 when a GDR

Gedenkstätte
Berliner Mauer

Ⓢ Nordbahnhof

❶ Need to Know

A double row of cobblestones guides you along 5.7km of the Wall's course. Track down remaining fragments of the Wall using Memorial Landscape Berlin Wall (www.berlin-wall-map.com).

✕ Take a Break

Not far from the Gedenkstätte Berliner Mauer is the famous Konnopke's Imbiss (p59).

★ Top Tip

There's a great view from the Documentation Centre's viewing platform.

---

spokesperson (mistakenly, it later turned out) announced during a press conference that all travel restrictions to the West would be lifted. When asked when, he said simply 'Immediately'. Amid scenes of wild partying, the two Berlins came together again.

In the course of 1990 the Wall almost disappeared from Berlin, some bits were smashed up and flogged to tourists, other sections were carted off to museums, parks, embassies, exhibitions and even private gardens across the globe. The longest section to survive intact is the East Side Gallery.

Gedenkstätte Berliner Mauer

The outdoor **Berlin Wall Memorial** (☏030-467 986 666; www.berliner-mauer-gedenkstaette.de; Bernauer Strasse btwn Schwedter Strasse & Gartenstrasse; ☺visitor & documentation centre 10am-6pm Tue-Sun, open-air exhibit 8am-10pm daily; ⑤Nordbahnhof, Bernauer Strasse,

Eberswalder Strasse) **FREE** extends for 1.4km along Bernauer Strasse and integrates an original section of Wall, vestiges of the border installations and escape tunnels, a chapel and a monument. Multimedia stations, panels, excavations and a Documentation Centre provide context and explain what the border fortifications looked like and how they shaped the lives of people on both sides.

East Side Gallery

The year was 1989. After 28 years, the Berlin Wall, that grim and grey divider of humanity, finally met its maker. Most of it was quickly dismantled, but along Mühlenstrasse, paralleling the Spree, a 1.3km stretch became the **East Side Gallery** (Map p63; www.eastsidegallery-berlin.de; Mühlenstrasse btwn Oberbaumbrücke & Ostbahnhof; ☺24hr; ⓊWarschauer Strasse, ⑤Ostbahnhof, Warschauer Strasse) **FREE**, the world's largest open-air mural collection. In more than 100 paintings, dozens of international artists translated the era's global euphoria and optimism into a mix of political statements, drug-induced musings and truly artistic visions.

The Berlin Wall

The construction of the Berlin Wall was a unique event in human history, not only for physically bisecting a city but by becoming a dividing line between competing ideologies and political systems. It's this global impact and universal legacy that continue to fascinate people more than a quarter century after its triumphant tear-down. Fortunately, plenty of original Wall segments and other vestiges remain, along with museums and memorials, to help fathom the realities and challenges of daily life in Berlin during the Cold War.

Our illustration points out the top highlights you can visit to learn about different aspects of these often tense decades. The best place to start is the ❶ **Gedenkstätte Berliner Mauer** for an excellent introduction to what the inner-city border really looked liked and what it meant to live in its shadow. Reflect upon what you've learned while relaxing along the former death strip, now the ❷ **Mauerpark**, before heading to the emotionally charged exhibit at the ❸ **Tränenpalast**, an actual border-crossing pavilion. Relive the euphoria of the

Tränenpalast
This modernist 1962 glass-and-steel border pavilion was dubbed 'Palace of Tears' because of the many tearful farewells that took place outside the building as East Germans and their western visitors had to say goodbye.

Brandenburg Tor
People around the world cheered as East and West Berliners partied together atop the Berlin Wall in front of the iconic city gate, which today is a photogenic symbol of united Germany.

Potsdamer Platz
Nowhere was the death strip as wide as on the former no-man's-land around Potsdamer Platz from which sprouted a new postmodern city quarter in the 1990s. A tiny section of the Berlin Wall serves as a reminder.

Checkpoint Charlie
Only diplomats and foreigners were allowed to use this border crossing. Weeks after the Wall was built, US and Soviet tanks faced off here in one of the hottest moments of the Cold War.

Wall's demise at the ④ **Brandenburg Tor**, then marvel at the revival of ⑤ **Potsdamer Platz**, which was nothing but death-strip wasteland until the 1990s. The Wall's geopolitical significance is the focus at ⑥ **Checkpoint Charlie**, which saw some of the tensest moments of the Cold War. Wrap up with finding your favourite mural motif at the ⑦ **East Side Gallery**.

It's possible to explore these sights by using a combination of walking and public transport, but a bike ride is the best method for gaining a sense of the former Wall's erratic flow through the central city.

FAST FACTS

Beginning of construction 13 August 1961
Total length 155km
Height 3.6m
Weight of each segment 2.6 tonnes
Number of watchtowers 300

② ·

Remnants of the Wall →

Mauerpark
Famous for its flea market and karaoke, this popular park actually occupies a converted section of death strip. A 30m segment of surviving Wall is now an official practice ground for budding graffiti artists.

Gedenkstätte Berliner Mauer
Germany's central memorial to the Berlin Wall and its victims exposes the complexity and barbaric nature of the border installation along a 1.4km stretch of the barrier's course.

Alexanderplatz

Alexanderstr

East Side Gallery
Paralleling the Spree for 1.3km, this is the longest Wall vestige. After its collapse, more than a hundred international artists expressed their feelings about this historic moment in a series of colourful murals.

⑦

The Reichstag

Reinstated as the home of the German parliament in 1999, the late-19th-century Reichstag is one of Berlin's most iconic buildings.

The Reichstag's Beginnings

It's been burned, bombed, rebuilt, buttressed by the Wall, wrapped in plastic and finally brought back from the dead by Norman Foster: 'turbulent history' just doesn't do it when describing the life this most famous of Berlin's landmarks has endured. This neo-baroque edifice was finished in 1894 to house the German Imperial Diet and served its purpose until 1933 when it was badly damaged by fire in an arson attack carried out by Marinus van der Lubbe, a young Dutch communist. This shocking event conveniently gave Hitler a pretext to tighten his grip on the German state. In 1945 the building was a major target for the Red Army who raised the red flag from the Reichstag, an act that became a symbol of the Soviet defeat of the Nazis.

Great For...

☑ Don't Miss

Free auto-activated audio guides provide info on the building, its landmarks and the workings of parliament.

❶ Need to Know

Map p50; www.bundestag.de; Platz der
Republik 1, Visitors' Service, Scheidemannstrasse; ⏰ lift ride 8am-midnight, last entry
10pm, Visitors' Service 8am-8pm Apr-Oct,
to 6pm Nov-Mar; 🚌 100, Ⓢ Brandenburger
Tor, Hauptbahnhof, Ⓤ Brandenburger Tor,
Bundestag; **FREE**

✕ Take a Break

For quick feeds, tourist-geared,
self-service **Berlin Pavillon** (Map p50;
☎ 030-2065 4737; www.berlin-pavillon.
de; Scheidemannstrasse 1; mains €3.50-9;
⏰ 8am-9pm; 🚌 100) comes in handy.

> ### ★ Top Tip
> For guaranteed access, make free tick-
> et reservations online before you leave
> home. Note that all visitors must show
> ID to enter the building.

The Cold War Years

Although in West Berlin, the Reichstag
found itself very near the dividing line
between East and West Berlin and, from the
early 1960s, the Berlin Wall. With the German government sitting safely in faraway
Bonn, this grand facade lost its purpose
and in the 1950s some in West Berlin
thought it should be demolished. However,
the wrecking balls never had their day and
the Reichstag was restored, albeit without
a lot of the decoration that had adorned the
old building.

Reunification & Norman Foster

Almost a year after the Wall came down,
the official reunification ceremony was
symbolically held at the Reichstag which, it
was later decided, would become the seat of
the German Bundestag (parliament) once

again. Before Norman Foster began his reconstruction work, the entire Reichstag was
spectacularly wrapped in plastic sheeting
by the Bulgarian-American artist Christo
in the summer of 1995. The following four
years saw the erection of Norman Foster's
now famous glittering glass cupola, the
centrepiece of the visitor experience today.
It is the Reichstag's most distinctive feature,
serviced by lift and providing fabulous
360-degree city views and the opportunity
to peer down into the parliament chamber.
To reach the top, follow the ramp spiralling
up around the dome's mirror-clad central
cone. The cupola is a spanking-new
feature, but Foster's brief also stipulated
that some parts of the building were to be
preserved. One example is the Cyrillic graffiti
left by Soviet soldiers in 1945.

Berlin Nightlife

With its well-deserved reputation as one of Europe's primo party capitals, Berlin offers a thousand-and-one scenarios for getting your cocktails and kicks (or wine or beer, for that matter).

Great For

☑ **Don't Miss**

Café am Neuen See (p62), generally regarded as Berlin's best beer garden.

Bars & Cafes

Berlin is a notoriously late city: bars stay packed from dusk to dawn and beyond, and some clubs don't hit their stride until 4am. The lack of a curfew never created a tradition of binge drinking.

Edgier, more underground venues cluster in Kreuzberg, Friedrichshain, Neukölln and up-and-coming outer boroughs like Wedding (north of Mitte) and Lichtenberg (past Friedrichshain). Places in Charlottenburg, Mitte and Prenzlauer Berg tend to be quieter and close earlier. Some proprietors have gone to extraordinary lengths to come up with special design concepts.

The line between cafe and bar is often blurred, with many changing stripes as the hands move around the clock. Alcohol, however, is served pretty much all day. Cocktail bars are booming in Berlin and

❶ Need to Know

Regular bars start up around 6pm and close at 1am or 2am the next day. Trendy places and cocktail bars don't open until 8pm or 9pm and stay open until the last tippler leaves. Clubs open at 11pm or midnight, but don't fill up until 1am or 2am, reaching their peak between 4am and 6am.

✖ Take a Break

Check out the food offerings while you're chilling out in one of Berlin's beer gardens or enjoying the views from a rooftop bar.

★ Top Tip

There's generally no need to dress up at Berlin's clubs, and getting past bouncers is fairly easy.

several new arrivals have measurably elevated the 'liquid art' scene. Dedicated drinking dens tend to be elegant cocoons with mellow lighting and low sound levels. A good cocktail will set you back between €10 and €15.

Beaches & Outdoor Drinking

Berliners are sun cravers and as soon as the first rays spray their way into spring, outdoor tables show up faster than you can pour a pint of beer. The most traditional places for outdoor chilling are of course the beer gardens with long wooden benches set up beneath leafy old chestnuts and with cold beer and bratwurst on the menu. In 2002, Berlin also jumped on the 'sandwagon' with the opening of its first beach bar, Strandbar Mitte (p61), in a prime location on the Spree River. Many that followed

have since been displaced by development, which has partly fuelled the latest trend: rooftop bars.

Clubbing

Over the past 25 years, Berlin's club culture has put the city firmly on the map of hedonists. With more than 200 venues, finding one to match your mood isn't difficult. Electronic music in its infinite varieties continues to define Berlin's after-dark action but other sounds, like hip-hop, dancehall, rock, swing and funk, have also made inroads. The edgiest clubs have taken up residence in power plants, transformer stations, abandoned apartment buildings and other repurposed locations. The scene is in constant flux as experienced club owners look for new challenges and a younger generation of promoters enters the scene with new ideas and impetus.

Historical Highlights

This walk checks off Berlin's block-buster landmarks as it cuts right through the historic city centre, Mitte (literally 'Middle'). This is the birth-place and glamorous heart of Berlin, a high-octane cocktail of culture, architecture and commerce.

Start Reichstag
Distance 3.5km
Duration three hours

1 The sparkling glass dome of the **Reichstag** (p43) has become a shining beacon of unified Berlin.

Classic Photo The iconic Brandenburg Gate is now a cheery symbol of German reunification.

2 The **Brandenburger Tor** (p48) became an involuntary neighbour of the Berlin Wall during the Cold War.

3 **Unter den Linden** has been Berlin's showpiece road since the 18th century.

Take a Break... Stop in at Augustiner am Gendarmenmarkt (p58) for German fare.

Friedrichstr

Bahnhof Friedrichstr

Friedrichstr

Platz der Republik

START

Scheidemannstr

Reichstagufer

Dorotheenstr

Tiergarten

Brandenburger Tor

Pariser Platz

Ebertstr

Wilhelmstr

Behrenstr

Französische Str

Mohrenstr

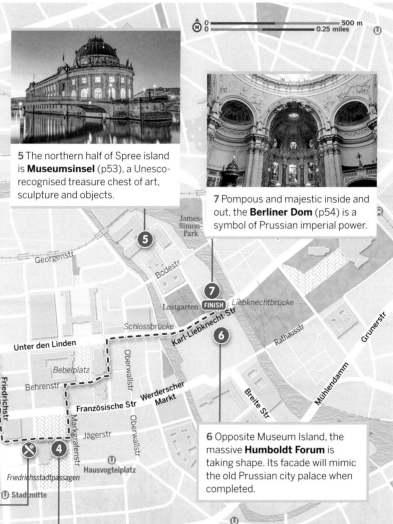

5 The northern half of Spree island is **Museumsinsel** (p53), a Unesco-recognised treasure chest of art, sculpture and objects.

7 Pompous and majestic inside and out, the **Berliner Dom** (p54) is a symbol of Prussian imperial power.

6 Opposite Museum Island, the massive **Humboldt Forum** is taking shape. Its facade will mimic the old Prussian city palace when completed.

4 Berlin's most beautiful square, **Gendarmenmarkt** (p49) is bookended by domed cathedrals with the famous Konzerthaus (Concert Hall) in between.

⊙ SIGHTS

◎ Mitte

With the mother lode of sights clustered within a walkable area, the most historic part of Berlin is naturally a prime port of call for most visitors.

Deutsches Historisches Museum
Museum

(German Historical Museum; Map p50; ☎030-203 040; www.dhm.de; Unter den Linden 2; adult/concession/under 18yr €8/4/free; ⊙10am-6pm; 🚌100, 200, Ⓤ Hausvogteiplatz, Ⓢ Hackescher Markt) If you're wondering what the Germans have been up to for the past two millennia, take a spin around this engaging museum in the baroque Zeughaus, former-ly the Prussian arsenal and now home of the German Historical Museum. Upstairs, displays concentrate on the period from the 1st century AD to the end of WWI in 1918, while the ground floor tracks the 20th

this compelling exhibit chronicles the stages of terror and persecution

century all the way through to German reunification.

Brandenburger Tor
Landmark

(Brandenburger Gate; Map p50; Pariser Platz; Ⓢ Brandenburger Tor, Ⓤ Brandenburger Tor) A symbol of division during the Cold War, the landmark Brandenburg Gate now epitomises German reunification. Carl Gotthard Langhans found inspiration in Athens' Acropolis for the elegant triumphal arch, completed in 1791 as the royal city gate. It stands sentinel over Pariser Platz, a harmoniously proportioned square once again framed by banks, a hotel and the US, British and French embassies, just as it was during its 19th-century heyday.

Holocaust Memorial
Memorial

(Memorial to the Murdered Jews of Europe; Map p50; ☎030-2639 4336; www.stiftung-denkmal.de; Cora-Berliner-Strasse 1; audio guide adult/concession €4/2; ⊙field 24hr; Ⓢ Brandenburger Tor, Ⓤ Brandenburger Tor) **FREE** Inaugurated in 2005, this football-field-sized memorial by American architect Peter Eisenman consists of 2711 sarcophagi-like concrete columns

Topographie des Terrors

rising in sombre silence from undulating ground. You're free to access this maze at any point and make your individual journey through it. For context visit the subterranean **Ort der Information** (Information Centre; Map p50; 030-7407 2929; www.holocaust-mahnmal. de; Cora-Berliner-Strasse 1; audio guide adult/concession €4/2; 10am-8pm Tue-Sun Apr-Sep, to 7pm Oct-Mar, last admission 45min before closing) **FREE** whose exhibits will leave no one untouched. Audio guides and audio translations of exhibit panels are available.

Gendarmenmarkt Square
(Map p50; U Französische Strasse, Stadtmitte) The Gendarmenmarkt area is Berlin at its ritziest, dappled with luxury hotels, fancy restaurants and bars. The graceful square is bookended by the domed 18th-century German and French cathedrals and punctuated by a grandly porticoed concert hall, the **Konzerthaus** (Map p50; 030-203 092 333; www.konzerthaus.de; Gendarmenmarkt 2; tours €3). It was named for the Gens d'Armes, an 18th-century Prussian regiment consisting of French Huguenot refugees whose story is chronicled in a museum inside the **French cathedral** (Map p50; www.franzoesischer-dom.de; church free, museum adult/concession €3.50/2, tower adult/child €3/1; church & museum noon-5pm Tue-Sun, tower 10am-7pm Apr-Oct, noon-5pm Jan-Mar, last entry 1hr before closing). Climb the tower here for grand views of historic Berlin.

Topographie des Terrors Museum
(Topography of Terror; Map p55; 030-2548 0950; www.topographie.de; Niederkirchner Strasse 8; 10am-8pm, grounds close at dusk or 8pm at the latest; S Potsdamer Platz, U Potsdamer Platz) **FREE** In the same spot where the most feared institutions of Nazi Germany (including the Gestapo headquarters and the SS central command) once stood, this compelling exhibit chronicles the stages of terror and persecution, puts a face on the perpetrators and details the impact these brutal institutions had on all of Europe. A second exhibit outside zeroes in on how life changed for Berlin and its people after the Nazis made it their capital.

East Berlin's Stasi Museum

This **exhibit** (Map p63; 030-553 6854; www.stasimuseum.de; Haus 1, Ruschestrasse 103; adult/concession €6/4.50; 10am-6pm Mon-Fri, 11am-6pm Sat & Sun; U Magdalenenstrasse) provides an overview of the structure, methods and impact of the Ministry of State Security (Stasi), former East Germany's secret police, inside the feared institution's fortress-like headquarters. Marvel at cunningly low-tech surveillance devices (hidden in watering cans, rocks, even neckties), a prisoner transport van with tiny, lightless cells, and the stuffy offices of Stasi chief Erich Mielke. Panelling is partly in English. Free English tours at 3pm Saturday and Sunday. The museum is in the eastern district of Lichtenberg, just north of U-Bahn station Magdalenenstrasse.

Tools of the spy trade
WALTER BIBIKOW/ALAMY ©

Checkpoint Charlie Historic Site
(Map p55; cnr Zimmerstrasse & Friedrichstrasse; 24hr; U Kochstrasse) **FREE** Checkpoint Charlie was the principal gateway for foreigners and diplomats between the two Berlins from 1961 to 1990. Unfortunately, this potent symbol of the Cold War has degenerated into a tacky tourist trap, though a free open-air exhibit that illustrates milestones in Cold War history is one redeeming aspect.

⊙ Scheunenviertel

Hackesche Höfe Historic Site
(Map p50; 030-2809 8010; www.hackeschehoefe.com; enter from Rosenthaler Strasse 40/41 or Sophienstrasse 6; M1, S Hackescher Markt,

Mitte

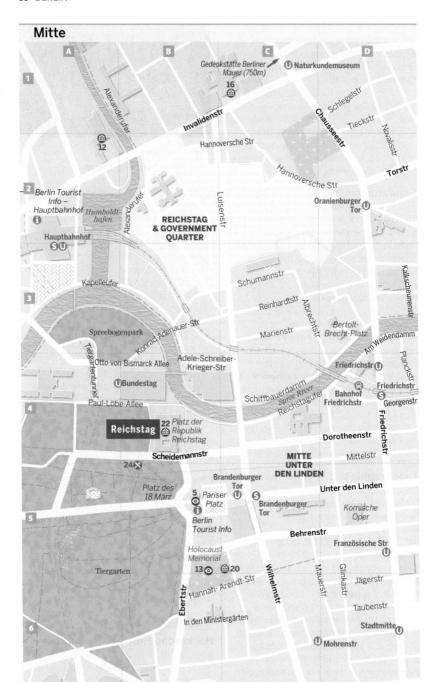

Gedenkstätte Berliner Mauer (750m)

Naturkundemuseum

16

Schlegelstr

Tieckstr

Chausseestr

Novalisstr

Invalidenstr

Hannoversche Str

Hannoversche Str

Torstr

12

Berlin Tourist Info – Hauptbahnhof

Humboldt-hafen

Alexanderufer

Luisenstr

REICHSTAG & GOVERNMENT QUARTER

Oranienburger Tor

Hauptbahnhof

Kapelleufer

Schumannstr

Reinhardtstr

Albrechtstr

Kalkscheunenstr

Spreebogenpark

Konrad-Adenauer-Str

Marienstr

Bertolt-Brecht-Platz

Am Weidendamm

Tiergartentunnel

Otto-von-Bismarck-Allee

Adele-Schreiber-Krieger-Str

Friedrichstr

Planckstr

Bundestag

Schiffbauerdamm

Spree River

Reichstagufer

Bahnhof Friedrichstr

Friedrichstr

Georgenstr

Paul-Löbe-Allee

Reichstag 22 Platz der Republik Reichstag

Dorotheenstr

Friedrichstr

Scheidemannstr

MITTE UNTER DEN LINDEN

Mittelstr

24

Brandenburger Tor

Unter den Linden

Platz des 18 März

5 Pariser Platz

Brandenburger Tor

Komische Oper

Berlin Tourist Info

Behrenstr

Französische Str

Holocaust Memorial

13

20

Wilhelmstr

Mauerstr

Glinkastr

Jägerstr

Tiergarten

Hannah-Arendt-Str

Taubenstr

In den Ministergärten

Ebertstr

Stadtmitte

Mohrenstr

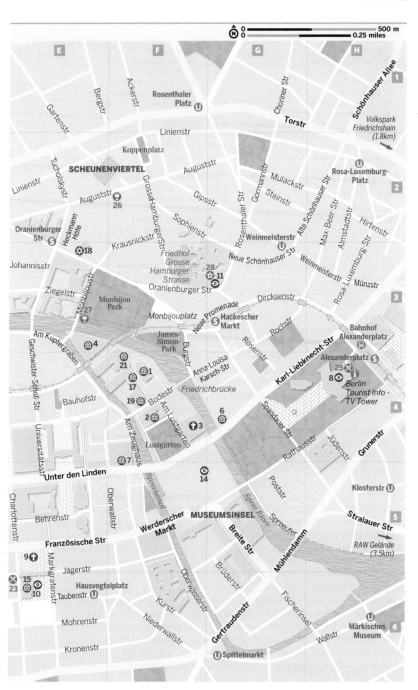

Mitte

U Weinmeisterstrasse) **FREE** The Hackesche Höfe is the largest and most famous of the courtyard ensembles peppered throughout the Scheunenviertel. Built in 1907, the eight interlinked *Höfe* reopened in 1996 with a congenial mix of cafes, galleries, boutiques and entertainment venues. The main entrance on Rosenthaler Strasse leads to **Court I**, prettily festooned with art nouveau tiles, while Court VII segues to the romantic **Rosenhöfe** with a sunken rose garden and tendril-like balustrades.

Museum für Naturkunde   Museum
(Museum of Natural History; Map p50; ☏030-2093 8591; www.naturkundemuseum.berlin; Invalidenstrasse 43; adult/concession incl audio guide €8/5; ◷9.30am-6pm Tue-Fri, 10am-6pm Sat & Sun; 🚇M5, M8, M10, 12, U Naturkundemuseum) Fossils and minerals don't quicken your pulse? Well, how about Tristan, one of the best-preserved *Tyrannosaurus rex* skeletons in the world, or the 12m-high *Brachiosaurus branchai*, the world's largest mounted dino skeleton? These Jurassic superstars are joined by a dozen other buddies, some of which are brought to virtual flesh-and-bone life with the help of clever 'Juraskopes'. Other crowd favourites in this excellent museum include Knut, the world's most famous dead polar bear, and an ultrarare archaeopteryx.

Neue Synagoge   Synagogue
(Map p50; ☏030-8802 8300; www.centrumjudaicum.de; Oranienburger Strasse 28-30; adult/concession €5/4; ◷10am-6pm Mon-Fri, to 7pm Sun, closes 3pm Fri & 6pm Sun Oct-Mar; 🚇M1, U Oranienburger Tor, S Oranienburger Strasse) The gleaming gold dome of the Neue Synagoge is the most visible symbol of Berlin's revitalised Jewish community. The 1866 original was Germany's largest synagogue but its modern incarnation is not so much a house of worship (although prayer services do take place), as a museum and place of remembrance called **Centrum Judaicum**. The dome can be climbed from April to September (adult/concession €3/2.50). An audio guide costs €3.

Hamburger Bahnhof – Museum für Gegenwart   Museum
(Contemporary Art Museum; Map p50; ☏030-266 424 242; www.smb.museum; Invalidenstrasse 50-51; adult/concession €14/7; ◷10am-6pm Tue, Wed & Fri, 10am-8pm Thu, 11am-6pm Sat & Sun; 🚇M5, M8, M10, S Hauptbahnhof, U Hauptbahnhof) Berlin's contemporary art showcase opened in 1996 in an old railway station, whose loft and grandeur are a great backdrop for this Aladdin's cave of paintings, installations, sculptures and video art. Changing exhibits span the arc of post-1950 artistic movements – from

conceptual art and pop art to minimal art and Fluxus – and include seminal works by such major players as Andy Warhol, Cy Twombly, Joseph Beuys and Robert Rauschenberg.

◎ Alexanderplatz

It's practically impossible to visit Berlin without spending time in this area, which packs some of Berlin's must-see sights into a very compact frame.

Museumsinsel   Museum
(Map p50; ☑030-266 424 242; www.smb. museum; day tickets for all 5 museums adult/ concession/under 18yr €18/9/free; ☺varies by museum; ☐100, 200, TXL, ⓤHackescher Markt, Friedrichstrasse) Walk through ancient Babylon, meet an Egyptian queen, clamber up a Greek altar or be mesmerised by Monet's ethereal landscapes. Welcome to Museumsinsel (Museum Island), Berlin's most important treasure trove, spanning 6000 years' worth of art, artefacts, sculpture and architecture from Europe and beyond. Spread across five grand museums built between 1830 and 1930, the complex takes up the entire northern half of the little Spree Island where Berlin's settlement began in the 13th century.

The first repository to open was the **Altes Museum** (Old Museum; Map p50; Am Lustgarten; adult/concession €10/5; ☺10am-6pm Tue, Wed & Fri-Sun, to 8pm Thu), which presents Greek, Etruscan and Roman antiquities. Behind it, the **Neues Museum** (New Museum; Map p50; Bodestrasse 1-3; adult/ concession €12/6; ☺10am-6pm, to 8pm Thu) showcases the Egyptian collection, most famously the bust of Queen Nefertiti, and also houses the Museum of Pre- and Early History. The temple-like **Alte Nationalgalerie** (Old National Gallery; Map p50; Bodestrasse 1-3; adult/concession €12/6; ☺10am-6pm Tue, Wed & Fri-Sun, to 8pm Thu) trains the focus on 19th-century European art. The island's top draw is the **Pergamonmuseum** (Map p50; Bodestrasse 1-3; adult/ concession €12/6; ☺10am-6pm Fri-Wed, to 8pm Thu), with its monumental architecture from

Sachsenhausen Concentration Camp

About 35km north of Berlin, **Sachsenhausen** (Memorial & Museum Sachsenhausen; ☑03301-200 200; www.stiftung-bg. de; Strasse der Nationen 22, Oranienburg; ☺8.30am-6pm mid-Mar–mid-Oct, to 4.30pm mid-Oct–mid-Mar, museums closed Mon mid-Oct–mid-Mar; Ⓟ; ⓈOranienburg) **FREE** was built by prisoners and opened in 1936 as a prototype for other concentration camps. By 1945, some 200,000 people had passed through its sinister gates, most of them political opponents, Jews, Roma people and, after 1939, POWs. Tens of thousands died here from hunger, exhaustion, illness, exposure, medical experiments and executions. Thousands more succumbed during the death march of April 1945, when the Nazis evacuated the camp in advance of the Red Army.

A tour of the memorial site with its remaining buildings and exhibits will leave no one untouched.

The S1 makes the trip thrice hourly from central Berlin (eg Friedrichstrasse station) to Oranienburg (€3.30, 45 minutes). Hourly regional RE5 and RB12 trains leaving from Hauptbahnhof are faster (€3.30, 25 minutes). The camp is about 2km from the Oranienburg train station.

Sachsenhausen memorial

ancient worlds, including the namesake Pergamonaltar. The **Bode-Museum** (Map p50; cnr Am Kupfergraben & Monbijoubrücke; adult/concession €12/6; ☺10am-6pm Tue, Wed

& Fri-Sun, to 8pm Thu), at the island's northern tip, is famous for its medieval sculptures.

DDR Museum
Museum

(GDR Museum; Map p50; ☑030-847 123 731; www.ddr-museum.de; Karl-Liebknecht-Strasse 1; adult/concession €9.50/6; ☉10am-8pm Sun-Fri, to 10pm Sat; ☐100, 200, TXL, ⑤Hackescher Markt) This interactive museum does an entertaining job of pulling back the iron curtain on an extinct society. You'll learn how, under communism, kids were put through collective potty training, engineers earned little more than farmers, and everyone, it seems, went on nudist holidays. A highlight is a simulated ride in a Trabi (an East German car).

Fernsehturm
Landmark

(TV Tower; Map p50; ☑030-247 575 875; www.tv-turm.de; Panoramastrasse 1a; adult/child €13/8.50, premium ticket €19.50/12; ☉9am-midnight Mar-Oct, 10am-midnight Nov-Feb, last ascent 11.30pm; ☐100, 200, TXL, Ⓤ Alexanderplatz, ⑤ Alexanderplatz) Germany's tallest structure, the TV Tower has been soaring 368m high since 1969 and is as iconic to Berlin as the Eiffel Tower is to Paris. On clear days, views are stunning from the panorama level at 203m or from the upstairs **restaurant** (Map p50; ☑030-247 5750; www.tv-turm.de/en/bar-restaurant; mains lunch €9.50-18.50, dinner €14.50-28.50; ☉10am-midnight), which makes one revolution per hour. To shorten the wait, buy a timed ticket online.

Berliner Dom
Church

(Berlin Cathedral; Map p50; ☑030-2026 9136; www.berlinerdom.de; Am Lustgarten; adult/concession/under 18yr €7/5/free; ☉9am-8pm Apr-Oct, to 7pm Nov-Mar; ☐100, 200, TXL, ⑤ Hackescher Markt) Pompous yet majestic, the Italian Renaissance–style former royal court church (1905) does triple duty as house of worship, museum and concert hall. Inside it's gilt to the hilt and outfitted with a lavish marble-and-onyx altar, a 7269-pipe Sauer organ and elaborate royal sarcophagi. Climb up the 267 steps to the gallery for glorious city views.

◎ Potsdamer Platz & Tiergarten

Potsdamer Platz
Area

(Map p55; Alte Potsdamer Strasse; ☐200, ⑤Potsdamer Platz, Ⓤ Potsdamer Platz) The rebirth of the historic Potsdamer Platz was Europe's biggest building project of the 1990s, a showcase of urban renewal masterminded by such top international architects as Renzo Piano and Helmut Jahn. An entire city quarter sprouted on terrain once bifurcated by the Berlin Wall and today houses offices, theatres and cinemas, hotels, apartments and museums. Highlights include the glass-tented **Sony Center** (Map p55; Potsdamer Strasse) and the **Panoramapunkt** (Map p55; ☑030-2593 7080; www.panoramapunkt.de; Potsdamer Platz 1; adult/concession €6.50/5, without wait €10.50/8; ☉10am-8pm Apr-Oct, to 6pm Nov-Mar) observation deck.

Tiergarten
Park

(Map p55; Strasse des 17 Juni; ☐100, 200, ⑤Potsdamer Platz, Brandenburger Tor, Ⓤ Brandenburger Tor) **FREE** Berlin's rulers used to hunt boar and pheasants in the rambling Tiergarten until garden architect Peter Lenné landscaped the grounds in the 18th century. Today it's one of the world's largest urban parks, popular for strolling, jogging, picnicking, Frisbee tossing and, yes, nude sunbathing and gay cruising (especially around the Löwenbrücke). It is bisected by a major artery, the Strasse des 17 Juni. Walking across the entire park takes about an hour, but even a shorter stroll has its rewards.

Gemäldegalerie
Gallery

(Gallery of Old Masters; Map p55; ☑030-266 424 242; www.smb.museum/gg; Matthäikirch-platz; adult/concession €10/5; ☉10am-6pm Tue, Wed & Fri, 10am-8pm Thu, 11am-6pm Sat & Sun; ♿; ☐M29, M48, M85, 200, ⑤Potsdamer Platz, Ⓤ Potsdamer Platz) This museum ranks among the world's finest and most comprehensive collections of European art with about 1500 paintings spanning the arc of artistic vision from the 13th to the 18th century. Wear comfy shoes when exploring

Kreuzberg & Potsdamer Platz

Kreuzberg & Potsdamer Platz

the 72 galleries: a walk past masterpieces by Titian, Dürer, Hals, Vermeer, Gainsborough and many more Old Masters covers almost 2km. Don't miss the Rembrandt Room (Room X).

◎ Prenzlauer Berg

Prenzlauer Berg doesn't have any blockbuster sights, and most of what it does have is concentrated in the pretty southern section around Kollwitzplatz. The neighbourhood does include the city's most

important exhibit on the Berlin Wall, the Gedenkstätte Berliner Mauer (p39), which begins in Wedding and stretches for 1.4km all the way into Prenzlauer Berg.

◎ Kreuzberg

Jüdisches Museum   Museum
(Jewish Museum; Map p55; ☏030-2599 3300; www.jmberlin.de; Lindenstrasse 9-14; adult/concession €8/3, audio guide €3; ⊙10am-8pm Tue-Sun, to 10pm Mon, last entry 1hr before closing; ⓤHallesches Tor, Kochstrasse) In a landmark

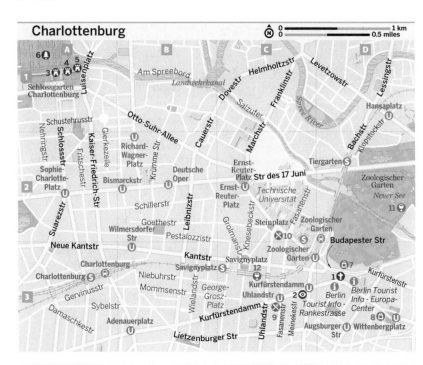

Charlottenburg

building by American-Polish architect
Daniel Libeskind, Berlin's Jewish Museum
offers a chronicle of the trials and triumphs
in 2000 years of Jewish life in Germany.
The exhibit smoothly navigates all major
periods, from the Middle Ages via the En-
lightenment to the community's post-1990
renaissance. Find out about Jewish cultural
contributions, holiday traditions, the difficult road to emancipation and outstanding

individuals (eg Moses Mendelssohn, Levi
Strauss) and the fates of ordinary people.

◎ Charlottenburg

Schloss Charlottenburg   Palace
(Map p56; ☎030-320 910; www.spsg.de; Spandau-
er Damm 10-22; day passes to all 4 buildings adult/
concession €12/9; ☺hours vary by building; P;
▣M45, 109, 309, ⓤRichard-Wagner-Platz, So-
phie-Charlotte-Platz) Charlottenburg Palace is

one of the few sites in Berlin that still reflects the one-time grandeur of the Hohenzollern clan that ruled the region from 1415 to 1918. Originally a petite summer retreat, it grew into an exquisite baroque pile with opulent private apartments, richly festooned festival halls, collections of precious porcelain and paintings by French 18th-century masters. It's lovely in fine weather when you can fold a stroll in the palace park into a day of peeking at royal treasures.

Kaiser-Wilhelm-Gedächtniskirche
Church

(Kaiser Wilhelm Memorial Church; Map p56; ☏030-218 5023; www.gedaechtniskirche.com; Breitscheidplatz; ☉church 9am-7pm, memorial hall 10am-6pm Mon-Fri, 10am-5.30pm Sat, noon-5.30pm Sun; 🚌100, 200, Ⓤ Zoologischer Garten, Kurfürstendamm, Ⓢ Zoologischer Garten) **FREE** Allied bombing in 1943 left only the husk of the west tower of this once magnificent neo-Romanesque church standing. Now an antiwar memorial, it stands quiet and dignified amid the roaring traffic. Historic photographs displayed in the **Gedenkhalle** (Hall of Remembrance), at the bottom of the tower, help you visualise the former grandeur of this 1895 church. The adjacent octagonal hall of worship, added in 1961, has glowing midnight-blue glass walls and a giant 'floating' Jesus.

⊙ TOURS

Berliner Unterwelten
History

(☏030-4991 0517; www.berliner-unterwelten. de; Brunnenstrasse 105; adult/concession €11/9; ☉Dark Worlds tours in English 1pm Mon & 11am Thu-Mon year-round, 11am Wed Mar-Nov, 3pm Wed-Mon & 1pm Wed-Sun Apr-Oct; Ⓢ Gesundbrunnen, Ⓤ Gesundbrunnen) After you've checked off the Brandenburg Gate and the TV Tower, why not explore Berlin's dark and dank underbelly? Join Berliner Unterwelten on its 'Dark Worlds' tour of a WWII underground bunker (available in English) and pick your way through a warren of claustrophobic rooms, past heavy steel doors, hospital beds, helmets, guns, boots and lots of other wartime artefacts.

Berlin on Bike
Cycling

(☏030-4373 9999; www.berlinonbike.de; Knaackstrasse 97, Kulturbrauerei, Court 4; tours incl bike adult/concession €21/18; ☉8am-8pm mid-Mar–mid-Nov, 10am-4pm Mon-Sat mid-Nov–mid-Mar; 🚋M1, Ⓤ Eberswalder Strasse) This well-established company has a busy schedule of insightful and fun bike tours led by locals. There are daily English-language city tours (Berlin's Best) and Berlin Wall tours as well as an Alternative Berlin tour three times weekly. Other tours (eg street art, night tours) run in German or in English on request.

Original Berlin Walks
Walking

(☏030-301 9194; www.berlinwalks.de; adult/concession from €14/12) Berlin's longest-running English-language walking tour company has a large roster of general and themed tours (eg Hitler's Germany, Jewish Life, Berlin Wall), as well as trips out to Sachsenhausen concentration camp, Potsdam and Wittenberg. The website has details on timings and meeting points.

🔴 SHOPPING

KaDeWe
Department Store

(Map p56; ☏030-212 10; www.kadewe.de; Tauentzienstrasse 21-24; ☉10am-8pm Mon-Thu, 10am-9pm Fri, 9.30am-8pm Sat; Ⓤ Wittenbergplatz) Every day some 180,000 shoppers invade continental Europe's largest department store. Going strong since 1907, it boasts an assortment so vast that a pirate-style campaign is the best way to plunder its bounty. If pushed for time, at least hurry up to the legendary 6th-floor gourmet food hall. The name, by the way, stands for *Kaufhaus des Westens* (department store of the West).

Ta(u)sche
Fashion & Accessories

(☏030-4030 1770; www.tausche.de; Raumerstrasse 8; ☉10am-8pm Mon-Fri, to 6pm Sat; Ⓤ Eberswalder Strasse) Heike Braun and Antje Strubels now sell their ingenious messenger-style bags around the world, but this is the shop where it all began. Bags come in 11 sizes with exchangeable flaps that zip off

Explore Berlin's Flea Markets

Berlin's numerous flea markets set up on weekends (usually Sunday) year-round – rain or shine – and are also the purview of fledgling local fashion designers and jewellery makers.

Flohmarkt im Mauerpark (www.flohmarktimmauerpark.de; Bernauer Strasse 63-64; ⊙9am-6pm Sun; 🚋M1, M10, 12, Ⓤ Eberswalder Strasse) Join the throngs of thrifty trinket hunters, bleary-eyed clubbers and excited tourists sifting for treasure at this always busy flea market with cult status, running right where the Berlin Wall once ran. Source new faves among retro threads, local-designer T-shirts, vintage vinyl and offbeat stuff. Street-food stands and beer gardens, including **Mauersegler** (📞030-9788 0904; www.mauersegler-berlin.de; Bernauer Strasse 63-64; ⊙2pm-2am May-Oct; 🚩; 🚋M10, Ⓤ Eberswalder Strasse), provide sustenance.

Nowkoelln Flowmarkt (Map p63; www.nowkoelln.de; Maybachufer; ⊙10am-6pm 2nd & 4th Sun of month Mar-Oct or later; Ⓤ Kottbusser Tor, Schönleinstrasse) This hipster-heavy flea market sets up twice-monthly along the scenic Landwehrkanal and delivers second-hand bargains galore along with handmade threads and jewellery.

RAW Flohmarkt (Map p63; www.raw-flohmarkt-berlin.de; Revaler Strasse 99, RAW Gelände; ⊙9am-7pm Sun; 🚋M10, M13, Ⓢ Warschauer Strasse, Ⓤ Warschauer Strasse) Bargains abound at this smallish flea market right on the grounds of **RAW Gelände** (Map p63; www.raw-tempel.de; along Revaler St), a former train repair station turned party village. It's wonderfully free of professional sellers, meaning you'll find everything from the proverbial kitchen sink to 1970s go-go boots. Bargains are plentiful, and food, a beer garden and cafes are nearby.

and on in seconds. There's a huge range of designs to match your mood or outfit, plus various inserts, depending on whether you need to lug a laptop, a camera or nappies (diapers).

Bikini Berlin Mall
(Map p56; www.bikiniberlin.de; Budapester Strasse 38-50; ⊙shops 10am-8pm Mon-Sat, building 9am-9pm Mon-Sat, 1-6pm Sun; 🚩; 🚌100, 200, Ⓤ Zoologischer Garten, Ⓢ Zoologischer Garten) Germany's first concept mall opened in 2014 in a spectacularly rehabilitated 1950s architectural icon nicknamed 'Bikini' because of its design: 200m-long upper and lower sections separated by an open floor, now chastely covered by a glass facade. Inside are three floors of urban indie boutiques and short-lease pop-up 'boxes' that offer a platform for up-and-coming designers.

EATING
Mitte

Augustiner am Gendarmenmarkt German €€
(Map p50; 📞030-2045 4020; www.augustiner-braeu-berlin.de; Charlottenstrasse 55; mains €6.50-26.50; ⊙10am-2am; Ⓤ Französische Strasse) Tourists, concert-goers and hearty-food lovers rub shoulders at rustic tables in this authentic Bavarian beer hall. Soak up the down-to-earth vibe right along with a mug of full-bodied Augustiner brew. Sausages, roast pork and pretzels provide rib-sticking sustenance, but there's also plenty of lighter (even meat-free) fare as well as good-value lunch specials.

Nobelhart & Schmutzig International €€€
(Map p55; 📞030-2594 0610; www.nobelhartund-schmutzig.com; Friedrichstrasse 218; 10-course menu €80; ⊙6.30pm-midnight; Ⓤ Kochstrasse) 'Brutally local' is the motto at the Michelin-starred restaurant of star sommelier Billy Wagner. All ingredients hail – without exception – from producers in and around Berlin and the nearby Baltic Sea. Hence, no

pepper or lemons. The intellectually ambitious food is fresh and seasonal or naturally preserved by using such traditional methods as pickling, brining and fermenting.

Prenzlauer Berg

Konnopke's Imbiss German €

(☏030-442 7765; www.konnopke-imbiss.de; Schönhauser Allee 44a; sausages €1.30-2; ☺9am-8pm Mon-Fri, 11.30am-8pm Sat; ☒M1, M10, ☒Eberswalder Strasse) Brave the inevitable queue at this famous sausage kitchen, ensconced in the same spot below the elevated U-Bahn tracks since 1930, but now equipped with a heated pavilion and an English menu. The 'secret' sauce topping its classic *Currywurst* comes in a four-tier heat scale from mild to wild.

Lucky Leek Vegan €€

(☏030-6640 8710; www.lucky-leek.de; Kollwitzstrasse 54; mains €14-20, 3-/5-course dinners €33/55; ☺6-10pm Wed-Sun; ☝; ☒Senefelderplatz) Josita Hartanto has a knack for coaxing maximum flavour out of the vegetable kingdom and for boldly combining

ingredients in unexpected ways. Hers is one of the best vegan restaurants in town and is especially lovely in the summer, when seating expands to a leafy pavement terrace. No à la carte on Fridays and Saturdays.

Oderquelle German €€

(☏030-4400 8080; www.oderquelle.de; Oderberger Strasse 27; mains €12-20; ☺6-11pm Mon-Sat, noon-11pm Sun; ☒M1, 12, ☒Eberswalder Strasse) It's always fun to pop by this woodsy resto and see what's inspired the chef today. Most likely it will be a well-crafted hearty German meal, perhaps with a slight Mediterranean nuance. On the standard menu, the crispy *Flammkuche* (Alsatian pizza) is a reliable standby. Best seat: on the pavement so you can keep an eye on the parade of passers-by.

Zum Schusterjungen German €€

(☏030-442 7654; www.zumschusterjungen.com; Danziger Strasse 9; mains €9-17; ☺11am-midnight; ☒Eberswalder Strasse) At this old-school gastropub, rustic Berlin charm is doled out with as much abandon as the delish home cooking. Big platters of goulash,

Konnopke's Imbiss

Clärchens Ballhaus

roast pork and *sauerbraten* (pot roas) feed both tummy and soul, as do the regionally brewed Berliner Schusterjunge Pilsner and Märkischer Landmann black beer.

⊗ Kreuzberg

Curry 36 German €

(Map p55; ✆030-2580 088 336; www.curry36.de; Mehringdamm 36; snacks €2-6; ⊙9am-5am; Ⓤ Mehringdamm) Day after day, night after night, a motley crowd – cops, cabbies, queens, office jockeys, savvy tourists etc – wait their turn at this top-ranked *Currywurst* snack shop that's been frying 'em up since 1981.

eins44 French, German €€€

(Map p63; ✆030-6298 1212; www.eins44.com; Elbestrasse 28/29, 2nd courtyard; mains lunch €8-10, dinner €26, 3-/4-/5-course dinner €43/53/63; ⊙12.30-2.30pm Tue-Fri, 7pm-midnight Tue-Sat; 🛜; 🚍M41, 104, 167, Ⓤ Rathaus Neukölln) This outpost in a late-19th-century distillery serves 'elevated Franco-German bistro fare' that ticks all the boxes from old-fashioned to postmodern. Metal lamps,

tiles and heavy wooden tables create industrial charm enhanced by large black-and-white photos. Lunches feature just a few classic dishes, while dinners are more elaborate.

Volt German €€€

(Map p63; ✆030-338 402 320; www.restaurant-volt.de; Paul-Lincke-Ufer 21; mains €32, 5-course dinner €78; ⊙6pm-midnight Mon-Sat; 🍴; Ⓤ Görlitzer Bahnhof, Schönleinstrasse) The theatrical setting in a 1928 transformer station would be enough to seek out Matthias Gleiss' sophisticated culinary outpost. More drama awaits on the plates where traditional Berlin dishes and German classics get a contemporary kick while putting on an artful show in honest-to-goodness ways.

⊗ Charlottenburg

Café-Restaurant Wintergarten im Literaturhaus International €€

(Map p56; ✆030-882 5414; www.literaturhaus-berlin.de/wintergarten-cafe-restaurant.html; Fasanenstrasse 23; mains €8-16; ⊙9am-midnight; 🍴; Ⓤ Uhlandstrasse) The hustle and bustle of Ku'damm is only a block away from this genteel art nouveau villa with attached literary salon and bookshop. Tuck into seasonal bistro cuisine amid elegant Old Berlin flair in the gracefully stucco-ornamented rooms or, if weather permits, in the idyllic garden. Breakfast is served until 2pm.

Restaurant am Steinplatz
German €€€

(Map p56; ☑030-5544 447 053; www.hotel steinplatz.com; Steinplatz 4; mains €18-38, 4-/5-course dinner €56/65; ☺noon-2.30pm & 6.30-10.30pm; P; ☒M45, ⓤErnst-Reuter-Platz, Zoologischer Garten, ⓢZoologischer Garten) The 1920s get a 21st-century makeover at this stylish outpost with an open kitchen where Marcus Zimmer feeds regional products into classic German and Berlin recipes. Even rustic beer-hall dishes such as *Eisbein* (boiled pork knuckle) are imaginatively reinterpreted and beautifully plated. A perennial favourite is the *Königsberger Klopse* (veal dumplings with capers, beetroot and mashed potatoes).

🍸 DRINKING & NIGHTLIFE

Mitte

Clärchens Ballhaus
Club

(Map p50; ☑030-282 9295; www.ballhaus.de; Auguststrasse 24; ☺11am-late; ☒M1, ⓢOranienburger Strasse) Yesteryear is right now at this late, great 19th-century dance hall where groovers and grannies hoof it across the parquet without even a touch of irony. There are different sounds nightly – salsa to swing, tango to disco – and a live band on Saturday. Dancing kicks off from 9pm or 9.30pm. Easy door but often packed, so book a table.

Strandbar Mitte
Bar

(Map p50; ☑030-2838 5588; www.strandbar-mitte.de; Monbijoustrasse 3; dancing €4; ☺10am-late May-Sep; ☒M1, ⓢOranienburger Strasse) With a full-on view of the Bode-Museum, palm trees and a relaxed ambience, Germany's first beach bar (since

🍴 Berlin's Eclectic Cuisine

Alongside Hamburg, Berlin has one of the country's most dynamic and swiftly evolving restaurant scenes, but it can still lay claim to local delicacies. First up is *Eisbein* (pork knuckles with sauerkraut), then *Kohlsuppe* (cabbage soup) and *Erbsensuppe* (pea soup). Then there's the classic meaty treat on the hoof: the *Boulette,* a German-style hamburger, eaten with a dry bun and ketchup or mustard. Don't bypass the chance to give *Königsberger Klopse* (veal dumplings in caper sauce) a whirl, either.

Berlin is also where you'll find the country's highest concentration of Turkish *Döner Kebab* (doner kebab)spots, an essential end to any drink-fuelled night on the town. Germany's Turkish population invented the modern doner, adding salad and garlicky yoghurt sauce to spit-roasted lamb, veal or chicken in pita bread.

Pork knuckle and sauerkraut

2002) is great for balancing a surfeit of sightseeing stimulus with a reviving drink and thin-crust pizza. At night, there's dancing under the stars with tango, cha-cha, swing and salsa, often preceded by dance lessons.

🍸 Potsdamer Platz & Tiergarten

Fragrances
Cocktail Bar

(Map p55; ☑030-337 777; www.ritzcarlton. com; Ritz-Carlton, Potsdamer Platz 3; ☺from

LGBT Berlin

Berlin's legendary liberalism has spawned one of the world's biggest, most divine and diverse LGBT playgrounds. Anything goes in 'Homopolis' (and we do mean anything!), from the highbrow to the hands-on, the bourgeois to the bizarre, the mainstream to the flamboyant. Except for the most hardcore places, gay spots get their share of opposite-sex and straight patrons.

Generally speaking, Berlin's gayscape runs the entire spectrum from mellow cafes, campy bars and cinemas to saunas, cruising areas, clubs with darkrooms and all-out sex venues. In fact, sex and sexuality are entirely everyday matters to the unshockable city folks and there are very few, if any, itches that can't be quite openly and legally scratched. As elsewhere, gay men have more options for having fun, but grrrrls of all stripes won't feel left out either.

Christopher Street Day celebrations
SERGEY KOHL/SHUTTERSTOCK ©

7pm Wed-Sat; ⊛; 🚌200, Ⓢ Potsdamer Platz, Ⓤ Potsdamer Platz) Berlin cocktail maven Arnd Heissen's newest baby is the world's first 'perfume bar', a libation station where he mixes potable potions mimicking famous scents. The black-mirrored space in the Ritz-Carlton is a like a 3D menu where adventurous drinkers sniff out their favourite from among a row of perfume bottles, then settle back into flocked couches to enjoy exotic blends served in unusual vessels, including a birdhouse.

Café am Neuen See   Beer Garden

(Map p56; ☑030-254 4930; www.cafeamneuen see.de; Lichtensteinallee 2; ☺restaurant 9am-11pm, beer garden 11am-late Mon-Fri, 10am-late Sat & Sun; ⓯; 🚌200, Ⓤ Zoologischer Garten, Ⓢ Zoologischer Garten, Tiergarten) Next to an idyllic pond in Tiergarten, this restaurant gets jammed year-round for its sumptuous breakfast and seasonal fare, but it really comes into its own during beer garden season. Enjoy a microvacation over a cold one and a pretzel or pizza, then take your sweetie for a spin in a rowing boat.

Prenzlauer Berg

Prater Biergarten   Beer Garden

(☑030-448 5688; www.pratergarten.de; Kastanienallee 7-9; snacks €2.50-6; ☺noon-late Apr-Sep, weather permitting; Ⓤ Eberswalder Strasse) Berlin's oldest beer garden has seen beer-soaked nights since 1837 and is still a charismatic spot for guzzling a custom-brewed Prater Pilsner beneath the ancient chestnut trees (self-service). Kids can romp around the small play area.

Weinerei Forum   Wine Bar

(☑030-440 6983; www.weinerei.com; Fehrbelliner Strasse 57; ☺10am-midnight; ☎; 🚌M1, Ⓤ Rosenthaler Platz) After 8pm, this living-room-style cafe turns into a wine bar that works on the honour principle: you 'rent' a wine glass for €2, then help yourself to as much vino as you like and in the end decide what you want to pay. Please be fair to keep this fantastic concept going.

Kreuzberg

Schwarze Traube   Cocktail Bar

(Map p63; ☑030-2313 5569; www.schwarze traube.de; Wrangelstrasse 24; ☺7pm-2am Sun-Thu, to 5am Fri & Sat; Ⓤ Görlitzer Bahnhof) Mixologist Atalay Aktas was Germany's Best Bartender of 2013 and this pint-sized drinking parlour is where he and his staff create their magic potions. Since there's no menu, each drink is calibrated to the taste and mood of each patron using premium spirits, expertise and a dash of psychology.

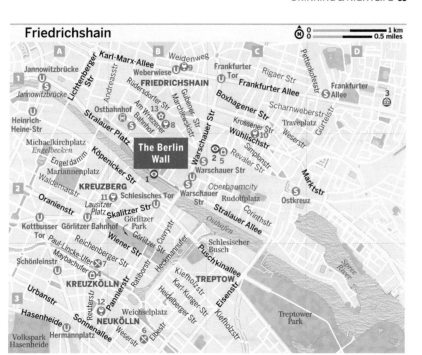

Friedrichshain

Thelonius　　　　　Cocktail Bar

(Map p63; 📞030-5561 8232; www.facebook.
com/theloniousbarberlin; Weserstrasse
202; ⏰7pm-2am or later; ⓤHermannplatz)
Embraced by a mellow soundscape and
complexion-friendly lighting, well-
mannered patrons pack this narrow burrow
named for American jazz giant Thelonius
Monk. Owner Laura Maria, who travelled
the world before returning to her Neukölln
roots, is the consummate host and creator

of the drinks menu that ticks all the boxes,
from classics to the adventurous.

🟢 Friedrichshain

Berghain/Panorama Bar　　Club

(Map p63; www.berghain.de; Am Wriezener Bahnhof; ⏰midnight Fri-Mon morning; ⑤Ostbahnhof) Only world-class spinmasters heat up
this hedonistic bass-junkie hellhole inside
a labyrinthine ex–power plant. Hard-edged
minimal techno dominates the ex–turbine

hall (Berghain) while house dominates at Panorama Bar, one floor up. Strict door, no cameras. Check the website for midweek concerts and record-release parties at the main venue and the adjacent **Kantine am Berghain** (Map p63; 030-2936 0210; www. berghain.de; Am Wriezener Bahnhof; admission varies; hours vary; Ostbahnhof).

Briefmarken Weine
Wine Bar

(Map p63; 030-4202 5292; www.briefmarken weine.de; Karl-Marx-Allee 99; 7pm-midnight; Weberwiese) For *dolce vita* right on socialist Karl-Marx-Allee, head to this charmingly nostalgic Italian wine bar ensconced in a former stamp shop. The original wooden cabinets cradle a hand-picked selection of Italian bottles that complement a snack menu of yummy cheeses, prosciutto and salami, plus a pasta dish of the day.

Hops & Barley
Pub

(Map p63; 030-2936 7534; www.hopsand barley-berlin.de; Wühlischstrasse 22/23; from 5pm Mon-Fri, from 3pm Sat & Sun; M13, Warschauer Strasse, Warschauer Strasse) Conversation flows as freely as the unfiltered Pilsner, malty *Dunkel* (dark) and fruity

Weizen (wheat) produced right here at one of Berlin's oldest craft breweries. The pub is inside a former butcher's shop and still has the tiled walls to prove it. Two projectors show football (soccer) games.

Charlottenburg

Bar am Steinplatz
Bar

(Map p56; 030-554 4440; www.hotelamstein platz.com; Steinplatz 4; 4pm-late; Ernst-Reuter-Platz) Christian Gentemann's liquid playground may reside at art deco Hotel am Steinplatz, but it hardly whispers 'stuffy hotel bar'. The classic and creative drinks (how about a Red Beet Old Fashioned?) often showcase regionally produced spirits and ingredients, and even the draught beer hails from the Berlin-based Rollberg brewery. Inventive bar bites complement the drinks.

Diener Tattersall
Pub

(Map p56; 030-881 5329; www.diener-berlin. de; Grolmanstrasse 47; 6pm-2am; Savignyplatz) In business for over a century, this Old Berlin haunt was taken over by German heavyweight champion Franz Diener in

From left: Hotel am Steinplatz; Chamäleon Varieté; Berliner Philharmonie

the 1950s and has since been one of West Berlin's pre-eminent artist pubs. From Billy Wilder to Harry Belafonte, they all came for beer and *Bulette* (meat patties), and left behind signed black-and-white photographs that grace Diener's walls to this day.

✪ ENTERTAINMENT

Berliner Philharmonie — Classical Music

(Map p55; ☏ tickets 030-254 888 999; www.berliner-philharmoniker.de; Herbert-von-Karajan-Strasse 1; tickets €30-100; ☒M29, M48, M85, 200, Ⓢ Potsdamer Platz, Ⓤ Potsdamer Platz) This world-famous concert hall has supreme acoustics and, thanks to Hans Scharoun's terraced vineyard configuration, not a bad seat in the house. It's the home turf of the Berliner Philharmoniker, which will be led by Sir Simon Rattle until 2018. One year later, Russia-born Kirill Petrenko will pick up the baton as music director.

Chamäleon Varieté — Cabaret

(Map p50; ☏ 030-400 0590; www.chamaeleonberlin.com; Rosenthaler Strasse 40/41; tickets €29-69; ☒M1, Ⓢ Hackescher Markt) A marriage of art nouveau charms and high-tech theatre trappings, this intimate 1920s-style venue in an old ballroom hosts classy variety shows – comedy, juggling acts and singing – often in sassy, sexy and unconventional fashion.

❶ INFORMATION

Visit Berlin (www.visitberlin.de), the Berlin tourist board, operates five walk-in offices and info offices at the airports.

Brandenburger Tor (Map p50; ☏ 030-250 025; www.visitberlin.de; Brandenburger Tor, south wing, Pariser Platz; ⊙9.30am-7pm Apr-Oct, to 6pm Nov-Mar; Ⓢ Brandenburger Tor, Ⓤ Brandenburger Tor)

Europa-Center (Map p56; ☏ 030-250 025; Tauentzienstrasse 9, Europa-Center, ground fl; ⊙10am-8pm Mon-Sat; ☒100, 200, Ⓤ Kurfürstendamm)

Hauptbahnhof (Map p50; ☏ 030-250 025; www.visitberlin.de; Hauptbahnhof, Europaplatz entrance, ground fl; ⊙8am-10pm; Ⓢ Hauptbahnhof, Ⓡ Hauptbahnhof)

Rankestrasse (Map p56; ☎030-250 025; www.
visitberlin.de; cnr Rankestrasse & Kurfürstendamm; ⊙10am-6pm Apr-Oct, to 4pm Nov-Mar;
🚌100, 200, Ⓤ Kurfürstendamm)

TV Tower (Map p50; ☎030-250 025; www.visit-
berlin.de; Panoramastrasse 1a, TV Tower, ground
fl; ⊙10am-6pm Apr-Oct, to 4pm Nov-Mar; 🚌100,
200, TXL, Ⓤ Alexanderplatz, Ⓢ Alexanderplatz)

 ## GETTING THERE & AWAY

AIR

Most visitors arrive in Berlin by air. The opening
of Berlin's new central airport has been delayed;
check www.berlin-airport.de for the latest. In the
meantime, flights continue to land at the city's
Tegel (TXL; ☎030-6091 1150; www.berlin-
airport.de; 🚌 Tegel Flughafen) and **Schönefeld**
(SXF; ☎030-6091 1150; www.berlin-airport.de;
🚆 Airport-Express, RE7 & RB14) airports.

TRAIN

Berlin's **Hauptbahnhof** (Main Train Station; www.
berliner-hbf.de; Europaplatz, Washingtonplatz;
Ⓢ Hauptbahnhof, Ⓤ Hauptbahnhof) is in the
heart of the city, just north of the Government
Quarter and within walking distance of major
sights and hotels. From here, the U-Bahn, the
S-Bahn, trams and buses provide links to all

parts of town. Taxi ranks are located outside
the north exit (Europaplatz) and the south exit
(Washingtonplatz).

 ## GETTING AROUND

Berlin's extensive and efficient public transport
system is operated by BVG (www.bvg.de) and
consists of the U-Bahn (underground, or sub-
way), the S-Bahn (light rail), buses and trams.

U-Bahn Most efficient way to travel; operates
4am to 12.30am and all night Friday, Saturday
and public holidays. From Sunday to Thursday,
half-hourly night buses take over in the interim.

S-Bahn Less frequent than U-Bahn trains but
with fewer stops, and thus useful for longer
distances. Same operating hours as the U-Bahn.

Bus Slow but useful for sightseeing on the
cheap. Run frequently 4.30am to 12.30am;
half-hourly night buses in the interim. MetroBus-
es (designated eg M1, M19) operate 24/7.

Tram Only in the eastern districts; MetroTrams
(designated eg M1, M2) run 24/7.

Cycling Bike lanes and rental stations abound;
bikes allowed in specially marked U-Bahn and
S-Bahn carriages.

Taxi Can be hailed; fairly inexpensive; avoid
during daytime rush hour.

Where to Stay

Berlin offers the full gamut of places to unpack your suitcase – you can even sleep in a former bank, boat or factory, in the home of a silent-movie diva or in a 'flying bed'.

Neighbourhood	Atmosphere
Historic Mitte	Close to major sights such as the Reichstag and Brandenburger Tor; great transport links; mostly high-end hotels; top restaurants; touristy, expensive, pretty dead at night
Museumsinsel & Alexanderplatz	Supercentral sightseeing quarter; easy transport access; close to blockbuster sights and mainstream shopping; noisy, busy and dusty thanks to lots of major construction; hardly any nightlife
Potsdamer Platz & Tiergarten	Urban flair in Berlin's newest quarter; cutting-edge architecture; high-end hotels; top museums; limited eating options; pricey
Scheunenviertel	Hipster quarter; trendy, historic, central; brims with boutique and designer hotels; strong cafe scene; top galleries and plenty of great street art; pricey, busy, noisy, no parking, bit touristy
City West & Charlottenburg	Great shopping; 'Old Berlin' bars and top restaurants; best range of good-value lodging; historic B&Bs; far from key sights and nightlife
Kreuzberg & Northern Neukölln	Best for bar-hopping and clubbing; cheap; lots of hostels; great foodie scene; excellent street art; gritty, noisy and busy
Friedrichshain	Student and young family quarter; bubbling nightlife; limited sleeping options; not so central; transport difficult in some areas
Prenzlauer Berg	Charming residential area; lively cafe and restaurant scene; indie boutiques and Mauerpark flea market; limited late-night action

AMSTERDAM, THE NETHERLANDS

Amsterdam at a Glance...

Amsterdam works its fairy-tale magic in many ways: via the gabled, Golden Age buildings; glinting, boat-filled canals; and especially the cosy, centuries-old bruin cafés (traditional pubs), where candles burn low and beers froth high. Add in mega art museums and cool street markets, and it's easy to see why this atmospheric city is one of Europe's most popular.

With One Day in Port

Begin with the biggies: head to the Museum Quarter to ogle the masterpieces at the **Van Gogh Museum** (p72) and **Rijksmuseum** (p78). They'll be crowded, so make sure you've prebooked tickets. In the afternoon, immerse yourself in the **Negen Straatjes** (Nine Streets; p83), a noughts-and-crosses board of speciality shops. The **Anne Frank Huis** (p74) is also in the neighbourhood, and it's a must.

Best Places for...

Traditional local food Bistro Bij Ons (p85)

Quick snacks Vleminckx (p84)

Traditional bar In 't Aepjen (p86)

Fine dining D'Vijff Vlieghen (p85)

Cakes De Laatste Kruimel (p84)

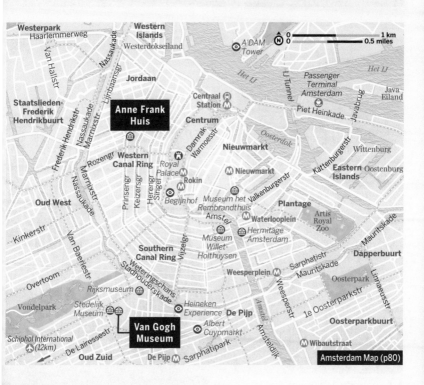

Amsterdam Map (p80)

Getting from the Port

Amsterdam's main passenger terminal is just one stop on tram 26 from the Centraal Station transport hub. If you fancy the stroll, it's around 15 minutes. From Centraal Station, you can access the rest of the transport network. A one-day public transport ticket is €7.50 and can be bought at the terminal, which also hires bikes.

Fast Facts

Currency Euro (€)

Language Dutch. English widely spoken.

Free wi-fi Most cafes; Instabridge app is also very useful.

Tourist information Information desk in passenger terminal. I Amsterdam Visitor Centre (is located outside Centraal Station.

Transport Locals use bikes to get around. Trams are fast, frequent and the main public transport option.

Van Gogh Museum

The world's largest Van Gogh collection is a superb line-up of masterworks. Opened in 1973 to house the collection of Vincent's younger brother, Theo, the museum comprises some 200 paintings and 500 drawings by Vincent and his contemporaries.

Great For...

☑ Don't Miss

The Potato Eaters, The Yellow House, Wheatfield with Crows and Sunflowers.

Entrance & Set-Up

The museum is spread over four levels, moving chronologically from Floor 0 (aka the ground floor) to Floor 3. It's still a manageable size. The audio guide is helpful and there's a separate version for children. The following sections include coverage of seminal works.

The Potato Eaters & Skeleton with Burning Cigarette

Van Gogh's earliest works – showing raw, if unrefined, talent – are from his time in the Dutch countryside and in Antwerp between 1883 and 1885. He painted peasant life, exalting their existence in works such as *The Potato Eaters* (1885). The symbolic *Still Life with Bible* (1885), painted after his father's death, shows a burnt-out candle, his Protestant minister father's bible and a much-thumbed smaller book, *La Joi*

SARAH COGHILL/LONELY PLANET ©

⚓

Explore Ashore

The museum is a 15-minute tram ride (tram 2 or 5; stop Van Baerlestraat) from Centraal Station. Trams run every few minutes. Allow about 1½ hours for the visit. Prebooking tickets will save the long queue, but you may still wait up to 15 minutes when busy.

❶ Need to Know

☏020-570 52 00; www.vangoghmuseum. com; Museumplein 6; adult/child €18/free, audio guide €5/3; ☺9am-7pm Sun-Thu, to 9pm Sat mid-Jul–Aug, to 6pm Sat-Thu Sep–mid-Jul, to 5pm Jan-Mar, to 10pm Fri; 🚊2/3/5/12 Van Baerlestraat

de Vivre, representing Van Gogh's more secular philosophy. *Skeleton with Burning Cigarette* (1886) was painted when Van Gogh was a student in Antwerp.

Self-Portraits

In 1886 Van Gogh moved to Paris, where his brother, Theo, was working as an art dealer. Vincent wanted to master the art of portraiture, but was too poor to pay for models. Several self-portraits resulted. You can see his palette begin to brighten as he comes under the influence of local Impressionists.

Sunflowers & The Yellow House

In 1888 Van Gogh left for Arles in Provence to paint its colourful landscapes and try to achieve his dream of creating an artists colony in the countryside. *Sunflowers* (1889) and other blossoms that shimmer with intense Mediterranean light are from this

period. So is *The Yellow House* (1888), a rendering of the abode Van Gogh rented in Arles. The artist Paul Gauguin came to stay, but they quarrelled terribly. *The Bedroom* (1888) depicts Van Gogh's sleeping quarters at the house. In 1888 Van Gogh sliced off part of his ear during a bout of psychosis.

Wheatfield with Crows

Van Gogh had himself committed to an asylum in Saint-Rémy in 1889. While there, his work became ever more extraordinary. His wildly expressive, yet tightly controlled landscapes are based on the surrounding countryside, with its cypress and olive trees. This period includes the sinuous, pulsating *Irises*. In 1890 he went north to Auvers-sur-Oise. One of his last paintings, *Wheatfield with Crows* (1890), is particularly menacing and ominous, and was finished shortly before his suicide, though it wasn't his final work.

Anne Frank Huis

It is one of the 20th century's most compelling stories: a young Jewish girl forced into hiding with her family and their friends to escape deportation by the Nazis. Walking through the bookcase-door is stepping back into a time that seems both distant and tragically real.

Great For...

☑ Don't Miss

Details including Anne's red-plaid diary, WWII news reels and a video of Anne's schoolmate Hanneli Gosler.

Background

It took the German army just five days to occupy all of the Netherlands. Once Hitler's forces had swept across the country, many Jews – like Anne Frank and her family – eventually went into hiding. Anne's diary describes how restrictions were gradually imposed on Dutch Jews: from being forbidden to ride streetcars and being forced to turn in their bicycles, to not being allowed to visit Christian friends.

The Franks moved into the upper floors of the specially prepared rear of the building on Prinsengracht, along with another couple, the Van Pels (the Van Daans in Anne's diary), and their son Peter. Four months later Fritz Pfeffer (called Mr Dussel in the diary) joined the household. Here they survived until they were discovered by the Gestapo in August 1944.

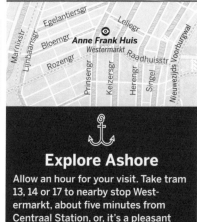

Explore Ashore

Allow an hour for your visit. Take tram 13, 14 or 17 to nearby stop Westermarkt, about five minutes from Centraal Station, or, it's a pleasant 20-minute walk.

ⓘ Need to Know

☏ 020-556 71 05; www.annefrank.org; Prinsengracht 263-267; adult/child €9/4.50; ⊙9am-10pm Apr-Oct, 9am-7pm Sun-Fri, to 9pm Sat Nov-Mar; 🚊13/14/17 Westermarkt

Ground Floor

After several renovations, the house itself is now contained within a modern, square shell that attempts to retain the original feel of the building (it was used during WWII as offices and a warehouse).

Offices & Warehouse

The building originally held Otto Frank's pectin (a substance used in jelly-making) business. On the lower floors you'll see the former offices of Victor Kugler, Otto's business partner, and the desks of Miep Gies, Bep Voskuijl and Jo Kleiman, all of whom worked in the office and provided food, clothing and other goods for the household.

Secret Annexe

The upper floors in the *achterhuis* (rear house) contain the Secret Annexe, where the living quarters have been preserved in powerful austerity. As you enter Anne's small bedroom, you can still sense the remnants of a young girl's dreams: view the photos of Hollywood stars and postcards of the Dutch royal family that she pasted on the wall.

The Diary

More haunting exhibits and videos await after you return to the front house – including Anne's red-plaid diary itself, sitting alone in a glass case. Watch the video of Anne's old schoolmate Hanneli Gosler, who describes encountering Anne at Bergen-Belsen concentration camp. Read heartbreaking letters from Otto, the only Secret Annexe occupant to survive the camps.

Tickets

At the time of research the only way to visit was with a ticket purchased online, although this may change, so check the website. Tickets are released two months in advance. You can print them or show them on your phone. You'll receive a set time for entry on a specific date.

Exploring the Jordaan

A former workers' quarter, the Jordaan teems with cosy pubs, galleries and markets crammed into a grid of tiny lanes. It's a wonderfully atmospheric place for a stroll.

Start Noorderkerk
Distance 2.7km
Duration one hour

3 Through a red door, **Rapenhofje** is a little courtyard that was home to one of Amsterdam's oldest almshouses (1648).

STAATSLIEDEN -
FREDERIK
HENDRIKBUURT

Take a Break... Grab a bite and a drink at scruffy yet alluring **Café 't Monumentje** (www.monument je.nl; ☺8.30am-1am Mon-Thu, to 3am Fri, 9am-3am Sat, 11am-1am Sun).

4 Westerstraat is a main drag of the Jordaan, with a weekly clothing market and **Pianola Museum** (www.pianola.nl; Westerstraat 106; museum adult/child €5/3, concert tickets from €7.50; ☺2-5pm Sun).

6 Johnny Jordaanplein is a square dedicated to a local hero and singer of schmaltzy tunes.

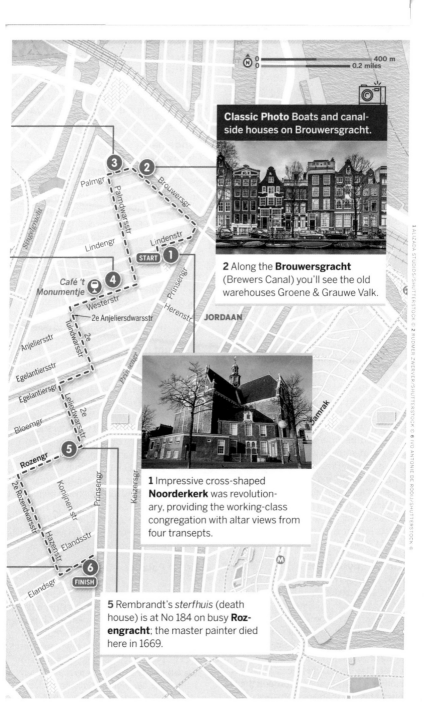

Classic Photo Boats and canalside houses on Brouwersgracht.

2 Along the **Brouwersgracht** (Brewers Canal) you'll see the old warehouses Groene & Grauwe Valk.

1 Impressive cross-shaped **Noorderkerk** was revolutionary, providing the working-class congregation with altar views from four transepts.

5 Rembrandt's *sterfhuis* (death house) is at No 184 on busy **Rozengracht**; the master painter died here in 1669.

JORDAAN

Café 't Monumentje

START

FINISH

SIGHTS

Rijksmuseum · Museum

(National Museum; 020-674 70 00; www.
rijksmuseum.nl; Museumstraat 1; adult/child
€17.50/free, audio guide €5; 9am-5pm; 2/5
Rijksmuseum) The Rijksmuseum is among
the world's finest art museums, packing in
works by local heroes Rembrandt, Vermeer
and Van Gogh as well as 7500 other masterpieces over 1.5km of galleries. To avoid
the biggest crowds, come before 10am or
after 3pm. Prebook tickets online, which
provides fast-track entry.

Start on the 2nd floor, with the astound-
ing Golden Age works. Intimate paintings
by Vermeer and de Hooch allow insight
into everyday life in the 17th century, while
Rembrandt's *The Night Watch* (1642) takes
pride of place.

Heineken Experience · Brewery

(020-523 92 22; https://tickets.heineken
experience.com; Stadhouderskade 78; adult/child
self-guided tour €18/12.50, VIP guided tour €49,
Rock the City ticket €25; 10.30am-7.30pm Mon-
Thu, to 9pm Fri-Sun; 16/24 Stadhouderskade)
On the site of the company's old brewery, Heineken's self-guided 'Experience'
provides an entertaining overview of the
brewing process, with a multimedia exhibit
where you 'become' a beer by getting
shaken up, sprayed with water and sub-
jected to heat. Prebooking tickets online
saves adults €2 and, crucially, allows you
to skip the ticket queues. Guided 2½-hour
VIP tours end with a five-beer tasting and
cheese pairing. Great-value Rock the City
tickets include a 45-minute canal cruise to
A'DAM Tower.

Albert Cuypmarkt · Market

(www.albertcuyp-markt.amsterdam; Albert
Cuypstraat, btwn Ferdinand Bolstraat & Van
Woustraat; 9.30am-5pm Mon-Sat; 16/24
Albert Cuypstraat) Some 260 stalls fill the Albert Cuypmarkt, Amsterdam's largest and
busiest market. Vendors loudly tout their
array of gadgets, homewares, flowers, fruit,
vegetables, herbs and spices. Many sell
clothes and other goods, too, and they're
often cheaper than anywhere else. Snack

vendors tempt passers-by with raw-herring
sandwiches, *frites* (fries), *poffertjes* (tiny
Dutch pancakes dusted with icing sugar)
and caramel-syrup-filled *stroopwafels*. If
you have room after all that, the surrounding area teems with cosy *cafés* (pubs) and
eateries.

Vondelpark · Park

(www.hetvondelpark.net; 2 Amstelveenseweg)
A private park for the wealthy until 1953,
Vondelpark now occupies a special place in
Amsterdam's heart. It's a magical escape,
but also supplies a busy social scene,
encompassing cycle ways, pristine lawns,
ponds with swans, quaint cafes, footbridg-
es and winding footpaths. On a sunny day,
an open-air party atmosphere ensues
when tourists, lovers, cyclists, in-line
skaters, pram-pushing parents, cartwheel-
ing children, football-kicking teenagers,
spliff-sharing friends and champagne-
swilling picnickers all come out to play.

Museum het Rembrandthuis · Museum

(Rembrandt House Museum; 020-520 04 00;
www.rembrandthuis.nl; Jodenbreestraat 4; adult/
child €13/4; 10am-6pm; 9/14 Waterlooplein)
Housed in Rembrandt's former home, where
the master painter spent his most successful years, painting big commissions such as
the *Night Watch* and running the Netherlands' largest painting studio. It wasn't to
last, however: his work fell out of fashion, he
had some expensive relationship problems
and bankruptcy came a-knocking. The
inventory drawn up when he had to leave the
house is the reason curators have been able
to refurnish the house so faithfully.

Royal Palace · Palace

(Koninklijk Paleis; 020-522 61 61; www.
paleisamsterdam.nl; Dam; adult/child €10/free;
10am-5pm; 4/9/16/24 Dam) Opened as a
town hall in 1655, this resplendent building
became a palace in the 19th century. The
interiors gleam, especially the marble work
– at its best in a floor inlaid with maps of
the world in the great *burgerzaal* (citizens'
hall) at the heart of the building. Pick up
a free audio guide at the desk when you

enter; it explains everything you see in vivid detail. King Willem-Alexander uses the palace only for ceremonies; check for periodic closures.

A'DAM Tower · Notable Building

(www.adamtoren.nl; Overhoeksplein 1; Lookout adult/child €12.50/6.50, premium €15/7.50, family ticket min 3 people €10/5; ⊙Lookout 10am-10pm; ⚲Badhuiskade) The 22-storey A'DAM Tower used to be the Royal Dutch Shell oil company offices, but has been funked up to become Amsterdam's newest big attraction. Take the trippy lift to the rooftop for awe-inspiring views in all directions, with a giant four-person swing that kicks out over the edge for those who have a head for heights (you're well secured and strapped in).

Hermitage Amsterdam · Museum

(☏020-530 74 88; www.hermitage.nl; Amstel 51; single exhibitions adult/child €17.50/free, all exhibitions adult/child €25/free; ⊙10am-5pm; MWaterlooplein, ⮕9/14 Waterlooplein) There have long been links between Russia and the Netherlands – Tsar Peter the Great learned shipbuilding here in 1697 – hence this branch of St Petersburg's State Hermitage Museum. Blockbuster temporary exhibitions show works from the Hermitage's vast treasure trove, while the permanent Portrait Gallery of the Golden Age has formal group portraits of the 17th-century Dutch A-list; the Outsider Gallery also has temporary shows. I Amsterdam and Museum cards allow free entrance or a discount, depending on the exhibition.

Museum Willet-Holthuysen · Museum

(☏020-523 18 22; www.willetholthuysen.nl; Herengracht 605; adult/child €9/4.50, free with Museum & I Amsterdam cards, audio guide €1; ⊙10am-5pm Mon-Fri, from 11am Sat & Sun; MWaterlooplein, ⮕4/9/14 Rembrandtplein) This exquisite canal house was built in 1687 for Amsterdam mayor Jacob Hop, then remodelled in 1739. It's named after Louisa Willet-Holthuysen, who inherited the house from her coal and glass-merchant father, and lived a lavish, bohemian life here with her husband. She bequeathed the property to the city in 1895. With displays including part of the family's

Rijksmuseum

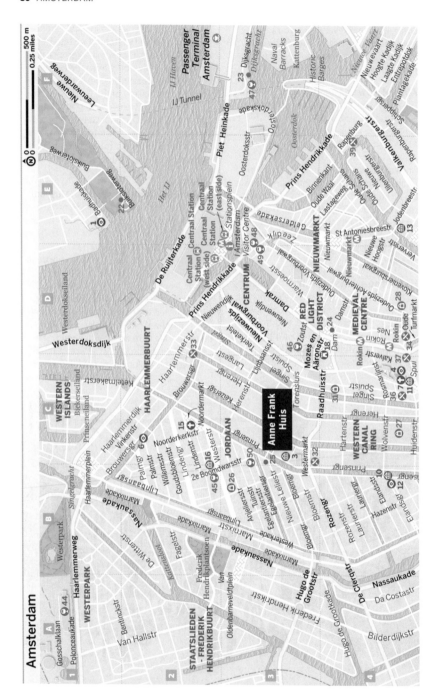

Amsterdam

WESTERN ISLANDS

Anne Frank Huis

RED LIGHT DISTRICT

MEDIEVAL CENTRE

CENTRUM

Passenger Terminal Amsterdam

HAARLEMMERBUURT

JORDAAN

WESTERN CANAL RING

STAATSLIEDEN - FREDERIK HENDRIKBUURT

WESTERPARK

NIEUWMARKT

500 m
0.25 miles

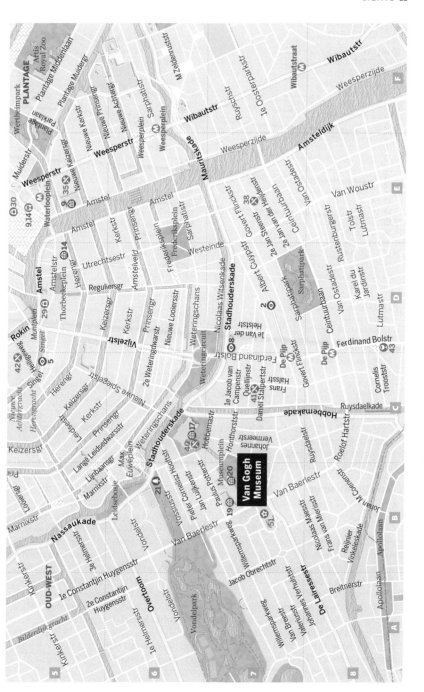

Amsterdam

275-piece Meissen table service, and an immaculate French-style garden, the museum is a fascinating window into the 19th-century world of the super-rich.

Stedelijk Museum   Museum

(☎ 020-573 29 11; www.stedelijk.nl; Museumplein 10; adult/child €17.50/free; ⊙10am-6pm Sat-Thu, to 10pm Fri; 🚊2/3/5/12 Van Baerlestraat) This fabulous museum houses the collection amassed by postwar curator Willem Sandberg. Displays rotate but you'll see an amazing selection featuring works by Picasso, Matisse, Mondrian, Van Gogh, Rothko, De Kooning, Warhol and more, plus an exuberant De Appel mural and great temporary exhibitions. The building was originally a bank, built in 1895 to a neo-Renaissance design by AM Weissman, and the modern extension is nicknamed 'the

bathtub' for reasons that will be obvious when you see it.

Begijnhof   Courtyard

(www.nicolaas-parochie.nl; ⊙9am-5pm; 🚊1/2/5 Spui) FREE Dating from the early 14th century, this enclosed former convent is a surreal oasis of peace, with tiny houses and postage-stamp gardens around a well-kept courtyard off Gedempte Begijnensloot. The Beguines, a Catholic order of unmarried or widowed women who cared for the elderly, lived a religious life without taking monastic vows. The last Beguine died in 1971. Within the *hof* (courtyard) is the charming 1671 **Begijnhof Kapel** (Begijnhof 30; ⊙1-6.30pm Mon, 9am-6.30pm Tue-Fri, 9am-6pm Sat & Sun), and the **Engelse Kerk** (English Church; www.ercadam.nl; Begijnhof 48; ⊙9am-5pm), built around 1392.

🍃 TOURS

The following tours provide a good introduction to Amsterdam, particularly if you're
short on time.

Sandeman's New
Amsterdam Tours   Walking

(www.neweuropetours.eu; tours by donation; ☺up
to 8 tours daily; 🚊4/9/16/24 Dam) Pay-what-
you-can walking tours that cover the Medieval Centre, Red Light District and Jordaan.

Hungry Birds Street
Food Tours   Walking, Food

(🔗06 1898 6268; www.hungrybirds.nl; day/
night tour per person €79/89; ☺11am Mon-Sat)
Guides take you 'off the eaten track' to chow
on Dutch and ethnic specialities. Tours visit
around 10 spots over four hours in De Pijp,
Utrechtsestraat, Rembrandtplein and the
Spui, from family-run eateries to street
vendors. Prices include all food. The meet-up
location is given after you make reservations.

Orangebike   Cycling

(🔗06 4684 2083; www.orange-bike.nl; Buik-
sloterweg 5c; tours €22.50-37.50, hire per hr/day
from €5/11; ☺9am-6pm; ⛴Buiksloterweg) Easy
cycling jaunts that take in the city's sights,
architecture and windmills.

Rederji Lampedusa   Boating

(www.rederjilampedusa.nl; canal tour 1-2hr €17,
VIP tours by donation; ☺canal tours Sat & Sun,
VIP tours Fri fortnightly May-Sep; 🚊26 Muziekgebouw) Take a canal-boat tour or a sunset
trip around Amsterdam harbour in former
refugee boats, brought from Lampedu-
sa. The tours are full of heart and offer a
fascinating insight, not only into stories
of contemporary migration, but of how
immigration shaped Amsterdam's history
– especially the canal tour. Both leave from
next to Mediamatic, just across the road
from the cruise terminal.

Those Dam Boat Guys   Cruise

(🔗06 1885 5219; www.thosedamboatguys.com;
tours €25; ☺11am, 1pm, 3pm, 5pm & 7pm Mar-
Sep; 🚊13/14/17 Westermarkt) Low-key canal
tours on small, electric boats where you
bring your own picnic.

🛍 SHOPPING

During the Golden Age, Amsterdam was
the world's warehouse, stuffed with riches
from the far corners of the earth. The
capital's cupboards are still stocked with all
kinds of exotica (just look at that Red Light
gear!), but the real pleasure here is finding
some odd, tiny shop selling something you
wouldn't find anywhere else.

Negen Straatjes   Area

(Nine Streets; www.de9straatjes.nl; 🚊1/2/5
Spui) In a city packed with countless shopping opportunities, each seemingly more
alluring than the last, the Negen Straatjes
represent the very densest concentration
of consumer pleasures. These nine little
streets are indeed small, each just a block
long. The shops are tiny too, and many are
highly specialised. Eyeglasses? Cheese?
Single-edition art books? Each has its own
dedicated boutique.

Moooi Gallery   Design

(🔗020-528 77 60; www.moooi.com; Westerstraat
187; ☺10am-6pm Tue-Sat; 🚊3/10 Marnixplein)
Founded by Marcel Wanders, this gallery-
shop features Dutch design at its most
over-the-top, from the life-size black horse
lamp to the 'blow away vase' (a whimsical
twist on the classic Delft vase) and the
'killing of the piggy bank' ceramic pig (with
a gold hammer).

X Bank   Design

(http://xbank.amsterdam; Spuistraat 172;
☺10am-6pm Mon-Wed, to 9pm Thu-Sat, noon-
8pm Sun; 🚊1/2/5/13/14/17 Dam) More than
just a concept store showcasing Dutch-
designed haute couture and ready-to-wear
fashion, furniture, art, gadgets and homewares, the 700-sq-metre X Bank also hosts
exhibitions, workshops, launches and lectures. Interior displays change every month;
check the website for upcoming events.

Vlieger   Stationery

(www.vliegerpapier.nl; Amstel 34; ☺noon-6pm
Mon, from 9am Tue-Fri, 11am-5.30pm Sat;
🚊4/9/14 Rembrandtplein) Love stationery
and paper? Make a beeline for Vlieger.

Daily Markets

No visit to Amsterdam is complete if you haven't experienced one of its lively outdoor markets.

Amsterdam's daily markets are open every day except Sunday. Albert Cuypmarkt (p78) in De Pijp is the largest, busiest market, offering food, clothing and everything else. Multi-product **Dappermarkt** (www.dappermarkt.nl; Dapperstraat, btwn Mauritskade & Wijttenbachstraat; ⊘9am-5pm Mon-Sat; ⏸3/7 Dapperstraat), near Oosterpark, is similar but smaller.

There's bric-a-brac galore at **Waterlooplein Flea Market** (www.waterlooplein.amsterdam; Waterlooplein; ⊘9.30am-6pm Mon-Sat; ⏸9/14 Waterlooplein) in Nieuwmarkt. **Ten Katemarkt** (www.tenkatemarkt.nl; Ten Katestraat; ⊘9am-5pm Mon-Sat; ⏸17 Ten Katestraat) adjoins the cultural and design complex De Hallen, with fresh food, flowers and more. The Flower Market, **Bloemenmarkt** (Singel, btwn Muntplein & Koningsplein; ⊘8.30am-7pm Mon-Sat, to 7.30pm Sun Apr-Oct, 9am-5.30pm Mon-Sat, 11am-5.30pm Sun Nov-Mar; ⏸1/2/5 Koningsplein), specialises in bulbs (and kitsch souvenirs); it's located in the Southern Canal Ring and open every day, *including* Sunday. Old tomes, maps and sheet music are the speciality at **Oudemanhuispoort Book Market** (Oudemanhuispoort; ⊘11am-4pm Mon-Sat; ⏸4/9/14/16/24 Spui/Rokin) in the centre.

Cheese, Albert Cuypmarkt

Since 1869, this two-storey shop has been supplying it all: Egyptian papyrus, beautiful handmade papers from Asia and Central America, papers inlaid with flower petals or bamboo, and paper textured like snakeskin.

 EATING

Amsterdam's food scene is woefully underrated. Beyond pancakes and potatoes, Dutch chefs put their spin on all kinds of regional and global dishes using ingredients plucked from local seas and farms.

De Laatste Kruimel   Cafe, Bakery €
(☎020-423 04 99; www.delaatstekruimel.nl; Langebrugsteeg 4; dishes €3-8; ⊘8am-8pm Mon-Sat, 9am-8pm Sun; ⏸4/9/14/16/24 Spui) Decorated with vintage finds from the Noordermarkt and wooden pallets upcycled as furniture, and opening to a tiny canalside terrace, the 'Last Crumb' has glass display cases piled high with pies, quiches, breads, cakes and lemon-and-poppy-seed scones. Grandmothers, children, couples on dates and just about everyone else crowds in for sweet treats and fantastic organic sandwiches.

Gartine   Cafe €
(☎020-320 41 32; www.gartine.nl; Taksteeg 7; dishes €6-12, high tea €17-25; ⊘10am-6pm Wed-Sat; ☝; ⏸4/9/14/16/24 Spui/Rokin) ⦿ Gartine is magical, from its covert location in an alley off busy Kalverstraat to its mismatched antique tableware and its sublime breakfast pastries, sandwiches and salads (made from produce grown in its garden plot and eggs from its chickens). The sweet-and-savoury high tea, from 2pm to 5pm, is a treat.

Vleminckx   Fast Food €
(http://vleminckxdesausmeester.nl; Voetboogstraat 33; fries €3-5, sauces €0.70; ⊘noon-7pm Sun & Mon, 11am-7pm Tue, Wed, Fri & Sat, to 8pm Thu; ⏸1/2/5 Koningsplein) Frying up *frites* since 1887, Amsterdam's best *friterie* has been based at this hole-in-the-wall takeaway shack near the Spui since 1957. The standard order of perfectly cooked crispy, fluffy *frites* is smothered in mayonnaise,

National Tulip Day at the Royal Palace (p78)

though its 28 sauces also include apple, green pepper, ketchup, peanut, sambal and mustard. Queues almost always stretch down the block, but they move fast.

De Belhamel   European €€

(☎020-622 10 95; www.belhamel.nl; Brouwersgracht 60; mains €23-27, 3-/4-course menus €35/45; ⊙noon-4pm & 6-10pm Sun-Thu, to 10.30pm Fri & Sat; ☐18/21/22 Buiten Brouwersstraat) In warm weather the canal-side tables here at the head of the Herengracht are an aphrodisiac, and the richly wallpapered art-nouveau interior set over two levels provides the perfect backdrop for exquisitely presented dishes such as poached sole with wild-spinach bisque, veal sweetbreads with crispy bacon, onion confit and deep-fried sage, or a half lobster with velvety salmon mayonnaise.

Bistro Bij Ons   Dutch €€

(☎020-627 90 16; http://bistrobijons.nl; Prinsengracht 287; mains €14-20; ⊙10am-10pm Tue-Sun; ✈; ☐13/14/17 Westermarkt) If you're not in town visiting your Dutch *oma* (grandma), try the honest-to-goodness cooking at this

charming retro bistro instead. Classics include *stamppot* (potatoes mashed with another vegetable) with sausage, *raasdonders* (split peas with bacon, onion and pickles) and *poffertjes*. House-made liqueurs include plum and *drop* (liquorice) varieties.

Van 't Spit   Rotisserie €€

(www.vantspit.nl; Frans Halsstraat 42; half/full roast chicken €11/21, sides €3-4; ⊙5pm-midnight; ☐16/24 Marie Heinekenplein) Van 't Spit does one thing – chicken (half or full), marinated overnight and spit-roasted over a wood-burning fire, with optional sides like salad or fries – but it does it so well that it's always packed. No reservations, so get in early or head to the bar for a cocktail such as a kickin' vodka-and-ginger-beer Dutch Mule while you wait.

D'Vijff Vlieghen   Dutch €€€

(☎020-530 40 60; http://vijffvlieghen.nl; Spuistraat 294-302; mains €23-29; ⊙6-10pm; ☐1/2/5 Spui) Spread across five 17th-century canal houses, the 'Five Flies' is a jewel. Old-wood dining rooms overflow with character, featuring Delft-blue tiles and original works by Rembrandt; chairs have copper plates inscribed with the names of famous guests (Walt Disney, Mick Jagger...). Exquisite dishes range from goose breast with apple, sauerkraut and smoked butter to candied haddock with liquorice sauce.

Greetje   Dutch €€€

(⌨020-779 74 50; www.restaurantgreetje. nl; Peperstraat 23-25; mains €23-29; ☺kitchen 6-10pm Sun-Thu, to 11pm Fri & Sat; 🚌22/34/35/48 Prins Hendrikkade) 🍴 Greetje is Amsterdam's most creative Dutch restaurant, using the best seasonal produce to resurrect and recreate traditional Dutch recipes, like pickled beef, braised veal with apricots and leek *stamppot*, and pork belly with Dutch mustard sauce. Kick off with the Big Beginning (€18), with a sampling of hot and cold starters.

Graham's Kitchen Gastronomy €€€

(⌨020-364 25 60; www.grahamskitchen. amsterdam; Hemonystraat 38; lunch mains €12-17, 3-/4-/5-/6-course menus €38/47/56/62; ☺6-10pm Tue & Wed, noon-2.30pm & 6-10pm Thu-Sat; 🚌4 Stadhouderskade) A veteran of Michelin-starred kitchens, chef Graham Mee now crafts intricate dishes at his own premises. Most produce is organic and sourced from the Amsterdam area. Lunch options include a gourmet take on fish and chips. The intimate space is small, so reserve well ahead. Tables are set up on the pavement in summer. Evenings see degustation sensations.

🍸 DRINKING & NIGHTLIFE

Amsterdam is one of the wildest nightlife cities in Europe and the world, and the testosterone-fuelled stag parties of young chaps roaming the Red Light District know exactly what they're doing here. Yet you can easily avoid the hardcore party scene if you choose to: Amsterdam remains a *café* (pub) society where the pursuit of pleasure centres on cosiness and charm.

In 't Aepjen   Brown Cafe

(Zeedijk 1; ☺noon-1am Mon-Thu, to 3am Fri & Sat; 🚌1/2/4/5/9/13/16/17/24 Centraal Station) Candles burn even during the day in this 15th-century building – one of two remain-

Heineken Experience (p78)

ing wooden buildings in the city – which has been a tavern since 1519: in the 16th and 17th centuries it served as an inn for sailors from the Far East, who often brought *aapjes* (monkeys) to trade for lodging. Vintage jazz on the stereo enhances the time-warp feel.

't Smalle   Brown Cafe

(www.t-smalle.nl; Egelantiersgracht 12; ☺10am-1am Sun-Thu, to 2am Fri & Sat; 🚊13/14/17 Westermarkt) Dating back to 1786 as a *jenever* (Dutch gin) distillery and tasting house, and restored during the 1970s with antique porcelain beer pumps and lead-framed windows, locals' favourite 't Smalle is one of Amsterdam's most charming *bruin cafés*. Dock your boat right by the pretty stone terrace, which is wonderfully convivial by day and impossibly romantic at night.

Hannekes Boom   Beer Garden

(www.hannekesboom.nl; Dijksgracht 4; ☺10am-1am Sun-Thu, to 3am Fri & Sat; 🚊26 Muziekgebouw) Handily close to the passenger terminal and thus ideal for a last Amsterdam beer, this nonchalantly cool, laid-back waterside *café* built from recycled materials has a beer garden that really feels like a garden, with timber benches, picnic tables under the trees and a hipster, arty crowd enjoying sitting out in the sunshine (it comes into its own in summer).

Brouwerij Troost   Brewery

(☎020-760 58 20; www.brouwerijtroost.nl; Cornelis Troostplein 21; ☺4pm-1am Mon-Thu, to 3am Fri, 2pm-3am Sat, to midnight Sun; 🛜; 🚊12 Cornelis Troostplein) 🍺 Watch beer being brewed in copper vats behind a glass wall at this outstanding craft brewery. Its dozen beers include a summery blonde, a smoked porter, a strong tripel and a deep-red Imperial IPA; it also distils cucumber and juniper gin from its beer, and serves fantastic bar food, including crispy prawn tacos and humongous burgers.

Proeflokaal de Ooievaar   Distillery

(www.proeflokaaldeooievaar.nl; St Olofspoort 1; ☺noon-midnight; 🚊1/2/4/5/9/13/16/17/24 Centraal Station) Not much bigger than a vat of *jenever*, this magnificent little tasting

 Brown Cafes

For the quintessential Amsterdam experience, pull up a stool in one of the city's famed *bruin cafés* (brown cafes). The true specimens have been in business a while and ge their name from the centuries' worth of smoke stains on the walls. *Bruin cafés* have candle-topped tables, sandy wooden floors and sometimes a house cat that sidles up for a scratch. Most importantly, they induce a cosy vibe that prompts friends to linger and chat for hours over drinks – the same enchantment the *cafés* have cast for 300 years.

't Smalle in the Jordaan

house has been going strong since 1782. On offer are 14 *jenevers* and liqueurs (such as Bride's Tears with gold and silver leaf) from the De Ooievaar distillery, still located in the Jordaan. Despite appearances, the house has not subsided but was built leaning over.

De Drie Fleschjes   Distillery

(www.dedriefleschjes.nl; Gravenstraat 18; ☺4-8.30pm Mon-Wed, 2-8.30pm Thu-Sat, 3-7pm Sun; 🚊1/2/5/13/14/17 Dam) A treasure dating from 1650, with a wall of barrels made by master shipbuilders, the tasting room of distiller Bootz specialises in liqueurs, including its signature almond-flavoured *bitterkoekje* (Dutch-style macaroon) liqueur, as well as superb *jenever*. Take a peek at the collection of *kalkoentjes* (small bottles with hand-painted portraits of former mayors).

 **Understand**

Amsterdam's Canals

Amsterdammers have always known their Canal Ring, built during the Golden Age, is extraordinary. Unesco made it official in 2010, when it listed the waterways as a World Heritage site. Today the city has 165 canals spanned by 1753 bridges – more than any other city in the world.

Far from being simply decorative or picturesque, or even waterways for transport, the canals were crucial to drain and reclaim the waterlogged land. They solved Amsterdam's essential problem: keeping the land and sea separate.

In Dutch a canal is a *gracht* (pronounced 'khrakht') and the main canals form the central *grachtengordel* (canal ring). These beauties came to life in the early 1600s, after Amsterdam's population grew beyond its medieval walls and city planners put together an ambitious design for expansion. The concentric waterways they built are the same ones you see today.

Starting from the core, the major semicircular canals are the Singel, Herengracht, Keizersgracht and Prinsengracht. The **Herengracht** is where Amsterdam's wealthiest residents moved once the canals were completed. They built their mansions alongside it (particularly around the Golden Bend), hence its name, which translates to Gentlemen's Canal.

The canals that cut across the core canals like spokes on a bicycle wheel are known as radial canals. Of these, the **Brouwersgracht** (Brewers Canal) is one of Amsterdam's most beautiful waterways. It takes its name from the many breweries that lined the banks in the 16th and 17th centuries.

Sure they're touristy, but **canal cruises** are also a delightful way to see the city. Several operators depart from moorings at Centraal Station, Damrak, Rokin and opposite the Rijksmuseum. Costs are similar. To avoid the steamed-up-glass-window effect, look for a boat with an open seating area.

Some 3050 houseboats line Amsterdam's canals. Living on the water became popular after WWII, when a surplus of old cargo ships helped fill the gap of a housing shortage on land. The Prinsengracht displays a particularly diverse mix of houseboats. You can climb aboard one and explore the cosy (ie cramped) interior at the **Houseboat Museum** (020-427 07 50; www.houseboatmuseum.nl; Prinsengracht 296k; adult/child €4.50/3.50; 10am-5pm daily Jul & Aug, Tue-Sun Sep-Dec & Jan-Jun; 13/14/17 Westermarkt), or book to stay overnight on the water yourself in true Amsterdam style.

⊗ ENTERTAINMENT

Amsterdam supports a flourishing arts scene, with loads of big concert halls, theatres, cinemas and other performance venues filled on a regular basis. Music fans will be in their glory, as there's a fervent subculture for just about every genre, especially jazz, classical and avant-garde beats.

Concertgebouw   Classical Music
(Concert Hall; 020-671 83 45; www.concert gebouw.nl; Concertgebouwplein 10; box office

1-7pm Mon-Fri, to 7pm Sat & Sun; 3/5/12/16/24 Museumplein) The Concert Hall was built in 1888 by AL van Gendt, who managed to engineer its near-perfect acoustics. Bernard Haitink, former conductor of the Royal Concertgebouw Orchestra, remarked that the world-famous hall was the orchestra's best instrument. Free half-hour concerts take place Wednesdays at 12.30pm from September to June; arrive early. Try the Last Minute Ticket Shop (www.lastminute

ticketshop.nl) for half-price seats to all other performances.

INFORMATION

DANGERS & ANNOYANCES

Amsterdam is a safe and manageable city and if you use common sense, you should have no problems.

○ Be alert for pickpockets in tourist-heavy zones such as Centraal Station, the Bloemenmarkt and Red Light District.

○ It is forbidden to take photos of women in the Red Light District windows; this is strictly enforced.

○ Be careful around the canals. Almost none of them have fences or barriers.

○ Watch out for bicycles; never walk in bicycle lanes and always look carefully before you cross one.

DISCOUNT CARDS

Seniors over 65 years, and their partners of 60 or older, benefit from reductions on public transport, museum admissions, concerts and more. You may look younger, so bring your passport.

I Amsterdam Card (€49/59/69 per 24/48/72 hours) provides admission to more than 30 museums (though not the Rijksmuseum), a canal cruise, and discounts at shops, entertainment venues and restaurants. Also includes a GVB transit pass. Useful for quick visits to the city. Available at VVV I Amsterdam Visitor Centres and some hotels.

LEGAL MATTERS

○ Technically, marijuana is illegal. However, possession of soft drugs (eg cannabis) up to 5g is tolerated. Larger amounts are subject to prosecution.

○ Don't light up in an establishment other than a coffeeshop (cafe authorised to sell cannabis) without checking that it's OK to do so.

○ Never buy drugs of any kind on the street.

TAXES & REFUNDS

Value-added tax (BTW in Dutch) is levied on most goods and services at 6% for restaurants, hotels, books, transport, medicines and museum admissions, and 21% for most other items. It should already be included in stated prices.

Non-EU residents may be able to claim a refund on a minimum €50 spent per shop per day. The website www.belastingdienst.nl has details.

TOILETS

○ Public toilets are not a widespread facility on Dutch streets, apart from the free-standing public urinals for men in places such as the Red Light District.

○ Many people duck into a *café* or department store.

○ The standard fee for toilet attendants is €0.50.

GETTING AROUND

GVB passes in chip-card form are the most convenient option for public transport. Buy them at visitor centres or from tram conductors. Always wave your card at the pink machine when entering and departing.

Walking Central Amsterdam is compact and very easy to cover by foot.

Bicycle This is the locals' main mode of getting around. Rental companies are all over town; bikes cost about €11 per day.

Tram Fast, frequent and ubiquitous, operating between 6am and 12.30am.

Bus & Metro Primarily serve the outer districts; not much use in the city centre.

Ferry Free ferries depart for northern Amsterdam from docks behind Centraal Station.

Taxi Expensive and not very speedy given Amsterdam's maze of streets.

COPENHAGEN, DENMARK

Copenhagen at a Glance...

Copenhagen is not only the coolest kid on the Nordic block, it's also consistently ranked as the happiest city in the world. Ask a dozen locals why and they would probably all zone in on the hygge, which generally means 'cosiness', but encompasses far more. But it is this laid-back contentment that helps give the Danish capital the X factor. The backdrop is pretty cool as well: its cobblestoned, bike-friendly streets are an enticing concoction of sherbet-hued town houses, craft studios and candlelit cafes. Add to this its compact size and it is possibly Europe's most seamless urban experience.

With One Day in Port

Head to salty **Nyhavn** (p100), former haunt of Hans Christian Andersen. Capture the perfect snap of the colourful canal, then hop on a **canal and harbour tour** (p104) of the city. Grab a smørrebrød for lunch. In the afternoon, head to the **Designmuseum Danmark** (p97) or stroll the all-ages **Tivoli Gardens** (p95), Copenhagen's vintage amusement park.

Best Places for...

Coffee Coffee Collective (p108)
Wine Ved Stranden 10 (p108)
Smørrebrød Schønnemann (p106)
Danish degustation Kadeau (p107)
Markets Torvehallerne KBH (p106)

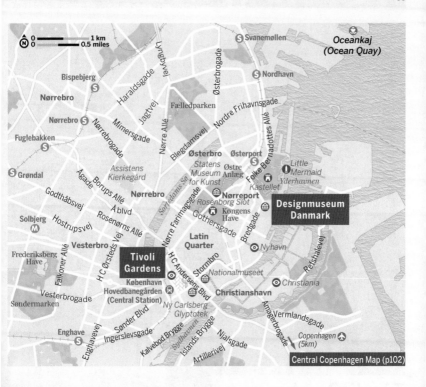

Central Copenhagen Map (p102)

Getting from the Port

From the principal cruise terminal, Oceankaj (Ocean Quay), cruise-specific shuttle bus 27 runs to Østerport station (10 minutes), handy for the design museum, and on to more central Nørreport station (20 minutes). Regular bus 25 also runs to Østerport. A single ticket/24-hour pass costs 24/80kr. You can buy tickets at Town Shop by the cruise terminal, where you can also hire bikes.

Fast Facts

Currency Danish krone (kr).

Language Danish. English very widely spoken.

Free wi-fi Cruise terminal, most cafes and the Copenhagen Visitors Centre (p109).

Tourist information Visitor service at cruise terminal. Copenhagen Visitors Centre, across the road from Tivoli.

Transport Integrated bus, metro and tram system. Locals widely use bikes to get around.

SEAN PAVONE/SHUTTERSTOCK ©

Tivoli Gardens

The country's top-ranking tourist draw, tasteful Tivoli Gardens has been eliciting gleeful thrills since 1843. Whatever your idea of fun – hair-raising rides, twinkling pavilions, open-air stage shows or alfresco pantomime and beer – this old-timer has you covered.

Great For...

☑ Don't Miss

The city views, taken at 70km/h, from the Star Flyer, one of the world's tallest carousels.

Roller Coasters

The Rutschebanen is the best loved of Tivoli's roller coasters, rollicking its way through and around a faux 'mountain' and reaching speeds of 60km/h. Built in 1914 it claims to be the world's oldest operating wooden roller coaster. If you're after something a little more hardcore, the Dæmonen (Demon) is a 21st-century beast with faster speeds and a trio of hair-raising loops.

Star Flyer

One of the world's tallest carousels, the Star Flyer will have you whizzing round and round at heights of up to 80m. It's a bit like being on a skyscraping swing, travelling at 70km/h and taking in a breathtaking view of Copenhagen's rooftops. The astrological symbols, quadrants and planets on the ride are a tribute to Danish astronomer Tycho Brahe.

Star Flyer carousel

⚓ Explore Ashore

Cruise shuttle bus 27 stops at Nørreport, from where it's a 15-minute stroll from Tivoli. To shorten your journey, jump on tram A, B or E and get off at Vesterport, 250m from Tivoli. A leisurely three hours at Tivoli is typical, but a briefer visit is also possible.

❶ Need to Know

📱33 15 10 01; www.tivoli.dk; Vesterbrogade 3; adult/child under 8yr 120kr/free, Fri after 7pm 160kr/free; ⊙11am-11pm Sun-Thu, to midnight Fri & Sat early Apr-late Sep, reduced hours rest of year; 🚻; 🚌2A, 5C, 9A, 12, 14, 26, 250S, Ⓢ København H

The Grounds

Beyond the carousels and side stalls is a Tivoli of landscaped gardens, tranquil nooks and eclectic architecture. Lower the adrenaline under beautiful old chestnut and elm trees, and amble around Tivoli Lake. Formed out of the old city moat, the lake is a top spot to snap pictures of Tivoli's Chinese Tower.

Illuminations & Fireworks

Throughout the summer season, Tivoli Lake wows the crowds with its nightly laser and water spectacular. The Saturday evening fireworks are a summer-season must, repeated again from 26 to 30 December for Tivoli's annual Fireworks Festival.

Live Performances

The indoor **Tivolis Koncertsal** (Concert Hall) hosts mainly classical music, with the odd musical and big-name pop or rock act. All tickets are sold at the **Tivoli Billetcenter** (⊙10am-10.45pm Sun-Thu, to 11.45pm Fri & Sat summer, 10am-6pm Mon-Fri rest of year) or through the Tivoli website.

Pantomime Theatre

Tivoli's criminally charming Pantomime Theatre debuted in 1874. It's the work of prolific architect Vilhelm Dahlerup, responsible for many of Copenhagen's most iconic buildings, including the Ny Carlsberg Glyptotek and Statens Museum for Kunst. Dahlerup's historicist style shines bright in his Tivoli creation, a colour-bursting ode to the Far East. While plays in the tradition of Italy's Commedia dell'arte are presented here, the stage also plays host to other styles of performances, including modern ballet. See the Tivoli website for details.

Designmuseum Danmark

Don't know your Egg from your Swan? Your PH4 from your PH5? For a crash course in Denmark's incredible design heritage, make an elegant beeline for this museum. Its shop is also one of the best places to pick up savvy gifts and easy-to-carry souvenirs.

Great For...

☑ Don't Miss

The iconic 1959 vintage poster 'Wonderful Copenhagen' – a duck and her little ones stopping traffic.

Housed in a converted 18th-century hospital, the museum is a must for fans of the applied arts and industrial design. Its booty includes Danish silver and porcelain, textiles and the iconic design pieces of modern innovators such as Kaare Klint, Poul Henningsen, Arne Jacobsen and Verner Panton.

20th-Century Crafts & Design

This is the museum's hero permanent exhibition, exploring 20th-century industrial design and crafts in the context of social, economic, technological and theoretical changes. You'll find a wealth of Danish design classics, among them Børge Mogensen's Shaker table, Verner Panton's Flowerpot Pendant lamp and S-shaped Panton chair, and Poul Henningsen's Table lamp 4/3. One small room dedicated to Arne Jacobsen features objects the architect specifically created for his SAS Royal Hotel,

HANNE FUGL BJERG/DESIGNMUSEUM DANMARK ©

Designmuseum Danmark

⚓

Explore Ashore

Get off the cruise shuttle bus at the first stop, Østerport. From here, it's an 800m walk on Grønningen along the fortress park to the museum. Plan to spend 1½ hours here, longer if lingering in the cafe.

ℹ Need to Know

www.designmuseum.dk; Bredgade 68; adult/child 100kr/free; ⊙11am-5pm Tue & Thu-Sun, to 9pm Wed; 🚌1A, MKongens Nytorv

including the Egg and Swan chairs, and the hotel's drapes. More unusual highlights include Henningsen's steel, timber and leather PH Grand Piano, as well as a wall of vintage graphic posters that includes the work of Viggo Vagnby, creator of the iconic 1959 'Wonderful Copenhagen' poster. The exhibition leads into the Danish Design Now exhibition, focused on the country's current innovators in numerous design fields, including urban, industrial and fashion.

Fashion & Fabric

This permanent exhibition showcases around 350 objects from the museum's rich textile and fashion collections. Spanning four centuries, the collection's treasures include French and Italian silks, ikat and batik weaving, and two extraordinary mid-20th-century tapestries based on cartoons by Henri Matisse. As would you expect, Danish textiles and fashion feature prominently, including Danish *hedebo* embroidery from the 18th to 20th centuries, and Erik Mortensen's collection of haute couture frocks from French fashion houses Balmain and Jean-Louis Scherrer.

Temporary Exhibitions

The museum's rotating temporary exhibitions provide fresh insights into the collection and design in general. Recent shows include *Learning from Japan,* an exploration of the role traditional Japanese crafts and applied arts have played in the development of Danish design. Juxtaposed against Japanese woodcuts, ceramics and furniture, this influence is brought to the fore in objects as diverse as Thorvald Bindesbøll's late-19th-century embroidered chair, Finn Juhl's 1953 Japanese sofa and Hans Sandgren Jakobsen Eri's 1993 tea-ceremony floor chair. Other recent temporary offerings have included a pop-up exhibition dedicated to Finnish architect Alvar Aalto and his modernist masterpiece, Paimio Sanatorium.

Cobbles & Cosiness

This walk follows Copenhagen's beautiful canalside through to the historic centre, taking in the city's noble architecture.

Start Nyhavn
Distance 2.7km
Duration two hours

4 Cobbled **Magstræde** is Copenhagen's oldest street.

5 Copenhagen's neoclassical courthouse, **Domhuset** (⊙8.30am-3pm Mon-Fri), is linked by bridge to cells across the road on Slutterigade.

Skindergade

Hyskenstræde

neltorv

Knabrostræde

Nytorv

Kompagnistræde

Læderstræde

Gammel
Strand (under
construction)

Højbro
Plads Ⓜ

Snaregade

Nybrogade

Vindebrogade

Rådhusstræde

Slotsholms Kanal

Rådhuspladsen
(under Ⓜ
construction)

STRØGET

Lavendelstræde

Farvergade

Løngangstræde

Frederiksholms Kanal

SLOTSHOLMEN

FINISH **6**

Vester Voldgade

Stormgade

ⓢ

6 The architectural flourish that is the **Rådhus** (town hall; www.kk.dk; 9am-4pm Mon-Fri, ⊙9.30am-1pm Sat) contains the very unusual World Clock.

3 Home to the Danish parliament, **Christiansborg Slot** (www.christiansborg.dk; adult/child 90kr/free; ⊙10am-5pm daily May-Sep, closed Mon Oct-Apr) has opulent interiors and picturesque courtyards.

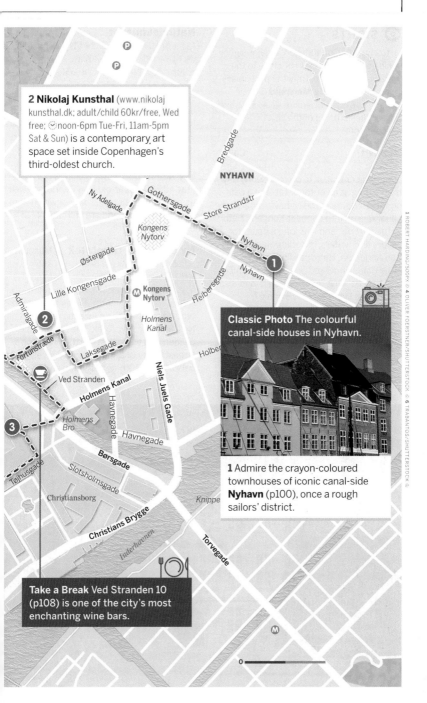

2 Nikolaj Kunsthal (www.nikolaj kunsthal.dk; adult/child 60kr/free, Wed free; ⊙noon-6pm Tue-Fri, 11am-5pm Sat & Sun) is a contemporary art space set inside Copenhagen's third-oldest church.

NYHAVN

Classic Photo The colourful canal-side houses in Nyhavn.

1 Admire the crayon-coloured townhouses of iconic canal-side **Nyhavn** (p100), once a rough sailors' district.

Take a Break Ved Stranden 10 (p108) is one of the city's most enchanting wine bars.

◎ SIGHTS

Virtually all of Copenhagen's major sight-seeing attractions are in or close to the medieval city centre. Only the perennially disappointing **Little Mermaid** (Den Lille Havfrue; Langelinie, Østerport; 🚌1A, 🚢Nordre Toldbod) lies outside of the city, on the harbourfront.

Nyhavn   Canal

(🚌1A, 26, 66, 350S, Ⓜ Kongens Nytorv) There are few nicer places to be on a sunny day than sitting at an outdoor table at a cafe on the quayside of the Nyhavn canal. The canal was built to connect Kongens Nytorv to the harbour and was long a haunt for sailors and writers, including Hans Christian Andersen. He wrote *The Tinderbox, Little Claus and Big Claus* and *The Princess and the Pea* while living at No 20, and also spent time living at Nos 18 and 67.

> *It has first claims on virtually every antiquity uncovered on Danish soil*

Nationalmuseet   Museum

(National Museum; 🖉33 13 44 11; www.natmus. dk; Ny Vestergade 10; adult/child 75kr/free; ⏰10am-5pm Tue-Sun, also open Mon Jul & Aug; 👶; 🚌1A, 2A, 9A, 14, 26, 37, Ⓢ København H) For a crash course in Danish history and culture, spend an afternoon at Denmark's National Museum. It has first claims on virtually every antiquity uncovered on Danish soil, including Stone Age tools, Viking weaponry, rune stones and medieval jewellery. Among the many highlights is a finely crafted 3500-year-old Sun Chariot, as well as bronze *lurs* (horns), some of which date back 3000 years and are still capable of blowing a tune.

Ny Carlsberg Glyptotek   Museum

(🖉33 41 81 41; www.glyptoteket.dk; Dantes Plads 7, HC Andersens Blvd; adult/child 95kr/free, Tue free; ⏰11am-6pm Tue-Sun, until 10pm Thu; 🚌1A, 2A, 9A, 37, Ⓢ København H) Fin de siècle architecture meets with an eclectic mix of art at Ny Carlsberg Glyptotek. The collection is divided into two parts: Northern Europe's largest booty of antiquities, and an elegant collection of 19th-century Danish and

Nationalmuseet

French art. The latter includes the largest collection of Rodin sculptures outside of France and no less than 47 Gauguin paintings. These are displayed along with works by greats like Cézanne, Van Gogh, Pissarro, Monet and Renoir.

Rosenborg Slot
Castle

(☎33 15 32 86; www.kongernessamling.dk/en/rosenborg; Øster Voldgade 4A; adult/child 110kr/free, incl Amalienborg Slot 145kr/free; ⏱9am-5pm mid-Jun–mid-Sep, reduced hours rest of year; 🚌6A, 42, 184, 185, 350S, Ⓜ Nørreport, Ⓢ Nørreport) A 'once-upon-a-time' combo of turrets, gables and moat, the early-17th-century Rosenborg Slot was built in Dutch Renaissance style between 1606 and 1633 by King Christian IV to serve as his summer home. Today the castle's 24 upper rooms are chronologically arranged, housing the furnishings and portraits of each monarch from Christian IV to Frederik VII. The *pièce de résistance* is the basement Treasury, home to the dazzling crown jewels, among them Christian IV's glorious crown and Christian III's jewel-studded sword.

Statens Museum for Kunst
Museum

(☎33 74 84 94; www.smk.dk; Sølvgade 48-50; adult/child 110kr/free; ⏱11am-5pm Tue & Thu-Sun, to 8pm Wed; 🚌6A, 26, 42, 184, 185) FREE Denmark's National Gallery straddles two contrasting, interconnected buildings: a late-19th-century 'palazzo' and a sharply minimalist extension. The museum houses medieval and Renaissance works and impressive collections of Dutch and Flemish artists, including Rubens, Brueghel and Rembrandt. It claims the world's finest collection of 19th-century Danish 'Golden Age' artists, among them Eckersberg and Hammershøi, foreign greats like Matisse and Picasso, and modern Danish heavyweights including Per Kirkeby.

Christiania
Area

(www.christiania.org; Prinsessegade; 🚌9A, Ⓜ Christianshavn) Escape the capitalist crunch at Freetown Christiania, a hash-scented commune straddling the eastern side of Christianshavn. Since its es-

 The Changing of the Guard

The Royal Life Guard is charged with protecting the Danish royal family and their city residence, Amalienborg Palace. Every day of the year, these soldiers march from their barracks through the streets of Copenhagen to perform the **Changing of the Guard** (www.kongehuset.dk/en/changing-of-the-guard-at-amalienborg; Amalienborg Slotsplads; ⏱noon daily; 🚌1A) FREE. Clad in 19th-century tunics and bearskin helmets, their performance of intricate manoeuvres is an impressive sight. If Queen Margrethe is in residence, the ceremony is even more grandiose, with the addition of a full marching band.

If you miss out on the noon ceremony, a smaller-scale shift change is performed every two hours thereafter, around the clock.

BIRUTĖ VIJEIKIENE/SHUTTERSTOCK ©

tablishment by squatters in 1971, the area has drawn nonconformists from across the globe, attracted by the concept of collective business, workshops and communal living. Explore beyond the settlement's infamous 'Pusher St' – lined with shady hash and marijuana dealers who do not appreciate photographs – and you'll stumble upon a semi-bucolic wonderland of whimsical DIY homes, cosy garden plots, eateries, beer gardens and music venues.

 TOURS

You can't visit Copenhagen and not take a canal boat trip. Not only is it a fantastic way

Central Copenhagen (København)

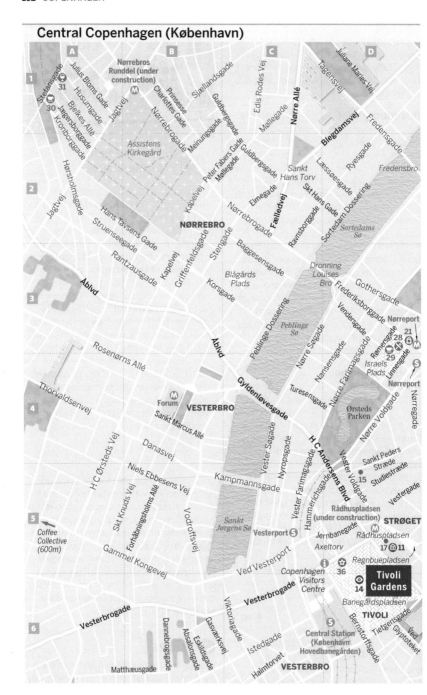

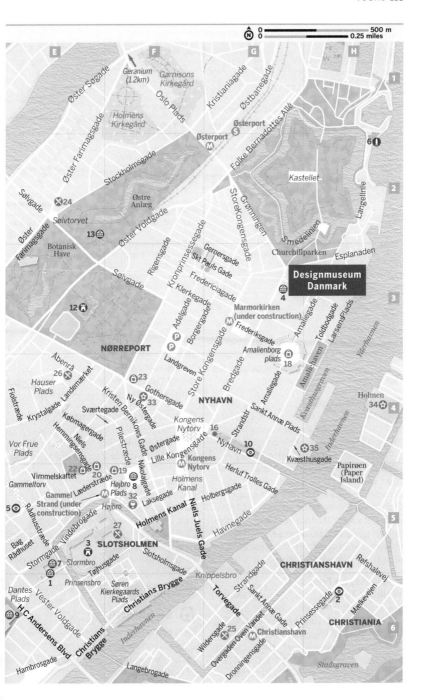

0 500 m
0 0.25 miles

E F G H

1

Geranium (1.2km)

Garnisons Kirkegård

Øster Søgade

Oslo Plads

Holmens Kirkegård

Østerport

Østerport M

Kristianiagade

Østbanegade

Folke Bernadottes Allé

6 ❶

Østre Anlæg

Øster Farimagsgade

Stockholmsgade

Kastellet

2

Langelinie

Sølvgade

⊗24

Søltorvet

13🏛

Øster Voldgade

Grønningen

Storkongensgade

Smedelinien

Churchillparken

Esplanaden

Østre Farimagsgade

Botanisk Have

Sølvgade

Rigensgade

Kronprinsessegade

Skt Pauls Gade

Gernersgade

Fredericiagade

Designmuseum Danmark

🏛4

3

12🏛

Adelgade

Klerkegade

Borgergade

Marmorkirken (under construction)

M Frederiksgade

Amaliegade

Toldbodgade

Larsens Plads

Ydrehavnen

NØRREPORT

Ⓟ

Ⓟ

Landgreven

Store Kongensgade

Amalienborg plads

Bredgade

🏠18

Amalienhaven

Amaliegade

Kvæsthusgraven

Åbenrå

26⊗

Hauser Plads

Kristen Bernikows Gade

Landemærket

Gothersgade

Ny Østergade

🔒23

33

NYHAVN

Kongens Nytorv

16

Strandstr

Sankt Annæ Plads

Holmen

34🏵

4

Fiolstræde

Krystalgade

Købmagergade

Hemmingsensgade

Sværtegade

Pilestræde

Niels

Nikolajgade

Østergade

Lille Kongensgade

Kongens Nytorv M

Nyhavn

10 ⊚

🏵35

Kvæsthusgade

Papirøen (Paper Island)

Vor Frue Plads

Vimmelskaftet

22🔒

20

🔒19

Gammeltorv

Læderstræde

Højbro 8

M Plads 32

Holmens Kanal

Herluf Trolles Gade

Holbergsgade

5

5⊚

Rådhusstræde

Gammel Strand (under construction)

Højbro

Laksegade

Niels Juels Gade

27

Havnegade

Bag Rådhuset

Stormgade

Vindebrogade

3 **SLOTSHOLMEN**

Slotsholmsgade

CHRISTIANSHAVN

Refshalevej

🏛7

Stormbro

Tøjhusgade

Knippelsbro

Strandgade

2 ⊚

1

Prinsensbro

Søren Kierkegaards Plads

Christians Brygge

Torvegade

Sankt Annæ Gade

Prinsessegade

Mælkevejen

Dantes Plads

Vester Voldgade

CHRISTIANIA

6

🏛9

H C Andersens Blvd

Christians Brygge

Inderhavnen

Wildersgade

25

Overgaden Oven Vandet

Christianshavn ⊚

Dronningensgade

Hambrosgade

Langebrogade

Stadsgraven

Central Copenhagen (København)

to see the city, but you get a perspective that landlubbers never see. Be aware that in most boats you are totally exposed to the elements (even during summer).

Bike Copenhagen with Mike
Cycling

(☑ 26 39 56 88; www.bikecopenhagenwithmike. dk; Sankt Peders Stræde 47; per person 299kr; 🚌 2A, 5C, 6A, 14, 250S) If you don't fancy walking, Bike Mike runs three-hour cycling tours of the city, departing Sankt Peders Stræde 47 in the city centre, just east of Ørstedsparken (which is southwest of Nørreport Station). The tour cost includes bike, helmet rental and Mike himself, a great character with deep, attention-grabbing knowledge of the city. Cash only.

Copenhagen Free Walking Tours
Walking

(www.copenhagenfreewalkingtours.dk; Rådhuspladsen) This outfit runs free daily walking tours of the city. The three-hour Grand Tour of Copenhagen departs daily at 10am, 11am and 3pm from outside Rådhus (Town Hall), taking in famous landmarks and

featuring interesting anecdotes. There's also a 90-minute Classical Copenhagen Tour, departing daily at noon. A 90-minute tour of Christianshavn departs daily at 4pm from Højbro Plads. A tip is expected.

Canal Tours Copenhagen
Boating

(☑ 32 96 30 00; www.stromma.dk; Nyhavn; adult/child 80/40kr; ⏰ 9.30am-9pm late Jun–mid-Aug, reduced hours rest of year; 🚸; 🚌 1A, 26, 66, 350S, Ⓜ Kongens Nytorv) Canal Tours Copenhagen runs one-hour cruises of the city's canals and harbour, taking in numerous major sights, including Christiansborg Slot, Christianshavn, the Royal Library, Opera House, Amalienborg Palace and the *Little Mermaid*. Embark at Nyhavn or Ved Stranden. Boats depart up to six times per hour from late June to late August, with reduced frequency the rest of the year.

🛍 SHOPPING

Most of the big retail names and homegrown heavyweights are found on the main pedestrian shopping strip, Strøget. The streets running parallel are dotted with interesting jewellery and antique stores while the so-called Latin Quarter, to the north, is worth a wander for books and clothing. Arty Nørrebro is home to Elmegade and Jægersborggade, two streets lined with interesting shops.

Bornholmer Butikken Food & Drinks
(📞30 72 00 07; www.bornholmerbutikken.dk; Stall F6, Hall 1, Torvehallerne KBH; ☺10am-7pm Mon-Thu, to 8pm Fri, to 6pm Sat, 11am-5pm Sun; 🛜; 🚍15E, 150S, 185, Ⓜ Nørreport, Ⓢ Nørreport) The Bornholm Store in Torvehallerne Market peddles specialities from the Danish island of Bornholm, famed for its prized local edibles. Tasty treats to bring home include honeys, relishes and jams, Johan Bülow liquorice, charcuterie, cheeses, herring, liquors and craft beers.

Hay House Design
(📞42 82 08 20; www.hay.dk; Østergade 61; ☺10am-6pm Mon-Fri, to 5pm Sat; 🚍1A, 2A, 9A, 14, 26, 37, 66, Ⓜ Kongens Nytorv) Rolf Hay's fabulous interior-design store sells its own coveted line of furniture, textiles and design objects, as well as those of other fresh, innovative Danish designers. Easy-to-pack gifts include anything from notebooks and ceramic cups, to building blocks for style-savvy kids.

Stilleben Design
(📞22 45 11 31; https://stilleben.dk; Frederiksborggade 22; ☺10am-6pm Mon-Fri, to 5pm Sat; 🚍350S, Ⓜ Nørreport, Ⓢ Nørreport) One of Copenhagen's top design stores, Stilleben is famed for its graphic prints, not to mention its stock of unique objects from mostly smaller-scale Scandi designers. Go gaga over all things beautiful and kooky, from boldly patterned cups, jugs, vases and tea cosies to striking sofa cushions, sculptural candle holders, jewellery, bags, socks and more.

There's another location just off **Strøget** (📞33 91 11 31; Niels Hemmingsensgade 3; ☺10am-6pm Mon-Fri, to 5pm Sat; 🚍1A, 2A, 9A, 14, 26, 37, 66, Ⓜ Kongens Nytorv).

Illums Bolighus Design
(📞33 14 19 41; www.illumsbolighus.dk; Amagertorv 8-10; ☺10am-7pm Mon-Thu & Sat, to 8pm Fri,

11am-6pm Sun; 🛜; 🚍1A, 2A, 9A, 14, 26, 37, 66, Ⓜ Kongens Nytorv) Design fans hyperventilate over this sprawling department store, its four floors packed with all things Nordic and beautiful. You'll find everything from ceramics, glassware, jewellery and fashion to throws, lamps, furniture and more. It's also a handy spot to pick up some X-factor souvenirs, from posters, postcards and notebooks adorned with vintage Danish graphics to design-literate Danish wallets and key rings.

Hoff Jewellery
(📞33 15 30 02; www.gallerihoff.dk; Østerbrogade 44, Østerbro; ☺noon-6pm Tue-Fri, to 3pm Sat; 🚍1A, 14, 37) Ingrid Hoff showcases some of the most innovative and talented jewellery designers in Denmark and Europe. Each item is a veritable conversation piece, and though the designers mix gold and silver with acrylic and nylon, this is by no means 'of-the-moment' fashion jewellery but one-off and limited-run pieces to covet for a lifetime.

Stine Goya Fashion & Accessories
(📞32 17 10 00; www.stinegoya.com; Gothersgade 58; ☺11am-6pm Mon-Fri, to 4pm Sat; 🚍350S, Ⓜ Kongens Nytorv) The winner of numerous prestigious design awards, Stine Goya is one of Denmark's hottest names in women's fashion. What makes her collections unique is the ability to marry clean Nordic simplicity with quirky details. Memorable recent offerings include silky 'oversized' frocks printed with painted human faces, svelte bee-print jumpsuits and a canary-yellow bomber jacket featuring contemporary local artwork. Not cheap but highly collectable.

🍴 EATING

Copenhagen remains one of the hottest culinary destinations in Europe, with more Michelin stars than any other Scandinavian city. These days it's not all New Nordic faves like sea buckthorn, *skyr* (strained yoghurt) curd and pickled quail eggs featuring on Danish menus, with old-school

From left: Torvehallerne KBH; Christiania (p101); Rosenborg Slot (p101)

Danish fare still a major player on the city's tables. Indeed, tucking into classics such as *frikadeller* (meatballs), *sild* (pickled herring) and the iconic Danish smørrebrød (open sandwiches) is an integral part of the Copenhagen experience.

Torvehallerne KBH   Market $

(www.torvehallernekbh.dk; Israels Plads, Nørreport; dishes from around 50kr; ⊙10am-7pm Mon-Thu, to 8pm Fri, to 6pm Sat, 11am-5pm Sun; ⊟15E, 150S, 185, MNørreport, SNørreport) Food market Torvehallerne KBH is an essential stop on the Copenhagen foodie trail. A delicious ode to the fresh, the tasty and the artisanal, the market's beautiful stalls peddle everything from seasonal herbs and berries to smoked meats, seafood and cheeses, smørrebrød, fresh pasta and hand-brewed coffee. You could easily spend an hour or more exploring its twin halls.

Schønnemann   Danish $$

(☎33 12 07 85; www.restaurantschonnemann. dk; Hauser Plads 16; smørrebrød 75-185kr; ⊙11.30am-5pm Mon-Sat; ☎; ⊟6A, 42, 150S, 184, 185, 350S, MNørreport, SNørreport) A ver-

itable institution, Schønnemann has been lining bellies with smørrebrød and *snaps* since 1877. Originally a hit with farmers in town selling their produce, the restaurant's current fan base includes revered chefs like René Redzepi; try the smørrebrød named after him: smoked halibut with creamed cucumber, radishes and chives on caraway bread.

Aamanns Takeaway   Danish $$

(☎20 80 52 01; www.aamanns.dk; Øster Farimagsgade 10; smørrebrød 65-115kr; ⊙11am-5.30pm daily, take away 11am-7pm Mon-Fri, to 4pm Sat & Sun; ⊟6A, 14, 37, 42, 150S, 184, 185) Get your contemporary smørrebrød fix at Aamanns, where open sandwiches are seasonal, artful and served on Aamanns' organic sourdough bread (arrive before 1pm to avoid waiting). If you can't decide between the braised pork belly with rhubarb and bacon crumble, the avocado with lemon cream, or the smoked cheese with cherry/onion compote, the tasting menu offers four smaller smørrebrød for a scrumptious overview. If you're eating in, the kitchen closes at 4pm.

Tårnet   Danish $$
(🖊33 37 31 00; http://taarnet.dk/restauranten; Christiansborg Slotsplads, Christiansborg Slot; lunch smørrebrød 85-135kr, dinner mains 235kr; ⊙11.30am-11pm Tue-Sun, kitchen closes 10pm; 🛜; 🚌1A, 2A, 9A, 26, 37, 66, 🚊Det Kongelige Bibliotek) Book ahead for lunch at Tårnet, owned by prolific restaurateur Rasmus Bo Bojesen and memorably set inside Christiansborg Slot's commanding tower. Lunch here is better value than dinner, with superlative, contemporary smørrebrød that is among the city's best. While the general guideline is two smørrebrød per person, some of the are quite substantial (especially the tartare), so check before ordering.

Kadeau   New Nordic $$$
(🖊33 25 22 23; www.kadeau.dk; Wildersgade 10B; tasting menu 1800kr; ⊙6.30pm-midnight Wed-Fri, noon-4pm & 6.30pm-midnight Sat; 🚌2A, 9A, 37, 350S, 🅜Christianshavn) The big-city spin-off of the Bornholm original, this Michelin-two-starred standout has firmly established itself as one of Scandinavia's top New Nordic restaurants. Whether it's salted and burnt scallops drizzled with clam bouillon, or an unexpected combination of toffee, crème fraiche, potatoes, radish and elderflower, each dish evokes Nordic flavours, moods and landscapes with extraordinary creativity and skill.

Geranium   New Nordic $$$
(🖊69 96 00 20; www.geranium.dk; Per Henrik Lings Allé 4, Østerbro; lunch or dinner tasting menu 2000kr, wine/juice pairings 1400/700kr; ⊙noon-3.30pm & 6.30pm-midnight Wed-Sat; 🛜🍴; 🚌14) 🌿 On the 8th floor of Parken Stadium, Geranium is the only restaurant in town sporting three Michelin stars. At the helm is Bocuse d'Or prize-winning chef Rasmus Kofoed, who transforms local ingredients into edible Nordic artworks like lobster paired with milk and the juice of fermented carrots and sea buckthorn, or cabbage sprouts and chicken served with quail egg, cep mushrooms and hay beer.

🍷 DRINKING & NIGHTLIFE
Copenhagen is packed with a diverse range of drinking options. Vibrant drinking areas include Kødbyen (the 'Meatpacking

 **Understand**

Hygge

Befriend a Dane or two and chances are you'll be invited to partake in a little *hygge*. Usually it translates as 'cosiness' but in reality, *hygge* (pronounced *hoo*-guh) means much more than that. Indeed, there really is no equivalent in English. *Hygge* refers to a sense of friendly, warm companionship of a kind fostered when Danes gather together in groups of two or more, although you can actually *hygge* on your own, too. The participants don't have to be friends (indeed, you might only have just met), but if the conversation flows – avoiding potentially divisive topics like politics – the bonhomie blossoms and toasts are raised before an open fire (or, at the very least, lots of candles), you are probably coming close. Atmosphere, harmony and comfort are key.

Most Danes experience *hygge* in the comfort of their own home, but many cafes, bars and restaurants do their utmost to foster a *hyggelig* atmosphere (note: *hyggelig* is the adjectival form of *hygge*). This comes with open fires or tea lights lit no matter what time of day or year, plus free-flowing drinks and comfort food served in a warm, softly lit, attractive setting. Christmas is the most *hyggelig* time of year.

Interestingly, the word's origin is not Danish but Norwegian. Originally meaning something along the lines of 'well-being', *hygge* first appeared in Danish writing in the early 1800s, and it might originate from the word '*hugge*' (to embrace). Remarkably, after becoming a hot trend for lifestyle magazines and wellness bloggers around the globe in 2015–16, the term *hygge* was added to the Oxford English Dictionary in 2017.

The international 'discovery' of *hygge* has prompted the publication of a handful of books explaining the concept, plus manuals on how non-Danish *hygge*-seekers can create and experience it. To find out more, don some woollen socks, light a few candles, make a cup of cocoa and get comfy on your sofa (blankets and cushions essential), then take lessons from *The Little Book of Hygge* by Meik Wiking. Wiking is the CEO of the Happiness Research Institute in Copenhagen, so the man knows *hygge*.

District') and Istedgade in Vesterbro, Ravnsborggade, Elmegade and Sankt Hans Torv in Nørrebro, and especially gay-friendly Studiestræde.

Coffee Collective — Coffee

(www.coffeecollective.dk; Jægersborggade 57, Nørrebro; ☺7am-8pm Mon-Fri, 8am-7pm Sat & Sun; 🚌8A) Copenhagen's most prolific microroastery, Coffee Collective has helped revolutionise the city's coffee culture in recent years. Head in for rich, complex cups of caffeinated magic. The baristas are passionate about their single-origin beans and the venue itself sits at one end of creative Jægersborggade in Nørrebro. There are three other outlets, including at gourmet food market **Torvehallerne KBH** (www.

coffeecollective.dk; Stall C1, Hall 2, Torvehallerne KBH; ☺7am-8pm Mon-Fri, 8am-7pm Sat, 8am-6pm Sun) 🍃 and in **Frederiksberg** (☎60 15 15 25; https://coffeecollective.dk; Godthåbsvej 34b, Frederiksberg; ☺7.30am-6pm Mon-Fri, from 9am Sat, from 10am Sun).

Ved Stranden 10 — Wine Bar

(☎35 42 40 40; www.vedstranden10.dk; Ved Stranden 10; ☺noon-10pm Mon-Sat; 🛜; 🚌1A, 2A, 9A, 26, 37, 66, 350S, 🅜Kongens Nytorv) Politicians and well-versed oenophiles make a beeline for this canal-side wine bar, its enviable cellar stocked with classic European vintages, biodynamic wines and more obscure drops. With modernist Danish design and friendly, clued-in staff, its string of rooms lend an intimate, civilised air that's perfect for grown-up conversation. Discuss terroir and tannins over vino-friendly nibbles like olives, cheeses and smoked meats.

Mikkeller & Friends   Microbrewery
(☏35 83 10 20; www.mikkeller.dk/location/mikkeller-friends; Stefansgade 35, Nørrebro; ◷2pm-midnight Sun-Wed, to 2am Thu & Fri, noon-2am Sat; 🛜; 🚌5C, 8A) Looking suitably cool with its turquoise floors and pale ribbed wood, Mikkeller & Friends is a joint venture of the Mikkeller and To Øl breweries. Beer geeks go gaga over the 40 artisan draught beers and circa 200 bottled varieties, which might include a chipotle porter or an imperial stout aged in tequila barrels. Limited snacks include dried gourmet sausage and cheese.

ENTERTAINMENT

Copenhagen is home to thriving live-music and club scenes that range from intimate jazz and blues clubs to mega rock venues. Blockbuster cultural venues such as **Operaen** (Copenhagen Opera House; ☏box office 33 69 69 69; www.kglteater.dk; Ekvipagemestervej 10; 🚌9A, ⛴Operaen) and **Skuespilhuset** (Royal Danish Playhouse; ☏33 69 69 69; https://kglteater.dk; Sankt Anne Plads 36; 🚌66, ⛴Nyhavn, Ⓜ Kongens Nytorv) deliver top-tier opera and theatre.

Jazzhus Montmartre   Jazz
(☏70 26 32 67; www.jazzhusmontmartre.dk; Store Regnegade 19A; ◷6pm-midnight Thu-Sat; 🚌1A, 26, 350S, Ⓜ Kongens Nytorv) Saxing things up since the late 1950s, this is one of Scandinavia's great jazz venues, with past performers including Dexter Gordon, Ben Webster and Kenny Drew. Today, it continues to host local and international talent. On concert nights, you can also tuck into a decent, three-course set menu (375kr) at the **cafe-restaurant**.

INFORMATION

DISCOUNT CARDS

The **Copenhagen Card** (www.copenhagencard.com; adult/child 10-15yr 24hr 389/199kr, 48hr 549/279kr, 72hr 659/329kr, 120hr 889/449kr) gives you access to 79 museums and attractions, as well as free public transport. Each adult card includes up to two children aged under 10. The card can be purchased at the visitor service at the Oceankaj cruise terminal, the Copenhagen Visitors Centre, many other places or online.

TOURIST INFORMATION

Copenhagen Visitors Centre (☏70 22 24 42; www.visitcopenhagen.com; Vesterbrogade 4A, Vesterbro; ◷9am-8pm Mon-Fri, to 6pm Sat & Sun Jul & Aug, reduced hours rest of year; 🛜; 🚌2A, 6A, 12, 14, 26, 250S, Ⓢ København H) Copenhagen's excellent and informative information centre has a cafe and lounge with free wi-fi; it also sells the Copenhagen Card.

🛈 GETTING AROUND

Foot Central Copenhagen is relatively compact and best navigated on foot; most major sights are within walking distance.

Bicycle World-class cycling infrastructure. The superb, city-wide rental system is **Bycyklen** (City Bikes; www.bycyklen.dk; per 1hr 30kr). Check the website for more details.

Bus Frequent services and great views.

Metro Efficient, 24/7 service. Handy connections between Nørreport, Nyhavn, Christianshavn, Island Brygge, Amager Strand and Copenhagen Airport.

Public Transport Extensive, efficient and handy for crossing town. City buses, the metro, S-train and Harbour Buses (ferries) all use the same ticket system.

Taxi Can be hailed on the street; numerous ranks across the city, including at Central Station. Alternatively, call ☏70 25 25 25 or 35 35 35 35.

OSLO, NORWAY

Oslo at a Glance...

Surrounded by mountains and the sea, this compact, cultured and fun city is Europe's fastest-growing capital, with a palpable sense of reinvention. Oslo is also home to world-class museums and galleries to rival anywhere else on the European art trail. But even here Mother Nature has managed to make her mark, and Oslo is fringed with forests, hills and lakes awash with opportunities for hiking, cycling, skiing and boating. Add to this mix a thriving cafe-and-bar culture, top-notch restaurants and nightlife options ranging from opera to indie rock, and the result is a thoroughly intoxicating place.

With One Day in Port

Start your day at **Akershus Fortress** (p118), then wander along Nedre Slottsgate and window shop, ending at the **Nasjonalgalleriet** (p118) and Edvard Munch's *The Scream*.

After lunch, take the ferry to pretty Bygdøy Peninsula, and spend your afternoon at **Vikingskipshuset** (p114) and catching up on Norwegian folk culture at the **Norsk Folkemuseum** (p115).

Best Places for...

Street food Syverkiosken (p123)
Food court Mathallen Oslo (p124)
Degustation Maaemo (p125)
Cafe Tim Wendelboe (p125)
Wine bar Territoriet (p125)

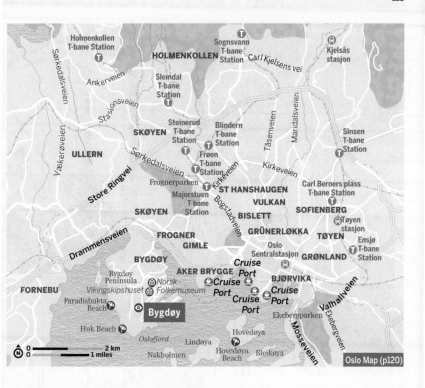

Oslo Map (p120)

Getting from the Port

Most cruises dock at one of three very
central docks around the Akershus
fortress. From here, the centre of town
is very walkable. The extensive tram
network is the best public transport
option in this area.

Fast Facts

Currency Norwegian kroner (kr)

Language Norwegian

Free wi-fi Most bars and cafes have free
wi-fi for customers.

Tourist Information Oslo Visitor
Centre (p125) is beside the main train
station.

Transport Trams, trains and the underground T-bane are covered by the Ruter
ticketing system.

Oseberg ship, Vikingshipshuset

History on Bygdøy

Best accessed by ferry, pretty, residential and rural-feeling Bygdøy is home to the city's most fascinating, quintessentially Norwegian, museums, featuring Vikings, traditional architecture and modern-day explorers.

Great For...

☑ Don't Miss

The most impressive and ostentatious of the three Viking ships, the *Oseberg*.

Vikingskipshuset

Prepare yourself for one of the most affecting **historical experiences** (Viking Ship Museum; ☎22 13 52 80; www.khm.uio.no; Huk Aveny 35; adult/child 80kr/free; ☻9am-6pm May-Sep, 10am-4pm Oct-Apr) of your life. Three Viking ships – two in impossibly pristine condition – sit proudly in a light, purpose-built hall from the 1930s. Their dignified, dark presence makes the life of the much mythologised Vikings seem vividly present.

The reason we have these ships today is that they were dragged up from their docks and used as the centrepiece of massive burial sites. This means that not only were the vessels preserved, but they were preserved with caches of the things a Viking might like to take with them to Valhalla. Thus their great archaeological gift tells us much about a whole range of aspects of

Viking relic, Vikingshipshuset

Kon-Tiki Museum

A favourite with children, this worthwhile **museum** (☏23 08 67 67; www.kon-tiki.no; Bygdøynesveien 36; adult/child 100/40kr, with Oslo Pass free; ⊗9.30am-6pm Jun-Aug, 10am-5pm Mar-May, Sep & Oct, 10am-4pm Nov-Feb) is dedicated to the balsa raft *Kon-Tiki*, which Norwegian explorer Thor Heyerdahl sailed from Peru to Polynesia in 1947. The museum also displays the totora-reed boat *Ra II*, built by Aymara people on the Bolivian island of Suriqui in Lake Titicaca. Heyerdahl used it to cross the Atlantic in 1970.

Norsk Folkemuseum

This **folk museum** (Norwegian Folk Museum; ☏22 12 37 00; www.norskfolkemuseum.no; Museumsveien 10; adult/child 130/40kr, with Oslo Pass free; ⊗10am-6pm mid-May–mid-Sep, 11am-3pm Mon-Fri, 11am-4pm Sat & Sun mid-Sep–mid-May) is Norway's largest open-air and one of Oslo's most popular attractions. The museum includes more than 140 buildings, mostly from the 17th and 18th centuries, gathered from around the country, rebuilt and organised according to region of origin. Paths wind past old barns, elevated *stabbur* (raised storehouses) and rough-timbered farmhouses with sod roofs sprouting wildflowers. Little people will be entertained by the numerous farm animals, horse and cart rides, and other activities.

Viking life, from their nautical engineering capabilities, their seacraft and their mercantile and military ambition, to a snapshot of a high-ranking citizen's everyday desires and tastes and their spiritual life.

Polarship Fram Museum

A **museum** (Frammuseet; ☏23 28 29 50; www.frammuseum.no; Bygdøynesveien 36; adult/child 100/40kr, with Oslo Pass free; ⊗9am-6pm Jun-Aug, 10am-5pm May & Sep, to 4pm Oct-May) dedicated to one of the most enduring symbols of early polar exploration, the 39m schooner Fram (meaning 'Forward'). You can wander the decks, peek inside the cramped bunk rooms and imagine life at sea and among the polar ice. There are detailed exhibits complete with maps, pictures and artefacts of various expeditions, from Nansen's attempt to ski across the North Pole to Amundsen's discovery of the Northwest Passage.

All Along the Waterfront

Once a heavily industrialised port area, Oslo's waterfront has been totally transformed over the last 20 years and is still in the process of rapid change. It makes for a heady mix of the new and the historic, and the industrial and the natural.

Start Ekebergparken
Distance 4.5km
Duration 2½ hours

5 At charming **Pipervika** (p124) you can eat the morning's catch straight from the boats while enjoying views across the harbour.

4 Akerhusstranda makes for a nice waterfront stroll, with the fortress looming above.

Take a Break. Try the prime waterfront stools at Vingen (p124).

6 The city's most-visited stretch of waterfront gives way to the serene sails of Renzo Piano's **Astrup Fearnley Museet** (p119).

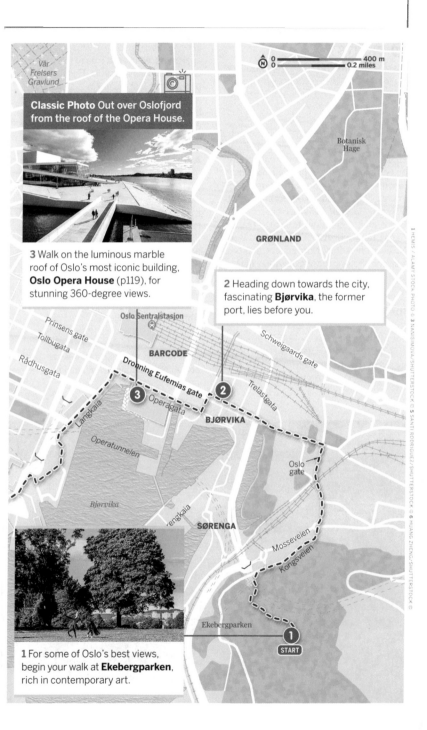

Classic Photo Out over Oslofjord from the roof of the Opera House.

3 Walk on the luminous marble roof of Oslo's most iconic building, **Oslo Opera House** (p119), for stunning 360-degree views.

2 Heading down towards the city, fascinating **Bjørvika**, the former port, lies before you.

1 For some of Oslo's best views, begin your walk at **Ekebergparken**, rich in contemporary art.

Vår Frelsers Gravlund

Botanisk Hage

GRØNLAND

Prinsens gate

Tollbugata

Rådhusgata

Oslo Sentralstasjon

BARCODE

Dronning Eufemias gate

Schweigaards gate

Trelastgata

Operagata

BJØRVIKA

Langkaia

Operatunnelen

Oslo gate

Bjørvika

engkaia

SØRENGA

Mosseveien

Kongsveien

Ekebergparken

START

1 HEMIS / ALAMY STOCK PHOTO © 3 NANISIMOVA/SHUTTERSTOCK © 5 SANTI RODRIGUEZ/SHUTTERSTOCK © 6 HUANG ZHENG/SHUTTERSTOCK ©

⊙ SIGHTS

Nasjonalgalleriet
Gallery

(National Gallery; ☎21 98 20 00; www.nasjonal
museet.no; Universitetsgata 13; adult/child 100kr/
free, Thu free; ⊙10am-6pm Tue, Wed & Fri, to 7pm
Thu, 11am-5pm Sat & Sun; ☒Tullinløkka) The
gallery houses the nation's largest collection
of traditional and modern art and many of
Edvard Munch's best-known creations are
on permanent display, including his most
renowned work, *The Scream*. There's also an
impressive collection of European art, with
works by Gauguin, Claudel, Picasso and El
Greco, plus Impressionists such as Manet,
Degas, Renoir, Matisse, Cézanne and Monet.
Nineteenth-century Norwegian artists have
a strong showing too, including key figures
such as JC Dahl and Christian Krohg.

The gallery is set to relocate in 2020.

Ibsen Museet
Museum

(Ibsen Museum; ☎40 02 36 30; www.ibsen
museet.no; Henrik Ibsens Gate 26; adult/child
115/30kr; ⊙11am-6pm May-Sep, to 4pm Oct-Apr,
guided tours hourly; ☒Slottsparken) While
downstairs houses a small and rather

idiosyncratic museum, it's Ibsen's former
apartment, which you'll need to join a tour
to see, that is unmissable. This was the
playwright's last residence and his study
remains exactly as he left it, as does the
bedroom where he uttered his famously
enigmatic last words, *'Tvert imot!'* ('To the
contrary!'), before dying on 23 May 1906.

Akershus Festning
Fortress

(Akershus Fortress; ⊙6am-9pm; ☒Christiania
Sq) **FREE** When Oslo was named capital
of Norway in 1299, King Håkon V ordered
the construction of Akershus, strategically
located on the eastern side of the harbour,
to protect the city from external threats.
It has, over the centuries, been extended,
modified and had its defences beefed up
a number of times. Still dominating the
Oslo harbourfront, the sprawling complex
consists of a medieval castle, **Akershus
Slott** (Akershus Castle; ☎22 41 25 21; www.
nasjonalefestningsverk.no; Kongens gate; adult/
child 60/30kr, with Oslo Pass free; ⊙11am-4pm
Mon-Sat, noon-5pm Sun), a fortress and as-
sorted other buildings, including still-active
military installations.

Akershus Festning

Royal Palace
Palace

(Det Kongelige Slott; ☑81 53 31 33; www.royal
court.no; Slottsparken 1; palace tours adult/child
135/105kr, with Queen Sonja Art Stable 200kr;
⊙guided tours in English noon, 2pm, 2.20pm
& 4pm Jun–mid-Aug; ⊕Slottsparken) The
Norwegian royal family's seat of residence
emerges from the wood-like **Slottsparken**
(⊙24hr) `FREE`, a relatively modest, pale
buttercup neoclassical pile. Built for
the Swedish (in fact, French) king Karl
Johan, the palace was never continuously
occupied before King Håkon VII and Queen
Maud were installed in 1905.

Astrup Fearnley Museet
Gallery

(Astrup Fearnley Museum; ☑22 93 60 60; www.
afmuseet.no; Strandpromenaden 2; adult/
child 120kr/free; ⊙noon-5pm Tue, Wed & Fri, to
7pm Thu, 11am-5pm Sat & Sun; ⊕Aker brygge)
Designed by Renzo Piano, this private
contemporary art museum is housed in a
wonderful building of silvered wood, with a
sail-like glass roof that feels both maritime
and at one with the Oslofjord landscape.
While the museum's original collecting
brief was conceptual American work from
the 1980s (with artists of the ilk of Jeff
Koons, Tom Sachs, Cindy Sherman and
Richard Prince well represented), it has in
recent times broadened beyond that, with,
for example, a room dedicated to Sigmar
Polke and Anselm Kiefer.

Its most famous piece remains, however,
the gilded ceramic sculpture *Michael
Jackson and Bubbles,* by Koons, and there
are also large works by Damien Hirst.
The temporary shows range from the
monographic, say Matthew Barney or
young Norwegian artist Matias Faldbakken,
to thematically tight curated surveys
such as New Norwegian Abstraction or
Chinese conceptual work. The museum is
surrounded by a fabulous park of contemporary sculpture.

Nobels Fredssenter
Museum

(Nobel Peace Center; ☑48 30 10 00; www.
nobelpeacecenter.org; Rådhusplassen 1; adult/
student 100/65kr; ⊙10am-6pm; ⊕Aker brygge)
Norwegians take pride in their role as

Oslo's Iconic Opera House

The centrepiece of the city's rapidly de-
veloping waterfront is the magnificent
Oslo Opera House (Den Norske Opera
& Ballett; ☑21 42 21 21; www.operaen.no;
Kirsten Flagstads plass 1; foyer free; ⊙foyer
10am-9pm Mon-Fri, 11am-9pm Sat, noon-9pm
Sun; ⓉSentralstasjonen), considered one
of the most iconic modern buildings of
Scandinavia. Designed by Oslo-based
architectural firm Snøhetta and costing
around €500 million to build, the Opera
House opened in 2008, and resembles
a glacier floating in the waters of the
Oslofjord. Its design is a thoughtful
meditation on the notion of monumen-
tality, the dignity of cultural production,
Norway's unique place in the world and
the conversation between public life and
personal experience.

The opera house hosts world-class
ballet and opera **performances** (tickets
100-795kr). Book ahead or try for the
last-minute 100kr standing seats.

international peacemakers, and the Nobel
Peace Prize is their gift to the men and
women judged to have done the most to
promote world peace over the course of the
previous year. This state-of-the-art museum celebrates the lives and achievements
of the winners with an array of digital
displays that offer as much or as little information as you feel like taking in.

Vigelandsanlegget
Park

(Vigeland Sculpture Park; www.vigeland.museum.
no/no/vigelandsparken; Nobels gate 32; ⊙Tue-
Sun noon-4pm; ⓉBorgen) The centrepiece of
the westside park of Frognerparken is an
extraordinary open-air showcase of work
by Norway's best-loved sculptor, Gustav
Vigeland. Statistically one of the top tourist
attractions in Norway, Vigeland Park is
brimming with 212 granite and bronze
Vigeland works. His highly charged oeuvre
includes entwined lovers, tranquil elderly

Oslo

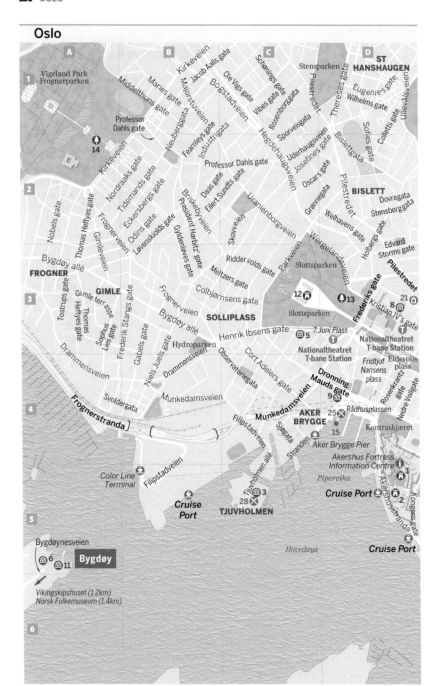

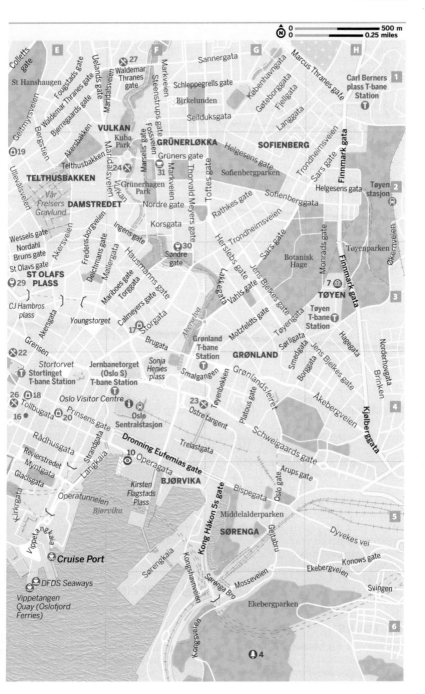

0   500 m
0   0.25 miles

E   F   G   H

Colletts gate
St Hanshaugen
Geitmyrsveien
Bergsten
Fougstads gate
Waldemar Thranes gate
Bjerregaards gate
Ueland gate
Maridalsveien
Steenstrups gate
Markveien
Waldemar Thranes gate
Sannergata
Schleppegrells gate
Birkelunden
Seilduksgata
Marcus Thranes gate
København gata
Gøteborggata
Fjellgata
Langgata
Carl Berners plass T-bane Station 1

19
VULKAN
Kuba Park
Telthusbakken
TELTHUSBAKKEN
Akersbakken
27
Fossveien
Marselis gate
24
Grüners gate
31
GRÜNERLØKKA
Grünerhagen Park
Markveien
Thorvald Meyers gate
Tottes gate
Helgesens gate
SOFIENBERG
Sofienbergparken
Sofienbergg gata
Trondheimsveien
Sars gate
Helgesens gata
Finnmark gata
Tøyen stasjon 2

Vår Frelsers Gravlund
DAMSTREDET
Maridalsveien
Vulkan
Nordre gate
Korsgata
Rathkes gate
Sofienberggata
Okerveien
Tøyenparken

Wessels gate
Nordahl Bruns gate
St Olavs gate
ST OLAFS PLASS
29
CJ Hambros plass
Akersgata
Grensen
22
Fredensborgveien
Deichmans gate
Mariboes gate
Akersveien
Ingens gate
Hausmanns gate
Mollergata
Torggata
Calmeyers gate
Youngstorget
17
Søndre gate
30
Brugata
Storgata
Herslebs gate
Trondheimsveien
Lakkegata
Vahls gate
Jens Bjelkes gate
Sars gate
Botanisk Hage
Monrads gate
Finnmark gata
7
TØYEN
Tøyen T-bane Station 3
Haggata
Norderhovgata
Brinken
Kjølberggata

Stortorvet
Stortinget T-bane Station
26   18
16
20
Tollbugata
Prinsens gate
Jernbanetorget (Oslo S) T-bane Station
Sonja Henies plass
Smalgangen
Grønland T-bane Station
GRØNLAND
Grønlandsleiret
Motzfeldts gate
Tøyengata
Sørligata
Smedgata
Borggata
Jens Bjelkes gate
Platous gate
Åkebergveien
4

Oslo Visitor Centre
Oslo Sentralstasjon
23
Østre tangent
Tøyenbekken
Trelastgata
Schweigaards gate
Arups gate
Oslo gate

Rådhusgata
Revierstredet
Myntgata
Glacisgata
Strandgata
Langkaia
Operatunnelen
Bjørvika
10
Operagata
Dronning Eufemias gate
BJØRVIKA
Kirsten Flagstads Plass
Kong Håkon 5s gate
Bispegata
Middelalderparken
SØRENGA
Getabru
Dyvekes vei
5

Kirkgata
Vippetangkaia
Cruise Port
DFDS Seaways
Vippetangen Quay (Oslofjord Ferries)
Sørengkaia
Kongshavnveien
Sørenga Bro
Mosseveien
Konows gate
Ekebergveien
Svingen
Ekebergparken
4
6

Oslo

couples, bawling babies and contempt-ridden beggars. Speaking of bawling babies, his most famous work here, *Sinataggen* (Little Hot-Head), portrays a child in a mood of particular ill humour.

To get here, take tram 12 to Vigelandsparken from the city centre.

Munchmuseet   Gallery
(Munch Museum; ☏23 49 35 00; www.munchmuseet.no; Tøyengata 53; adult/child 100kr/free; ☺10am-4pm, to 5pm mid-Jun–late Sep; Ⓣ Tøyen) A monographic museum dedicated to Norway's greatest artist Edvard Munch (1863–1944), and housing the largest collection of his work in the world: 28,000 items including 1100 paintings and 4500 watercolours, many of which were gifted to the city by Munch himself (although his best-known pieces, including *The Scream*, are held in the Nasjonalgalleriet; p118).

To get here, take a bus or the T-bane to Tøyen, followed by a 300m signposted walk.

🅖 TOURS

Båtservice Sightseeing   Boating
(☏23 35 68 90; www.boatsightseeing.com; Pier 3, Rådhusbrygge; per person 215-650kr; 🚢Aker brygge) For a watery view of Oslo and the Oslofjord, Båtservice Sightseeing offers a whole array of tours aboard either a traditional wooden schooner or a more up-to-date motorboat. There's a hop-on, hop-off service from May to September (24-hour ticket 215kr).

Viking Biking   Cycling
(☏412 66 496; www.vikingbikingoslo.com; Nedre Slottsgate 4; 3hr tour adult/child 350/200kr; ☺9.30am-6pm; 🚲Øvre Slottsgate) This excellent outfit is a great place to head if you want to explore Oslo on two wheels. It runs a range of guided bike tours, including a three-hour 'City Highlights' route through some of Oslo's parks and backstreets, plus a 'River Tour' along the path beside the Akerselva River, both designed to avoid traffic wherever possible.

🅐 SHOPPING

Oslo's centre and its inner neighbourhoods have a great selection of small shops if you're not into the malls. The city centre's Kirkegaten, Nedre Slottsgate and Prinsens gate are home to a well-considered collection of Scandinavian and international fashion and homewares shops, with Frogner and St Hanshaugen also having some good upmarket choices. Grünerløkka is great for vintage and Scandinavian fashion too.

Norwegian Rain
Fashion & Accessories

(✆996 03 411; http://norwegianrain.com; Kirkegata 20; ⊙10am-6pm Mon-Fri, to 5pm Sat; 🚊Nationaltheatret) Bergen comes to Oslo! This west coast design superstar creates what might be the world's most covetable raincoats. This Oslo outpost stocks the complete range as well as creative director T-Michael's woollen suits, detachable-collar shirts, leather shoes and bags, not to mention limited editions of Kings of Convenience LPs.

Cappelens Forslag
Books

(✆908 81 106; www.cappelensforslag.no; Bernt Ankers gate 4; ⊙11am-6pm Mon-Fri, to 4pm Sat; 🚊Brugata) Both a rare and cult lit dealer and cafe, this bookshop is set to be your new favourite. Make yourself at home on the front-room sofa with a good coffee and browse your way through its first editions and other gems, most of which are in English. It also hosts readings, book launches and concerts.

FWSS
Fashion & Accessories

(Fall Winter Spring Summer; http://fallwinterspringsummer.com; Prinsens gate 22; ⊙10am-7pm Mon-Fri, to 6pm Sat; 🚊Øvre Slottsgate) New flagship of this fast-growing Norwegian label, known for its easy basics as well as seasonal collections that combine Scandinavian simplicity with a pretty, playful edge.

Gutta På Haugen
Food & Drinks

(✆22 60 85 12; http://gutta.no; Ullevålsveien 45; ⊙8am-7pm; 🚌37) For picnic or self-catering supplies, head to this well-stocked St Hanshaugen institution. There's a huge cheese selection with both Norwegian and European produce, a lovely array of local sausages and boxes of the must-try Norwegian flat bread. Its fresh produce is the best of the season and you can grab an excellent soft serve to take away at its ice-cream van across the road.

 Exploring the Wild Side of Oslo

Avid skiers, hikers and sailors, Oslo residents will do just about anything to get outside. That's not too hard given that there are over 240 sq km of woodland, 40 islands and 343 lakes within the city limits. And you can jump on a train with your skis and be on the slopes in less than 30 minutes.

Cross-country skiing near Oslo
MORTEN NORMANN ALMELAND/SHUTTERSTOCK ©

Tronsmo
Books

(✆22 99 03 99; www.tronsmo.no; Universitetsgata 12; ⊙9am-5pm Mon-Wed, to 6pm Thu & Fri, 10am-4pm Sat; 🚊Tullinløkka) A social hub as much as a bookshop, come for its large range of English-language books and stay for a reading or performance. There's a large LGBT section and a basement full of comics and graphic novels.

EATING

Oslo's food scene has come into its own in recent years, attracting curious culinary-minded travellers who've eaten their way round Copenhagen or Stockholm and are looking for new sensations. Dining out here can involve a Michelin-starred place, a hot-dog stand, peel-and-eat shrimp, a place doing innovative Neo Nordic small plates or a convincingly authentic Japanese, Italian, French, Indian or Mexican dish.

Syverkiosken
Hot Dogs $

(✆967 08 699; Maridalsveien 45; hot dogs from 20kr; ⊙9am-11.30pm Mon-Fri, from 11am Sat &

Oslo: Unexpected Art Capital

Something of an insider's secret, Oslo has an art scene that cities five times its size would be proud of. Like the country itself, it's egalitarian, flush with cash, vibrant, unpretentious if sometimes very serious, and often fearless. From its contemporary collections full of heavy-hitting international names (which you'll find ridiculously uncrowded) to a flourishing, fun artist-run scene (which you'll often find happily full of crowds of young artists), everything is easily accessible.

Munchmuseet (p122)

KIEV.VICTOR/SHUTTERSTOCK ©

Sun; 🚊34) It might look like a hipster replica, but this hole-in-the-wall *pølser* (hot dogs) place is absolutely authentic and one of the last of its kind in Oslo. Dogs can be had in a potato bread wrap in lieu of the usual roll, or with both, and there's a large range of old-school accompaniments beyond sauce and mustard.

Sentralen Restaurant
New Nordic $$

(📞22 33 33 22; www.sentralen.no; Øvre Slottsgate 3; small plates 85-195kr; ⊙11am-10pm Mon-Sat; 🚊Øvre Slottsgate) One of Oslo's best dining experiences is also its most relaxed. A large dining room with a bustling open kitchen, filled with old social club chairs and painted in tones of deep, earthy green, draws city workers, visitors and natural-wine-obsessed locals in equal measure. Small-plate dining makes it easy to sample across the appealing Neo Nordic menu.

Grand Café
Norwegian $$

(📞23 21 20 18; www.grand.no; Karl Johans gate 31; mains 145-295kr; ⊙11am-11pm Mon-Fri, from noon Sat, noon-9pm Sun; 🚊Stortinget) At 11am sharp, Henrik Ibsen would leave his apartment and walk to Grand Café for a lunch of herring, beer and one shot of aquavit (an alcoholic drink made from potatoes and caraway liquor). His table is still here. Don't worry, though, today you can take your pick from perfectly plated, elegantly sauced cod and mussels, spelt risotto with mushrooms or cured lamb and potato.

Mathallen Oslo
Food Hall $$

(www.mathallenoslo.no; Maridalsveien 17, Vulkan; ⊙8am-1am Tue-Fri, from 9.30am Sat & Sun; 🚊54) Down by the river, this former industrial space is now a food court dedicated to showcasing the very best of Norwegian regional cuisine, as well as some excellent internationals. There are dozens of delis, cafes and miniature restaurants, and the place buzzes throughout the day and well into the evening.

Vingen
New Nordic $$

(📞901 51 595; http://vingenbar.no; Strandpromenaden 2; mains 145-240kr; ⊙10am-9pm Sun-Wed, to midnight Thu-Sat; 🚊Aker brygge) While honouring its role as museum cafe for Astrup Fearnley (p119) and a super-scenic pit stop, Vingen is so much more. Do drop in for excellent coffee, but also come for lunch or dinner with small, interesting menus subtly themed in homage to the museum's current temporary show. Nightfall brings cocktails, and sometimes DJs and dancing in the museum lobby and, in summer, on the waterfront terrace.

Pipervika
Seafood $$

(www.pipervika.no; Rådhusbrygge 4; mains 175-250kr, shrimp per kg 130kr; ⊙7am-11pm; 🚊Aker brygge) If the weather is nice, nothing beats a shrimp lunch, with fresh shrimp on a baguette with mayonnaise and a spritz of lemon eaten dockside. The revamped fisherman's co-op still does takeaway peel-and-eat shrimp by the kilo, but you can now also relax with a sushi plate, oysters or a full seafood menu including fish burger on brioche or killer fish and chips.

Everything is prepared with daily bounty from the Oslofjord.

Maaemo   New Nordic $$$
(☑22 17 99 69; https://maaemo.no; Schweigaards gate 15; menu 2600kr; ☺6pm-midnight Wed & Thu, from noon Sat & Sun; ☒Bussterminalen Grønland) This is not a meal to be taken lightly: first, you'll need to book many months in advance, and second, there will, for most of us, be the indenting of funds. But go if you can, not for the three Michelin star accolades but for Esben Holmboe Bang's 20 or so courses that are one of the world's most potent culinary experiences and a sensual articulation of what it means to be Norwegian.

⊙ DRINKING & NIGHTLIFE

The locals definitely don't seem to mind the high price of alcohol: Oslo has a ridiculously rich nightlife scene, with a huge range of bars and clubs, and most open until 3am or later on weekends. The compact nature of the city and its interconnecting inner neighbourhoods means bar crawling is a joy, if expensive.

Tim Wendelboe   Cafe
(☑400 04 062; www.timwendelboe.no; Grüners gate 1; ☺8.30am-6pm Mon-Fri, 11am-5pm Sat & Sun; ☒Schous plass) Tim Wendelboe is often credited with kick-starting the Scandinavian coffee revolution and his eponymous cafe and roastery is both a local freelancers' hang-out and an international coffee-fiend pilgrimage site. All the beans are, of course, self-sourced and handroasted (the roaster is part of the furniture), and all coffees – from an iced pour-over to a regular cappuccino – are world-class.

Fuglen   Cocktail Bar, Cafe
(www.fuglen.com; Universitetsgaten 2; ☺7.30am-10pm Mon & Tue, to 1am Wed & Thu, to 3am Fri, 11am-3am Sat, to 10pm Sun; ☒17B) Fuglen and its crew of merry, young entrepreneurs are part of Oslo's dour-to-dreamily cool reinvention. Since taking over a traditional cafe, they've launched a coffee and Norwegian design mini-empire in Japan, while in their home city they continue to roast and brew as well as mix some of the best cocktails around.

Territoriet   Wine Bar
(http://territoriet.no/; Markveien 58; ☺4pm-1am Mon-Fri, from noon Sat & Sun; ☒Schous plass) A true neighbourhood wine bar that's also the city's most exciting. The grape-loving owners offer up more than 300 wines by the glass and do so without a list. Talk to the staff about your preferences and – yes, this is Norway – your budget, and they'll find something you'll adore. Ordering beer or gin and tonic won't raise an eyebrow, we promise.

⊙ INFORMATION

Oslo Visitor Centre (☑81 53 05 55; www.visit oslo.com; Jernbanetorget 1; ☺9am-6pm; ☒Sentralstasjon) Right beside the main train station. Sells transport tickets as well as the useful Oslo Pass (adult/child 24hr 395/595/745kr); publishes free guides to the city.

⊙ GETTING AROUND

All public transport is covered off by the Ruter (https://ruter.no/en/) ticketing system; schedules and route maps are available online or at **Trafikanten** (☑177; www.ruter.no; Jernbanetorget; ☺7am-8pm Mon-Fri, 8am-6pm Sat & Sun).

Tram Oslo's tram network is extensive and runs 24 hours.

T-bane The six-line Tunnelbanen underground system, better known as the T-bane, is faster and extends further from the city centre than most city buses or tram lines.

Train Suburban trains and services to the Oslofjord where the T-bane doesn't reach.

BERGEN, NORWAY

Bergen at a Glance...

Surrounded by seven hills and seven fjords, Bergen is a beguiling city. During the early Middle Ages, it was an important seaport and a member of the Hanseatic League, as well as Norway's capital – a heritage that can still be glimpsed in the beautifully preserved wooden houses of Bryggen, now protected as a Unesco World Heritage Site. Colourful houses creep up the hillsides, ferry-boats flit around the fjords, and a cluster of excellent art museums provide a welcome detour in case Bergen's notoriously fickle weather sets in. Meanwhile, a large student population ensures the city has a buzzy cafe and bar scene.

With One Day in Port

Walk around Bergen's heart, the historic harbour, until you reach the old port of **Bryggen** (p130) and its lovely wooden warehouses. Drop in to the **Bryggens Museum** (p131) to put the area in historical context, then have lunch at the **Torget fish market** (p140), where you can dine handsomely on whatever the day's catch has brought in. Spend the afternoon exploring the stellar art collection at **KODE** (p133).

Best Places for...

Seafood Torget Fish Market (p140)

Home cooking Pingvinen (p140)

Modern gastronomy Lysverket (p141)

Whisky Terminus Bar (p142)

Craft beer Bryggeriet (p142)

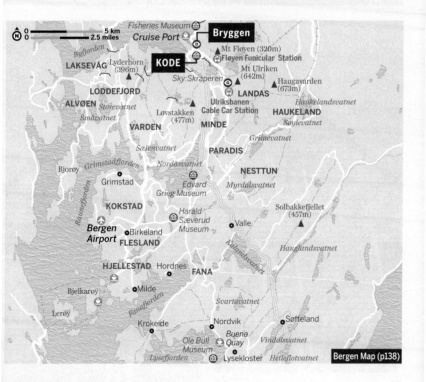

Getting from the Port

The most-frequently used cruise terminal, Skolten, is very central, an easy 750m stroll to Bryggen and similarly close to other sights. Buses also run past and there's a taxi rank.

Fast Facts

Currency Norwegian kroner (kr)

Language Norwegian

Free wi-fi Tourist office, and most cafes and restaurants.

Tourist information Bergen's tourist office (p143) is excellent. There's also a visitor centre (p143) in Bryggen.

Transport Buses and trams operated by Skyss (p143).

Bryggen

The picturesque and colourful wooden warehouses of this historic district are a beautiful sight. They have their origins in the 14th century when Bergen was part of the Hanseatic trade league.

Great For...

☑ Don't Miss

Walking around the harbour to get the best shots from the other side of the water.

Wooden Quarter

Bergen's oldest quarter runs along the eastern shore of Vågen Harbour (*bryggen* translates as 'wharf') in long, parallel and often leaning rows of gabled buildings. Each has stacked-stone or wooden foundations and reconstructed rough-plank construction. It's enchanting, no doubt about it, but can be exhausting if you hit a crush when there are multiple ships in port and bus tours rolling in.

The wooden alleyways of Bryggen have become a haven for artists and craftspeople, and there are bijou shops and boutiques at every turn. The atmosphere of an intimate waterfront community remains intact; losing yourself here is one of Bergen's pleasures.

History

The current 58 buildings (25% of the original, although some claim there are now 61) cover 13,000 sq metres and date from

Bryggen 🅞

⚓

Explore Ashore

It's a short, pleasant 10-minute stroll to Bryggen from the principal cruise terminal, or take bus 5 or 6. Plan on an hour or two wandering the area.

❶ Need to Know

Bryggen is free to visit.

museum (🕿55 55 20 80; Enhjørningsgården; adult/child 20/10kr; ⊙2-4pm Tue, Sat & Sun Jun-Aug). It's an atmospheric experience, with vintage radios and wartime memorabilia. Fittingly, finding it is still a challenge. It's behind the Enhjørningen restaurant; pass through the alley and up the stairs to the 3rd floor.

Bryggens Museum

This archaeological **museum** (🕿55 30 80 30; www.bymuseet.no; Dreggsallmenning 3; adult/child 80kr/free; ⊙10am-4pm mid-May–Aug, shorter hours rest of year) was built on the site of Bergen's first settlement, and the 800-year-old foundations unearthed during its construction have been incorporated into the exhibits, which include medieval tools, pottery, skulls and runes. It gives a good insight into the history of the Bryggen area; the permanent exhibition documenting Bergen c 1300 is particularly fascinating.

Bergen Steinsenter

Statisfy your inner troll at this eccentric gem and crystal merchant, which stocks some stunning geological specimens from around Norway and further afield. It's one of several quirky shops that make wandering Bryggen such an appealing experience.

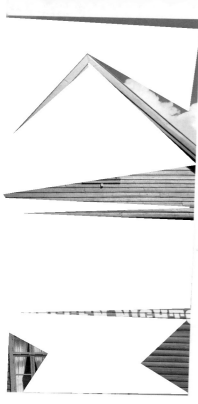

...er the first big fire in 1702, although the ...ilding pattern is from the 12th century. The ...chaeological excavations suggest that the ...ay was once 140m further inland than its ...esent location.

In the early 14th century, there were ...out 30 wooden buildings, each usually ...ared by several *stuer* (trading firms). They ...se two or three stories above the wharf ...d combined business premises with living ...arters and warehouses. Each building ...d a crane for loading and unloading ships, ... well as a *schøtstue* (large assembly ...om) where employees met and ate.

...heta Museum

...amed after the Norwegian Resistance ...oup that occupied it between 1940 and ...45, this excellent reconstruction of a clan-...stine Resistance headquarters, uncovered ...the Nazis in 1942, is now Bryggen's tiniest

SAIKO3P/SHUTTERSTOCK ©

KODE

A catch-all umbrella for Bergen's art museums, KODE showcases one of the largest art-and-design collections in Scandinavia. Each of the four buildings has its own focus.

Great For...

☑ **Don't Miss**

Munch's *Frieze of Life* paintings in KODE 3.

KODE 1

This impressive renovated museum makes a good place to start your explorations of KODE's collection. Exhibitions here include one showcasing Norwegian gold and silverwork, and another exploring the eclectic arts and antiques hoard amassed by 19th-century collectors William and Anna Brugh Singer. There's also a collection amassed by Queen Sonja of Norway, herself a keen amateur artist.

The revamp also added a series of new glass-fronted shelves, made to look like a museum's store cupboard, that are loaded with fascinating treasures, with a new exhibition showcasing a fabulous array of Chinese art and craft spanning many centuries. The building itself has an interesting history: originally known as 'Permanenten', the museum was built in 1896 for the Bergen National Fair.

Paintings in KODE 3

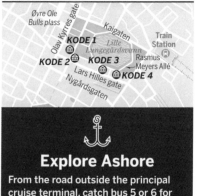

Øvre Ole Bulls plass
Olav Kyrres gate
Kaigaten
Train Station
KODE 1
Lille Lungegårdsvann
Rasmus
KODE 2
KODE 3
Meyers Allé
Lars Hilles gate
KODE 4
Nygårdsgaten

Explore Ashore

From the road outside the principal cruise terminal, catch bus 5 or 6 for the 10-minute ride to Olav Kyrres gate, from where it's a short stroll across the park to the KODE sites.

❶ Need to Know

☑ 53 00 97 04; www.kodebergen.no; Rasmus Meyers allé; adult/child 100kr/free, includes all 4 museums, valid 2 days

KODE 2

KODE 2 hosts several temporary exhibitions every year, as well as a contemporary art collection with a focus on Norwegian and Scandinavian artists from the 1980s onwards. Cafe Smakverket and a great gallery shop are at street level.

KODE 3

KODE 3 is all about Edvard Munch: overall, the collection here is arguably even better than Oslo's Munch Museum. The rooms are fabulously intimate: highlights include several pieces from his *Frieze of Life* – a series of paintings depicting various aspects of the psyche. The core of the collection was amassed by Rasmus Meyer, a local businessman and philanthropist, who was among the first significant collectors of Munch's art, securing major works from all of his artistic periods. The 1924 building was designed by Ole Landmark and purpose-built to house Meyer's extraordinary gift.

Elsewhere around the museum, works from 18th- and 19th-century Norwegian painters such as JC Dahl, Harriet Backer, Erik Werenskiold and Gerhard Munthe are interesting as well as atmospheric, as are the complete rooms of strange and wonderful historical interiors from the Bergen area.

KODE 4

A home to a large permanent collection of European modernist works including the odd Klee, Picasso and Miró; there is also a gallery dedicated to Norwegian landscape painter Nikoli Astrup. The arresting 1930s building was the head office of Bergen's electrical power company.

Astrup's paintings are perhaps the highlight here. His neo-romantic, almost naive, paintings, drawings and woodcuts depict the fjords, fields and mountains of his home region of Jølster, as well as traditional life in the early 20th century. Viewing his work makes for an evocative background to your own exploration of Norway's west.

Exploring the Fjords

Exploring Norway's fjord country has all the hallmarks of being Scandinavia's most beautiful journey. You'll leave wondering if this truly is God's own country.

Great For...

☑ **Don't Miss**

The scenic majesty of Geirangerfjord.

Hardangerfjord

Running from the Atlantic to the steep wall of central Norway's Hardangervidda Plateau, Hardangerfjord is classic Norwegian fjord country. There are many beautiful corners, although our picks would take in Eidfjord, Ulvik and Utne, while Folgefonna National Park offers glacier walks and top-level hiking. It's also well-known for its many fruit farms, especially apples – Hardanger is sometimes known as the orchard of Norway. The fjord is an easy day trip from Bergen.

Sognefjorden

Sognefjorden, the world's second-longest (203km) and Norway's deepest (1308m) fjord, cuts a deep slash across the map of western Norway. In places, sheer walls rise

Preikestolen, Lysefjord

PE3N/SHUTTERSTOCK ©

❶ Need to Know

Fjord Tours (p140) makes it easy to see the best fjord scenery in a short space of time.

more than 1000m above the water, while elsewhere a gentler shoreline supports farms, orchards and villages.

The broad, main waterway is impressive but it's worth detouring into its narrower arms, such as the deep and lovely Nærøy-fjord, for idyllic views of abrupt cliff faces and cascading waterfalls.

Aurlandsfjorden

Branching off the main thrust of Sogne-forden, the deep, narrow Aurlandsfjorden runs for about 29km, but is barely 2km across at its widest point – which means it crams an awful lot of scenery into a rela-tively compact space. The view is best seen from the amazing Stegastein viewpoint, which juts out from the hillside along the stunning Aurlandsfjellet road.

Geirangerfjord

Well, this is the big one: the world-famous, Unesco-listed, oft-photographed fjord that every visitor to Norway simply has to tick off their bucket list. And in purely scenic terms, it's impossible to argue against the case for its inclusion: it is, quite simply, one of the world's great natural features, a majestic combination of huge cliffs, tumbling water-falls and deep blue water that's guaranteed to make a lasting imprint on your memory.

Unfortunately with prestige comes pop-ularity. Some 600,000 visitors come here to see the sights every year and your cruise ship will be one of a small armada if you visit in summer. The main port of Geiranger is often very busy but thankfully, out on the fjord itself, peace and tranquillity remains.

Lysefjord

All along the 42km-long Lysefjord (Light Fjord), the granite rock glows with an ethe-real light and even on dull days it's offset by almost-luminous mist. This is the favourite fjord of many visitors, and there's no doubt that it has a captivating beauty. Take a cruise along the fjord, or the four-hour hike to the top of **Preikestolen**, the plunging cliff-face that's graced a million postcards from Norway.

⊙ SIGHTS

Making time just to wander Bergen's historic neighbourhoods is a must. Beyond Bryggen, the most picturesque are the steep streets climbing the hill behind the Fløibanen funicular station, Nordnes (the peninsula that runs northwest of the centre, including along the southern shore of the main harbour) and Sandviken (the area north of Håkonshallen). It's a maze of winding lanes and clapboard houses, perfect for a quiet wander.

Edvard Grieg Museum   Museum

(Troldhaugen; ☑55 92 29 92; http://griegmuseum.no; Troldhaugvegen 65, Paradis-Bergen; adult/child 100kr/free; ⊙9am-6pm May-Sep, 10am-4pm Oct-Apr) Composer Edvard Grieg and his wife Nina Hagerup spent summers at this charming Swiss-style wooden villa from 1885 until Grieg's death in 1907. Surrounded by fragrant, tumbling gardens and occupying a semi-rural setting – on a peninsula by coastal Nordåsvatnet lake, south of Bergen – it's a truly lovely place to visit.

Apart from Grieg's original home, there is a modern exhibition centre, a 200-seat concert hall and perhaps the most compelling feature of them all, the tiny, lakeside Composer's Hut. Here the composer was always guaranteed silence, if not his muse.

From June to mid-September, there is a daily bus tour (adult/child/student/senior 250/100/200/200kr) departing from the tourist office (p143) at 11.30am. It includes transport, entrance and a short piano concert, and it's wise to pre-purchase tickets. Also see the website or visit the tourist office for details of summer recitals; there is a free shuttle bus for evening performances. The best public transport access is via a city-centre tram to Nesttun (two-hour ticket 36kr), alighting at the stop 'Hop'; from there it's a 2km signed walk.

Ole Bull Museum   Museum

(Museet Lysøen; ☑56 30 90 77; www.lysoen.no; adult/child incl guided tour 60/30kr; ⊙11am-4pm mid-May–Aug, Sun only Sep) This beautiful estate was built in 1873 as the summer residence of Norway's first musical superstar, violinist Ole Bull. Languishing on its own

Edvard Grieg Museum

private island, it's a fairy-tale concoction of turrets, onion domes, columns and marble inspired by Moorish architecture. Of particular note is the soaring pine music hall: it's hard not to imagine Bull practising his concertos in here.

Outside, the grounds are criss-crossed with 13km of lovely walks, and there's a small cafe.

The best way to arrive is aboard the passenger ferry (adult/child 60/30kr, eight minutes, hourly 11am to 3pm), which runs from Buena Quay to the island.

Hanseatic Museum   Museum

(Finnegårdsgaten 1a; adult/child 160/60kr; ⊙9am-6pm Jul-Aug, 11am-2pm Tue-Sat, to 4pm Sun Sep-May) This interesting museum provides a window into the world of Hanseatic traders. Housed in a rough-timber building dating from 1704, it starkly reveals the contrast between the austere living and working conditions of the merchant sailors and apprentices, and the comfortable lifestyle of the trade partners.

Highlights include the manager's office, private liquor cabinet and summer bedroom; the apprentices' quarters, where beds were shared by two men; the fish storage room; and the *fiskeskrue* (fish press), which pressed and processed over a million pounds (450,000kg) of fish a month.

An essential complement to the Hanseatic Museum, **Schøtstuene** (Øvregaten 50; adult/child 160/60kr incl Hanseatic Museum; ⊙9am-6pm Jul-Aug, 11am-2pm Tue-Sat, to 4pm Sun Sep-May) is a reconstruction of one of the original assembly halls where the fraternity of Hanseatic merchants once met for their business meetings and beer guzzling.

The admission price also includes entry to the **Fisheries Museum** (Norges Fiskerimuseum; ☎53 00 61 60; http://fiskerimuseum.museumvest.no; Sandviksboder 23; adult/child 90kr/free; ⊙10am-6pm Jun-Aug), and transport in the free shuttle bus, which runs half-hourly from Bryggen.

 The Creation of Norway's Fjords

Norway's signature landscape, the fjords rank among the most astonishing natural landforms anywhere in the world. The Norwegian coast is cut deeply with these inlets distinguished by plunging cliffs, isolated farms high on forested ledges and an abundance of ice-blue water extending deep into the Norwegian interior.

Norway's fjords are a relatively recent phenomenon in geological terms. Although Norwegian geological history stretches back 1.8 billion years, the fjords were not carved out until much later. During the glacial periods over this time, the elevated highland plateaus that ranged across central Norway subsided at least 700m due to an ice sheet up to 2km thick. The movement of this ice, driven by gravity down former river courses, gouged out the fjords and valleys and created the surrounding mountains by sharpening peaks and exposing high cliffs of bare rock. The fjords took on their present form when sea levels rose as the climate warmed following the last ice age (which ended around 10,000 years ago), flooding into the new valleys left behind by melting and retreating glaciers. Sea levels are thought to have risen by as much as 100m, creating fjords whose waters can seem impossibly deep.

Northern Lights over Hardangerfjord
TRAVFI/SHUTTERSTOCK ©

Bergen Kunsthall   Gallery

(☎940 15 050; www.kunsthall.no; Rasmus Meyers allé 5; adult/child 50kr/free, from 5pm

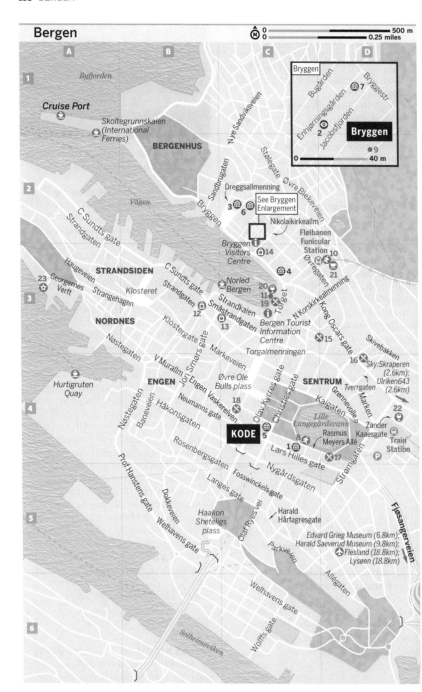

Bergen

Buffjorden

Cruise Port

Skoltegrunnskaien
(International
Ferries)

BERGENHUS

Vågen

STRANDSIDEN

C-Sundts gate
Strandgaten

Haugeveien
Georgernes
Verft
23

Strangehagen

Klosteret

NORDNES

Klostergate

Nøstegaten

Nøstegaten

Hurtigruten
Quay

Baneveien

ENGEN

V Muralln

Jon Smørs gate

Håkonsgaten

Prof Hansten gate

Dokkeveien

Welhavens gate

Haakon
Sheteligs
plass

Olaf Ryes vei

Langes gate

Solheimsviken

Wolffs gate

Sandbrugaten

Bryggen

Nye Sandviksveien

Skottegate Øvre Blekeveien

Dreggsallmenning

3 6

See Bryggen
Enlargement

Nikolaikirkeallm

Bryggen
Visitors
Centre
14

Fløibanen
Funicular
Station
10

Øvregaten
21

C-Sundts gate
Strandgaten

Norled
Bergen
20
11
19

Strandkaien
Småstrandgaten
13

12

Markeveien

Bergen Tourist
Information
Centre

N Korskirkeallmenning

Kong Oskars gate

Torget

4

15

Torgallmenningen

Øvre Ole
Bulls plass

Neumanns gate

18

Rosenberggaten

Fosswinckels gate

Olav Kyrres gate

Christies gate

KODE
5

Lars Hilles gate

Nygårdsgaten

Lille
Lungegårdsvann

SENTRUM

Grønnevolle

Kaigaten

Kalfaret

Tverrgaten

Skivebakken
16
Sky:Skraperen
(2.6km);
Ulriken643
(2.6km)

Marken

Zander
Kaaesgate
Rasmus
Meyers Allé
1

17

22
Train
Station

Strømgaten

Flisangerveien

Harald
Hårfagresgate

Parkveien

Edvard Grieg Museum (6.8km);
Harald Saeverud Museum (9.8km);
Flesland (18.8km);
Lysøen (18.8km)

Allégaten

Welhavens gate

Bryggen

Bryggen

Bugården

Bryggestr

7

Enhjørningsgården
2
Jacobsfjorden

Bryggen

9

0 ____ 40 m

0 ____ 500 m
0 ____ 0.25 miles

Bergen

Thu free; ⊘11am-5pm Tue-Sun, to 8pm Thu) Bergen's major contemporary-art institution hosts significant exhibitions of international and Norwegian artists, often with a single artist's work utilising the entire space. The cleanly glamorous 1930s architecture is worth a look in itself. The attached venue and bar, Landmark (p142), also hosts video and electronic art, concerts, film, performances and lectures.

😊 ACTIVITIES

Fløibanen Funicular   Cable Car
(⌕55 33 68 00; www.floibanen.no; Vetrlidsalmenning 21; adult/child return 90/45kr; ⊘7.30am-11pm Mon-Fri, 8am-11pm Sat & Sun) For an unbeatable view of the city, ride the 26-degree Fløibanen funicular to the top of Mt Fløyen (320m), with departures every 15 minutes. From the top, well-marked hiking tracks lead into the forest; the possibilities are mapped out on the free *Walking Map of Mount Fløyen,* available from the Bergen tourist office (p143).

Ulriken643   Cable Car
(⌕53 64 36 43; www.ulriken643.no; adult/child/family return 170/100/460kr; ⊘9am-9pm May-Sep, 9am-5pm Tue-Sun Oct-Apr) Look up to the mountains from the harbour, and you'll spy a radio mast clad in satellite dishes. That's the top of Mt Ulriken (643m) you're spying, and on a clear day it offers a stunning panorama over city, fjords and mountains. Thankfully you don't have to climb it; a cable car speeds from bottom to top in just seven minutes.

At the top, there's an excellent restaurant, **Sky:Skraperen** (⌕55 32 04 04; Ulrikens topp; mains 155-250kr; ⊘9am-9pm May-Sep, 10am-4pm Oct-Apr), as well as a gift shop and a zipline.

The easiest way to get to the cable-car station is to catch the double-decker shuttle bus which leaves every half-hour from the Torget fish market from 9am to 9pm mid-May to September.

🌀 TOURS

Bergen Guide Service (⌕55 30 10 60; www. bergenguideservice.no; Holmedalsgården 4; adult/child 130kr/free; ⊘office 9am-3pm Mon-Fri) offers guided walking tours of the city year-round, and in summer, **Bryggen Guiding** (⌕55 30 80 30; www.bymuseet.no; Bryggens Museum, Dreggsallm 3; adult/child 150kr/free), run by the Bryggens Museum, has historical walking tours of the Bryggen area.

Fonnafly   Scenic Flights
(⌕55 34 60 00; www.fonnafly.no; for 3 passengers from 5500kr) This national group will

Fjord Tours from Bergen

There are dozens of tours of the fjords from Bergen; the tourist office (p143) has a full list and you can buy tickets there or purchase them online. Most offer discounts if you have a Bergen Card (p143). For a good overview, browse the tourist office website.

Fjord Tours (☑81 56 82 22; www. fjordtours.com) and **Rodne Fjord Cruises** (☑55 25 90 00; www.rodne.no; Torget; adult/ child/family 550/350/1250kr; ☺10am & 2.30pm daily Mar-Oct, 10am Wed-Fri, noon Sat & Sun Nov-Feb) are the key operators.

Whale-watching tour
ANDREI ANDRITCU/SHUTTERSTOCK ©

put together a custom sightseeing trip in a helicopter – the aerial views over the fjords are once-in-a-lifetime stuff, but they don't come cheap.

Bergen Food Tours Food

(☑960 44 892; www.bergenfoodtours.com; adult/child 800/700kr) These three-hour food tours are a great way to ease yourself into Nordic cuisine. The classic walk includes stops at around eight different spots around the city, where you get to sample the goods: seafood, reindeer, pastries, craft beer and *trekroneren* (hot dogs), as well as fish soup made by none other than Bergen's top chef, Christopher Håtuft of Lysverket.

🅐 SHOPPING

Aksdal i Muren Clothing

(☑55 24 24 55; www.aksdalimuren.no; Østre Muralmenning 23; ☺10am-5pm Mon-Fri, 10am-

6pm Sat) This enticing shop in a historic landmark building has been ensuring the good people of Bergen are warm and dry since 1883. The city's best selection of rainwear includes cult Swedish labels such as Didriksons, big names like Helly Hansen and Barbour, but also local gems such as Blæst by Lillebøe. We can't think of a better Bergen souvenir than a stripey sou'wester.

Colonialen Strandgaten 18 Deli

(☑55 90 16 00; www.colonialen.no; Strandgaten 18; ☺8am-6pm Mon-Fri, 10am-6pm Sat) This impeccably cool cafe-deli serves up lavish lunchtime sandwiches, plus an irresistible selection of cold cuts, cheeses, oils, smoked fish and so much more. It's also the best place in town to try baked goodies and breads from Colonialen's own bakery – including its to-die-for cinnamon buns.

Røst Gifts & Souvenirs

(☑488 94 499; www.butikkenrost.no; Bryggen 15; ☺10am-8pm Mon-Fri, 10am-7pm Sat & Sun) Short on souvenir-buying time and want something a bit more upmarket than a troll doll? This bright boutique right in the centre of Bryggen has a large range of well-designed Norwegian and Scandinavian objects and homewares, as well as local fashion for women, children and babies.

✖ EATING

Torget Fish Market Seafood $

(Torget; lunches 99-169kr; ☺7am-7pm Jun-Aug, 7am-4pm Mon-Sat Sep-May) For most of its history, Bergen has survived on the fruits of the sea, so there's no better place for lunch than the town's lively fish market, where you'll find everything from salmon to calamari, fish and chips, prawn baguettes and seafood salads. If you can afford it, the sides of smoked salmon are some of the best in Norway.

Pingvinen Norwegian $$

(☑55 60 46 46; www.pingvinen.no; Vaskerelven 14; daily specials 119kr; mains 159-269kr; ☺noon-3am) Devoted to Norwegian home cooking, Pingvinen is the old favourite of *everyone* in

Bergen. They come for meals their mothers and grandparents used to cook, and the menu always features at least one of the following: fish-cake sandwiches, reindeer, fish pie, salmon, lamb shank and *raspeballer* (sometimes called *komle*) – west-coast potato dumplings. Note that whale is served here.

Colonialen Litteraturhuset Norwegian $$

(☎55 90 16 00; www.colonialen.no/litteraturhuset; Østre skostredet 5-7; lunch 145-245kr, dinner 180-280kr; ☺9-11pm Tue-Fri, 11am-midnight Sat) The more laid-back, bistro sister to Colonialen Restaurant, this is a favourite for Bergeners looking for a relaxed but refined lunch. It's a quietly elegant space, with neutral walls and blonde-wood tables creating that essential too-cool-for-school Nordic atmosphere, and dishes are full of flavour: leeky fish soup or meat-and-cheese platters for lunch; mountain trout or duck-leg confit for dinner.

Lysverket Norwegian $$$

(☎55 60 31 00; www.lysverket.no; KODE 4, Rasmus Meyers allé 9; lunch mains 165-195kr, lunch sharing menu with/without dessert 295/395kr, 4-/7-course menu 745/995kr; ☺11am-1am Tue-Sat) If you're going to blow the budget on one meal in Norway, make it here. Chef Christopher Håtuft is pioneering his own brand of Nordic cuisine, which he dubs 'neo-fjordic' – in other words, combining modern techniques with the best fjord-sourced produce. His food is highly seasonal, incredibly creative and full of surprising textures, combinations and flavours. Savour every mouthful.

Colonialen Restaurant Norwegian $$$

(☎55 90 16 00; www.colonialen.no/restaurant/; Kong Oscars gate 44; 6-/8-course tasting menu 895/1195kr; ☺6-11pm Mon-Sat) Part of an ever-expanding culinary empire, this flagship fine-diner showcases the cream of New Nordic cuisine. It's playful and pushes boundaries, sure, but the underlying flavours are classic, and employ the very best Norwegian ingredients, especially from the west coast. Presentation is impeccable – expect edible flowers and unexpected

Ole Bull Museum (p136)

Bergen market

ingredients aplenty. Strange it's on the dingy side of town.

🍷 DRINKING & NIGHTLIFE

Bergen has a great bar scene and locals are enthusiastic drinking companions. Most of them favour the places in the centre or southwest of Øvre Ole Bulls plass. Big, multilevel nightclubs cluster around here, too; they are easy to spot, often fabulously trashy, and only admit those aged over 24.

Landmark   Bar, Cafe
(📞940 15 050; Bergen Kunsthalle, Rasmus Meyers allé 5; ⏲cafe 11am-5pm Tue-Sun, bar 7pm-1am Tue-Thu, to 3.30am Fri & Sat) This large, airy room is a beautiful example of 1930s Norwegian design and is named for architect Ole Landmark. It multitasks: daytime cafe, lecture and screening hall; live-performance space, bar and venue for Bergen's best club nights. It's a favourite with the city's large creative scene. The cafe serves yummy lunches, with a choice of open-faced sandwiches and a weekly melt (995kr to 1295kr).

Terminus Bar   Bar
(Zander Kaaesgate 6, Grand Terminus Hotel; ⏲5pm-midnight) Consistently voted one of the word's best whisky bars, this grand old bar in the Grand Hotel Terminus is the perfect place for a quiet dram. It promises over 500 different drams. The 1928 room looks gorgeous both before and after you've sampled a few.

Bryggeriet   Microbrewery
(📞55 55 31 55; www.bryggeriet.biz; Torget 2; ⏲4-10pm Tue-Thu, 6-10.30pm Fri & Sat) Bergen's brewheads and beer-nuts hold this downtown microbrewery in high esteem for its creative, interesting beers, mostly brewed in the Germanic tradition, and developed in partnership with the head chef to match the Teutonic-flavoured food. Up on the 3rd floor near the fish market, it's a rustic, cosy space with fine water views – and the beers are barnstorming.

Det Lille Kaffekompaniet   Cafe
(Nedre Fjellsmug 2; ⏲10am-8pm Mon-Fri, 10am-6pm Sat & Sun) This was one of Bergen's first third-wave coffee places and retains a

super local feel. Everyone overflows onto the neighbouring stairs when the sun's out and you're not sure which table belongs to whom.

 ENTERTAINMENT

Bergen has a busy program of concerts throughout summer, many of them focusing on Bergen's favourite son, composer Edvard Grieg. Most take place at evocative open-air venues such as the Grieg Museum (p136), the **Harald Sæverud Museum** (Siljustøl; ☎55 92 29 92; www.siljustolmuseum. no; Siljustølveien 50, Råda; adult/child 60kr/free; ⊙noon-4pm Sun late Jun–mid-Aug), atop Mt Fløyen and in the park adjacent to Håkonshallen. Bergen Cathedral also offers free organ recitals on Sunday and Thursday from mid-June until the end of August.

USF Vertfet   Live Music
(USF; ☎55 31 00 60; www.usf.no; Georgernes Verft 12; ⊙11am-11pm) This huge arts and culture complex in a renovated warehouse space hosts a varied program of contemporary art exhibitions, theatre, dance, gigs and other cultural happenings, and also has an excellent on-site cafe, **Kippers** (⊙11am-11pm Mon-Thu, noon-midnight Fri & Sat, noon-11pm Sun).

INFORMATION

DISCOUNT CARDS

The **Bergen Card** (www.visitbergen.com/bergencard; adult/child 24hr pass 240/90kr, 48hr 310/1120kr, 72hr 380/150kr) gives you free entrance to most of Bergen's main museums, plus discounted entry to the rest. You also get free travel on public transport, free or discounted

return trips on the Fløibanen funicular (p139), depending on the time of year; free guided tours of Bergen; and discounts on city- and boat-sightseeing tours, concerts and cultural performances. It's available from the tourist office, some hotels, the bus terminal and online.

TOURIST INFORMATION

Bergen Tourist Information Centre (☎55 55 20 00; www.visitbergen.com; Strandkaien 3; ⊙8.30am-10pm Jun-Aug, 9am-8pm May & Sep, 9am-4pm Mon-Sat Oct-Apr) One of the best and busiest in the country, Bergen's tourist office distributes the free and worthwhile *Bergen Guide* booklet, as well as a huge stock of information on the entire region.

Bryggen Visitors Centre (Jacobsfjorden, Bryggen; ⊙9am-5pm mid-May–mid-Sep) Maps and activities in the Bryggen neighbourhood.

GETTING AROUND

BICYCLE

Bergen Bike (☎400 04 059; www.norwayactive. no; Bontelabo 2; adult per 2hr/day 200/500kr) Rental bikes near the quay.

Sykkelbutikken (www.sykkelbutikken.no; Kong Oscars gate 81; touring bikes per day/week 250/850kr; ⊙10am-8pm Mon-Fri, 10am-4pm Sat) Bicycle hire near the train station.

BUS & TRAM

Skyss (☎177; www.skyss.no) operates buses and light-rail trams throughout Bergen. Fares are based on a zone system; one-trip tickets cost 37kr to 62kr, and can be bought from the machines at tram stops. Ten-trip tickets are also available, and you get free travel with the Bergen Card.

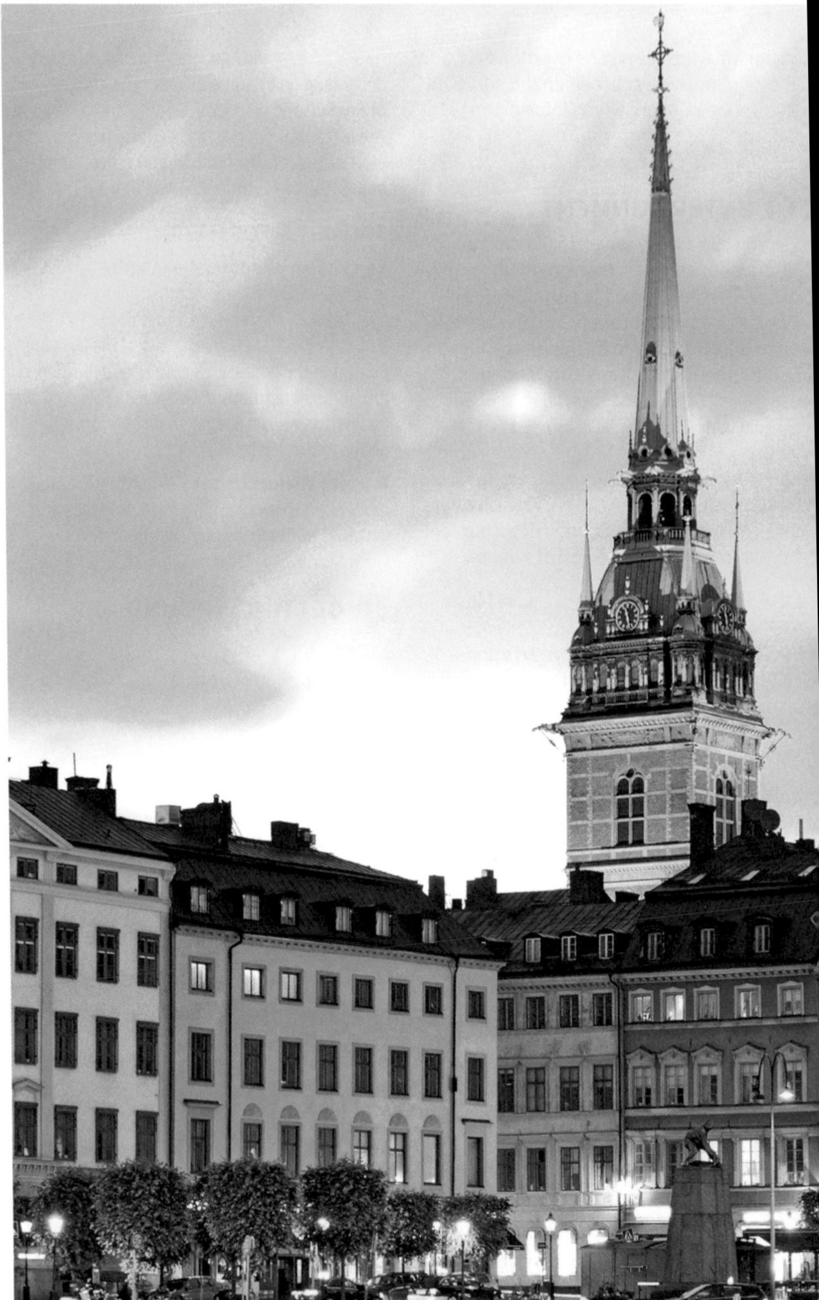

STOCKHOLM, SWEDEN

Stockholm at a Glance...

Stockholmers call their city 'beauty on water'. But despite the well-preserved historic core, Stockholm is no museum piece: it's modern, dynamic and ever-changing. Gamla Stan is a saffron-and-spice vision from the storybooks, one of Europe's most arresting historic hubs, with an imposing palace, looming cathedrals and razor-thin cobblestone streets. Stockholm's beauty and fashion sense are also legendary, with good design a given. Travellers also quickly discover this is a city of food obsessives. If a food trend appears anywhere in the world, Stockholm is on to it. The result is one of Europe's most memorable cities.

With One Day in Port

Start the day with a walk through the old town, **Gamla Stan** (p150) and take in a tour of the royal palace, **Kungliga Slottet** (p152). In the afternoon, head to Djurgården and its standout **Vasam-useet** (p148), home to an hubristic 17th-century warship.

Best Places for...

Picturesque dining Under Kastanjen (p159)

Vegetarians Rutabaga (p160)

Cafe Rosendals Trädgårdskafe (p158)

Beer Akkurat (p160)

Wine Monks Wine Room (p161)

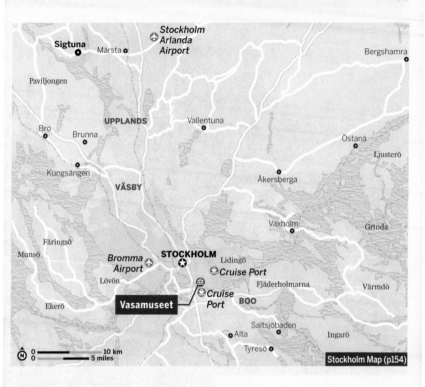

Stockholm Map (p154)

Getting from the Port

Stockholm has several cruise docks. Commonly used is central Stadsgården, from where it's a 200m walk to buses that run you to Gamla Stan (a 15- to 20-minute walk) in under 10 minutes. Hop-on, hop-off boats also run.

From Frihamnen or nearby Värtahamnen, bus 76 heads to near Djurgården (10 minutes) and Gamla Stan (15 minutes).

Shuttles are also usually available. More remote terminals have train connections with Stockholm.

Fast Facts

Currency Swedish kronor (kr)

Language Swedish. English very widely spoken.

Free wi-fi Centralstationen and most cafes.

Tourist information Stockholm Visitor Center (p161) occupies a space inside Kulturhuset on Sergels Torg.

Transport Storstockholms Lokaltrafik (p161) runs the tunnelbana (metro), local trains and buses.

Vasamuseet

Learn about the short maiden voyage of the massive 17th-century warship Vasa, which sank within minutes of setting sail. It's one of the most popular museums on Djurgården.

Great For...

☑ Don't Miss

Guided tours, a scale model of the ship, the short film screening, and exploring the upper deck

The Ship

A good-humoured glorification of some dodgy calculations, Vasamuseet is the custom-built home of the massive warship *Vasa*. The ship, a whopping 69m long and 48.8m tall, was the pride of the Swedish crown when it set off on its maiden voyage on 10 August 1628. Within minutes, the top-heavy vessel tipped and sank to the bottom of Saltsjön, along with many of the people on board. The museum details its painstaking retrieval and restoration, as well as putting the whole thing into historical context.

Tours

Tour guides explain the extraordinary and controversial 300-year story of the ship's death and resurrection – check schedules online to find one of the tours in English.

Replica of the *Vasa*

Explore Ashore

The easiest way to get here from Stadsgården terminal is to jump on a hop-on, hop-off boat service, which stops right here (day ticket 200kr). From Frihamnen, jump on bus 76 (43kr), get off at the Djurgårdsbron stop, then stroll across the bridge.

ℹ️ Need to Know

www.vasamuseet.se; Galärvarvsvägen 14; adult/child 130kr/free; ⊘8.30am-6pm Jun-Aug, 10am-5pm Thu-Tue, to 8pm Wed Sep-May; P; 🚌44, ⛴Djurgårdsfärjan, 🚊7

Exhibits

Five levels of exhibits cover artefacts salvaged from *Vasa*, life on board, naval warfare and 17th-century sailing and navigation, plus sculptures and temporary exhibitions. The bottom-floor exhibition is particularly fascinating, using modern forensic science to recreate the faces and life stories of several of the ill-fated passengers. The ship was painstakingly raised in 1961 and reassembled like a giant 14,000-piece jigsaw. Almost all of what you see today is original.

Meanwhile

Putting the catastrophic fate of *Vasa* in historical context is a permanent multimedia exhibit, *Meanwhile*. With images of events and moments happening simultaneously around the globe – from China to France to 'New Amsterdam', from traders and settlers to royal families to working mothers and put-upon merchants – it establishes a vivid setting for the story at hand.

Scale Model

On the entrance level is a model of the ship at scale 1:10, painted according to a thoroughly researched understanding of how the original would have looked. Once you've studied it, look for the intricately carved decorations adorning the actual *Vasa*. The stern in particular is gorgeous – it was badly damaged but has been slowly and carefully restored.

Upper Deck

A reconstruction of the upper gun deck allows visitors to get a feel for what it might have been like to be on a vessel this size. *Vasa* had two gun decks, which held an atypically large number of cannons – thought to be part of the reason it capsized.

Old Town

This exploration of Stockholm's city centre takes you past the best the city has to offer, with a focus on the beguiling old city.

Start Centralstationen
Distance 3km
Duration two hours

1 From Centralstationen, head to **Sergels Torg**, with frenzied commuters, casual shoppers and the odd demonstration.

2 Pop into arts hub **Kulturhuset** (www.kulturhusetstadsteatern.se; 11am-5pm, some sections closed Mon), with its exhibitions, theatres, cafes and creative spaces.

4 Head for the city's medieval core, into Storkyrkobrinken and the city's oldest building, **Storkyrkan**.

7 Explore the old town to **Mårten Trotzigs Gränd**, Stockholm's narrowest lane, on your way back to Centralstationen.

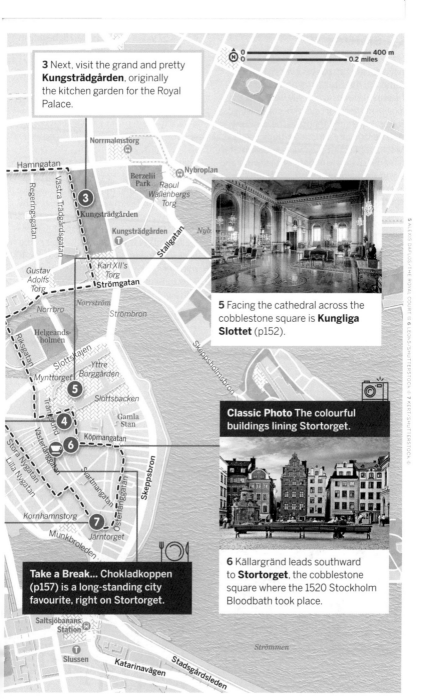

3 Next, visit the grand and pretty **Kungsträdgården**, originally the kitchen garden for the Royal Palace.

5 Facing the cathedral across the cobblestone square is **Kungliga Slottet** (p152).

Classic Photo The colourful buildings lining Stortorget.

6 Källargränd leads southward to **Stortorget**, the cobblestone square where the 1520 Stockholm Bloodbath took place.

Take a Break... Chokladkoppen (p157) is a long-standing city favourite, right on Stortorget.

Map labels:
- Norrmalmstorg
- Hamngatan
- Regeringsgatan
- Västra Trädgårdsgatan
- Berzelii Park
- Nybroplan
- Raoul Wallenbergs Torg
- Kungsträdgården
- Kungsträdgården
- Stallgatan
- Nyb.
- Gustav Adolfs Torg
- Karl XII's Torg
- Strömgatan
- Norrbro
- Norrström
- Strömbron
- Skeppsholmsbron
- Riksgatan
- Helgeands-holmen
- Slottskajen
- Yttre Borggården
- Mynttorget
- Trångsund
- Slottsbacken
- Gamla Stan
- Köpmangatan
- Västerlånggatan
- Stora Nygatan
- Lilla Nygatan
- Skeppsbron
- Svartmangatan
- Österlånggatan
- Kornhamnstorg
- Munkbroleden
- Järntorget
- Saltsjöbanans Station
- Slussen
- Katarinavägen
- Stadsgårdsleden
- Strömmen

0 / 0   400 m / 0.2 miles

⊙ SIGHTS

Stockholm can seem a baffling city to navigate at first, strewn over 14 islands. Although the city centre and other neighbourhoods are easily walkable, the excellent transport system, comprising trams, buses and metro, is the best way to cover the city's more far-flung sights. Most people start their visit at Gamla Stan, a medieval tangle of narrow alleyways and colourful buildings which, although touristy, is extremely picturesque and home to several truly splendid sights.

Kungliga Slottet   Palace

(Royal Palace; ☏08-402 61 30; www.theroyalpalace.se; Slottsbacken; adult/child 160/80kr, combo ticket incl Riddarholmen adult/child 180/90kr; ⊙9am-5pm daily Jul & Aug, 10am-5pm daily May-Jun & Sep, 10am-4pm Tue-Sun Oct-Apr; 🚌43, 46, 55, 59 Slottsbacken, 🚇Gamla Stan) Kungliga Slottet was built on the ruins of Tre Kronor castle, which burned down in 1697. The north wing survived and was incorporated into the new building. Designed by court architect Nicodemus Tessin the Younger,

it took 57 years to complete. Highlights include the decadent Karl XI Gallery, inspired by Versailles' Hall of Mirrors, and Queen Kristina's silver throne in the Hall of State.

Stadshuset   Notable Building

(City Hall; www.stockholm.se/stadshuset; Hantverkargatan 1; adult/child 100/50kr, tower 50kr/free; ⊙9am-3.30pm, admission by tour only; 🚌3, 62 Stadshuset, 🚇Rådhuset) The mighty Stadshuset dominates Stockholm's architecture. Topping off its square tower is a golden spire and the symbol of Swedish power: the three royal crowns. Entry is by guided tour only; tours in English take place every 30 minutes from 9am until 3.30pm in summer, less frequently the rest of the year. The **tower** is open for visits every 40 minutes from 9.15am to 4pm or 5pm from May to September; it offers stellar views and a great thigh workout.

Moderna Museet   Museum

(☏08-52 02 35 00; www.modernamuseet.se; Exercisplan 4; ⊙10am-8pm Tue & Fri, to 6pm Wed-Thu, 11am-6pm Sat & Sun; 🅿; 🚌65, ⛴Djurgårdsfärjan) FREE Moderna Museet

Kungliga Slottet

is Stockholm's modern-art maverick, its permanent collection ranging from paintings and sculptures to photography, video art and installations. Highlights include works by Pablo Picasso, Salvador Dalí, Andy Warhol, Damien Hirst and Robert Rauschenberg, plus several key figures in the Scandinavian and Russian art worlds and beyond. There are important pieces by Francis Bacon, Marcel Duchamp and Henri Matisse, as well as their contemporaries, both household names and otherwise.

Skansen   Museum

(www.skansen.se; Djurgårdsvägen; adult/child 180/60kr; ⊙10am-6pm, extended hours in summer; P; ⬚69, ⬚Djurgårdsfärjan, ⬚7) The world's first open-air museum, Skansen was founded in 1891 by Artur Hazelius to provide an insight into how Swedes once lived. You could easily spend a day here and not see it all. Around 150 traditional houses and other exhibits dot the hilltop – it's meant to be 'Sweden in miniature', complete with villages, nature, commerce and industry. Note that prices and opening hours vary seasonally; check the website before you go.

ABBA: The Museum   Museum

(⬚08-12 13 28 60; www.abbathemuseum. com; Djurgårdsvägen 68; adult/child 250/95kr; ⊙9am-7pm Mon-Fri Jun-Aug, shorter hours rest of year; ⬚67, ⬚Djurgårdsfärjan, Emelie, ⬚7) A sensory-overload experience that might appeal only to devoted ABBA fans, this long-awaited and wildly hyped cathedral to the demigods of Swedish pop is almost aggressively entertaining. It's packed to the gills with memorabilia and interactivity – every square inch has something new to look at, be it a glittering guitar, a vintage photo of Benny, Björn, Frida or Agnetha, a classic music video, an outlandish costume or a tour van from the band members' early days.

Fotografiska   Gallery

(www.fotografiska.eu; Stadsgårdshamnen 22; adult/child 135kr/free; ⊙9am-11pm Sun-Wed, to 1am Thu-Sat; ⬚Slussen) A stylish photography museum, Fotografiska is a must for shutterbugs. Its constantly changing exhibitions

Shopping Swedish Design

Now that Ingvar Kamprad's unmistakably huge blue-and-yellow Ikea stores have sprouted up all over the world, Swedish design may have lost some of its exotic appeal. But that just means more people can know the sleek, utilitarian joy of invisible drawers, paper chandeliers and round squares.

Most of the clever designs Ikea brings to the masses originated among Stockholm's relentlessly inventive designers, and you can see these artefacts in their undiluted form all over the city in museums, shops, and a few shops that are so exclusive they may as well be museums.

Functional elegance defines Swedish design, although in recent decades a refreshing tendency towards the whimsical has lightened the mood. For a good collection of design objects arranged chronologically and by theme, head to **Nordiska Museet** (⬚08-51 95 47 70; www.nordiskamuseet.se; Djurgårdsvägen 6-16; adult/child 120kr/free; ⊙10am-5pm Sep-May, 9am-5pm rest of year, to 8pm Wed; ⬚44, 69, ⬚Djurgårdsfärjan, ⬚7). You can also find examples of both historic and contemporary design at upmarket shops like **Svenskt Tenn** (p157), home to floral fabric prints by design legend Josef Frank, and **Nordiska Galleriet** (⬚08-442 83 60; www.nordiskagalleriet.se; Nybrogatan 11; ⊙10am-6pm Mon-Fri, to 5pm Sat; ⬚Östermalmstorg), with its dizzying array of neat things to look at.

For something a little more accessible, Södermalm's main drag, Götgatan, is home to democratically priced **DesignTorget** (www.designtorget.se; Götgatan 31; ⊙10am-7pm Mon-Fri, 10am-6pm Sat, 11am-5.30pm Sun; ⬚Slussen), with several other locations around town.

are huge, interestingly chosen and well presented; examples have included a Robert Mapplethorpe retrospective, portraits by

Stockholm

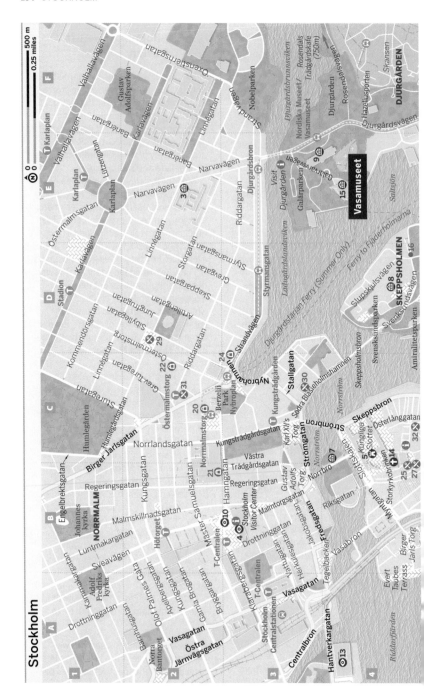

500 m
0.25 miles

Stockholm

indie filmmaker Gus Van Sant and an enormous collection of black-and-white photos by Sebastião Salgado. The attached cafe-bar draws a crowd on summer evenings, with DJs, good cocktails and outdoor seating. It's especially handy if you dock at Stadsgården.

Historiska Museet   Museum
(☏08-51 95 56 20; www.historiska.se; Narvavägen 13-17; ☺10am-5pm Jun-Aug, 11am-5pm Tue-Sun, to 8pm Wed Sep-May; ☒44, 56, ☒Djurgårdsbron, ☒Karlaplan, Östermalmstorg) **FREE** The national historical collection awaits at this enthralling museum. From Iron Age skates and a Viking boat to medieval textiles and Renaissance triptychs, it spans over 10,000 years of Swedish culture and history. There's an exhibit about the medieval Battle of Gotland (1361), an excellent multimedia display on the Vikings, a room of breathtaking altarpieces from the Middle Ages, a vast textile collection and a section on prehistoric culture.

⊕ TOURS

Fjäderholmarna   Boating
(Feather Islands; ☏08-21 55 00; www.fjaderholmslinjen.se; Nybroplan, Berth 13; adult/child round-trip 145/70kr; ☺hourly 10.30am-10.30pm May–early Sep) A trip to the Feather Islands takes about 25 minutes from Stockholm, and is a fantastic way to get a taste of the archipelago in a very short time. You can swim and sunbathe, visit traditional workshops including smiths and glassblowers, admire old boats, visit a brewery and stuff yourself on smoked fish. Recommended!

Millennium Tour   Walking
(www.stadsmuseum.stockholm.se; per person 130kr; ☺11.30am Sat year-round, 6pm Thu Jul-Sep) Fans of Stieg Larsson's madly popular crime novels (eg *The Girl with the Dragon Tattoo*) will enjoy this walking tour (in English) pointing out key locations from the books and films. While the Stadsmuseum is closed for renovations, buy tickets online or at the **Medieval Museum** (www.medeltidsmuseet.stockholm.se; Strömparterren; ☺noon-5pm Tue-Sun, to 8pm Wed; ☒62, 65, Gustav Adolfs torg) **FREE**. Tour meeting points are on the tickets.

Strömma Kanalbolaget   Boating
(☏08-12 00 40 00; www.stromma.se; Svensksundsvägen 17; 200-400kr) This ubiquitous company offers tours large and small, from a 50-minute 'royal canal tour' around

Djurgården (200kr) to a 50-minute ABBA tour (315kr), which visits places where the *ABBA* movie was shot and drops you off at the ABBA museum (p153). There are also hop-on, hop-off tours by bus (from 300kr), boat (180kr) or both (400kr).

Recommended: 'Under the Bridges of Stockholm' (250kr), a two-hour canal tour running daily 10am to 7pm mid-April to October. Book ahead if possible, as this tour sometimes sells out.

🅐 SHOPPING

Svenskt Tenn   Arts, Homewares

(☑08-670 16 00; www.svenskttenn.se; Nybrogatan 15; ⊙10am-6pm Mon-Fri, 10am-4pm Sat; 🚇Kungsträdgården) As much a museum of design as an actual shop, this iconic store is home to the signature fabrics and furniture of Josef Frank and his contemporaries. Browsing here is a great way to get a quick handle on what people mean by 'classic Swedish design' – and it's owned by a foundation that contributes heavily to arts funding.

NK   Department Store

(☑08-762 80 00; www.nk.se; Hamngatan 12-18; ⊙10am-8pm Mon-Fri, 10am-6pm Sat, 11am-5pm Sun; 🚇T-Centralen) An ultraclassy department store founded in 1902, NK (Nordiska Kompaniet) is a city landmark – you can see its rotating neon sign from most parts of Stockholm. You'll find top-name brands and several nice cafes, and the basement levels are great for stocking up on souvenirs and gourmet groceries. Around Christmas, check out its inventive window displays.

E Torndahl   Design

(www.etorndahl.se; Västerlånggatan 63; ⊙10am-8pm; 🚇Gamla Stan) This spacious design shop, run by the women of the Torndahl family since 1864, is a calm and civilised oasis on busy Västerlånggatan, offering jewellery, textiles and clever Scandinavian household objects.

Studio Lena M   Gifts & Souvenirs

(www.studiolenam.wordpress.com; Kindstugan 14; ⊙10am-6pm, to 5pm Sat; 🚇Gamla Stan) This tiny, dimly lit shop is chockfull of adorable prints and products featuring the distinctive graphic design work of Lena M. It's a great place to find a unique – and uniquely Swedish – gift to bring home, or even just a cute postcard.

Marimekko   Clothing, Homewares

(☑08-440 32 75; www.marimekko.com; Norrmalmstorg 4; ⊙10am-7pm Mon-Fri, to 5pm Sat; 🚇Östermalmstorg) Marimekko's bright, bold, retro patterns are the stuff of legend. The Finnish textile company has plastered almost everything with its iconic prints, from towels, cups and coasters to notebooks, bags, napkins and clothes.

Chokladfabriken   Chocolate

(www.chokladfabriken.com; Renstiernas Gata 12; ⊙10am-6.30pm Mon-Fri, 10am-5pm Sat; 🚇Medborgarplatsen, Slussen) For an edible souvenir, head to this chocolate shop, where seasonal Nordic ingredients are used to make heavenly treats. In addition to chocolate boxes and hot-cocoa mix in gift boxes, there's a cafe for an on-the-spot fix, occasional tastings, and a stash of speciality ingredients and utensils for home baking.

🅧 EATING

Chokladkoppen   Cafe $

(www.chokladkoppen.se; Stortorget 18; cakes & coffees from 35kr, mains 85-125kr; ⊙9am-11pm Jun-Aug, shorter hours rest of year; 🛜; 🚇Gamla Stan) Arguably Stockholm's best-loved cafe, hole-in-the-wall Chokladkoppen sits slap bang on the old town's enchanting main square. It's an atmospheric spot with a sprawling terrace and pocket-sized interior with low-beamed ceilings, custard-coloured walls and edgy artwork. The menu includes savoury treats like broccoli-and-blue-cheese pie and scrumptious cakes.

Östermalms Saluhall   Market $

(www.saluhallen.com; Östermalmstorg; ⊙9.30am-7pm Mon-Fri, to 5pm Sat; 🚇Östermalmstorg) Östermalms Saluhall is a gourmet food hall that inhabits a delightful many-spired brick building. It's

Understand

Classic Swedish Cuisine

Traditional Swedish cuisine is based on simple, everyday dishes known generally as *husmanskost* (basic home cooking). The most famous example of this, naturally, is Swedish meatballs. Other classic *husmanskost* dishes, largely built around seafood and potatoes, include various forms of pickled and fried herring, cured salmon, shrimp, roe and *pytt i panna* (potato hash served with sliced beets and a fried egg on top), which may be the ultimate comfort food. Open-face shrimp sandwiches are everywhere, piled high with varying degrees of art.

One speciality food that not many visitors (and not all that many Swedes, either) take to immediately is *surströmming*. It's a canned, fermented Baltic herring opened and consumed ritually once a year, during late August and early September. It may be wrapped in *tunnbröd* (soft, thin, unleavened bread like a tortilla) with boiled potato, onions and other condiments, all washed down with ample amounts of *snaps* (a distilled alcoholic beverage, such as vodka or aquavit). Cans of it make excellent souvenirs, as long as you wrap them well to avoid the truly nightmarish possibility of a leak into your suitcase. (And check with your airline first – flying with *surströmming* is not always allowed.)

The prevalence of preserved grub harks back to a time when Swedes had little choice but to store their spring and summer harvests for the long, icy winter.

Other traditional foods worth trying include *toast skagen* (toast with bleak roe, crème fraiche and chopped red onion), the classic *köttbullar och potatis* (meatballs and potatoes, usually served with lingonberry jam, known as *lingonsylt*), and *nässelsoppa* (nettle soup, traditionally served with hard-boiled eggs). Pea soup and pancakes are traditionally served on Thursday. Seafood staples include caviar, gravad or rimmad lax (cured salmon), and the ubiquitous *sill* (herring), eaten smoked, fried or pickled and often accompanied by Scandi trimmings such as capers, mustard and onion. Tucking into a plate of freshly fried Baltic herring with new potatoes and lingonberry sauce from an outdoor table overlooking the sea is a quintessential – and easily achieved – Swedish experience.

Swedes are devoted to their daily coffee ritual, *fika*, which inevitably also includes a pastry – often *kanelbullar* (cinnamon buns) or *kardemummabullar* (cardamom rolls). Gourmet *konditori* (old-fashioned bakery-cafes) and cafes offer their own variations on all the standard cakes and cookies – best to sample several.

a sophisticated take on the traditional market, with fresh produce, fish counters, baked goods, butcher shops and tea vendors and some top places to grab a meal. For best results, arrive hungry and curious.

Sturekatten   Cafe $

(☑08-611 16 12; www.sturekatten.se; Riddargatan 4; pastries from 35kr; ☺9am-7pm Mon-Fri, 9am-6pm Sat, 10am-6pm Sun; ☒Östermalmstorg) Looking like a life-size doll's house, this vintage cafe is a fetching blend of antique chairs, oil paintings, ladies who lunch

and servers in black-and-white garb. Slip into a salon chair, pour some tea and nibble on a piece of apple pie or a *kanelbulle* (cinnamon bun).

Rosendals Trädgårdskafe   Cafe $$

(☑08-54 58 12 70; www.rosendalstradgard.se; Rosendalsterrassen 12; mains 99-145kr; ☺11am-5pm Mon-Fri, to 6pm Sat & Sun May-Sep, closed Mon Feb-Apr & Oct-Dec; ℗♪; ☒44, 69, 76 Djurgårdsbron, ☒7) ✿ Set among the greenhouses of a pretty botanical garden, Rosendals is an idyllic spot for heavenly pastries and coffee or a meal and a glass of organic wine. Lunch includes a brief menu of soups, sandwiches (such as ground-lamb burger with chanterelles) and gorgeous salads. Much of the produce is biodynamic and grown onsite.

Under Kastanjen   Swedish $$

(☏08-21 50 04; www.underkastanjen.se; Kindstugatan 1, Gamla Stan; mains 182-289kr, dagens (daily special) lunch 105kr; ⏰8am-11pm Mon-Fri, 9am-11pm Sat, 9am-9pm Sun; 🛜; 🚆Gamla Stan) This has to be just about the most picturesque corner of Gamla Stan, with tables set on a cobbled square under a beautiful chestnut tree surrounded by ochre and yellow storybook houses. Enjoy classic Swedish dishes like homemade meatballs with mashed potato; the downstairs wine bar has a veritable Spanish bodega feel with its whitewashed brick arches and moody lighting.

Meatballs for the People   Swedish $$

(☏08-466 60 99; www.meatballs.se; Nytorgsgatan 30, Södermalm; mains 179-195kr; ⏰11am-

10pm Mon-Thu, to midnight Fri & Sat, limited hours Jul & Aug; 🛜; 🚆Medborgarplatsen) The name says it all. This restaurant serves serious meatballs, including moose, deer, wild boar and lamb, served with creamed potatoes and pickled vegetables, washed down with a pint of Sleepy Bulldog craft beer. It's a novel twist on a traditional Swedish dining experience, accentuated by the rustic decor and delightful waiting staff.

Woodstockholm   Swedish $$$

(☏08-36 93 99; www.woodstockholm.com; Mosebacketorg 9, Södermalm; mains 265-285kr; ⏰11.30am-2pm Mon, 11.30am-2pm & 5-11pm Tue-Sat; 🛜🖉; 🚆Slussen) ✹ This hip dining spot incorporates a wine bar and furniture store showcasing chairs and tables by local designers. The menu changes weekly and is themed, somewhat wackily: think Salvador Dalí or Aphrodisiac, the latter including scallops with oyster mushrooms and sweetbreads with yellow beets and horseradish cream. This is fast becoming one of the city's classic foodie destinations. Reservations essential.

Stadshuset (p152)

ABBA: The Museum (p153)

Rutabaga   Vegetarian $$$

(☑08-679 35 84; www.mdghs.se; Södra Blasie-
holmshamnen 6, Grand Hôtel Stockholm; dishes
125-295kr; ⊙5pm-midnight Mon-Sat Aug-Jun; ☑;
☒Kungsträdgården) At Rutabaga, celebrity
chef Mathias Dahlgren pushes vegetarian
cuisine into the realm of art: the menu
features vividly colourful salads and other
unusual combinations (an egg-truffle-
white-bean dish, a mango and mozzarella
salad) which, as always, Dahlgren presents
impeccably on the plate. Most dishes are
meant for sharing (if you can bear to give
any up). Closes in July.

Kryp In   Swedish $$$

(☑08-20 88 41; www.restaurangkrypin.nu; Präst-
gatan 17; lunch mains 135-168kr, dinner mains 198-
290kr; ⊙5-11pm Mon-Fri, noon-4pm & 5-11pm Sat
& Sun; ☜; ☒Gamla Stan) Small but perfectly
formed, this spot wows diners with creative
takes on traditional Swedish dishes. Expect
the likes of salmon carpaccio, Kalix roe,
reindeer roast or gorgeous, spirit-warming
saffron aioli shellfish stew. The service is
seamless and the atmosphere classy without being stuffy. The three-course set menu
(455kr) is superb. Book ahead.

🍷 DRINKING & NIGHTLIFE

Akkurat   Bar

(☑08-644 00 15; www.akkurat.se; Hornsgatan
18; ⊙3pm-midnight Mon, to 1am Tue-Sat, 6pm-
1am Sun; ☒Slussen) Valhalla for beer fiends,
Akkurat boasts a huge selection of Belgian
ales as well as a good range of Swedish-
made microbrews and hard ciders. It's
one of only two places in Sweden to be
recognised by a Cask Marque for its real
ale. Extras include a vast wall of whisky and
live music several nights a week.

Kvarnen   Bar

(☑08-643 03 80; www.kvarnen.com; Tjärhovs-
gatan 4; ⊙11am-1am Mon & Tue, to 3am Wed-Fri,
noon-3am Sat, noon-1am Sun; ☒Medborgarplat-
sen) An old-school Hammarby football fan
hang-out, Kvarnen is one of the best bars in
Söder. The gorgeous beer hall dates from
1907 and seeps tradition; if you're not the
clubbing type, get here early for a nice pint

and a meal (mains from 210kr). As the night progresses, the nightclub vibe takes over. Queues are fairly constant but justifiable.

Monks Wine Room   Wine Bar

(☑08-23 12 14; www.monkscafe.se; Lilla Nygatan 2; ☺5pm-midnight Tue-Thu, 4pm-midnight Fri & Sat; ⓡGamla Stan) Set in atmospheric 17th-century surroundings in the heart of the old town, Monks Wine Room has a well-stocked cellar with hundreds of bottles to choose from. Stop by for a quick glass of wine to recharge the batteries or take some time to sample a cheese and wine pairing.

INFORMATION

DISCOUNT CARDS

Destination Stockholm (☑08-663 00 80; www.stockholmpass.com; adult 1-/2-/3-/5-day pass 595/795/995/1295kr, children half-price) offers the Stockholm Pass, a discount package that includes free sightseeing tours and admission to 75 attractions.

TOURIST INFORMATION

Stockholm Visitor Center (☑08-50 82 85 08; www.visitstockholm.com; Kulturhuset, Sergels Torg 3; ☺9am-7pm Mon-Fri, 9am-4pm Sat, 10am-4pm Sun May–mid-Sep, shorter hours rest of year; ☎; ⓡT-Centralen) The main visitors centre occupies a space inside Kulturhuset on Sergels Torg.

Tourist Center (☑08-55 08 82 20; www.guide-stockholm.info; Köpmangatan 22; ☺10am-4pm Mon-Fri year-round, 11am-2pm Sat & Sun Jun-Sep; ⓡGamla Stan) Tiny office in Gamla Stan, with brochures and information.

Visit Djurgården (☑08-667 77 01; www.visitdjurgarden.se; Djurgårdsvägen 2; ☺9am-dusk) With tourist information specific to Djurgården, this office at the edge of the Djurgården bridge is attached to Sjöcaféet, so you can grab a bite or a beverage as you plot your day.

Cycling Around Stockholm

Stockholm is a very bicycle-friendly city. Cycling is best in the parks and away from the busy central streets and arterial roads, but even busy streets usually have dedicated cycle lanes. There's also a separate network of paved walking and cycling paths that reaches most parts of the city; these paths can be quite beautiful, taking you through green fields and peaceful forested areas. Tourist offices carry maps of cycle routes. Borrow a set of wheels from **City Bikes** (www.citybikes.se; 3-day/season card 165/300kr).

🛈 GETTING AROUND

Storstockholms Lokaltrafik (SL; ☑08-600 10 00; www.sl.se; Centralstationen; ☺SL Center Sergels Torg 7am-6.30pm Mon-Fri, 10am-5pm Sat & Sun, inside Centralstationen 6.30am-11.45pm Mon-Sat, from 7am Sun) runs the tunnelbana (metro), local trains and buses within Stockholm county. You can buy tickets and passes at SL counters, ticket machines at tunnelbana stations, and Pressbyrå kiosks. Refillable SL travel cards (20kr) can be loaded with single-trip or unlimited-travel credit. A single ticket costs 30kr to 60kr and is valid for 75 minutes; it covers transfers between bus and metro. A 24-/72-hour pass costs 120/240kr per adult.

Tunnelbana The city's underground rail system is efficient and extensive.

Bus Local buses thoroughly cover the city and surrounds.

Tram Tram lines serve Djurgården from Norrmalm.

Ferry In summer, ferries are the best way to get to Djurgården, and they serve the archipelago year-round.

HELSINKI, FINLAND

Helsinki at a Glance...

Spectacularly entwined with the Baltic Sea's bays, inlets and islands, Helsinki's boulevards and backstreets are awash with magnificent architecture, intriguing drinking and dining venues and groundbreaking design – its design scene is one of the most electrifying in the world today. Fresh Finnish flavours can be found all over Helsinki, from the historic kauppahalli (covered market) to venerable restaurants, creative bistros and Michelin-starred gastronomy labs. Helsinki is surrounded by a sublime natural environment that's easily reached from all across the city.

With One Day in Port

In the morning, investigate the waterfront **kauppatori** (p179) and nearby **Tuomiokirkko** (p170), then stroll up **Esplanadin Puisto** (p178), visiting major Finnish design shops, and along Mannerheimintie. Admire contemporary art in striking **Kiasma** (p170), then 'golden age' art at the nearby **Ateneum** (p170). Spend the afternoon at island **Suomenlinna** (p166), and a sauna at traditional **Kotiharjun Sauna** (p176) or modern **Allas Sea Pool** (p176).

Best Places for...

Modern Finnish Olo (p177)

Sustainable eating Grön (p176)

Sandwiches Karl Fazer Café (p175)

Food market Vanha Kauppahalli (p175)

Beer Birri (p178)

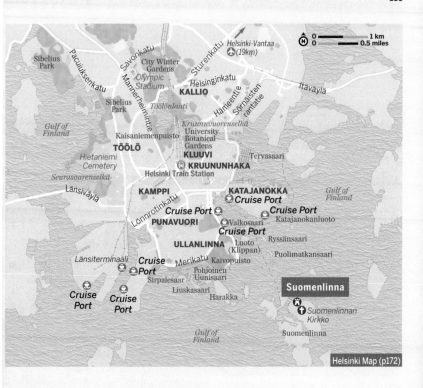

Helsinki Map (p172)

Getting from the Port

There are several cruise-ship docks. From the berths on either side of the main harbour, it's an easy waterfront stroll to the centre, though trams are available. From West Harbour, trams 7 and 6T take you downtown (€3.20, 10 to 15 minutes), while from Munkkisaari/ Hernesaari, catch bus 14 (€3.20, 15 minutes).

Fast Facts

Currency Euro (€)

Language Finnish, Swedish

Free wi-fi Large parts of the city centre have free wi-fi, as do many cafes and restaurants.

Tourist information Helsinki City Tourist Office (p179) is near the harbour in the centre of town.

Transport The city's public transport system, HSL (www.hsl.fi), operates buses, metro and local trains, trams and local ferries.

Suomenlinna

Suomenlinna, the 'fortress of Finland', straddles a cluster of car-free islands connected by bridges, and is a marvellous place to spend an afternoon or morning.

A Unesco World Heritage Site, Suomenlinna was built by the Swedes in the mid-18th century. Ferries from central Helsinki make the scenic journey to Suomenlinna, where you can explore museums, former bunkers and fortress walls, as well as Finland's only remaining WWII submarine.

Exploring Suomenlinna

From Suomenlinna's main quay, a blue-signposted walking path connects the key attractions. You'll immediately see the distinctive church, **Suomenlinnan Kirkko** (www.helsinginkirkot.fi; ⊙noon-4pm Wed-Sun, plus Tue Jun-Aug). Built by the Russians in 1854, it doubles as a lighthouse.

Suomenlinna's most atmospheric area, **Kustaanmiekka**, is at the end of the blue trail. Exploring the old bunkers, crumbling fortress walls and cannon gives you an

Great For...

☑ Don't Miss

The most atmospheric part of Suomenlinna, Kustaanmiekka, is at the end of the blue trail.

ANTON KUDELIN/SHUTTERSTOCK ©

insight into this fortress. The monumental King's Gate was built in 1753–54; in summer you can take a **water bus** (www.jt-line.fi; return €7) to Helsinki from here, saving the walk back to the main quay.

Guided tours are available, lasting an hour and departing from Rantakasarmi Information Centre.

Museums

On the main island, Susisaari, the **Ehrensvärd-Museo** (www.suomenlinna.fi; Suomenlinna; adult/child €5/2; ⏲10am-5pm Jun-Aug, 11am-4pm May & Sep) was once the home of Augustin Ehrensvärd, who designed the fortress. Opposite, sailmakers and other workers have been building ships since the 1750s at the picturesque **Viaporin Telakka** shipyard, today used for the maintenance of wooden vessels.

Explore Ashore

To get to Suomenlinna, make your way to Helsinki's kauppatori; this is walkable from central cruise terminals, a 10- to 15-minute bus/tram ride from others. Ferries (www.hsl.fi; single/return €3.20/5, 15 minutes, up to four hourly) depart regularly with waterbuses (www.jt-line.fi; return €7) running in summer, making three stops on Suomenlinna (20 minutes). Allow four hours if you'll investigate the museums; two if you just want a stroll around.

Need to Know

www.suomenlinna.fi

Along the shore, the **Vesikko** (www.suomenlinna.fi; adult/child incl Suomenlinna-Museo €7/4; ⏲11am-6pm May-Sep) is the only WWII-era submarine remaining in Finland. It's fascinating to climb inside and see how it all worked. Needless to say, there's not much room to move. A combined ticket here is also valid at the **Suomenlinna-Museo** (adult/child incl Vesikko €7/4; ⏲10am-6pm May-Sep, 10.30am-4.30pm Oct-Apr), a two-level museum covering the history of the fortress, located by the bridge that links Susisaari and Iso Mustasaari.

On Iso Mustasaari is **Sotamuseo Maneesi** (www.sotamuseo.fi; adult/child €7/4; ⏲11am-6pm early May-Sep), which has a comprehensive overview of Finnish military hardware. Nearby, inside a charming wooden building, the **Lelumuseo** (Toy Museum; www.lelumuseo.fi; adult/child €6/3; ⏲11am-6pm May-Sep) contains a delightful private collection of hundreds of dolls, teddy bears and wind-up toys.

Helsinki's Art & Design

Helsinki is renowned for its architecture, and this walk takes in many exemplars of the city's dramatically varying styles. It reveals the city's evolution from market town to the cutting-edge capital it is today.

Start Vanha Kauppahalli
Distance 3.2km
Duration Three hours

7 Continue walking northwest then west through leafy backstreets to the **Temppeliaukion Kirkko** (p171), an extraordinary rock-hewn church.

6 National Romantic splendour reaches its peak at Helsinki's spectacular **train station**, topped by a copper-caped clock tower.

5 Walk west to the country's finest art museum, the **Ateneum** (p170), in a palatial 1887 neo-Rennaissance building.

Olympic Stadium

Kaupunginpuutarha

City Winter Gardens

Töölönlahti

Mannerheimintie

Mechelinkatu

Runeberginkatu

Museokatu

Nervanderinkatu

Temppelikatu

Arkadiankatu

Mannerheimintie

Kampintori

Hietaniemi Cemetery

Eteläinen Rautatiekatu

Kamppi Ⓜ

Ruoholahti Ⓜ

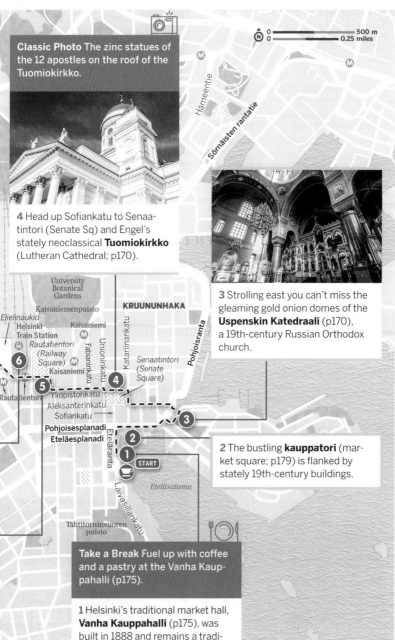

Classic Photo The zinc statues of the 12 apostles on the roof of the Tuomiokirkko.

4 Head up Sofiankatu to Senaatintori (Senate Sq) and Engel's stately neoclassical **Tuomiokirkko** (Lutheran Cathedral; p170).

3 Strolling east you can't miss the gleaming gold onion domes of the **Uspenskin Katedraali** (p170), a 19th-century Russian Orthodox church.

University Botanical Gardens

KRUUNUNHAKA

Kaisaniemenpuisto

Elielinaukio

Helsinki Train Station

Kaisaniemi

Rautatientori (Railway Square)

6

Kaisaniemi

M

Rautatientori

5

Yliopistonkatu

Aleksanterinkatu

Sofiankatu

4

Senaatintori (Senate Square)

Pohjoisranta

Katariinankatu

Unioninkatu

Fabianinkatu

Pohjoisesplanadi

Eteläesplanadi

2

1

START

3

2 The bustling **kauppatori** (market square; p179) is flanked by stately 19th-century buildings.

Eteläranta

Laivasillankatu

Eteläsatama

Tähtitorninvuoren puisto

Take a Break Fuel up with coffee and a pastry at the Vanha Kauppahalli (p175).

1 Helsinki's traditional market hall, **Vanha Kauppahalli** (p175), was built in 1888 and remains a traditional Finnish market.

Hämeentie

Sörnäisten rantatie

0   500 m
0   0.25 miles

◉ SIGHTS

Ateneum
Gallery

(www.ateneum.fi; Kaivokatu 2; adult/child €15/free; ⊘10am-6pm Tue & Fri, to 8pm Wed & Thu, to 5pm Sat & Sun) Occupying a palatial 1887 neo-Rennaissance building, Finland's premier art gallery offers a crash course in the nation's art. It houses Finnish paintings and sculptures from the 'golden age' of the late 19th century through to the 1950s, including works by Albert Edelfelt, Hugo Simberg, Helene Schjerfbeck, the von Wright brothers and Pekka Halonen. Pride of place goes to the prolific Akseli Gallen-Kallela's triptych from the Finnish national epic, the *Kalevala*, depicting Väinämöinen's pursuit of the maiden Aino.

Kiasma
Gallery

(www.kiasma.fi; Mannerheiminaukio 2; adult/child €14/free, 1st Sun of month free; ⊘10am-5pm Tue & Sun, to 8.30pm Wed-Fri, to 6pm Sat) Now one of a series of elegant contemporary buildings in this part of town, curvaceous and quirky metallic Kiasma, designed by Steven Holl and finished in 1998, is a symbol of the city's modernisation. It exhibits an eclectic collection of Finnish and international contemporary art, including digital art, and has excellent facilities for kids. Its outstanding success is that it has been embraced by the people of Helsinki, with a theatre and a hugely popular glass-sided cafe and terrace.

Tuomiokirkko
Church

(Lutheran Cathedral; www.helsinginseurakunnat.fi; Unioninkatu 29; ⊘9am-midnight Jun-Aug, to 6pm Sep-May) **FREE** One of CL Engel's finest creations, the chalk-white neoclassical Lutheran cathedral presides over Senaatintori. Created to serve as a reminder of God's supremacy, its high flight of stairs is now a popular meeting place. Zinc statues of the 12 apostles guard the city from the roof of the church. The spartan, almost mausoleum-like interior has little ornamentation under the lofty dome apart from an altar painting and three stern statues of Reformation heroes Martin Luther, Philip Melanchthon and Mikael Agricola.

Uspenskin Katedraali
Church

(Uspenski Cathedral; www.hos.fi/uspenskin-katedraali; Kanavakatu 1; ⊘9.30am-4pm Tue-Fri,

From left: Uspenskin Katedraali; Kiasma; Interior of the Temppeliaukion Kirkko

GRISHA BRUEV/SHUTTERSTOCK ©

10am-3pm Sat, noon-3pm Sun) `FREE` The eye-catching red-brick Uspenski Cathedral towers above Katajanokka island. Built as a Russian Orthodox church in 1868, it features classic golden onion-topped domes and now serves the Finnish Orthodox congregation. The high, square interior has a lavish iconostasis with the Evangelists flanking panels depicting the Last Supper and the Ascension.

Kansallismuseo   Museum

(National Museum of Finland; www.kansallismuseo.fi; Mannerheimintie 34; adult/child €10/free, 4-6pm Fri free; ⊘11am-6pm Tue-Sun) Built in National Romantic art nouveau style and opened in 1916, Finland's premier historical museum looks a bit like a Gothic church with its heavy stonework and tall square tower. A major overhaul is underway until 2019, but the museum will remain open throughout. Already-completed sections include an exceptional prehistory exhibition and the Realm, covering the 13th to the 19th century. Also here is a fantastic hands-on area for kids, Workshop Vintti.

Temppeliaukion Kirkko   Church

(☎09-2340-6320; www.helsinginseurakunnat.fi; Lutherinkatu 3; adult/child €3/free; ⊘9.30am-5.30pm Mon-Thu & Sat, to 8pm Fri, noon-5pm Sun Jun-Aug, shorter hours Sep-May) Hewn into solid stone, the Temppeliaukio church, designed by Timo and Tuomo Suomalainen in 1969, feels close to a Finnish ideal of spirituality in nature – you could be in a rocky glade were it not for the stunning 24m-diameter roof covered in 22km of copper stripping. Its acoustics are exceptional; regular concerts take place here. Opening times vary depending on events, so phone or search for its Facebook page for updates. There are fewer groups midweek.

Design Museum   Museum

(www.designmuseum.fi; Korkeavuorenkatu 23; combination ticket with Museum of Finnish Architecture adult/child €10/free; ⊘11am-6pm Jun-Aug, 11am-8pm Tue, to 6pm Wed-Sun Sep-May) An unmissable stop for Finnish design aficionados, Helsinki's Design Museum has a permanent collection that looks at the roots of Finnish design in the nation's traditions and nature. Changing exhibitions

Helsinki

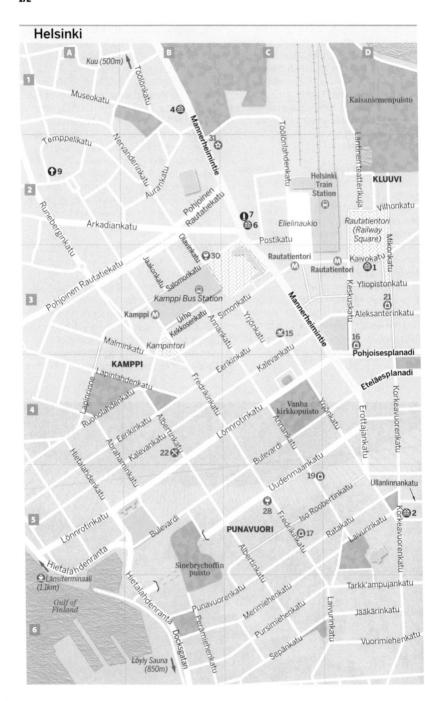

Kuu (500m)

Museokatu

Töölönkatu

Temppelikatu

Nervanderinkatu

Aurankatu

4

Mannerheimintie

31

Kaisaniemenpuisto

Läntinen teatterikuja

KLUUVI

9

Runeberginkatu

Arkadiankatu

Pohjoinen Rautatiekatu

Helsinki Train Station

Töölönlahdenkatu

Vilhonkatu

Mikonkatu

7
6

Elielinaukio

Rautatientori (Railway Square)

Postikatu

Kaivokatu

1

Olavinkatu

30

Rautatientori

Rautatientori

Yliopistonkatu

Pohjoinen Rautatiekatu

Jaakonkatu

Salomonkatu

Kamppi Bus Station

Simonkatu

Kamppi

Urho Kekkosenkatu

Annankatu

Yrjönkatu

Keskuskatu

Mannerheimintie

21

Aleksanterinkatu

15

Kampintori

Eerikinkatu

Kalevankatu

16

Pohjoisesplanadi

Malminkatu

KAMPPI

Lapinrinne

Lapinlahdenkatu

Ruoholahdenkatu

Eerikinkatu

Albertinkatu

Fredrikinkatu

Lönnrotinkatu

Vanha kirkkopuisto

Annankatu

Yrjönkatu

Eteläesplanadi

Korkeavuorenkatu

Erottajankatu

Hietalahdenkatu

Abrahaminkatu

Kalevankatu

22

Bulevardi

Uudenmaankatu

19

Ullanlinnankatu

28

Fredrikinkatu

Iso Roobertinkatu

Ratakatu

Laivurinkatu

Korkeavuorenkatu

2

Lönnrotinkatu

Bulevardi

PUNAVUORI

17

Hietalahdenranta

Länsiterminaali (1.1km)

Gulf of Finland

Sinebrychoffin puisto

Albertinkatu

Punavuorenkatu

Merimiehenkatu

Tarkk'ampujankatu

Jääkärinkatu

Hietalahdenranta

Docksgatan

Perämiehenkatu

Pursimiehenkatu

Sepänkatu

Laivurinkatu

Vuorimiehenkatu

Löyly Sauna (850m)

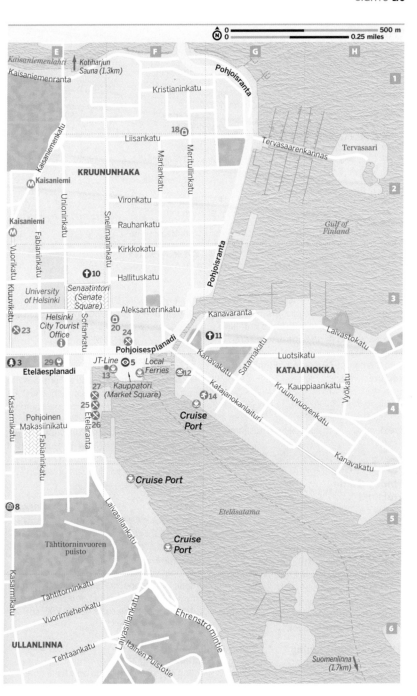

Helsinki

focus on contemporary design – everything from clothing to household furniture. From June to August, 30-minute tours in English take place at 2pm on Saturday and are included in admission. Combination tickets with the nearby **Museum of Finnish Architecture** (Arkkitehtuurimuseo; ☑045-7731-0474; www.mfa.fi; Kasarmikatu 24; adult/child €10/free, combination ticket with Design Museum €12/free; ☺11am-6pm Tue & Thu-Sun, to 8pm Wed) are a great-value way to see the two museums.

⊙ TOURS

Happy Guide Helsinki
Walking, Cycling

(☑044-502-0066; www.happyguidehelsinki. com; walking/bike tours from €20/55) Happy Guide Helsinki runs a range of original, light-hearted but informative cycling and walking tours around the city. Just some of its bike-tour options include berry picking or a sunset sauna tour; walking tours range from an old-town tour to food tours and craft-beer tours. Meeting points are confirmed when you book.

Helsinki Sightseeing
Cruise

(Gray Line; ☑09-2288-1600; www.stromma. fi; Kauppatori; 1½hr cruise adult/child €25/13;

☺late Apr-late Oct) One of several companies offering boat tours of Helsinki's maze of islands and waterways.

🔒 SHOPPING

Helsinki is a design epicentre, from fashion to furniture and homewares. Its hub is the Design District Helsinki (https://designdis-trict.fi), spread out between chic Esplanadi to the east, retro-hipster Punavuori to the south and Kamppi to the west. Hundreds of shops, studios and galleries are mapped on its website; you can also pick up a map at the tourist office.

Artek
Design

(www.artek.fi; Keskuskatu 1B; ☺10am-7pm Mon-Fri, to 6pm Sat) Originally founded by architect and designers Alvar Aalto and his wife Aino Aalto in 1935, this iconic Finnish company maintains the simple design principle of its founders. Textiles, lighting and furniture are among its homewares. Many items are only available at this 700-sq-metre, two-storey space.

Tre
Design

(www.worldoftre.com; Mikonkatu 6; ☺11am-7pm Mon-Fri, to 6pm Sat) If you only have time to visit one design store in Helsinki, this 2016-opened emporium is a brilliant bet. Showcasing the works of Finnish designers in fashion, jewellery and accessories, including umbrellas, furniture, ceramics, textiles, stationery and art, it also stocks a superb range of architectural and design books to fuel inspiration.

Lasikammari   Antiques

(www.lasikammari.fi; Liisankatu 9; ⊗noon-5pm Tue, Wed & Thu, to 2pm Mon, Fri & Sat) Vintage Finnish glassware from renowned brands such as Iittala, Nuutajärvi and Riihimäki, and individual designers such as Alvar Aalto and Tapio Wirkkala, make this tiny shop a diamond find for collectors. Along with glasses, you'll find vases, jugs, plates, bowls, light fittings and artistic sculptures. Prices are exceptionally reasonable; international shipping can be arranged on request.

Awake   Design

(www.awake-collective.com; Fredrikinkatu 25; ⊗12.30-6.30pm Tue-Fri, 11am-4pm Sat) ⚐ At this super-minimalist art gallery–concept store, changing displays of handmade, Finnish-only designs range from men's and women's fashion and accessories, including watches, jewellery, bags and shoes, to birch plywood furniture and homewares such as rugs, carpets, sheets and blankets. Everything is ecologically and sustainably produced. Regular evening art and fashion shows are accompanied by champagne – check the website for announcements.

Sweet Story   Food

(www.sweetstory.fi; Katariinankatu 3; ⊗10am-6pm Tue-Fri, 11am-4pm Sat) ⚐ Handmade caramels, liquorices (including a traditional Finnish variety with tar) and a rainbow of boiled sweets at this fantasy land are all organic and free from gluten, lactose and artificial colours and preservatives. Most are made at Sweet Story's own Helsinki workshop. There's also a handful of other specialities from Denmark, Lithuania and Austria.

Lokal   Design

(www.lokalhelsinki.com; Annankatu 9; ⊗11am-6pm Tue-Fri, 11am-4pm Sat, noon-4pm Sun) ⚐ A Design District standout, this hybrid design shop-gallery has rotating exhibitions from Finnish-based artists and designers, including traditional woodcarver Aimo Katajamäki, ceramicist Kristina Riska, birch-bark painter and jeweller Janna Syvänoja, contemporary painter Visa Norros and industrial furniture designer Jouko Kärkkäinen. All pieces exhibited are for sale.

⊗ EATING

Vanha Kauppahalli   Market €

(www.vanhakauppahalli.fi; Eteläranta 1; ⊗8am-6pm Mon-Sat, plus 10am-5pm Sun Jun-Aug; ⚐) ⚐ Alongside the harbour, this is Helsinki's iconic market hall. Built in 1888 it's still a traditional Finnish market, with wooden stalls selling local flavours such as liquorice, Finnish cheeses, smoked salmon and herring, berries, forest mushrooms and herbs. The centrepiece is its superb cafe, **Story** (www.restaurantstory.fi; snacks €3.20-10, mains €12.80-17; ⊗kitchen 8am-3pm Mon-Fri, to 5pm Sat, bar to 6pm Mon-Sat; ⚐) ⚐. Look out too for soups from **Soppakeittiö** (www.sopakeittio.fi; soups €9-10; ⊗11am-5pm Mon-Sat; ⚐).

Karl Fazer Café   Cafe €

(www.fazer.fi; Kluuvikatu 3; dishes €4-12; ⊗7.30am-10pm Mon-Fri, 9am-10pm Sat, 10am-6pm Sun; ⚐⚐⚐) Founded in 1891 and fronted by a striking art deco facade, this cavernous cafe is the flagship for Fazer's chocolate empire. The glass cupola reflects sound, so locals say it's a bad place to gossip. It's ideal, however, for buying dazzling confectionery, fresh bread, salmon or shrimp sandwiches, or digging into towering sundaes or spectacular cakes. Gluten-free dishes are available.

Kuu   Finnish €€

(⚐09-2709-0973; www.ravintolakuu.fi; Töölönkatu 27; mains €19-30, 2-/3-course lunch menus €24/28, 4-course dinner menus €47-51; ⊗11.30am-midnight Mon-Fri, 2pm-midnight Sat,

Understand

The Sauna

A sacred part of Finnish culture is the sauna (pronounced sah-oo-nah, not saw-nuh), prescribed to cure almost every ailment, used to seal business deals, or just socialise over a few beers.

Traditionally, saunas were used as a family bathhouse as well as a place to smoke meat and even give birth. The earliest references to the Finnish sauna date from chronicles of 1113 and there are numerous mentions of their use in the *Kalevala*, Finland's national epic.

The most common sauna is electric, which produces a fairly dry, harsh heat compared with the much-loved chimney sauna, driven by a log fire. Rarer is the chimneyless *savusauna* (smoke sauna). The soot-blackened walls are part of the experience.

Saunas are usually taken in the nude (public saunas are nearly always sex-segregated) and Finns are quite strict about its nonsexual – even sacred – nature. Shower first. Once inside (with a temperature of 80°C to 100°C), water is thrown onto the stove using a *kauhu* (ladle), producing *löyly* (steam). A *vihta* (whisk of birch twigs and leaves) is sometimes used to lightly strike the skin, improving circulation. Cool off with a cold shower or preferably by jumping into a lake (in the dead of winter Finns cut a hole in the ice and jump right in). Repeat. The sauna beer afterwards is also traditional.

Helsinki has several public saunas:

Kotiharjun Sauna (www.kotiharjunsauna.fi; Harjutorinkatu 1; adult/child €13/7; ⊗2-9.30pm Tue-Sun) Dating from 1928, this is Helsinki's only original traditional public wood-fired sauna.

Löyly Sauna (☑09-6128-6550; www.loylyhelsinki.fi; Hernesaarenranta 4; per 2hr incl towel €19; ⊗4-10pm Mon, 1-10pm Tue, Wed & Sun, 7.30-9.30am & 1-10pm Thu, 1-11pm Fri, 7.30am-9.30am & 1-11pm Sat) ✔ A smoke sauna is part of this sustainably powered timber complex. You can jump straight into the sea afterwards.

Sky Wheel (www.skywheel.fi; Katajanokanlaituri 2; adult/child €12/9; ⊗10am-9pm Mon-Fri, to 10pm Sat, 11am-7pm Sun May-Oct, shorter hours Nov-Apr) Helsinki's sightseeing Ferris wheel has a special 'SkySauna' gondola cabin.

Allas Sea Pool (www.allasseapool.fi; Katajanokanlaituri 2; day ticket adult/child €12/6, towel rental €5; ⊗6.15am-11pm Mon-Fri, 8am-11pm Sat & Sun) In addition to pools, this modern harbourfront complex has three saunas.

Yrjönkadun Uimahalli (www.hel.fi; Yrjönkatu 21B; adult/child swimming €5.50/2.50, swimming plus sauna €14/7; ⊗men 6.30am-8pm Tue & Thu, 7am-8pm Sat, women noon-8pm Sun & Mon, 6.30am-8pm Wed & Fri, closed Jun-Aug) This art deco complex's saunas are beloved by Helsinki locals.

4-11pm Sun) Traditional Finnish fare is given a sharp, contemporary twist at Kuu, which creates dishes from local ingredients such as smoked reindeer heart with pickled forest mushrooms, poached pike-perch with Lappish fingerling potatoes, and liquorice ice cream with cloudberry soup. Wines aren't cheap, but there are some interesting choices. Its casual bistro sibling, KuuKuu, is located 800m south.

Grön   Bistro €€

(☑050-328-9181; www.restaurantgron.com; Albertinkatu 36; mains €23-26, 4-course menu €49; ⊗5-10pm Tue-Sat; ☞🎵) ✔ Seasonal, often foraged ingredients are used in this exceptional bistro's plant, fish or meat starters and mains, and wild, plant or dairy desserts. Finnish artists not only provide the dining room's ceramic plates and paintings on the whitewashed walls, but also forage for the kitchen's wild herbs, berries, mushrooms and catch its fish. There are just 20 seats, so book ahead.

Suomenlinnan Panimo   Finnish €€

(☎020-742-5307; www.panimoravintola.fi; Suomenlinna C1; mains €15-30; ☺noon-10pm Mon-Sat, to 6pm Sun Jun-Aug, shorter hours Sep-May) By the main quay, this microbrewery is the best place to drink or dine on Suomenlinna. It brews three ciders and seven different beers, including a hefty porter, plus several seasonal varieties, and offers good food to accompany it, such as pike-perch with mustard tar sauce, or a game platter with bear salami, smoked reindeer and wild pheasant rillettes.

Olo   Finnish €€€

(☎010-320-6250; www.olo-ravintola.fi; Pohjois-esplanadi 5; 4-course lunch menu €53, dinner tasting menus short/long from €79/109, with paired wines €173/255; ☺6-11pm Tue-Sat Jun–mid-Aug, 11.30am-3pm & 6-11pm Tue-Fri, 6-11pm Sat mid-Aug–May) At the forefront of new Suomi cuisine, Michelin-starred Olo occupies a handsome 19th-century harbourside mansion. Its memorable degustation menus incorporate both the forage ethos and molecular gastronomy, and feature culinary jewels such as fennel-smoked salmon, herring with fermented cucumber, Åland lamb with blackcurrant leaves, juniper-marinated reindeer carpaccio, and Arctic crab with root celery. Book a few weeks ahead.

🍸 DRINKING & NIGHTLIFE

Diverse drinking and nightlife in Helsinki ranges from cosy bars to specialist craft-beer and cocktail venues, and clubs with live music and DJs. In summer early opening beer terraces sprout all over town.

Steam Hellsinki   Cocktail Bar

(www.steamhellsinki.fi; Olavinkatu 1; ☺4pm-4am Mon-Sat; 🛜) A wonderland of steampunk design, with futuristic-meets-19th-century industrial steam-powered machinery decor,

Ilmari Tapiovaara exhibition at the Design Museum (p171)

Ateneum (p170)

including a giant Zeppelin floating above the gondola-shaped bar, mechanical cogs and pulleys, globes, lanterns, radios, candelabras, Chesterfield sofas and a Zoltar fortune-telling machine, this extraordinary bar has dozens of varieties of gin and DJs spinning electro-swing. Ask about gin-appreciation and cocktail-making courses in English.

Birri
Microbrewery

(Il Birrificio; http://ilbirri.fi; Fredrikinkatu 22; ⊙11am-11pm Mon-Thu, to 1am Fri & Sat, to 4pm Sun) Birri brews three of its own beers on-site at any one time, stocks a fantastic range of Finnish-only craft beers and also handcrafts its own seasonally changing sausages. The space is strikingly done out with Arctic-white metro tiles, brown-and-white chequerboard floor tiles, exposed timber beams and gleaming silver kegs.

Kappeli
Bar

(www.kappeli.fi; Eteläesplanadi 1; ⊙10am-midnight; ⊛) Dating from 1867, this grand bar-cafe opens to an outdoor terrace seating 350 people and has regular jazz, blues

and folk music in the nearby bandstand in **Esplanadin Puisto** (Esplanadi Park) from May to August. Locals and visitors alike flock here on a sunny day.

⊕ ENTERTAINMENT

Musiikkitalo
Concert Venue

(Helsinki Music Centre; ☎020-707-0400; www.musiikkitalo.fi; Mannerheimintie 13; tickets free-€30) Home to the Helsinki Philharmonic Orchestra, Finnish Radio Symphony Orchestra and Sibelius Academy, the glass-and copper-fronted Helsinki Music Centre, opened in 2011, hosts a diverse program of classical, jazz, folk, pop and rock. The 1704-capacity main auditorium, visible from the foyer, has stunning acoustics. Five smaller halls seat 140 to 400. Buy tickets at the door or from www.ticketmaster.fi.

ⓘ INFORMATION

DISCOUNT CARDS

The **Helsinki Card** (www.helsinkicard.com; 1-/2-/3-day pass €46/56/66) gives you free public transport around the city and **local ferries** (Kau-ppatori) to Suomenlinna, entry to 28 attractions in and around Helsinki and a 24-hour hop-on, hop-off bus tour.

It's cheaper online; otherwise, buy them at tourist offices or transport terminals. To get value from it, you'd have to pack in a lot of sightseeing.

TOURIST INFORMATION

Between June and August, multilingual 'Helsinki Helpers' – easily spotted by their lime-green jackets – are a mine of tourist information.

Helsinki City Tourist Office (09-3101-3300; www.visithelsinki.fi; Pohjoisesplanadi 19; 9am-6pm Mon-Sat, to 4pm Sun mid-May–mid-Sep, 9am-6pm Mon-Fri, 10am-4pm Sat & Sun mid-Sep–mid-May) Busy multilingual office with a great quantity of information on the city.

Strömma (www.stromma.fi; Pohjoisesplanadi 19; 9am-6pm Mon-Sat, to 4pm Sun mid-May–mid-Sep, 9am-6pm Mon-Fri, 10am-4pm Sat & Sun mid-Sep–mid-May) In the city tourist office; sells various tours and local cruises.

GETTING AROUND

Walking Central Helsinki is compact and easily covered on foot.

Bicycle Helsinki's shared-bike scheme is City Bikes (www.hsl.fi/citybikes).

Tram Ten main routes cover the city.

Bus Most visitors won't need to use them.

 Do-It-Yourself Tram Tours

You can get a good overview of the city aboard a regular local tram on three main routes, accompanied by free downloadable guides from the tourist office website that briefly describe notable sights along the way.

Purchase tram tickets onboard, or at sales points such as **Kamppi bus station** (www.matkahuolto.fi; Salomonkatu), many R-Kiosks and the tourist office.

Tram 2 Get a classic overview of Helsinki on this loop from the kauppatori.

Tram 4 One-way architectural route.

Tram 6 A one-way design- and culinary-focused route.

KARASEV VICTOR/SHUTTERSTOCK ©

Metro Single line; the most useful stops for visitors are in the centre and Kallio.

Ferry Local ferries serve island destinations, including Suomenlinna.

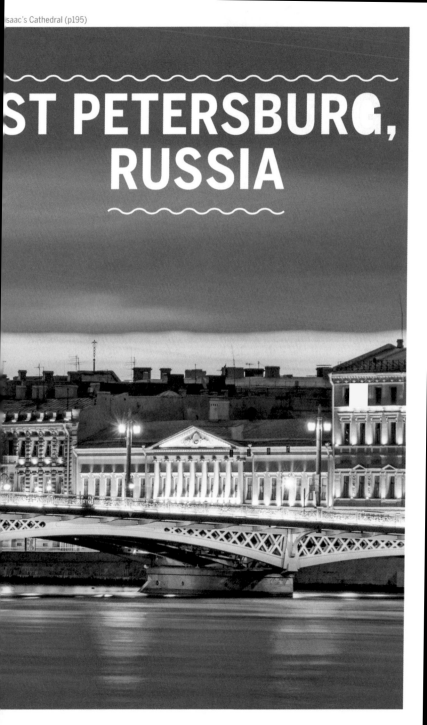

ST PETERSBURG, RUSSIA

St Petersburg at a Glance...

The sheer grandeur and history of Russia's imperial capital never fail to amaze. St Petersburg is an almost unrivalled treasure trove of art and culture on a picturesque canvas of canals, bridges and striking plazas adorned with baroque and neoclassical palaces. Its summer White Nights are legendary, when performing arts festivals pack out concert halls and the entire city seems to party all night long.

With One Day in Port

Start at the dazzling ensemble of **Palace Square** (p186), the **Winter Palace** (p186) and the **General Staff Building** (p186). Here, the **Hermitage** (p184) could fill the day; otherwise, focus on key interests and spend a couple of hours there. Then stroll down Nevsky Prospekt, drop into the **Kazan Cathedral** (p192) and detour to the **Church of the Saviour on the Spilled Blood** (p191). An afternoon **canal cruise** (p199) is a must.

Best Places for...

Cafe Zoom Café (p201)

Traditional food Yat (p201)

Modern Russian Gräs x Madbaren (p203)

Cocktails Kabinet (p204)

Craft beer Redrum (p203)

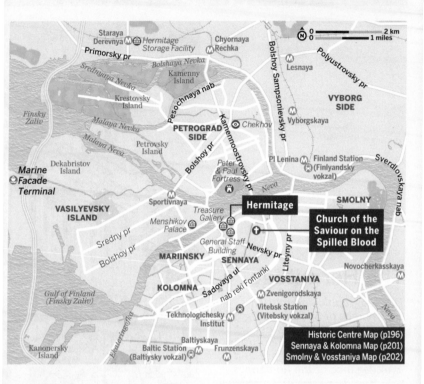

Getting from the Port

Visa-free passengers will be transported direct from the Marine Facade cruise terminal into the centre and back. If you have a Russian visa, you can catch bus 158 to the Primorskaya metro stop and access the city from there.

Fast Facts

Currency Rouble (R)

Language Russian

Tourist information The main bureau (p205) is just off Nevsky Prospekt in the historic centre.

Visas See p205.

Transport Metro is the fastest, while buses, minibuses and trolleybuses are good for shorter distances.

The Winter Palace

The Hermitage

The geographic and tourism centrepiece of St Petersburg is one of the world's greatest art collections. No other institution so embodies the opulence and extravagance of the Romanovs.

Great For...

ℹ **Need to Know**

Государственный Эрмитаж; Map p196; www.hermitagemuseum.org; Dvortsovaya pl 2; combined ticket R700; ⊙10.30am-6pm Tue, Thu, Sat & Sun, to 9pm Wed & Fri; Ⓜ Admiralteyskaya

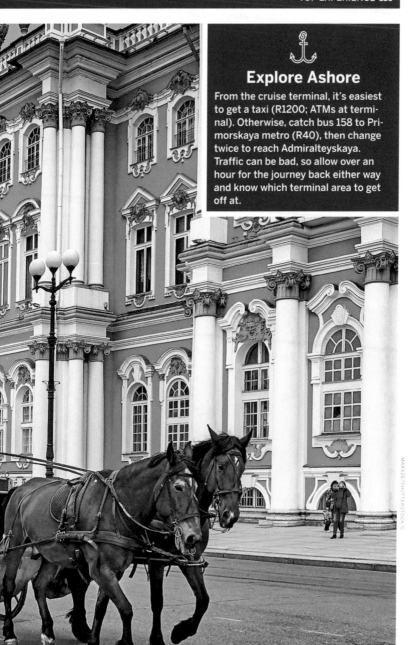

⚓ Explore Ashore

From the cruise terminal, it's easiest to get a taxi (R1200; ATMs at terminal). Otherwise, catch bus 158 to Primorskaya metro (R40), then change twice to reach Admiralteyskaya. Traffic can be bad, so allow over an hour for the journey back either way and know which terminal area to get off at.

MARAZE/SHUTTERSTOCK ©

The Hermitage first opened to the public in 1852. Today, for the price of admission (prebooking is a great idea), anybody can parade down the grand staircases and across parquet floors, gawping at crystal chandeliers, gilded furniture and an amazing art collection that once was for the eyes of the Tsar's court only.

Layout

The main complex consists of five connected buildings – the **Winter Palace** (Зимний дворец; Map p196), the **Small Hermitage** (Малый Эрмитаж; Map p196), the **Great (Old) Hermitage** (Большой (Старый) Эрмитаж; Map p196), also known as the Large Hermitage, the **New Hermitage** (Новый Эрмитаж; Map p196) and the **Hermitage Theatre** (Map p196; ☎ 812-408 1084; https://hermitagetheater.com; Dvortsovaya nab 32; online tickets from R8300) – and is devoted to items from prehistoric times up until the mid-19th century. Impressionist, postimpressionist and modern works are found in the new galleries of the **General Staff Building** (Здание Главного штаба; Map p196; Dvortsovaya pl 6-8; R300, incl main Hermitage museum & other buildings R700; ⊗10.30am-6pm Tue, Thu, Sat & Sun, to 9pm Wed & Fri; MAdmiralteyskaya) across **Palace Square** (Дворцовая площадь; Map p196).

Collection

The Western European Collection, in particular, does not miss much: Spanish, Flemish, Dutch, French, English and German art are all covered from the 15th to the 18th centuries, while the Italian collection goes back all the way to the 13th century, including the Florentine and

The Gold Drawing Room

Venetian Renaissance, with priceless works by Leonardo da Vinci, Raphael, Michelangelo and Titian. A highlight is the enormous collection of Dutch and Flemish painting, in particular the spectacular assortment of Rembrandt, most notably his masterpiece *Return of the Prodigal Son*.

As much as you will see in the museum, there's about 20 times more in its vaults, part of which you can visit at the Hermitage Storage Facility (p195). Other branches of the museum include the **Winter Palace of Peter I** (Зимний дворец Петра Первого; Map p196; Dvortsovaya nab 32; R150; ⊙10.30am-5pm Tue-Sat, 10am-4pm Sun; Ⓜ Admiralteyskaya),

> **☑ Don't Miss**
>
> Rembrandt (Room 254), Great Church (Room 271), Treasure Gallery and the Peacock Clock (Room 204).

ANTON_IVANOV/SHUTTERSTOCK ©

further east along the Neva, **Menshikov Palace** (Государственный Эрмитаж-Дворец Меншикова; ☎812-323 1112; Universitetskaya nab 15; R300; ⊙10.30am-6pm Tue, Thu, Sat & Sun, to 9pm Wed & Fri; Ⓜ Vasileostrovskaya) on Vasilyevsky Island, and the **Imperial Porcelain factory** (www.ipm.ru; pr Obukhovsky Oborony 151; R300; ⊙10am-7pm Mon-Fri; Ⓜ Lomonosovskaya) in the south of the city.

Treasure Gallery

For lovers of things that glitter and the applied arts, the Hermitage's **Treasure Gallery** (Map p196; ☎812-571 8446; Winter Palace, Dvortsovaya pl; tour of Diamond or Golden Rooms R350; Ⓜ Admiralteyskaya) should not be missed. These two special collections, guarded behind vault doors, are open only by guided tour, for which you should either call ahead to reserve a place, or buy a ticket at the entrance. The **Golden Rooms** collection focuses on a hoard of fabulous Scythian and Greek gold and silver from the Caucasus, Crimea and Ukraine, dating from the 7th to 2nd centuries BC; the **Diamond Rooms** section has fabulous jewellery from Western Europe and pieces from as far apart as China, India and Iran.

> **✕ Take a Break**
>
> Eating options in the Hermitage are poor. Nearby, Yat (p201) serves excellent Russian food in a charming atmosphere; prebook.

The Hermitage

A HALF-DAY TOUR

Successfully navigating the State Hermitage Museum, with its four vast interconnecting buildings and around 360 rooms, is an art form in itself. Our half-day tour of the highlights can be done in four hours, or easily extended to a full day.

Once past ticket control start by ascending the grand **❶ Jordan Staircase** to Neva Enfilade and Great Enfilade for the impressive staterooms, including the former throne room St George's Hall and the 1812 War Gallery (Room 197), and the Romanovs' private apartments. Admire the newly restored **❷ Great Church** then make your way back to the Neva side of the building via the Western Gallery (Room 262) to find the splendid **❸ Pavilion Hall** with its view onto the Hanging Garden and the gilded Peacock Clock, always a crowd pleaser.

Make your way along the series of smaller galleries in the Large Hermitage hung with Italian Renaissance art, including masterpieces by **❹ Da Vinci** and **❺ Caravaggio**. The Loggia of Raphael (Room 227) is also impressive. Linger a while in the galleries containing Spanish art before taking in the Dutch collection, the highlight of which is the hoard of **❻ Rembrandt** canvases in Room 254.

Descend the Council Staircase (Room 206), noting the giant malachite vase, to the ground floor where the fantastic Egyptian collection awaits in Room 100 as well as the galleries of Greek and Roman Antiquities. If you have extra time, it's well worth booking tours to see the special exhibition in the **❼ Gold Rooms** of the Treasure Gallery.

Jordan Staircase
Originally designed by Rastrelli, in the 18th century this incredible white marble construction was known as the Ambassadorial Staircase because it was the way into the palace for official receptions.

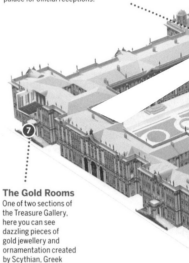

The Gold Rooms
One of two sections of the Treasure Gallery, here you can see dazzling pieces of gold jewellery and ornamentation created by Scythian, Greek and ancient Oriental craftsmen.

Great Church
This stunningly ornate church was the Romanovs' private place of worship and the venue for the marriage of the last tsar, Nicholas II, to Alexandra Feodorovna in 189[5]

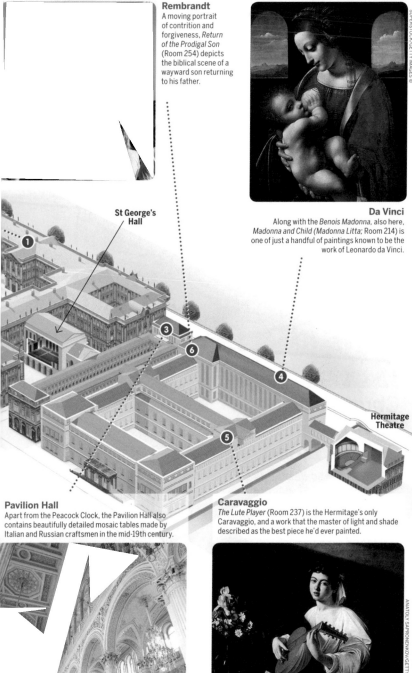

Rembrandt
A moving portrait of contrition and forgiveness, *Return of the Prodigal Son* (Room 254) depicts the biblical scene of a wayward son returning to his father.

Da Vinci
Along with the *Benois Madonna*, also here, *Madonna and Child (Madonna Litta;* Room 214) is one of just a handful of paintings known to be the work of Leonardo da Vinci.

St George's Hall

Hermitage Theatre

Pavilion Hall
Apart from the Peacock Clock, the Pavilion Hall also contains beautifully detailed mosaic tables made by Italian and Russian craftsmen in the mid-19th century.

Caravaggio
The Lute Player (Room 237) is the Hermitage's only Caravaggio, and a work that the master of light and shade described as the best piece he'd ever painted.

SUPERSTOCK/GETTY IMAGES ©

ANATOLY SAPRONENKOV/GETTY IMAGES ©

CHAN SRITHAWEEPORN/GETTY IMAGES ©

Church of the Saviour on the Spilled Blood

This five-domed dazzler is St Petersburg's most elaborate church, with a classic Russian Orthodox exterior and an interior decorated with some 7000 sq metres of mosaics.

Great For...

☑ Don't Miss

Canopy marking assassination spot and the mosaic murals.

History

Officially called the Church of the Resurrection of Christ, its colloquial name references the assassination attempt on Tsar Alexander II here in 1881. The church, which was consecrated in 1907, incorporates elements of 18th-century Russian architecture from Moscow and Yaroslavl, and is so lavish it took 24 years to build and was 1 million roubles over budget – an enormous sum for the times.

Renewal

Decades of abuse and neglect during most of the Soviet era ended in the 1970s when restoration began. When the doors reopened 27 years later on what is now a museum, visitors were astounded by the spectacular mosaics covering the walls and ceilings. Designs for the mosaics came from top artists of the day including Victor Vasnetsov, Mikhail Nesterov and Andrei Ryabushkin.

Konyushennaya pl Teatralny
Malo-Konyushenny *most* *Moyka* 1-y Sadovy
most *most*

**Church of
the Saviour on
the Spilled Blood**

Mikhailovsky
Gardens

Shvedsky per Mikhailovsky
Theatre
Russian
Museum

⚓ Explore Ashore

From the cruise terminal, it's easiest to get a taxi (R1200; ATMs at terminal). Otherwise, catch bus 158 to Primorskaya metro (R40), then go two stops to Gostiny Dvor. The church is a 15-minute walk. Traffic can be bad, so allow an 1½ hours for the taxi journey back.

❶ Need to Know

Храм Спаса на Крови; Map p196;
☏812-315 1636; http://eng.cathedral.ru/spasa_na_krovi; Konyushennaya pl; adult/student R250/150; ⊙10.30am-6pm Thu-Tue; Ⓜ Nevsky Prospekt

The polychromatic exterior – decorated with mosaics of detailed scenes from the New Testament and the coats of arms of the provinces, regions and towns of the Russian Empire of Alexander's time – is equally showstopping. Twenty granite plaques around the facade record the main events of Alexander's reign.

Around the Church

Administered by the Russian Museum, the 8.7-hectare **Mikhailovsky Garden** (Михайловский сад; Map p196; https://igardens.ru; ⊙10am-10pm May-Sep, 10am-8pm Oct-Mar, closed Apr; Ⓜ Nevsky Prospekt) **FREE** is lovely. The gardens are famous for their Style Moderne wrought-iron fence and gates, a profusion of metallic blooms and flourishes that wrap around one side of the church. You get an impressive perspective of **Mikhailovsky Castle** (Михайловский замок; Map p196;

☏812-595 4248; www.rusmuseum.ru; Sadovaya ul 2; adult/student R300/150; ⊙10am-6pm Mon, Wed & Fri-Sun, 1-9pm Thu; Ⓜ Gostiny Dvor), a branch of the Russian Museum (p194) that is worth visiting for its temporary exhibits as well as a few finely restored state rooms. The main building of the excellent museum, Mikhailovsky Palace, is along the park's southern side.

Did You Know?

● In the western apse, the spot of the assassination attempt on Alexander II is marked by a small but beautiful canopy made of rhodonite and jasper.

● Near the exit is a small exhibition of photos showing parts of the restoration process.

● There's a spectacular view of the church from Teatralny most near the intersection of the Moyka and Griboyedov Canal.

St Petersburg's Historic Heart

This stroll takes in the grandeur of central St Petersburg, with its magnificent palaces, churches, canals, bridges and statues.

Start Dvortsovaya pl
Distance 2km
Duration three hours

2 On the Moyka River is the **Pushkin Flat-Museum** (www.museumpushkin.ru; adult/student R250/150; ⊙10.30am-5pm Wed-Sun), former residence of Russia's most celebrated poet.

1 Magnificent **Palace Square** (p186) is simply one of the world's most striking plazas.

Classic Photo The must-have St Petersburg bridge shot from Bankovsky most.

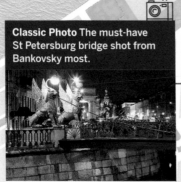

6 The **Kazan Cathedral** is a formidable sight. Behind it, **Bankovsky most** is the city's most picturesque bridge.

Take a Break Hit Gräs x Madbaren (p203) for great Scandi-Russian fusion dishes.

Winter Palace

Alexander Garden

General Staff Building

START

Admiralteyskaya

Malaya Morskaya ul

Bolshaya Morskaya ul

nab reki Moyki

nab reki Moyki

Moyka

Bolshaya Konyushennaya ul

Stroganov Palace

Gorokhovaya ul

Kazanskaya pl

Griboyedov Canal

SENNAYA

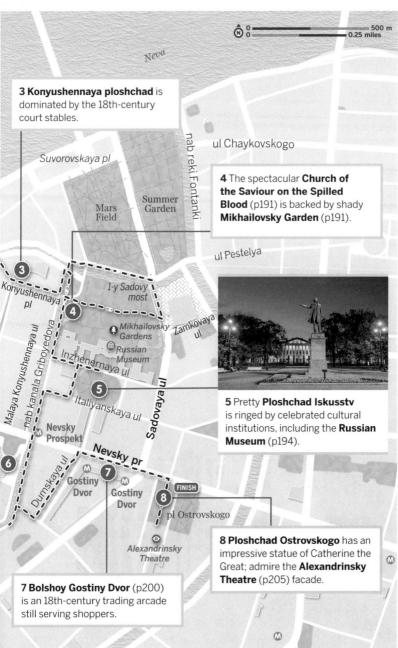

3 Konyushennaya ploshchad is dominated by the 18th-century court stables.

4 The spectacular **Church of the Saviour on the Spilled Blood** (p191) is backed by shady **Mikhailovsky Garden** (p191).

5 Pretty **Ploshchad Iskusstv** is ringed by celebrated cultural institutions, including the **Russian Museum** (p194).

7 Bolshoy Gostiny Dvor (p200) is an 18th-century trading arcade still serving shoppers.

8 Ploshchad Ostrovskogo has an impressive statue of Catherine the Great; admire the **Alexandrinsky Theatre** (p205) facade.

Neva

Suvorovskaya pl

ul Chaykovskogo

nab reki Fontanki

Mars Field

Summer Garden

ul Pestelya

Konyushennaya pl

1-y Sadovy most

Zamkovaya ul

Mikhailovsky Gardens

Russian Museum

Inzhenernaya ul

Malaya Konyushennaya ul

nab kanala Griboyedova

Italiyanskaya ul

Sadovaya ul

Nevsky Prospekt

Nevsky pr

Dumskaya ul

Gostiny Dvor

Gostiny Dvor

FINISH

pl Ostrovskogo

Alexandrinsky Theatre

500 m
0.25 miles

⊙ SIGHTS

Russian Museum   Museum

(Русский музей; Map p196; ☏812-595 4248; www.rusmuseum.ru; Inzhenernaya ul 4; adult/ student R450/200; ☉10am-8pm Mon, 10am-6pm Wed & Fri-Sun, 1-9pm Thu; Ⓜ Nevsky Prospekt) Focusing solely on Russian art, from ancient church icons to 20th-century paintings, the Russian Museum's collection is magnificent and can easily be viewed in half a day or less. The collection includes works by Karl Bryullov, Alexander Ivanov, Nicholas Ghe, Ilya Repin, Natalya Goncharova, Kazimir Malevich and Kuzma Petrov-Vodkin, among many others, and the masterpieces keep on coming as you tour the beautiful Carlo Rossi–designed Mikhailovsky Palace and its attached wings.

Entry is either from Arts Sq or via the connected **Benois Wing** (Map p196; ☏812-595 4248; www.rusmuseum.ru; nab kanala Griboyedova; adult/student R450/200; ☉10am-8pm Mon, 10am-6pm Wed & Fri-Sun, 1-9pm Thu; Ⓜ Nevsky Prospekt) on nab kanala Griboyedova. There's also an entrance from the lovely Mikhailovsky Gardens (p191) behind the palace. Permanent and temporary exhibitions by the Russian Museum are also held at the **Marble Palace** (Мраморный дворец; Map p196; ☏812-595 4248; www.rusmuseum. ru; Millionnaya ul 5; adult/student R300/150; ☉10am-6pm Mon, Wed & Fri-Sun, 1-9pm Thu; Ⓜ Nevsky Prospekt), the Mikhailovsky Castle (p191; also known as the Engineer's Castle) and the **Stroganov Palace** (Строгановский дворец; Map p196; www.rusmuseum.ru; Nevsky pr 17; adult/student R300/150; ☉10am-6pm Wed & Fri-Mon, 1-9pm Thu; Ⓜ Nevsky Prospekt). Combined tickets, available at each palace, cover entrance either to your choice of two the same day (adult/student R600/270) or to all four within a three-day period (R850/400).

Fabergé Museum   Museum

(Музей Фаберже; Map p196; ☏812-333 2655; http://fabergemuseum.ru; nab reki Fontanki 21; R450, incl tour R600; ☉10am-8.45pm Sat-Thu; Ⓜ Gostiny Dvor) The magnificently restored Shuvalovsky Palace is home to the world's largest collection of pieces manufactured by the jeweller Peter Carl Fabergé (including nine imperial Easter eggs) and fellow

Russian Museum

master craftspeople of pre-revolutionary Russia.

St Isaac's Cathedral Museum

(Исаакиевский собор; Map p196; ☑ 812-315 9732; www.cathedral.ru; Isaakievskaya pl; cathedral adult/student R250/150, colonnade R150; ◔ cathedral 10.30am-10.30pm Thu-Tue May-Sep, to 6pm Oct-Apr, colonnade 10.30am-10.30pm May-Oct, to 6pm Nov-Apr; Ⓜ Admiralteyskaya) The golden dome of St Isaac's Cathedral dominates the St Petersburg skyline. Its obscenely lavish interior is open as a museum, although services are held in the cathedral throughout the year. Most people bypass the museum to climb the 262 steps to the *kolonnada* (colonnade) around the drum of the dome, providing superb city views.

Peter & Paul Fortress Fortress

(Петропавловская крепость; www.spbmuseum. ru; grounds free, SS Peter & Paul Cathedral adult/ child R450/250, combined ticket for 5 exhibitions R600/350; ◔ grounds 8.30am-8pm, exhibitions 11am-6pm Mon & Thu-Sun, 10am-5pm Tue; Ⓜ Gorkovskaya) Housing a cathedral where the Romanovs are buried, a former prison and various exhibitions, this large defensive fortress on Zayachy Island is the kernel from which St Petersburg grew into the city it is today. History buffs will love it and everyone will swoon at the panoramic views from atop the fortress walls, at the foot of which lies a sandy riverside beach, a prime spot for sunbathing.

Hermitage Storage Facility Museum

(Реставрационно-хранительный центр Старая деревня; ☑ 812-340 1026; www.hermitage museum.org; Zausadebnaya ul 37a; tours R550; ◔ tours 11am, 1pm, 1.30pm & 3.30pm Wed-Sun; ⛨ Ⓜ Staraya Derevnya) Guided tours of the Hermitage's state-of-the-art restoration and storage facility are highly recommended. This is not a formal exhibition as such, but the guides are knowledgeable and the examples chosen for display (paintings, furniture and carriages) are wonderful.

The storage facility is directly behind the big shopping centre opposite the

Take a Day Trip to Peterhof

Peterhof, the 'Russian Versailles' 29km west of St Petersburg, is a palace surrounded by leafy gardens and a spectacular ensemble of gravity-powered fountains. It makes a perfect day trip if you have the time in port. It's largely a reconstruction, due to having been a major WWII casualty.

The **Grand Palace** (Большой дворец; www.peterhofmuseum.ru; ul Razvodnaya; adult/student R700/400, audio guide R600; ◔ 10.30am-6pm Tue-Sun, closed last Tue of month) is an imposing building. From June to September it is open to foreign tourists only from noon to 2pm, and 4.15pm to 5.45pm (to 7.45pm on Saturdays); guided tours are in Russian at other times.

The **Grand Cascade** (◔ 11am-5pm Mon-Fri, to 6pm Sat & Sun May-Oct) is a symphony of more than 140 fountains and canals partly engineered by Peter. You pay to enter the Lower Park, and they only work from mid-May to early October, but the gilded ensemble looks marvellous all year.

Peterhof is easy and cheap to reach. *Marshrutky* 300, 424 and 424A (R80) leave from outside Avtovo metro station, *marshrutka* 103 from outside Leninsky Prospekt station. From May to September, **Peterhof Express** (Map p196; www. peterhof-express.com; single/return adult R800/1500, student R600/1000; ◔ 10am-6pm) hydrofoils depart from the Admiralty jetty every 30 minutes from 10am: an expensive but highly enjoyable way to get to Peterhof, and you arrive right out front.

Grand Canal, Peterhof

Historic Centre

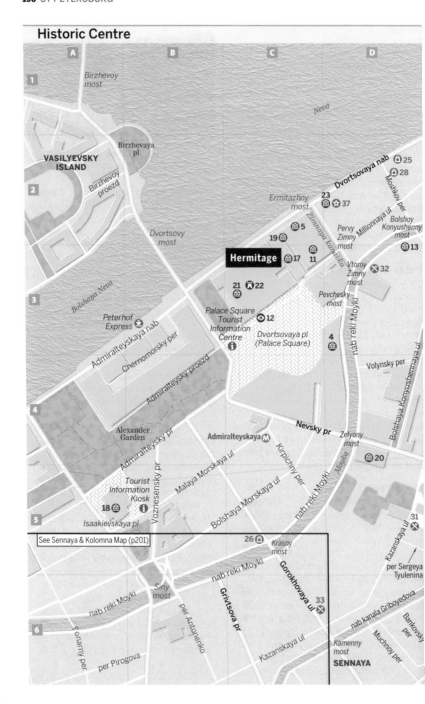

Birzhevoy most

Neva

Birzhevaya pl

VASILYEVSKY ISLAND

Birzhevoy proezd

Dvortsovy most

Bolshaya Neva

Dvortsovaya nab ● 25
🔒 28

Moshkov per

Ermitazhny most
23 🏛 ★ 37

Pervy Zimny most
Bolshoy Konyushenny most
Millionnaya ul
🏛 13

● 5
19 🏛
Hermitage 🏛 17 🏛 11

Vtoroy Zimny most ✕ 32

21 🏛 22

Pevchesky most

nab reki Moyki

Peterhof Express ●

Admiralteyskaya nab
Chernomorsky per
Admiralteysky proezd

Palace Square Tourist Information Centre 🅘

● 12

Dvortsovaya pl (Palace Square)
4 🏛

Volynsky per

Bolshaya Konyushennaya ul

Alexander Garden

Admiralteysky pr

Admiralteysky pr

Voznesensky pr

Malaya Morskaya ul

Admiralteyskaya Ⓜ

Kirpichny per

Nevsky pr

Zelyony most

🏛 20

Monika

nab reki Moyki

Tourist Information Kiosk 🅘
18 🏛
Isaakievskaya pl

Bolshaya Morskaya ul

31 ✕

Kazanskaya ul

per Sergeya Tyulenina

See Sennaya & Kolomna Map (p201)

26 🔒
Krasny most

nab reki Moyki

Gorokhovaya ul

33 ✕

nab kanala Griboyedova

Bankovsky per

Siny most

Grivtsova pr

per Antonenko

nab reki Moyki

ponarny per

per Pirogova

Kazanskaya ul

Kamenny most
SENNAYA

Muchnoy per

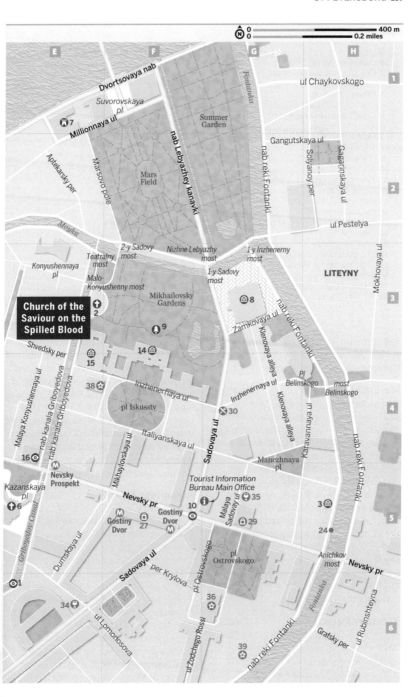

0   400 m
0   0.2 miles

E **F** **G** **H**

Dvortsovaya nab

Suvorovskaya pl

Millionnaya ul

7

Aptekarsky per

Marsovo pole

Moyka

Mars Field

nab Lebyazhey kanavki

Fontanka

Summer Garden

nab reki Fontanki

ul Chaykovskogo

Gangutskaya ul

Solyanoy per

Gagarinskaya ul

ul Pestelya

ul Chaykovskogo

Konyushennaya pl

Teatralny most

Malo-Konyushenny most

Shvedsky per

2-y Sadovy most

Nizhne Lebyazhy most

1-y Sadovy most

Mikhailovsky Gardens

Mikhaylovskaya ul

Zamkovaya ul

1-y Inzhenerny most

LITEYNY

Mokhovaya ul

Church of the Saviour on the Spilled Blood

2

9

8

14   15

Klenovaya alleya

nab reki Fontanki

38

pl Iskusstv

Inzhenernaya ul

Inzhenernaya ul

Pl Belinskogo

most Belinskogo

Italyanskaya ul

Manezhnaya pl

Klenovaya alleya

Karavannaya ul

nab reki Fontanki

Malaja Konyushennaya ul

nab kanala Griboyedova

16

Nevsky Prospekt

Nevsky pr

Kazanskaya pl

6

Griboyedov Canal

Dumskaya ul

Gostiny Dvor

27

30

Sadovaya ul

Tourist Information Bureau Main Office

10

Gostiny Dvor

Malaya Sadovay ul

35

29

3

24

Nevsky pr

Sadovaya ul

per Krylova

pl Ostrovskogo

Anichkov most

Fontanka

Grafsky per

ul Rubinshteyna

1

34

ul Lomonosova

ul Zodchego Rossi

36

39

nab reki Fontanki

Historic Centre

metro station – look for the enormous golden-yellow glass facility decorated with shapes inspired by petroglyphs.

Mariinsky Theatre   Theatre

(Мариинский театр; Map p201; ☏812-326 4141; www.mariinsky.ru; Teatralnaya pl; ☺box office 11am-7pm; Ⓜ Sadovaya) The Mariinsky Theatre has played a pivotal role in Russian ballet ever since it was built in 1859 and remains one of Russia's most loved and respected cultural institutions. Its pretty green-and-white main building on aptly named Teatralnaya pl (Theatre Sq) is a must for any visitor wanting to see one of the world's great ballet and opera stages, while its newer second stage, the **Mariinsky II** (Мариинский II; Map p201; ul Dekabristov 34; tickets R350-6000; ☺ticket office 11am-7pm; Ⓜ Sadovaya), is a state-of-the-art opera house for the 21st century.

Yusupov Palace   Palace

(Юсуповский дворец; Map p201; ☏8-921-970 3038; www.yusupov-palace.ru; nab reki Moyki 94; adult/student incl audio guide R700/500, Rasputin tour R350/250; ☺11am-6pm; Ⓜ Sadovaya)

This spectacular palace on the Moyka River has some of the best 19th-century interiors in the city, in addition to a fascinating and gruesome history. The palace's last owner was the eccentric Prince Felix Yusupov, a high-society darling and at one time the richest man in Russia. Most notoriously, the palace is the place where Grigory Rasputin was murdered in 1916, and the basement where this now infamous plot unravelled can be visited as part of a guided tour.

Alexander Nevsky Monastery   Monastery

(Александро-Невская лавра; Map p202; www. lavra.spb.ru; Nevsky pr 179/2; cemetery R400, pantheon R150; ☺grounds 6am-11pm summer, 8am-9pm winter, churches 6am-9pm, cemeteries 9.30am-6pm summer, 11am-4pm winter, pantheon 11am-5pm Tue, Wed & Fri-Sun; Ⓜ Ploshchad Aleksandra Nevskogo) The Alexander Nevsky Monastery – named for the patron saint of St Petersburg – is the city's most ancient and eminent monastery. Peter the Great made a mistake when he founded the monastery on this spot at the far end of Nevsky pr, thinking wrongly that it was the site where Alexander of Novgorod had beaten the Swedes in 1240. Nonetheless, in 1797 the monastery became a *lavra*, the most senior grade of Russian Orthodox monasteries.

 TOURS

Peterswalk Walking Tours Walking
(📞812-943 1229; http://peterswalk.com; from R1320) Going for over 20 years, Peter Kozyrev's innovative and passionately led tours are highly recommended as a way to see the city with knowledgeable locals. The daily Original Peterswalk (R1320) is one of the favourites and leaves daily from the **Julia Child Bistro** (Map p201; 📞812-929 0797; Grazhdanskaya ul 27; mains R310-490; ⏱9am-11pm Mon-Fri, from 10am Sat & Sun; 📶📷; ⓂSadovaya) at 10.30am from April to end of September. Other tours from around R2000.

The choice of tours available is enormous and includes a Rasputin Walk and a WWII and the Siege of Leningrad tour. There are also regular bicycle tours on Saturday and Sundays at 11am between June and September and departing near the Hermitage, and a night bike tour every Tuesday and Thursday from June to August departing the same location at 10.30pm.

Sputnik Tours Walking
(📞499-110 5266; www.sputnik8.com; price varies) This online tour agency is one with a difference: it acts as a marketplace for locals wanting to give their own unique tours of their own city. Browse, select a tour, register and pay a deposit and then you are given the contact number of the guide. A superb way to meet locals you'd never meet otherwise.

Anglo Tourismo Boating
(Map p196; 📞8-921-989 4722; http://anglotourismo.com; 27 nab reki Fontanki; 1hr cruise adult/student R1900/900; ⓂGostiny Dvor) There's a huge number of companies offering cruises all over the Historic Heart, all with similar prices and itineraries. Anglo Tourismo, however, is the only operator to run tours

 White Nights in St Petersburg

In mid-June the sun slumps lazily towards the horizon, but never fully sets, meaning that the magical nights are a wonderful whitish-grey. At this time Petersburgers indulge themselves in plenty of all-night revelry, several arts festivals take place including the spectacular **Scarlet Sails** (Алые паруса; http://parusaspb.ru; ⏱Jun) extravaganza and the **Stars of the White Nights** (www.mariinsky.ru; ⏱late May–mid-Jul) performing arts program. Though it's the busiest time to visit the city, there's nothing quite like it, so don't miss out – even if you come in May or July you'll be impressed by how late the sun stays out!

Fireworks during Scarlet Sails
DROZDIN VLADIMIR/SHUTTERSTOCK ©

with commentary in English. Between May and September the schedule runs every 1½ hours between 11am and 6.30pm. From 1 June to 31 August there are also additional night cruises.

The company also runs walking tours, including a free one starting daily from mid-May to end of September at 10.30am and lasting three hours.

DenRus Tours
(www.denrus.ru) This long-established shore-excursion operator offers a number of different tours angled specifically towards cruise passengers. Tours can often to be adapted to visitor needs and guides are well trained, experienced and speak good English.

 Performing Arts: How to Buy Tickets

By far the easiest way to buy tickets is online through a performance venue's own website; do this well in advance to make sure you get seats for shows you want to see when you're in St Petersburg. Outside of the busy White Nights season, last-minute tickets are generally easy to find. The standard way to buy tickets on the ground is from a theatre kiosk (театральная касса); these kiosks can be found all over the city, or you can also buy tickets in person from the individual theatre box offices.

Mariinsky Theatre Ballet
SERGEY PETROV/SHUTTERSTOCK ©

 SHOPPING

If *matryoshka* (nesting dolls) aren't your thing, you can enliven your souvenir shopping with pieces of Soviet chic, antiques, street fashion and contemporary arts and crafts.

Kupetz Eliseevs   Food & Drinks

(Map p196; ☑812-456 6666; www.kupetzeliseevs. ru; Nevsky pr 56; ⏱10am-11pm; 🛜; Ⓜ Gostiny Dvor) This Style Moderne stunner is St Petersburg's most elegant grocery store, selling plenty of branded goods from blends of tea to caviar and handmade chocolates as well as delicious freshly baked breads, pastries and cakes. Kids will love watching the animatronic figures in the window display and there are pleasant cafes on the ground floor and in the former wine cellar.

Au Pont Rouge   Department Store

(Map p196; https://aupontrouge.ru; nab reki Moyki 73-79; ⏱10am-10pm; Ⓜ Admiralteyskaya)

Dating from 1906–7, the one-time Esders and Scheefhaals department store has been beautifully restored and is one of the most glamorous places to shop in the city. This glorious Style Moderne building is now dubbed Au Pont Rouge after the Krasny most (Red Bridge) it stands beside. Inside you'll find choice fashions and accessories and top-notch souvenirs.

8 Store   Fashion & Accessories

(Map p196; ☑8-981-741 1880; http://8-store. ru; Dvortsovaya nab 20; ⏱1-9pm; Ⓜ Admiralteyskaya) If you're looking for affordable Russian designer fashions, accessories, interior objects and souvenirs, this chic boutique is worth searching out.

Imenno Lavka   Gifts & Souvenirs

(Именно-лавка; Map p196; ☑8-921-581 0466; www.imenno-lavka.ru; TAIGA, Dvortsovaya nab 20; ⏱11am-7pm; Ⓜ Admiralteyskaya) In front of this design office is a small boutique showcasing interesting gifts, accessories, books and interior-design products by local talents. Look out for the bear and wolf heads and wooden beard masks by Alexander Kanygin.

Bolshoy Gostiny Dvor   Mall

(Большой Гостиный Двор; Map p196; ☑812-630 5408; http://bgd.ru; Nevsky pr 35; ⏱10am-10pm; Ⓜ Gostiny Dvor) One of the world's first indoor shopping malls, the 'Big Merchant Yard' dates from between 1757 and 1785 and stretches 230m along Nevsky pr (its perimeter is more than 1km long). This Rastrelli creation is not as elaborate as some of his other work, finished as it was by Vallin de la Mothe in a more sober neoclassical style.

 EATING

Khachapuri i Vino   Georgian $

(Map p202; ☑812-273 6797; Mayokovskogo 56; mains R310-390; ⏱noon-midnight; 🛜 ✐; Ⓜ Chernyshevskaya) This welcoming, warmly lit space serves outstanding Georgian fare. The recipes aren't overly complicated and the fine ingredients speak for themselves

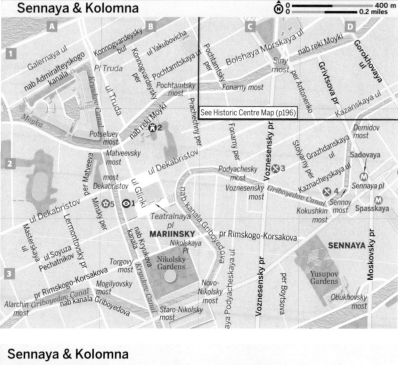

Sennaya & Kolomna

◎ **Sights**
1 Mariinsky Theatre B2
2 Yusupov Palace B2

✖ **Eating**
3 Julia Child Bistro C2

4 Severyanin D2

✪ **Entertainment**
5 Mariinsky II B2
  Mariinsky Theatre .... (see 1)

in flavour-rich dishes like aubergine baked with *suluguni* (a type of cheese), pork dumplings, and tender lamb stew with coriander. Don't miss the excellent *khachapuri* (cheese bread), which comes in a dozen varieties and is whipped up by the bakers in front.

Zoom Café
European $

(Map p196; ☎812-612 1329; www.cafezoom.ru; Gorokhovaya ul 22; mains R350-550; ☺9am-midnight Mon-Fri, from 11am Sat, from 1pm Sun; 🛜🍴👶; Ⓜ Nevsky Prospekt) A perennially popular cafe (expect to wait for a table at peak times) with a cosy feel and an interesting menu, ranging from Japanese-style

chicken in teriyaki sauce to potato pancakes with salmon and cream cheese. Well-stocked bookshelves, a range of board games and adorable cuddly toys (each with its own name) encourage lingering.

Yat
Russian $$

(Ять; Map p196; ☎812-957 0023; www.eatinyat. com; nab reki Moyki 16; mains R370-750; ☺11am-11pm; 🛜👶; Ⓜ Admiralteyskaya) Perfectly placed for eating near the Hermitage, this country-cottage-style restaurant has a very appealing menu of traditional dishes, presented with aplomb. The *shchi* (cabbage-based soup) is excellent, and there is also a tempting range of flavoured

Smolny & Vosstaniya

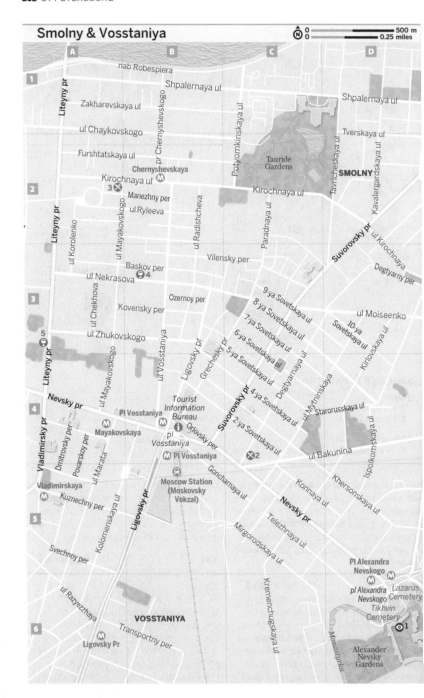

N
0 ————————— 500 m
0 ————————— 0.25 miles

nab Robespiera

Shpalernaya ul

Liteyny pr

Zakharevskaya ul

ul Chaykovskogo

pr Chernyshevskogo

Furshtatskaya ul

Chernyshevskaya Ⓜ

Kirochnaya ul

3 ✕

Manezhny per

ul Ryleeva

ul Korolenko

ul Mayakovskogo

Liteyny pr

ul Radishcheva

Baskov per

4 Ⓜ

ul Nekrasova

ul Chekhova

Ozernoy per

Kovensky per

ul Zhukovskogo

5 Ⓜ

Liteyny pr

ul Mayakovskogo

ul Vosstaniya

Ligovsky pr

Grechesky pr

Potyomkinskaya ul

Tauride Gardens

SMOLNY

Shpalernaya ul

Tverskaya ul

Tavricheskaya ul

Kirochnaya ul

Paradnaya ul

Vilensky per

9-ya Sovetskaya ul

8-ya Sovetskaya ul

7-ya Sovetskaya ul

6-ya Sovetskaya ul

5-ya Sovetskaya ul

4-ya Sovetskaya ul

Degtyarnaya ul

Suvorovsky pr

ul Kirochnaya

Kavalergardskaya ul

Degtyarny per

ul Moiseenko

10-ya Sovetskaya ul

Kirillovskaya ul

2-ya Sovetskaya ul

ul Mytninskaya

Starorusskaya ul

Nevsky pr

Pl Vosstaniya Ⓜ

Tourist Information Bureau
ⓘ

Orlovsky per

Mayakovskaya Ⓜ

pl Vosstaniya

Ⓜ Pl Vosstaniya

2 ✕

ul Bakunina

Vladimirsky pr

Dmitrovsky per

Povarskoy per

ul Marata

Moscow Station (Moskovsky Vokzal)

Goncharnaya ul

Konnaya ul

Khersonskaya ul

Ispolkomskaya ul

Vladimirskaya Ⓜ

Kuznechny per

Kolomenskaya ul

Nevsky pr

Telezhnaya ul

Svechnoy per

Mirgorodskaya ul

Kremenchugskaya ul

Pl Alexandra Nevskogo Ⓜ

pl Alexandra Nevskogo

Lazarus Cemetery

Tikhvin Cemetery

ul Razyezzhaya

VOSSTANIYA

Transportny per

Ligovsky Pr Ⓜ

1 ◉

Monastyrka

Alexander Nevsky Gardens

Smolny & Vosstaniya

vodkas. There's a fab kids area with pet rabbits for them to feed.

Gräs x Madbaren   Fusion $$

(Map p196; ☏812-928 1818; http://grasmad baren.com; ul Inzhenernaya 7; mains R420-550, tasting menu R2500; ⊗1-11pm Sun-Thu, until 1am Fri & Sat; 🛜; Ⓜ Gostiny Dvor) Anton Abrezov is the talented exec chef behind this Scandi-cool meets Russian locavore restaurant where you can sample dishes such as a delicious corned beef salad with black garlic and pickled vegetables or an upmarket twist on ramen noodles with succulent roast pork.

The connected cocktail bar Madbaren is equally inventive, offering libations such as Siberian Penicillin (horseradish vodka, pollen syrup and rhubarb).

Chekhov   Russian $$

(Чехов; ☏812-234 4511; http://restaurant-chekhov.ru; Petropavlovskaya ul 4; mains R550-890; ⊗noon-11pm; Ⓜ Petrogradskaya) Despite a totally nondescript appearance from the street, this restaurant's charming interior perfectly recalls that of a 19th-century dacha (summer country house) and makes for a wonderful setting for a meal. The menu, hidden inside classic novels, features lovingly prepared dishes such as roasted venison with bilberry sauce or Murmansk sole with dill potatoes and stewed leeks.

Severyanin   Russian $$

(Северянин; Map p201; ☏8-921-951 6396; www.severyanin.me; Stolyarny per 18; mains R620-1300; ⊗noon-midnight; 🛜; Ⓜ Sennaya Ploshchad) An old-fashioned elegance pre-vails at Severyanin, one of the top choices for Russian cuisine near Sennaya pl. Amid vintage wallpaper, mirrored armoires and tasselled lampshades, you might feel like you've stepped back a few decades. Start

off with the excellent mushroom soup or borsch (beetroot soup), before moving on to rabbit ragout in puff pastry or Baltic flounder with wine sauce.

Banshiki   Russian $$

(Банщики; Map p202; ☏8-921-941 1744; www. banshiki.spb.ru; Degtyanaya 1; mains R500-1100; ⊗11am-11pm; 🛜; Ⓜ Pl Vosstaniya) Although it opened in 2017, Banshiki has already earned a sterling reputation for its excellent Russian cuisine, serving up a huge variety of nostalgic dishes with a contemporary touch. Everything is made in-house, from its refreshing *kvas* (fermented rye bread water) to dried meats and eight types of smoked fish. Don't overlook cherry *vareniki* (dumplings) with sour cream, oxtail ragout or the rich borsch.

🍷 DRINKING & NIGHTLIFE

Redrum   Bar

(Map p202; ☏812-416 1126; www.facebook.com/ redrumbarspb; ul Nekrasova 26; ⊗4pm-1am Sun-Thu, to 3am Fri & Sat; Ⓜ Mayakovskaya) One of St Petersburg's best drinking dens, Red-rum hits all the right notes. It has a cosy, white brick interior, a welcoming, easygoing crowd, and a stellar selection of craft brews (some two dozen on tap). There's also good pub fare on hand to go with that creative line-up of Session Indian Pale Ales, sour ales, Berliner Weisse and porters.

Union Bar & Grill   Bar

(Map p202; www.facebook.com/barunion; Liteyny pr 55; ⊗6pm-4am Sun-Thu, to 6am Fri & Sat; 🛜; Ⓜ Mayakovskaya) The Union is a glamorous and fun place, characterised by one enor-mous long wooden bar, low lighting and a New York feel. It's all rather adult, with a serious cocktail list and designer beers on

Mariinsky Theatre

tap. The hip 20- and 30-something crowd packs in on weekends to catch live bands, but it's generally quiet during the week.

Kabinet   Cocktail Bar

(Map p196; ☎8-911-921 1944; www.instagram. com/kabinet_bar; Malaya Sadovaya ul 8; ⊙8am-6pm; ⓜGostiny Dvor) Bookings are essential for this speakeasy cocktail bar styled as a secret poker joint and hidden beneath the Grill Brothers burger restaurant. It's a fun, sophisticated place with the waiters dealing sets of cards to determine your choice of cocktail.

⭐ ENTERTAINMENT

The classical performing arts are one of the biggest draws to St Petersburg. Highly acclaimed professional artists stage productions in elegant theatres around the city, many of which have been recently revamped and look marvellous. Seeing a Russian opera, ballet or classical-music performance in a magnificent baroque theatre is a highlight of any trip.

Mariinsky Theatre   Ballet, Opera

(Мариинский театр; Map p201; ☎812-326 4141; www.mariinsky.ru; Teatralnaya pl 1; tickets R1200-6500; ⓜSadovaya) St Petersburg's most spectacular venue for ballet and opera, the Mariinsky Theatre is an attraction in its own right. Tickets can be bought online or in person; book in advance during the summer months. The magnificent interior is the epitome of imperial grandeur, and any evening here will be an impressive experience.

The Mariinsky Theatre will close at some point in 2018 or 2019 for a full (and, again, much needed) renovation.

Mikhailovsky
Theatre   Performing Arts

(Михайловский театр; Map p196; ☎812-595 4305; www.mikhailovsky.ru; pl Iskusstv 1; tickets R500-5000; ⓜNevsky Prospekt) This illustrious stage delivers the Russian ballet or operatic experience, complete with multitiered theatre, frescoed ceiling and elaborate productions. Pl Iskusstv (Arts Sq) is a lovely setting for this respected venue, which is home to the State Academic Opera & Ballet Company.

Alexandrinsky Theatre   Theatre

(Map p196; 812-710 4103; www.alexandrin-sky.ru; pl Ostrovskogo 2; tickets R900-6000; Gostiny Dvor) This magnificent venue is just one part of an immaculate architectural ensemble designed by Carlo Rossi. The theatre's interior oozes 19th-century elegance and style, and it's worth taking a peek even if you don't see a production here.

This is where Anton Chekhov premiered *The Seagull* in 1896; the play was so badly received on opening that the playwright fled to wander anonymously among the crowds on Nevsky pr. Chekhov is now a beloved part of the theatre's huge repertoire, ranging from Russian folktales to Shakespearean tragedies.

Head through the archway in the southwest corner of the square to find the Alexanderinsky's **New Stage** (Новая сцена; Map p196; 812-401 5341; nab reki Fontanki 49a; Gostiny Dvor).

ℹ INFORMATION

Tourist information is decent in St Petersburg, and in addition to the **Tourist Information Bureau's main office** (Map p196; 812-303 0555, 812-242 3909; http://eng.ispb.info; Sadovaya ul 14/52; 10am-7pm Mon-Sat; Gostiny Dvor), just off Nevsky pr in the Historic Heart, there is an office in **Smolny** (Map p202; pl Vosstaniya; 10am-7pm; Ploshchad Vosstaniya), and kiosks at **Palace Square** (Map p196; 8-931-326 5744; Dvortsovaya pl; 10am-7pm; Admiralteyskaya) and **St Isaac's Cathedral** (Map p196; Isaakievskaya pl; 10am-7pm; Admiralteyskaya).

ℹ GETTING AROUND

Metro Fastest way to cover long distances. Has around 70 stations and runs from approximately 5.45am to 12.45am. The flat fare for a trip is R45.

Organising a Russian Visa

Most nationalities (Israel, South Africa, South Korea and several South American nations are among those who do not) normally need a visa to enter Russia. Cruise passengers can enter St Petersburg visa-free for 72 hours, but you can only do so on condition that a tour is purchased through an officially recognised travel agency (which need not be the one offered by the cruise company), which gives you little freedom. Contracting a guided tour independently may allow you to negotiate some free time or even just pay for transport from and to the ship, but the best way to be truly independent is to get a Russian visa before you leave home. Allow at least a month; the most annoying part of the visa process is the need to provide an invitation (also called visa support) from a hotel or travel agency. Several online agencies do this for about US$30. There is also a hefty visa fee. The process probably isn't worth it if you're not at least overnighting in St Petersburg.

Bus, Trolleybus & Marshrutky Buses are best for shorter distances in areas without good metro coverage; they can be slow going, but the views are good. Trolleybuses are slower still, but are cheap and plentiful. *Marshrutky* are the private sector's contribution – fast fixed-route minibuses that you can get on or off anywhere along their routes. Fares vary; pay the driver directly.

Tram Largely obsolete and little used, but still useful in areas such as Kolomna and Vasilyevsky Island where there is little else available.

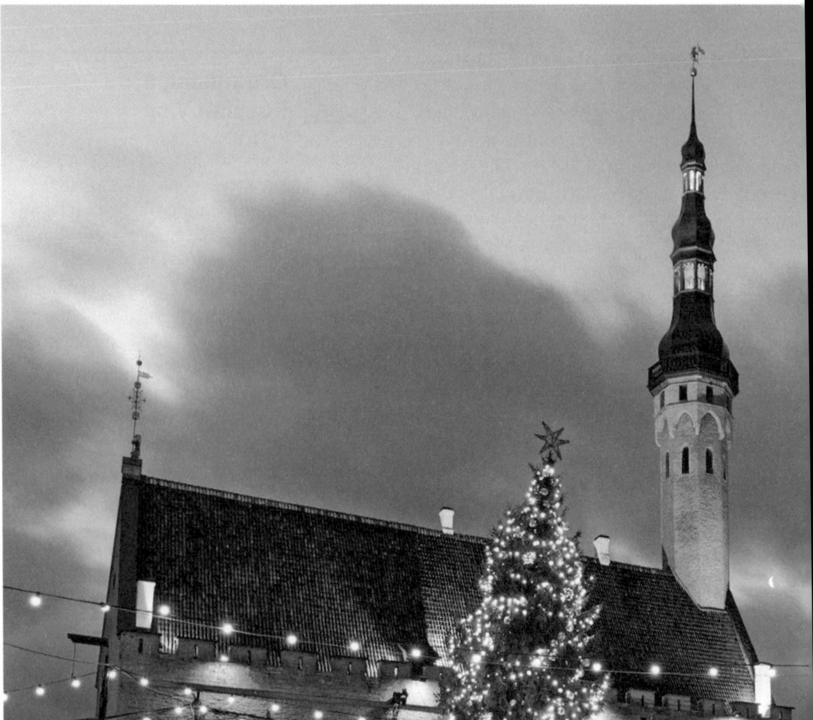

TALLINN, ESTONIA

Tallinn at a Glance...

Tallinn is a proud European capital with an allure that's all its own. The city is lively yet peaceful, absurdly photogenic and bursting with wonderful sights – ancient churches, medieval streetscapes and noble merchants' houses. Throw in delightful food and vibrant modern culture and it's no wonder Tallinn is so popular.

Despite the boom of 21st-century development, Tallinn safeguards the fairy-tale charms of its Unesco-listed Old Town – one of Europe's most complete walled cities. And the blossoming of first-rate restaurants, atmospheric hotels and a well-oiled tourist machine makes visiting a breeze.

With One Day in Port

Spend your first day exploring **Old Town** (p212). Tackle our **walking tour** (p212) in the morning, then spend your afternoon exploring one or two of the museums – perhaps the **Hotel Viru KGB Museum** (p215) and the branch of the Estonian History Museum at the **Great Guild Hall** (p214).

Best Places for...

Vegetarians/Vegans Vegan Restoran V (p220)

Coffee RØST Pagar & Kohvik (p220)

Classic Estonian food Rataskaevu 16 (p220)

New Estonian food Leib (p220)

Wine Gloria Wine Cellar (p221)

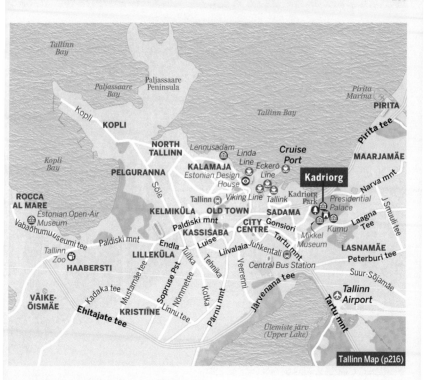

Tallinn Map (p216)

Getting from the Port

Cruise ships dock at the Old City Harbour, a pleasant 700m stroll to the Old Town. Free shuttles are also on hand to take you to the gate of that district. Dodge the organised tours and follow your own path.

Fast Facts

Currency Euro (€)

Language Estonian

Free wi-fi Ubiquitous in cafes, restaurants and bars. Many squares and other public places also have it.

Tourist information Tallinn Tourist Information Centre (p221) is in the Old Town.

Transport A compact and walkable city, with cheap, reliable public transport.

Kadriorg

Many visitors to Tallinn never make it out of the Old Town but Kadriorg, just to the east of central Tallinn, is blessed with wide parklands and great art galleries.

Great For...

☑ Don't Miss

Avant-garde contemporary exhibitions at Kumu.

Kadriorg Park

About 2km east of Old Town, this beautiful park's ample acreage is Tallinn's favourite patch of green. Together with the baroque Kadriorg Palace, it was commissioned by the Russian tsar Peter the Great for his wife Catherine I soon after his conquest of Estonia (Kadriorg means 'Catherine's Valley' in Estonian).

Nowadays the oak, lilac and horse chestnut trees give shade to strollers and picnickers, the formal pond and gardens provide a genteel backdrop for romantic promenades and wedding photos, and the children's playground is a favourite free-for-all for the city's youngsters. Stop by the **park's information centre** (Kadrioru pargi infopunkt; Weizenbergi 33; ⊘10am-5pm Wed-Sun), housed in a pretty 18th-century cottage near the main entrance, to see a scale model of the palace and its grounds.

Kadriorg Palace

⚓ Explore Ashore

It's a short ride from central Tallin. Tram 3 stops right by Kadriorg Park. Buses 1A and 34A (among others) stop at the J Poska stop on Narva mnt, near the foot of the park, while buses 31, 67 and 68 head to the Kumu end.

❶ Need to Know

Kadrioru park; www.kadriorupark.ee

Kadriorg Palace

Kadriorg Palace, a baroque beauty built by Peter the Great between 1718 and 1736, houses a branch of the **Estonian Art Museum** (Kardrioru kunstimuuseum; ☎606 6400; www.kadriorumuuseum.ekm.ee; A Weizenbergi 37, Kadriorg Palace; adult/child €6.50/4.50; ☺10am-6pm Tue & Thu-Sun May-Sep, to 5pm Thu-Sun Oct-Apr, to 8pm Wed year-round) devoted to Dutch, German and Italian paintings from the 16th to the 18th centuries, and Russian works from the 18th to early 20th centuries (check out the decorative porcelain with Communist imagery upstairs). The pink building is exactly as frilly and fabulous as a palace ought to be and there's a handsome French-style formal garden at the rear.

Mikkel Museum

The Estonian Art Museum's collection spills over into this former **kitchen for Kadriorg**

Palace (Mikkeli muuseum; ☎606 6400; www.mikkelimuuseum.ekm.ee; A Weizenbergi 28; adult/child €6/3.50; ☺10am-6pm Tue & Thu-Sun May-Sep, to 5pm Thu-Sun Oct-Apr, to 8pm Wed year-round; P). It displays a small but interesting assortment of paintings and porcelain, along with temporary exhibitions. There are several joint-admission ticketing options.

Presidential Palace

Echoing the style of Kadriorg Palace, this **grand building** (A Weizenbergi 39) was purpose-built in 1938 to serve as the official residence of the Estonian president – a role it once again fulfils. It's not open to the public, but you can peer through the gates at the honour guards out front.

Kumu

This futuristic, Finnish-designed, seven-storey **building** (☎602 6000; www.kumu.ekm.ee; A Weizenbergi 34; adult/student €8/6; ☺10am-8pm Thu, to 6pm Wed & Fri-Sun year-round, plus 10am-6pm Tue Apr-Sep) is a spectacular structure of limestone, glass and copper, nicely integrated into the landscape. Kumu (the name is short for *kunstimuuseum,* or art museum) contains the country's largest repository of Estonian art as well as constantly changing contemporary exhibits. There's everything from venerable painted altarpieces to the work of contemporary Estonian artists such as Adamson-Eric. The complex has an excellent shop and cafe.

Tallinn's Old Town

Wandering around the medieval streets of Tallinn is one of Scandinavia's most rewarding urban pastimes, although you could spend days in this pleasurable pursuit.

Start Kiek in de Kök
Distance 4km
Duration three hours

Classic Photo Lower Town Wall offers terrific red-rooftop views plus it is the most photogenic stretch of Tallinn's remaining walls.

5 Lower Town Wall (p214) links nine of the 26 remaining towers (there were once 45).

Take a Break... Stop for down-home Estonian cooking at **Vanaema Juures** (www.vonkrahl.ee/vanaemajuures; Rataskaevu 10/12; ⓧnoon-10pm).

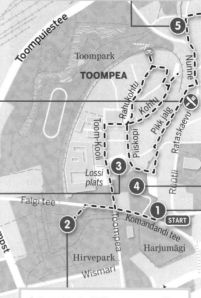

3 Castle Square (Lossi plats) is dominated by pretty, onion-domed **Alexander Nevsky Orthodox Cathedral** (p218).

2 From **Linda Hill** you can see the remaining medieval elements of Toompea Castle.

6 The 1860-built **St Canute's Guild Hall** is topped with zinc statues of Martin Luther and the guild's patron saint.

7 The 1410 headquarters of the **Great Guild** (p214), to which the most eminent merchants belonged, is now an intriguing museum.

4 At **Danish King's Garden**, artists set up their easels in summer to capture the ageless vista over Tallinn's rooftops.

1 The tall, stout 15th-century **Kiek in de Kök** cannon tower was one of Tallinn's most formidable defences.

⊙ SIGHTS

Town Hall Square
Square

(Raekoja plats) In Tallinn all roads lead to Raekoja plats, the city's pulsing heart since markets began setting up here in the 11th century. One side is dominated by the Gothic town hall, while the rest is ringed by pretty pastel-coloured buildings dating from the 15th to 17th centuries. Whether bathed in sunlight or sprinkled with snow, it's always a photogenic spot.

Tallinn Town Hall
Historic Building

(Tallinna raekoda; ☏ 645 7900; www.raekoda. tallinn.ee; Raekoja plats; adult/student €5/2; ☺ 10am-4pm Mon-Sat Jul & Aug, shorter hours rest of year; 🚹) Completed in 1404, this is the only surviving Gothic town hall in Northern Europe. Inside, you can visit the Trade Hall (whose visitor book drips with royal signatures), the Council Chamber (featuring Estonia's oldest woodcarvings, dating from 1374), the vaulted Citizens' Hall, a yellow-and-black-tiled councillor's office and a small kitchen. The steeply sloped attic has displays on the building and its restoration.

Details such as brightly painted columns and intricately carved wooden friezes give some sense of the original splendour.

Great Guild Hall
Museum

(Suurgildi hoone; ☏ 696 8693; www.ajaloomuu-seum.ee; Pikk 17; adult/child €6/3; ☺ 10am-6pm, closed Wed Oct-Apr) The Estonian History Museum has filled the striking 1410 Great Guild building with a series of ruminations on the Estonian psyche, presented through interactive and unusual displays. Coin collectors shouldn't miss the old excise chamber, with its numismatic relics stretching back to Viking times, while military nuts should head downstairs. The basement also covers the history of the Great Guild itself, while Estonian music, language, geography and deep history all win consideration.

Lower Town Wall
Fortress

(Linnamüür; ☏ 644 9867; Väike-Kloostri 1; adult/child €2/0.75; ☺ 11am-7pm Jun-Aug, shorter hours/days rest of year) The most photogenic stretch of Tallinn's remaining walls connects nine towers lining the western edge of Old Town. Visitors can explore the barren nooks

Estonian Open-Air Museum

and crannies of three of them (there are modest displays on weaponry and castle--craft inside) with cameras at the ready for the red-rooftop views. The gardens outside the wall are pretty and relaxing.

St Mary's Lutheran Cathedral   Church

(Tallinna Püha Neitsi Maarja Piiskoplik toomkirik; ☑644 4140; www.toomkirik.ee; Toom-Kooli 6; church/tower €2/5; ☺9am-5pm May & Sep, to 6pm Jun-Aug, shorter hours/days rest of year) Tallinn's cathedral (now Lutheran, originally Catholic) had been initially built by the Danes by at least 1233, although the exterior dates mainly from the 15th century, with the tower completed in 1779. This impressive building was a burial ground for the rich and titled, and the whitewashed walls are decorated with the elaborate coats-of-arms of Estonia's noble families. Fit view-seekers can climb the tower.

Hotel Viru KGB Museum   Museum

(☑680 9300; www.viru.ee; Viru väljak 4; tour €12; ☺daily May-Oct, Tue-Sun Nov-Apr) When the Hotel Viru was built in 1972, it was not only Estonia's first skyscraper, it was the only place for tourists to stay in Tallinn – and we mean that literally. Having all the foreigners in one place made it much easier to keep tabs on them and the locals they had contact with, which is exactly what the KGB did from its 23rd-floor spy base. The hotel offers fascinating tours of the facility in various languages; bookings essential.

St Catherine's Cloister   Church

(www.claustrum.eu; Müürivahe 33; adult/child €2/1; ☺11am-5pm mid-May–Sep) Perhaps Tallinn's oldest building, St Catherine's Monastery was founded by Dominican monks in 1246. In its glory days it had its own brewery and hospital. A mob of angry Lutherans torched the place in 1524 and the monastery languished for the next 400 years until its partial restoration in 1954. Today the ruined complex includes the gloomy shell of the barren church (which makes an atmospheric venue for occasional recitals) and a peaceful cloister lined with carved tombstones.

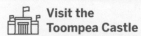

Visit the Toompea Castle

Lording it over the lower part of Old Town is the ancient hilltop citadel of **Toompea** (Lossi plats). In German times this was the preserve of the feudal nobility, literally looking down on the traders and lesser beings below. It's now almost completely given over to government buildings, churches, embassies and shops selling amber knick-knacks and fridge magnets, and is correspondingly quieter than the teeming streets below.

Estonian Open-Air Museum   Museum

(Eesti vabaõhumuuseum; ☑654 9101; www.evm. ee; Vabaõhumuuseumi tee 12, Rocca Al Mare; adult/child €9/6 high season, €7/5 low season; ☺10am-8pm 23 Apr-28 Sep, to 5pm 29 Sep-22 Apr) If tourists won't go to the countryside, let's bring the countryside to them. That's the modus operandi of this excellent, sprawling complex, where historic Estonian buildings have been plucked and transplanted among the tall trees. In summer the time-warping effect is highlighted by staff in period costume performing traditional activities among the wooden farmhouses and windmills. There's a chapel dating from 1699 and an old wooden tavern, Kolu Kõrts, serving traditional Estonian cuisine.

Activities such as weaving, blacksmithing, and traditional cooking are put on, kids love the horse-and-carriage rides (adult/child €9/6) and bikes can be hired (per hour €3). If you find yourself in Tallinn on Midsummer's Eve (23 June), come here to witness the traditional celebrations, bonfire and all.

To get here from the centre, take Paldiski mnt. When the road nears the water, veer right onto Vabaõhumuuseumi tee. Bus 21, which departs from the **railway station** (Balti Jaam; Toompuiestee 35) at least hourly, stops right out front. Combined family tickets are available that include **Tallinn Zoo** (Tallinna loomaaed; ☑694 3300; www.tallinnzoo.ee; Paldiski mnt 145, Veskimetsa; adult/child €8/5; ☺9am-

Tallinn

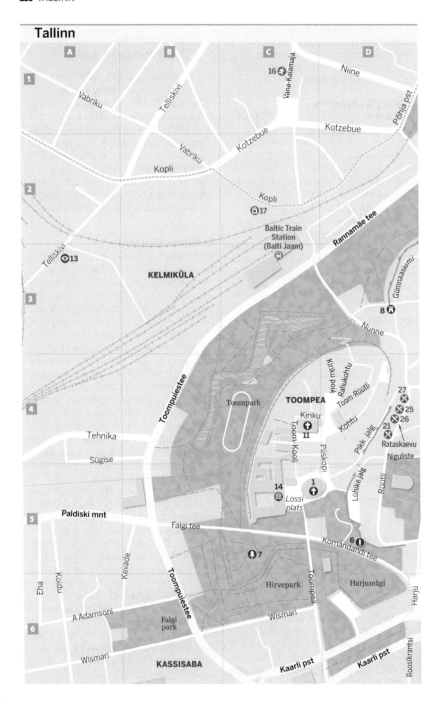

A
B
C
D

1

Vabriku
Telliskivi
Vana-Kalamaja
16
Niine
Kotzebue
Kotzebue
Põhja pst

2

Vabriku
Kopli
Kopli
17
Telliskivi
13
Baltic Train Station (Balti Jaam)
Rannamäe tee

KELMIKÜLA

3

Gümnaasiumi
8
Nunne

Toompuiestee
Toompark

4

TOOMPEA
Kiriku põik
Rahukohtu
Toom-Rüütli
27
25
26
Kiriku
Toom-Kooli
11
Kohtu
Pikk jalg
21
Rataskaevu
Piiskopi
Niguliste

5

Tehnika
Sügise
Paldiski mnt
Falgi tee
14
1
Lossi plats
Lühike jalg
Rüütli
6

KASSISABA

6

Eha
Koidu
Kevade
A Adamsoni
Toompuiestee
Falgi park
7
Hirvepark
Komandandi tee
Toompea
Wismari
Harjumägi
Harju
Wismari
Kaarli pst
Kaarli pst
Roosikrantsi

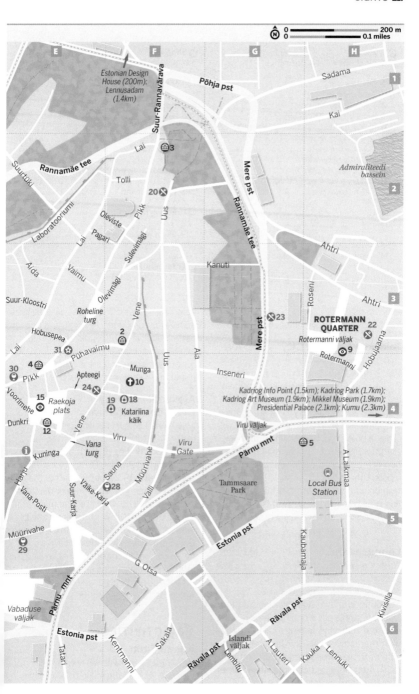

Tallinn

8pm May-Aug, to 7pm Mar, Apr, Sep & Oct, to 5pm Nov-Feb), which is a 20-minute walk away.

Telliskivi Creative City   Area

(Telliskivi Loomelinnak; www.telliskivi.eu; Telliskivi 60a; ⊘shops 10am-6pm Mon-Sat, 11am-5pm Sun; 🚲) Once literally on the wrong side of the tracks, this set of abandoned factory buildings is now Tallinn's most alternative shopping and entertainment precinct, with cafes, a bike shop, bars selling craft beer, graffiti walls, artist studios, food trucks and pop-up concept stores. But it's not only hipsters that flock to Telliskivi to peruse the fashion and design stores, drink espressos and riffle through the stalls at the weekly flea market – you're as likely to see families rummaging and sipping.

Lennusadam   Museum

(Seaplane Harbour; 🕿620 0550; www.meremuu-seum.ee; Vesilennuki 6; adult/child €14/7; ⊘10am-7pm daily May-Sep, to 6pm Tue-Sun Oct-Apr; P) Surrounded on two sides by island-dotted waters, Estonia has a rich maritime history, explored in this fascinating museum filled with interactive displays. When the building, with its triple-domed hangar, was completed in 1917, its reinforced-concrete shell frame construction was unique in the world. Re-sembling a classic Bond-villain lair, the vast space was completely restored and opened to the public in 2012. Highlights include exploring the cramped corridors of a 1930s naval submarine, and the icebreaker and minehunter ships moored outside.

Alexander Nevsky Orthodox Cathedral   Cathedral

(🕿644 3484; http://tallinnanevskikatedraal.eu; Lossi plats 10; ⊘8am-7pm, to 4pm winter) The positioning of this magnificent, onion-domed Russian Orthodox cathedral (completed in 1900) at the heart of the country's main administrative hub was no accident: the church was one of many built during the late 19th century as part of a general wave of Russification in the empire's Baltic provinces. Orthodox believers come here in droves, alongside tourists ogling the interior's striking icons and frescoes. Quiet, respectful, demurely dressed visitors are welcome, but cameras aren't.

ACTIVITIES

Kalma Saun   Spa

(🕿627 1811; www.kalmasaun.ee; Vana-Kalamaja 9a; €9-10; ⊘11am-10pm Mon-Fri, 10am-11pm

Sat & Sun) In a grand 1928 building behind the train station, Tallinn's oldest public sauna still has the aura of an old-fashioned, Russian-style *banya* (bathhouse) – flagellation with a birch branch is definitely on the cards. It has separate men's and women's sections (the women's is slightly cheaper) and private saunas are available (per hour €20; up to six people).

TOURS

Tallinn Traveller Tours　　Tours

(☑58374800; www.traveller.ee) This outfit runs entertaining tours – including a two-hour Old Town walk (private groups of 1-15 people from €80, or there's a larger free tour, for which you should tip the engaging guides) departing from outside the tourist office (p221). There are also ghost tours (€15), bike tours (from €19), pub crawls (€20) and day trips as far afield as Rīga (€55).

Euroaudioguide　　Walking

(www.euroaudioguide.com; iPod rental €15) Preloaded iPods available from the tourist office (p221) offer excellent commentary on most Old Town sights, with plenty of history thrown in. If you've got your own iPod, iPhone or iPad you can download the tour as an e-book (€10).

SHOPPING

The city's glitziest shopping precinct is the **Rotermann Quarter** (Rotermanni kvartal; ☑626 4200; www.rotermann.eu; Rotermanni 8), a clutch of former warehouses now sheltering dozens of small stores selling everything from streetwear to Scandinavian-designed furniture, artisanal cheese, good wines, top-notch bread and dry-aged beef. Telliskivi Creative City has fewer but more unusual shops, and you'll be tripping over *käsitöö* (handicraft) stores everywhere in Old Town.

Katariina Käik　　Arts & Crafts

(St Catherine's Passage; www.katariinagild.eu; off Vene 12; ⊙noon-6pm Mon-Sat) This lovely medieval lane is home to the Katariina Guild, comprising eight artisans' studios where you can happily browse the work of 14 female creators. Look for ceramics, textiles, patchwork quilts, hats, jewellery, stained glass and beautiful leather-bound books. Opening hours can vary among the different studios.

Masters' Courtyard　　Arts & Crafts

(Meistrite Hoov; www.hoov.ee; Vene 6; ⊙10am-6pm) Archetypal of Tallinn's amber-suspended medieval beauty, this cobbled 13th-century courtyard offers rich pickings – a cosy chocolaterie/cafe, a guesthouse, and artisans' stores and workshops selling quality ceramics, glass, jewellery, knitwear, woodwork and candles.

Balti Jaama Turg　　Market

(Baltic Station Market; https://astri.ee/bjt; Kopli 1; ⊙9am-7pm Mon-Sat, to 5pm Sun) The gentrification of the train station precinct is manifest in this sleek new market complex, where niche food vendors trade from tidy huts on the former site of a famed but slightly seedy outdoor market. There's also a supermarket, meat, dairy and seafood halls, green grocers, fashion retailers, a gym and underground parking.

Estonian Design House　　Gifts & Souvenirs

(Eesti Disaini Maja; www.estoniandesignhouse. ee; Kalasadama 8; ⊙11am-7pm Mon-Fri, to 6pm Sat & Sun) This slick little store showcases the work of over 100 Estonian designers – everything from shoes to lamps, furniture to ceramics. Keep an eye out for the 'slow fashion' of local designer Reet Aus, who creates clothes for her label out of offcuts from mass-production processes.

Chado　　Drinks

(☑648 4318; www.chado.ee; Uus 11; ⊙noon-6pm Mon-Fri, 11am-4pm Sat & Sun) These passionate provedores specialise in tea in all of its comforting forms, sourcing many of the shop's leaves directly from Asia. Drop by to chat chai with the clued-up staff or pick up delectable artisanal chocolate.

EATING

Vegan Restoran V   Vegan €
(☏626 9087; www.vonkrahl.ee; Rataskaevu 12;
mains €9-11; ◷noon-11pm Sun-Thu, to midnight
Fri & Sat; ✐) Visiting vegans are spoiled for
choice in this wonderful restaurant. In summer everyone wants one of the four tables on
the street, but the atmospheric interior is just
as appealing. The food is excellent – expect
the likes of tempeh and veggies on brown
rice with tomato-coconut sauce, and kale and
lentil pie with creamy hemp-seed sauce.

RØST Pagar & Kohvik   Bakery €
(☏55604732; http://rost.ee; Rotermanni 14;
snacks €3; ◷9am-6pm Tue-Fri, 10am-5pm Sat)
This fabulous little artisan bakery makes
dense, almost fruity Estonian bread,
sourdoughs, spiced pastries and other
delightful things to accompany its carefully
selected and expertly prepared coffee.

Rataskaevu 16   Estonian €€
(☏642 4025; www.rataskaevu16.ee; Rataskaevu 16; mains €14-16; ◷noon-11pm Sun-Thu, to
midnight Fri & Sat; ⛲) If you've ever had a
hankering for braised elk roast, this warm,
stone-walled place, named simply for its
Old Town address, can sate it. Although it's
hardly traditional, plenty of Estonian faves
fill the menu – fried Baltic herrings, grilled
pork tenderloin and Estonian cheeses
among them. Finish, if you can, with a serve
of the legendary warm chocolate cake.

Sfäär   Modern European €€
(☏56992200; www.sfaar.ee; Mere pst 6e; mains
€13-14; ◷8am-10pm Mon-Fri, from 10am Sat,
10am-5pm Sun; ☎) Chic Sfäär delivers an
inventive menu highlighting great Estonian
produce in dishes that gesture east (tempu-
ra) and west (beef tartare). The warehouse-
style setting is like something out of a
Nordic design catalogue, the cocktail and
wine list won't disappoint and if the lubrica-
tion loosens the purse strings sufficiently,
there's a pricey fashion store attached.

Von Krahli Aed Modern European €€
(☏58593839; www.vonkrahl.ee; Rataskaevu
8; mains €13-16; ◷noon-midnight Mon-Sat, to
11pm Sun; ☎✐) You'll find plenty of greenery
on your plate at this rustic, plant-filled
restaurant (aed means 'garden'), beneath
the rough beams of a medieval merchant's
house. Veggies star here (although all dishes can be ordered with some kind of fleshy
embellishment) and there's care taken to
offer vegan dishes and gluten-, lactose- and
egg-free options.

Leib   Estonian €€€
(☏611 9026; www.leibresto.ee; Uus 31; mains
€17-19; ◷noon-11pm) Leib (Estonian black
bread) is a thing of great beauty and quiet
national pride, and you'll find a peerless
rendition here: dense, moist, almost fruity
in its Christmas-cake complexity. Thick-
sliced and served with salt-flaked butter, it's
the ideal accompaniment to the delightful
New Nordic ('new Estonian'?) food at this
garden restaurant in the Old Town headquarters of Tallinn's Scottish club (really!).

Tchaikovsky   Russian, French €€€
(☏600 0600; www.telegraafhotel.com; Vene 9;
mains €24-25; ◷noon-3pm & 6-11pm Mon-Fri,
1-11pm Sat & Sun; ☎) Located in a glassed-in
pavilion within the Hotel Telegraaf, Tchaik-
ovsky offers a dazzling tableau of blinged-
up chandeliers, gilt frames and greenery.
Service is formal and faultless (as is the
carefully contemporised menu of Franco-
-Russian classics) and the experience is
capped by live chamber music. The €25
three-course weekday lunch is excellent value and there's terrace seating in summer.

🍷 DRINKING & NIGHTLIFE

Don't worry about Tallinn's reputation as a
stag-party paradise: it's easy to avoid the
'British' and 'Irish' pubs in the southeast
corner of Old Town where lager-louts
congregate (roughly the triangle formed by
Viru, Suur-Karja and the city walls).

No Ku Klubi   Bar
(☏631 3929; Pikk 5; ◷noon-1am Mon-Thu, to
3am Fri, 2pm-3am Sat, 6pm-1am Sun) A nondescript red-and-blue door, a key-code to
enter, a clubbable atmosphere of regulars

Alexander Nevsky Orthodox Cathedral (p218)

lounging in mismatched armchairs – could this be Tallinn's ultimate 'secret' bar? Once the surreptitious haunt of artists in Soviet times, it's now free for all to enter – just ask one of the smokers outside for the code. Occasional evenings of low-key music and film are arranged.

Gloria Wine Cellar   Wine Bar

(☑640 6804; www.gloria.ee; Müürivahe 2; ◷noon-11pm Mon-Sat) Set in a cellar beneath the inner face of the town wall, this atmospheric wine bar and shop stocks thousands of bottles across a series of vaulted stone chambers. Credenzas, heavy carpets, antique furniture and walls hung with paintings greet you inside, and the passing life of Tallinn outside, should the weather encourage an alfresco glass.

Frank   Bar

(☑623 3059; www.frankbistro.ee; Sauna 2; ◷noon-midnight Sun-Tue, to 2am Wed-Sat) Of all of Old Town's bars, this is a particular favourite of locals, whether for a burger, a cooked breakfast at dinnertime or just a quiet drink in a relaxed environment. A wide selection

of juleps and other cocktails and occasional events round out a delightful package.

ℹ INFORMATION

Tallinn Tourist Information Centre (☑645 7777; www.visittallinn.ee; Niguliste 2; ◷9am-7pm Mon-Sat, to 6pm Sun Jun-Aug, shorter hours rest of year) A very well-stocked and helpful office. Many Old Town walking tours leave from here.

ℹ GETTING AROUND

Tallinn has an excellent network of buses, trams and trolleybuses running from around 6am to 11pm or midnight. The major local bus station is beneath the Viru Keskus shopping centre. All local public transport timetables are online at www.tallinn.ee.

Buy a paper ticket from the driver (€2 for a single journey, exact change required) or buy a Ühiskaart (smartcard; €2) at an R-Kiosk, post office or the Tallinn City Government customer service desk, add credit, then validate the card at the start of each journey using the orange card-readers. E-ticket fares are €1.10/3 for an hour/day.

RĪGA, LATVIA

Rīga at a Glance...

The Gothic spires that dominate Rīga's cityscape might suggest austerity, but it is the flamboyant art nouveau that forms the flesh and the spirit of this vibrant cosmopolitan city, the largest of all three Baltic capitals. Like all northerners, it is quiet and reserved on the outside, but there is some powerful chemistry going on inside its hip bars, modern art centres, and in the kitchens of its cool experimental restaurants.

With One Day in Port

Start your adventure in the heart of the city with a stop at the much-loved **Blackheads House** (p232), then spend the rest of the morning wandering among the twisting, cobbled lanes of **Old Rīga**. In the afternoon, head to the **Quiet Centre**, where you'll find some of Rīga's finest examples of art nouveau architecture. Don't miss the **Rīga Art Nouveau Museum** (p229).

Best Places for...

Cafe Miit (p236)

Desserts Arbooz (p235)

Cosy dining Fazenda Bazārs (p236)

Modern 3 Pavaru (p237)

Beer hall Folksklub Ala Pagrabs (p237)

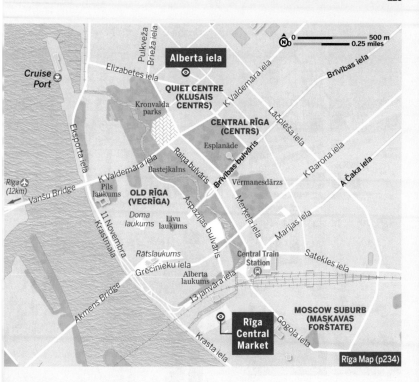

Getting from the Port

It's a short stroll from the Rīga Passenger Terminal, where most cruise ships dock, into central Rīga, with the old town close at hand about 1.2km away. Some cruise companies will provide shuttles, otherwise taxis are also available. It's about 400m to the nearest tram stop, from where several lines run past the old town.

Fast Facts

Currency Euro (€)

Language Latvian

Free wi-fi Most cafes and restaurants.

Tourist information Main office (p237) is near the river in the old town.

Transport The centre is very walkable, but trams, trolleybuses and buses all run. For routes, consult www.rigassatiksme.lv.

Rīga Central Market

Haggle for your huckleberries at this vast market, housed in a series of WWI Zeppelin hangars and spilling outdoors as well. It's an essential Rīga experience.

Great For...

☑ **Don't Miss**

Your wallet or purse...pickpockets prey on the unattentive here.

Around the Market

Strolling the market, known in the local lingo as Rīgas Centrāltirgus, is a pleasure, providing bountiful opportunities both for a spot of people-watching and to buy some quality food. Although the number of traders is dwindling, the dairy and fish departments, each occupying a separate hangar, present a colourful picture of abundance that activates ancient foraging instincts in the visitors. It's an excellent snapshot of local life.

History

In operation since 1570, the riverside market flourished during the mid-1600s when the city outgrew Stockholm to become the largest stronghold of the Swedish Empire. Laden with goods, boats travelling down the Daugava would meet those traversing the Baltic Sea for a mutually beneficial exchange.

⚓

Explore Ashore

From the passenger terminal, walk about 500m to Kronvalda bulvāris, from where the number 7 tram runs every 10 minutes to the market (€1.15, 10 minutes). Expect to spend an hour or so at the market, more if you explore Spīķeri.

❶ Need to Know

Rīgas Centrāltirgus; ☎6722 9985; www.rct.lv; Nēģu iela 7; ☺7am-6pm

In 1930 the market moved to its current location on the border of Central Rīga and the Russified Maskavas neighbourhood ('Little Moscow') to make use of the railway, which replaced the river as the principal trade route.

Confronted with the market's ever-growing size, the city of Rīga decided to bring in five enormous German-built hangars that had been designed to house Zeppelins, from the town of Vainode in Western Latvia. These hangars – each 35m high – added 57,000 sq metres of vending space, allowing an additional 1250 vendors to peddle their goods. The market can now house some 3000 stalls and is claimed to be Europe's largest. Together with Old Rīga, the market is included on Unesco's World Heritage list.

Eating the Catch

If it's a nice day, you could put together a great Latvian picnic from the various stalls

in the market. But if you've been tempted by the good-looking fish counters, one might ask: Where do I get it cooked? Well, luckily **Siļķītes un Dillītes** (www.facebook.com/SilkitesUnDillites; Centrāltirgus iela 3; mains €7-10; ☺9am-5pm), or Herring & Dill, as the name of this grungy kitchen-cum-bar translates, is right here and it'll do the cooking for you. Pick your fish and some minutes later it will be fried and served with veggies and chips.

Spīķeri

The shipping yard behind the Central Market is the latest **district** (www.spikeri.lv) to benefit from a generous dose of gentrification. These crumbling brick warehouses were once filled with swinging slabs of hanger meat; these days you'll find hip cafes and start-up companies. Stop by during the day to check out **Kim?** (☎6722 3321; www.kim.lv; Maskavas iela 12/1; €3; ☺noon-8pm Tue, to 6pm Wed-Sun) – an experimental art zone that dabbles with contemporary media – or come in the evening to peruse the surplus of farm produce at the **night market**.

Alberta iela 2a

PHILIP100/GETTY IMAGES ©

Alberta Iela

Rīga is known as one of Europe's capitals of art nouveau, with hundreds of buildings. This street is the finest example of it and one of the city's key sights.

Great For...

☑ **Don't Miss**

Looking up...most of the finest detail is well above street level.

It's like a huge painting, which you can spend hours staring at, as your eye dete more and more intriguing details. But in fact this must-see Rīga sight is a rather functional street with residential houses restaurants and shops. Art nouveau, oth wise known as Jugendstil, is the style and the master responsible for most of these Mikhail Eisenstein. Named after the foun er of Rīga, Bishop Albert von Buxthoeven, the street was the architect's gift to Rīga (its 700th anniversary.

Number 2a

At Alberta iela 2a, constructed in 1906, serene faces with chevalier helmets stand guard atop the facade, which noticea- bly extends far beyond the actual roof of the structure. Screaming masks and horrible goblins adorn the lower sections amid clean lines and surprising robot-like

Alberta iela 9

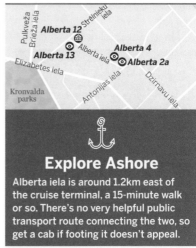

BALAKATE/SHUTTERSTOCK ©

⚓

Explore Ashore

Alberta iela is around 1.2km east of the cruise terminal, a 15-minute walk or so. There's no very helpful public transport route connecting the two, so get a cab if footing it doesn't appeal.

ℹ Need to Know

Alberta iela

shapes. Most noticeable are the two stone satyr phoenix-women that stand guard at the front. The facade of the building next door is in much better condition.

Number 4

The three heads on Alberta iela 4, two doors down from 2a, will surely capture your attention. If you look carefully, you'll see a nest of snakes slithering around their heads, evoking Medusa. All six eyes seem transfixed on some unseen horror, but only two of the faces are screaming in shock and fear. Two elaborate reliefs near the entrance feature majestic griffins, and ferocious lions with erect, fist-like tails keep watch on the roof.

Number 12

Once the home of Konstantīns Pēkšēns (a local architect responsible for over 250 of

the city's buildings), this is now the **Rīga Art Nouveau Museum** (Rīgas jūgendstila muzejs; www.jugendstils.riga.lv; Alberta iela 12; adult/child May-Sep €6/4, Oct-Apr €3.50/2.50; ☺10am-6pm Tue-Sun). The interiors have been completely restored to resemble a middle-class apartment from the 1920s. Enter from Strēlnieku iela; push No 12 on the doorbell.

Note the spectacular staircase, geometric stencils, rounded furniture, original stained glass in the dining room and the still-functioning stove in the kitchen. There's also a free 10-minute video detailing the city's distinct decor.

Number 13

The Rīga Graduate School of Law at Alberta iela 13 epitomises Jugendstil's attention to detail. Peacocks, tangled shrubs and bare-breasted heroines abound while cheery pastoral scenes are depicted in relief on Erykah Badu–like turbans atop the giant yawning masks. The triangular summit is a mishmash of nightmarish imagery: lion heads taper off into snake tails (like Chimera), sobbing faces weep in agony and a strange futuristic mask stoically stares out over the city from the apex.

Art Nouveau Rīga

After investigating the art nouveau magnificence of Alberta iela, this stroll takes you past some of Rīga's other examples of the style.

Start Alberta iela, Quiet Centre
Distance 3km
Duration two hours (leisurely pace)

1 Strēlnieku iela 4a is filled in with sumptuous blue brick and framed by garland-wielding goddesses.

6 At Smilšu iela 8, two women stand atop a protruding bay carrying an elaborate crown of leaves.

5 The building at **Smilšu iela 2** is considered to be one of the finest examples of Jugendstil in Old Rīga.

0   400 m
0   0.2 miles

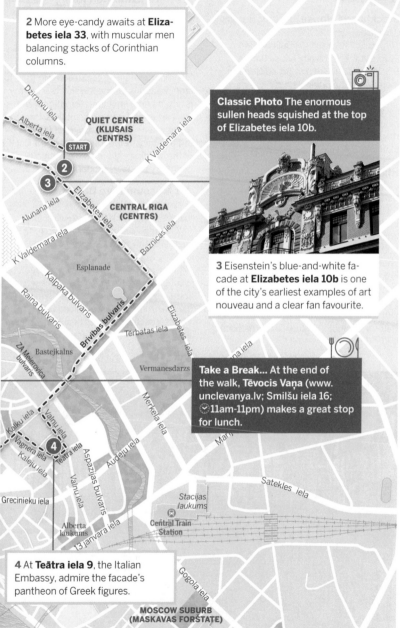

2 More eye-candy awaits at **Elizabetes iela 33**, with muscular men balancing stacks of Corinthian columns.

QUIET CENTRE (KLUSAIS CENTRS)

START

CENTRAL RIGA (CENTRS)

Esplanade

Bastejkalns

Vermanesdarzs

Classic Photo The enormous sullen heads squished at the top of Elizabetes iela 10b.

3 Eisenstein's blue-and-white facade at **Elizabetes iela 10b** is one of the city's earliest examples of art nouveau and a clear fan favourite.

Take a Break... At the end of the walk, Tēvocis Vaņa (www.unclevanya.lv; Smilšu iela 16; 11am-11pm) makes a great stop for lunch.

Stacijas laukums

Central Train Station

Alberta laukums

4 At **Teātra iela 9**, the Italian Embassy, admire the facade's pantheon of Greek figures.

MOSCOW SUBURB (MASKAVAS FORŠTATE)

Dzirnavu iela
Alberta iela
K Valdemara iela
Alunana iela
K Valdemara iela
Kalpaka bulvaris
Raina bulvaris
ZA Meierovica bulvaris
Brivibas bulvaris
Terbatas iela
Elizabetes iela
Baznicas iela
Merkela iela
Kaļķu iela
Vaļņu iela
Vagnera iela
Kaļeju iela
Teātra iela
Aspazijas bulvaris
Audēju iela
Vaļņu iela
Grecinieku iela
13 janvara iela
Satekles iela
Gogoļa iela

1 VELO JURA/SHUTTERSTOCK © 3 BUMIHILLS/SHUTTERSTOCK © 5 PETER FORSBERG / ALAMY STOCK PHOTO ©

⊙ SIGHTS

Blackheads House Historic Building
(Melngalvju nams; ☏6704 3678; www.melngal
vjunams.lv; Rātslaukums 7) Built in 1344
as a veritable fraternity house for the
Blackheads guild of unmarried German
merchants, the original house was deci-
mated in 1941 and flattened by the Soviets
seven years later. Somehow the original
blueprints survived and an exact replica of
this fantastically ornate structure was completed in 2001 for Rīga's 800th birthday.

Rīga Cathedral Church
(Rīgas Doms; ☏6722 7573; www.doms.lv; Doma
laukums 1; €3; ⊙10am-5pm Oct-Jun, 9am-6pm
Sat-Tue, 9am-5pm Wed-Fri Jul-Sep) Founded
in 1211 as the seat of the Rīga diocese, this
enormous (once Catholic, now Evangelical
Lutheran) cathedral is the largest medieval
church in the Baltic. The architecture is an
amalgam of styles from the 13th to the 18th
centuries: the eastern end, the oldest portion, has Romanesque features; the tower is
18th-century baroque; and much of the rest
dates from a 15th-century Gothic rebuilding.

Arsenāls Exhibition Hall Gallery
(Izstāžu zāle Arsenāls; ☏6732 4461; www.lnmm.
lv; Torņa iela 1; adult/child €3.50/2; ⊙11am-
6pm Tue, Wed & Fri, to 8pm Thu, noon-5pm Sat &
Sun) Behind a row of spooky granite heads
depicting Latvia's most prominent artists,
the imperial arsenal, constructed in 1832 to
store weapons for the Russian tsar's army,
is now a prime spot for international and
local art exhibitions, which makes it worth
a visit whenever you are in Rīga. Also check
out the massive wooden stairs at the back
of the building – their simple yet funky
geometry predates modern architecture.

Art Museum Rīga Bourse Museum
(Mākslas muzejs Rīgas Birža; ☏6732 4461; www.
lnmm.lv; Doma laukums 6; adult/child €6/3;
⊙10am-6pm Tue-Thu, Sat & Sun, to 8pm Fri)
Rīga's lavishly restored stock exchange
building is a worthy showcase for the city's
art treasures. The elaborate facade features
a coterie of deities that dance between
the windows, while inside, gilt chandeliers
sparkle from ornately moulded ceilings. The
Oriental section features beautiful Chinese
and Japanese ceramics and an Egyptian

SVETLANA MAHOVSKAYA/SHUTTERSTOCK ©

mummy, but the main halls are devoted to Western art, including a Monet painting and a scaled-down cast of Rodin's *The Kiss*.

Corner House   Museum

(Former KGB compound; Stūra Māja; okupaci-jasmuzejs.lv/en/kgb-building; Brīvības iela 69; adult/student €5/2; ⊙10am-5.30pm Mon, Tue, Thu & Fri, noon-7pm Wed, 10am-4pm Sat & Sun) The epitome of a haunted house, this imposing fin de siècle building is remembered by generations of Latvians as the local headquarters of the notorious Soviet secret police – NKVD/KGB. Arbitrary arrests, torture, executions – it saw it all. These days it houses an exhibition dedicated to victims and perpetrators of political repression, which directly affected 26,000 people. An English-language tour of torture dungeons is available daily at 10.30am, except Wednesdays, when it starts at noon.

Freedom Monument   Monument

(Brīvības bulvāris) Affectionately known as 'Milda', Rīga's Freedom Monument towers above the city between Old and Central Rīga. Paid for by public donations, the monument was designed by Kārlis Zāle and erected in 1935 where a statue of Russian ruler Peter the Great once stood.

Holocaust Memorial   Monument

Don't miss the moving Holocaust Memorial, sitting a block behind Akadēmijas laukums in a quiet garden. A large synagogue occupied this street corner until it was burned to the ground during WWII, tragically with the entire congregation trapped inside. No one survived. Today the concrete monument standing in its place is dedicated to the brave Latvians who risked their lives to help hide Jews during the war.

Latvian Ethnographic Open-Air Museum   Museum

(Latvijas etnogrāfiskais brīvdabas muzejs; ☏6799 4106; www.brivdabasmuzejs.lv; Brīvības gatve 440; adult/child €4/1.40; ⊙10am-5pm, to 8pm May-Oct) If you don't have time to visit the Latvian countryside, a stop at this open-air museum is a must. Sitting along the shores of Lake Jugla just northeast of the city limits, this stretch of forest contains more than 100 wooden buildings (churches, windmills, farmhouses etc) from each of Latvia's four cultural regions.

From left: Old church in the Latvian Ethnographic Open-Air Museum; Rīga Cathedral; Freedom Monument

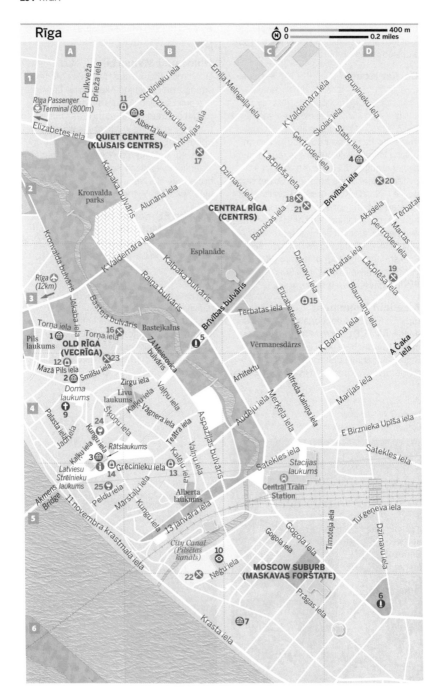

Rīga

N 0 — 400 m
0 — 0.2 miles

Rīga

TOURS

Rīga Culture Free Tour
Cultural Tour

(☏20338877; www.rigaculturefreetour.lv) **FREE**
A daily English-language walk conducted by local cultural experts. It lasts for two hours and begins at noon from Rainis monument on Esplanāde.

🔒 SHOPPING

Art Nouveau Rīga
Gifts & Souvenirs

(www.artnouveauriga.lv; Strēlnieku iela 9; ⊘10am-7pm) Sells a variety of art nouveau–related souvenirs, from guidebooks and postcards to stone gargoyles and bits of stained glass.

Riija
Fashion & Accessories

(www.riija.lv; Tērbatas iela 6/8; ⊘10am-7pm Mon-Fri, to 5pm Sat) Scandi-sleek design inhabits every polished nook and cranny at this new design enclave in the heart of Centrs. Look out Sweden, Latvian design is on the rise!

Hobbywool
Arts & Crafts

(☏27072707; www.hobbywool.com; Mazā Pils iela 6; ⊘10am-6pm Mon-Sat, 11am-3pm Sun) It feels like walking into a Mark Rothko painting – the little shop is filled from top to bottom with brightly coloured knitted shawls, mittens, socks and jackets.

Pienene
Beauty, Handicrafts

(Kungu iela 7/9; ⊘10am-8pm; 🛜) 'The Dandelion' is an airy boutique and cafe in the heart of Old Rīga where visitors can sample locally produced beauty products, try on floaty scarves and sniff scented candles.

Latvijas Balzāms
Drinks

(☏6708 1213; www.lb.lv; Audēju iela 8; ⊘9am-10pm) One of myriad branches of a popular chain of liquor stores selling the trademark Latvian Black Balzām.

⊗ EATING

For centuries in Latvia, food equalled fuel, energising peasants as they worked the fields, and warming their bellies during bone-chilling Baltic winters. Today, the era of boiled potatoes and pork gristle has faded away as food becomes a sensorial experience rather than a necessary evil. Although it will be a while before globetrotters stop qualifying local restaurants as being 'good for Rīga', the cuisine scene has improved by leaps and bounds over the last decade.

Arbooz
Desserts €

(www.facebook.com/arbOOz.lv; Dzirnavu iela 34A; macaroons €2, cupcakes €3.85; ⊘10am-8pm Mon-Fri, 11am-6pm Sat) We'd call this tiny place sweet even if it didn't make these light fruity cupcakes and meringues – just

 **Understand**

History of Art Nouveau

More than 750 buildings in Rīga (more than any other city in Europe) boast this flamboyant and haunting style of decor. Art nouveau is also known as Jugendstil, meaning 'Youth Style', named after a Munich-based magazine called *Die Jugend*, which popularised the design in its pages.

Art nouveau's early influence was Japanese print art disseminated throughout Western Europe, but as the movement gained momentum, the style became more ostentatious and freeform – design schemes started to feature mythical beasts, screaming masks, twisting flora, goddesses and goblins. The turn of the 20th century marked the movement's height as it swept through every major European city from Porto to Petersburg.

The movement in Rīga can be divided into three pronounced phases. The first was called 'Eclectic Decorative Art Nouveau'; it occurred during the first five years of the 20th century. During this time, the primary focus was the facade rather than the interior, as highly ornate patterns were imported from Germany by local architects who studied there. This design phase is the most pronounced in Central Rīga because the prevalence of the style coincided with the opening of a local architectural faculty.

After the revolution of 1905, however, this art nouveau style was quickly phased out as local architects furiously dabbled with the notion of establishing a design scheme with nationalistic flair. The so-called 'National Romanticism' was born out of this idea, and reflected Latvian ethnographic motifs. An affinity for natural materials flourished as urban facades were left unpainted to show the greys and browns of the building materials. Although this rather un-art nouveau style was only popular for four years, it coincided with a boom in the city's trading wealth, and thus a lot of structures exhibit this style, even today.

The final phase was known as 'Perpendicular Art Nouveau' – it flourished from around 1908 to 1912. The style was a hybrid design between the existing art nouveau traits and a return to classical motifs (presented in a heavily stylised fashion). An accentuation on verticality was pronounced, as was the penchant for balconies and bay windows.

In Rīga, the most noted Jugendstil architect was Mikhail Eisenstein (father of Sergei Eisenstein, the Soviet film director), who flexed his artistic muscles on Alberta iela.

for its looks. You might be able to occupy one of only four tables, otherwise opt for beautifully packaged takeaway and enjoy your coffee on a park bench.

Miit Cafe €

(www.miit.lv; Lāčplēša iela 10; mains €5; ☺7am-9pm Mon, to 11pm Tue & Wed, to 1am Thu, to 3am Fri, 9am-1am Sat, 10am-6pm Sun) Rīga's hipster students head here to sip espresso and blog about Nietzsche amid comfy couches and discarded bicycle parts. The two-course lunch is a fantastic deal for

penny-pinchers – expect a soup and a main course for under €5 (dishes change daily).

Fazenda Bazārs Modern European €€

(☎6724 0809; www.fazenda.lv; Baznīcas iela 14; mains €7-12; ☺9am-10pm Mon-Fri, 10am-10pm Sat, 11am-10pm Sun) Although right in the centre, this place feels like you've gone a long way and suddenly found a warm tavern in the middle of nowhere. Complete with a tiled stove, this wooden house oozes megatonnes of charm and the food on offer feels as homey as it gets, despite its globalist fusion nature.

Kasha Gourmet
Modern European €€

(☏20201444; www.kasha-gourmet.com; Stabu iela 14; mains €8-17; ☺10am-10pm Mon-Thu, 10am-11pm Fri & Sat, 10am-8pm Sun) It might be that it does succeed in making the food feel tastier by turning the plate into a piece of modern art, or perhaps it's the postmodernist mixture of ingredients, but this is one of the most unusual and undervalued restaurants in Rīga. We are particularly fond of its set breakfasts beautifully laid out on wooden slabs.

Istaba
Cafe €€€

(☏6728 1141; K Barona iela 31a; mains €17; ☺noon-11pm) Owned by local chef and TV personality Mārtiņš Sirmais, 'The Room' sits in the rafters above a gallery and occasional performance space. There's no set menu – you're subject to the cook's fancy – but expect lots of free extras (bread, dips, salad, veggies), adding up to a massive serving.

3 Pavaru
Modern European €€€

(☏20370537; www.3pavari.lv; Torņa iela 4; mains €17-28; ☺noon-11pm) The stellar trio of chefs who run the show have a jazzy approach to cooking, with improvisation at the heart of the compact and ever-changing menu. The emphasis is on experiment (baked cod with ox-tail stew, anyone?) and artful visual presentation that could have made Mark Rothko or Joan Miró gasp in admiration.

🍷 DRINKING & NIGHTLIFE

Folksklub Ala Pagrabs
Beer Hall

(☏27796914; www.folkklubs.lv; Peldu iela 19; ☺noon-midnight Sun, to 1am Mon & Tue, to 3am Wed, to 4am Thu & Fri, 2pm-4am Sat) A huge cavern filled with the bubbling magma of relentless beer-infused joy, folk-punk music, dancing and Latvian nationalism, this is an essential Rīga drinking venue, no matter what highbrowed locals say about it. The bar strives to reflect the full geography and diversity of Latvian beer production, but there is also plenty of local cider, fruit wine and *šmakouka* moonshine.

Egle
Beer Garden

(www.spogulegle.lv; Kaļķu iela 1a; ☺11am-1am) Split between a noisier half with live music most nights (everything from folk to rockabilly), and a quieter half (which generally closes early), this is the best of Old Rīga's open-air beer gardens. It shuts up shop when the weather gets really horrible.

ℹ️ INFORMATION

Tourist Information Centre (☏6703 7900; www.liveriga.com; Rātslaukums 6; ☺10am-6pm Oct-Apr, 9am-7pm May-Sep) Dispenses tourist maps and walking-tour brochures, helps with accommodation, books and day trips, and sells concert tickets. It also stocks the Rīga Pass, which offers discounts on sights and restaurants, and free rides on public transport.

ℹ️ GETTING AROUND

The centre of Rīga is too compact for most visitors even to consider public transport, but trams, buses or trolleybuses may come in handy if you are venturing further out. For routes and schedules, consult www.rigassatiksme.lv. Tickets cost €1.15; unlimited tickets are available for 24 hours (€5). Tickets are available from Narvessen newspaper kiosks as well as vending machines on board new trams.

GDAŃSK, POLAND

Gdańsk at a Glance...

Centuries of maritime ebb and flow as a port city; streets of distinctively un-Polish architecture influenced by a united nations of wealthy merchants who shaped the city's past; the to-ing and fro-ing of Danzig/Gdańsk between Teutonic Prussia and Slavic Poland; and the destruction of WWII have bequeathed the city a unique atmosphere.

Pace the Main Town's narrow, cobbled streets, gaze in wonder at monster red-brick churches, perambulate historic thoroughfares lined with grand, elegantly slender buildings, and wander in and out of characterful cafes, amber shops and intriguing museums.

With One Day in Port

Spend the morning strolling around the historic centre, appreciating **Długi Targ** (p244), pacing the waterfront and popping into museums. After lunching on Pomeranian cuisine in a local restaurant, in the afternoon visit the **European Solidarity Centre** (p243) to gain an appreciation of Poland's postwar history and Gdańsk's role in the unravelling of the Eastern Bloc.

Best Places for...

Regional dishes Tawerna Mestwin (p253)

Period dining Kresowa (p253)

Historic atmosphere Restauracja Pod Łososiem (p254)

Perry Józef K (p255)

Craft beer Brovarnia (p255)

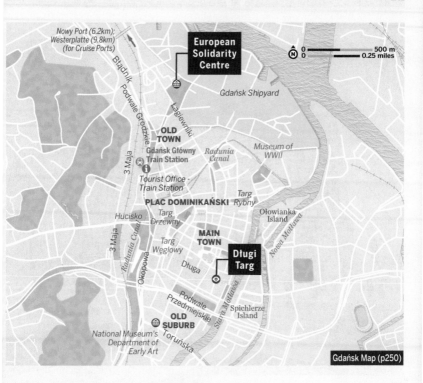

Gdańsk Map (p250)

Getting from the Port

Gdańsk has two cruise terminals. From Westerplatte to the centre, bus 106 runs about every 80 minutes (3zł, 25 minutes). A taxi is otherwise best. From Nowy Port, regular tram 10 goes to the train station (walk or take tram 8 from there). Larger ships dock in Gdynia, a 35-minute SKM train ride from Gdańsk.

Fast Facts

Currency Złoty (zł)

Language Polish

Free wi-fi Lots of free spots across the city. Check www.gdanskwifi.pl.

Tourist information There are tourist office branches downtown and at the train station.

Transport The SKM commuter train zips between the three cities with intermediate stops. Tram and bus services cover more bases in Gdańsk itself.

PATRYK KOSMIDER/SHUTTERSTOCK ©

European Solidarity Centre

This striking modern rusted-iron building by the shipyards is one of Gdańsk's unmissables. The seven halls examine Poland's postwar fight for freedom; displays blend state-of-the-art multimedia with period artefacts.

Great For...

☑ **Don't Miss**

Hall A covers the key story of the brave Polish dockers.

Hall A

Each hall is lettered and the exhibition runs chronologically from A to G. Hall A takes you to the 1970s shipyard, with yellow docker helmets lining the ceiling and a battered electric truck, the type Lech Wałęsa once worked on as an electrician, almost blocking your way. Footage includes the negotiations between dockers and the Communist regime and the signing of the 1980 agreements (the oversize comedy pen Wałęsa used to sign is sadly missing).

Halls B–D

Hall B is all Communist-era interiors, a fascinating retro experience that takes you to a prison cell, an interrogation room and a typical family living room. Solidarity and martial law are the themes of halls C and D.

European **Solidarity Centre**

Gdańsk Shipyard

Wałowa

⚓ Explore Ashore

Tram 8 from Podwale Przedmiejskie in central Gdańsk runs to the museum regularly, taking 10 minutes (3zł). If you are coming from Gdynia, the museum is very close to Gdańsk Główny railway station. Allow at least two hours for the museum.

❶ Need to Know

Europejskie Centrum Solidarności; ☑58 772 4112; www.ecs.gda.pl; Plac Solidarności 1; adult/concession 17/13zł; ⊙10am-8pm Jun-Sep, to 6pm Oct-May)

Halls E–G

Hall E is a large mock-up of the famous round table, complete with TV cameras and name badges. An interesting section on the various revolutions across Eastern Europe follows in hall F, while hall G is a spartan affair dedicated to Pope John Paul II.

The special hall opposite the ticket desk hosts Polish-themed exhibitions, which are usually free.

History of the Shipyard

Gdańsk's former Lenin **Shipyard** (Stocznia Gdańska) is a key fragment of 20th-century European history. It was here that the first major cracks in Eastern Europe's communist wall appeared when discontent with the regime boiled over into strikes and dissent, brutally stamped out by armed force in 1970. A decade later an electrician named Lech

Wałęsa emerged to rouse crowds of strikers here, leading to the formation of the Solidarity movement and ultimately to democracy for Poland and most of the Eastern Bloc.

However, since the giddy years of the Wałęsa presidency, the yard has largely lost its hallowed status and at one time the vast area was even slated for redevelopment and general gentrification. Nothing ever came of this and there has even been a minor revival in the shipbuilding industry, though nothing like the scale of the postwar years.

Just in front of the shipyard gates, the striking **Monument to the Fallen Shipyard Workers** (Plac Solidarności) commemorates the workers killed in the riots of 1970. Unveiled on 16 December 1980, 10 years after the massacre, the monument is a set of three 42m-tall steel crosses, with a series of bronze bas-reliefs in their bases. The first monument in a communist country to commemorate the regime's victims, it became an instant symbol and remains so today.

MATYAS REHAK/SHUTTERSTOCK ©

Długi Targ

'Long Market' was once the main city market and is now the major focus for visitors. It's pretty touristy but look up from the crowds to appreciate the wonderful period architecture, rebuilt postwar.

Great For...

☑ **Don't Miss**

The sumptuous facade of the Golden House.

Green Gate

Długi Targ is flanked from the east by the Green Gate, marking the end of the Royal Way. It was built in the 1560s on the site of a medieval defensive gate and was supposed to be the residence of the kings. But they never stayed in what turned out to be a cold and uncomfortable lodge; they preferred the houses nearby, particularly those opposite the Artus Court.

Town Hall

Dominating Długi Targ, Gdańsk's impressive Gothic-Renaissance town hall boasts the city's highest tower at 81.5m and is home to the Historical Museum of Gdańsk (p248).

Neptune Fountain

According to legend, the Neptune Fountain, next to the Town Hall, once gushed

Neptune Fountain

Długi Targ

Explore Ashore

Długi Targ is a short five-minute walk from where buses and trams from the port stop on Podwale Przedmiejskie. From Gdynia, disembark at Gdańsk Główny station and get tram 3, 8 or 9. Count on an hour from Gdynia Główna station to Długi Targ.

❶ Need to Know

The main tourist information centre (p255) is on this square.

forth with the trademark Gdańsk liqueur, Goldwasser. As the story goes, it spurted out of the trident one merry night and Neptune found himself endangered by crowds of drunken locals. The bronze statue was the work of Flemish artist Peter Husen; it was made between 1606 and 1613 and is the oldest secular monument in Poland. A menagerie of stone sea creatures was added in the 1750s.

Golden House

The 1618 Golden House, designed by Johan Voigt, has the richest facade in the city. In the friezes between storeys are 12 elaborately carved scenes interspersed with busts of famous historical figures, including two Polish kings. The four statues waving to you from the balustrade at the top are Cleopatra, Oedipus, Achilles and Antigone.

Artus Court

Rising in all its embellished grandeur behind the Neptune Fountain, the Artus Court, now a museum (p248), is perhaps the single best-known house in Gdańsk. The court has been an essential stop for passing luminaries ever since its earliest days, and a photo display in the entrance shows an enviable selection of famous visitors, from King Henry IV of England to a host of contemporary presidents. It was comprehensively destroyed during WWII but was painstakingly restored from old photographs and historical records.

Built in the middle of the 14th century, the court was given its monumental facade by Abraham van den Block in the 1610s. Inside, there's a huge hall topped by a Gothic vault supported on four slim granite columns, decorated with hunting murals and dominated by a vast painting depicting the Battle of Grunwald. Wealthy local merchants used the building as a communal guildhall, holding meetings, banquets and general revelries in the lavishly decorated interior.

Along the Mottawa

Lining the Mottawa River is Gdańsk's waterfront, once a busy quay crowded with hundreds of sailing ships loading and unloading their cargo.

Start Green Bridge
Distance 700m
Duration 20 minutes

Take a Break... Treat yourself to a sumptuous lunch at 16th-century Restauracja Pod Łososiem (p254).

MAIN TOWN

4 The 15th-century **St Mary's Gate** (Brama Mariacka) is one of the grandest on the city's waterfront.

3 The palatial **House Under the Angels** (Dom Pod Aniołami) was the largest burgher's house in Gdańsk in the 1600s.

1 The **Green Bridge** gives a wonderful view of the imposing Green Gate, guarding Długi Targ.

START

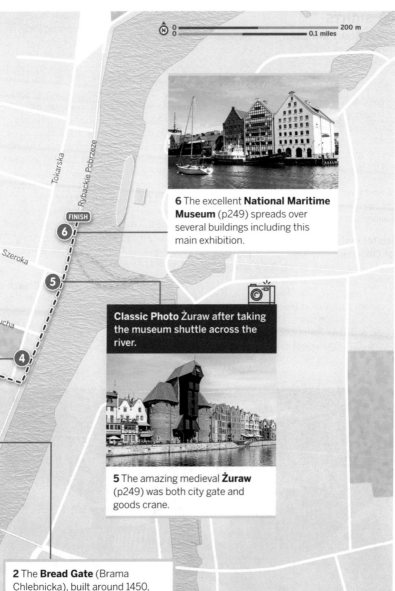

6 The excellent **National Maritime Museum** (p249) spreads over several buildings including this main exhibition.

Classic Photo Żuraw after taking the museum shuttle across the river.

5 The amazing medieval **Żuraw** (p249) was both city gate and goods crane.

2 The **Bread Gate** (Brama Chlebnicka), built around 1450, has the original city coat of arms consisting of two crosses.

Tokarska

Rybackie Pobrzeże

Szeroka

Ducha

FINISH

◉ SIGHTS

Artus Court Museum   Museum

(www.mhmg.gda.pl; ul Długi Targ 43/44; adult/ concession 10/5zł, free Mon; ⊘9am-1pm Mon, 9am-4pm Tue-Thu, 10am-6pm Fri & Sat, 10am-4pm Sun) In the plainly renovated upper floors of Artus House is a selection of historical exhibits, including a photographic 'simulacrum' of how the great hall would have looked at its peak, a breathtaking spectacle. One unique feature of the interior is its giant Renaissance tiled stove, standing in the corner of the hall and almost touching the ceiling. It's reputedly the highest stove of its kind in Europe containing 520 tiles, 437 of which are originals.

Historical Museum of Gdańsk   Museum

(www.mhmg.pl; Długa 46/47; adult/concession 12/6zł, tower 5zł; ⊘9am-1pm Tue, 10am-4pm Wed, Fri & Sat, to 6pm Thu, from 11am Sun) This museum is located in the historic **town hall** (Długi Targ), which claims Gdańsk's highest tower at 81.5m. The showpiece is the Red Room (Sala Czerwona), done up in Dutch mannerist style from the end of the 16th century. The 2nd floor houses exhibitions related to Gdańsk's history, including mock-ups of old Gdańsk interiors. From here you can access the tower for great views across the city.

The Red Room's interior is not an imitation but the real deal; it was dismantled in 1942 and hidden outside the city until the end of the bombing. The richly carved fireplace (1593) and the marvellous portal (1596) all attract the eye, but the centre of attention is the ornamented ceiling – 25 paintings dominated by an oval centrepiece entitled *The Glorification of the Unity of Gdańsk with Poland*. Other striking rooms include the Winter Hall with its portraits of Gdańsk's mayors up to the 17th century and the Great Council Chamber with its huge oils of Polish kings.

St Mary's Church   Church

(www.bazylikamariacka.gdansk.pl; ul Podkramarska 5; adult/concession 4/2zł, tower 6/3zł; ⊘8.30am-6.30pm Mon-Sat, 11am-noon & 1-5pm Sun May-Sep, slightly shorter hours Oct-Apr) Dominating the heart of the Main Town, St

Artus Court Museum

Mary's is often cited as the largest brick church in the world. Some 105m long and 66m wide at the transept, its massive squat tower climbs 78m high into the Gdańsk cityscape. Begun in 1343, St Mary's didn't reach its present proportions until 1502. Don't miss the 15th-century astronomical clock, placed in the northern transept, and the church tower (it's 405 steps above the city).

National Maritime Museum
Museum

(Narodowe Muzeum Morskie w Gdańsku; ☑ Maritime Cultural Centre 58 329 8700, information 58 301 8611; www.nmm.pl; ul Ołowianka 9-13; all sites adult/concession 18/10zł; ⓒ10am-6pm daily)
This is a sprawling exhibition of maritime history and Gdańsk's role through the centuries as a Baltic seaport. Headquarters is the multimillion-euro Maritime Cultural Centre, with a permanent interactive exhibition 'People-Ships-Ports'. Other exhibitions include the MS *Sołdek,* the first vessel to be built at the Gdańsk shipyard in the postwar years, and the Żuraw, a 15th-century loading crane that was the biggest in its day. The granaries across the river house more displays, which are highly recommended.

These exhibits on Ołowianka Island in the Motława River illustrate the history of Polish seafaring from the earliest times to the present. They include models of old sailing warships and ports, a 9th-century dugout, navigation instruments, ships' artillery, flags and the like.

Another interesting exhibit here is a collection of salvaged items from the *General Carleton,* a British ship that mysteriously disappeared in the Baltic in 1785.

The museum's ferry service (per trip 1.50zł, free with ticket for all sites) shuttles between the crane and the island.

Żuraw
Landmark

(Crane; www.nmm.pl; ul Szeroka 67/68; adult/concession 8/5zł; ⓒ10am-6pm daily Jul & Aug, closed Mon and shorter hours Sep-Jun) Part of the National Maritime Museum, the oh-so conspicuous Gdańsk Crane rises above the waterfront. Built in the mid-15th century

Old Town & Main Town

Gdańsk's crown jewel is the Main Town (Główne Miasto), which looks much as it did some 300 to 400 years ago, during the height of its prosperity. As the largest of the city's historic quarters and the richest architecturally, it was the most carefully restored after WWII. Prussian additions from the Partition period were airbrushed out of this remarkably impressive re-creation, so the result is a snapshot of Gdańsk up to the end of the 18th century.

Despite its name, Gdańsk's Old Town (Stare Miasto) was not the cradle of the city. The earliest inhabited site, according to archaeologists, was in what is now the Main Town area. Nonetheless, a settlement existed in the Old Town from the late 10th century and developed parallel to the Main Town.

Under the Teutonic order, the two parts merged into a single urban entity, but the Old Town was always poorer and had no defensive system of its own. One other difference was that the Main Town was more 'German' while the Old Town had a larger Polish population. During WWII it suffered as much as its wealthier cousin but, apart from a handful of buildings (mainly churches), it was not rebuilt.

as the biggest double-towered gate on the shoreline, it also served to shift heavy cargo directly onto vessels docked at the quay. Incredibly, this people-powered device could hoist loads of up to 2000kg, making it the largest crane in medieval Europe. Early-17th-century wheels were added higher up for installing masts.

Amber Museum
Museum

(☑58 301 4733; www.mhmg.pl; Targ Węglowy 26; adult/concession 10/5zł; ⓒ10am-1pm Mon, 10am-4pm Tue-Sat, 11am-4pm Sun) This museum is dedicated to all things amber and the craft of designing and creating

Gdańsk

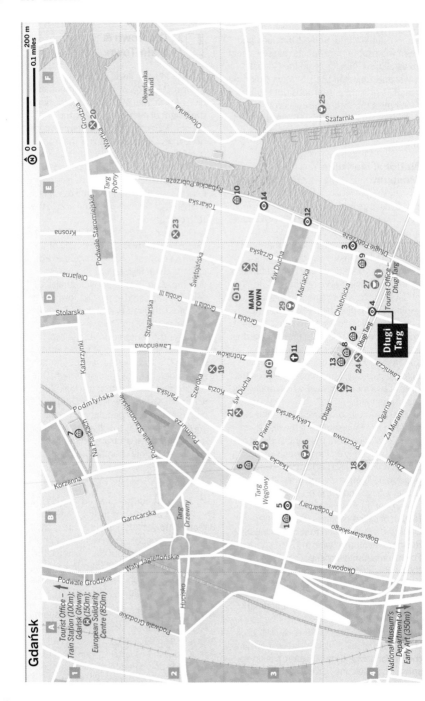

N

0   200 m
0   0.1 miles

Tourist Office –
Train Station (100m);
Gdańsk Główny
(150m);
European Solidarity
Centre (850m)

Podwale Grodzkie

Wały Jagiellońskie

Podwale Grodzkie

Hucisko

Garncarska

Korzenna

Na Piaskach

Podmłyńska

Podwale Staromiejskie

Podwale Staromiejskie

Targ Drzewny

Bogusławskiego

Okopowa

Za Murami

Zbytki

Ogarna

Pocztowa

Długa

Lektykarska

Pivna

Tkacka

Kozia

Szeroka

Złotników

Grobla I

Grobla II

Grobla III

Straganiarska

Ławendowa

Grobla I

Świętojańska

Grząska

Św. Ducha

Św. Ducha

Św. Ducha

Mariacka

Chlebnicka

Ławnicza

Podbądarski

Podgarbary

Targ Węglowy

MAIN TOWN

Szafarnia

Ołowianka Island

Ołowianka

Rybackie Pobrzeże

Targ Rybny

Podwale Staromiejskie

Krosna

Olejarna

Stolarska

Katarzynki

Panska

Podmłyńze

Podmłyńska

Warka

Grodzka

Tokarska

Długie Pobrzeże

Długie Pobrzeże

Długi Targ

Długi Targ

Długi Targ

Tourist Office –
Długi Targ

National Museum's
Department of
Early Art (350m)

A1 B1 C1 D1 E1 F1 — A2 B2 C2 D2 E2 — A3 B3 C3 D3 E3 — A4 B4

1, 5, 6, 7, 28, 26, 18, 21, 19, 16, 11, 17, 13, 24, 8, 2, 4, 27, 9, 3, 29, 15, 22, 23, 10, 14, 12, 20, 25

Gdańsk

amber jewellery. The musuem is located in the Foregate, a former prison and torture chamber, so in addition to amber displays, there's also some startlingly realistic displays of torture instruments. Two for one!

Golden Gate   Gate

(Złota Brama) Built in 1612, the Golden Gate was designed by Abraham van den Block, son of the man behind the decoration of the Upland Gate. It's a sort of triumphal arch ornamented with a double-storey colonnade and topped with eight allegorical statues.

Once you pass the Golden Gate, you are on the gently curving ulica Długa, one of the loveliest streets in Poland, which, despite its name (meaning 'Long Street'), is only 300m in length. In 1945 it was just a heap of smoking rubble.

Royal Way   Historic Site

Lined by the city's grandest facades, the Royal Way was the route along which the Polish kings traditionally paraded during their periodic visits. Of the three Royal Ways in Poland (Warsaw, Kraków and Gdańsk), Gdańsk's is the shortest – it's only 500m long, but architecturally it is perhaps the most refined.

Great Mill   Historic Building

(Wielki Młyn; ul Na Piaskach) Standing conspicuously opposite St Catherine's Church,

the Great Mill certainly lives up to its name. Created by the Teutonic Knights in northern Poland's typical red brick around 1350, it was medieval Europe's largest mill at over 40m long and 26m high. With a set of 18 monster millstones (now gone), each 5m in diameter, the mill produced 200 tonnes of flour per day right up until 1945.

No longer serving the purpose for which it was built, the mill has become a mall, containing a convenient supermarket and several low-grade eateries.

Great Arsenal   Historic Building

(Wielka Zbrojownia; ul Tkacka) Ul Piwna terminates at the Great Arsenal, an architectural gem. The work of Antonius van Opbergen, it was built at the beginning of the 17th century and, like most of Gdańsk's architecture, clearly shows the influence of the Low Countries. The main eastern facade, framed within two side towers, is floridly decorated and guarded by figures of soldiers on the top. Military motifs predominate, and the city's coat of arms guards the doorways.

National Museum's
Department of Early Art   Museum

(Muzeum Narodowe Oddział Sztuki Dawnej; www. mng.gda.pl; ul Toruńska 1; adult/concession 10/6zł, free Fri; ⊙10am-5pm Tue-Sun May-Sep, 9am-4pm Mon-Fri, 10am-5pm Sat & Sun Oct-Apr) Located just outside the Main Town, the

Shopping for Amber

For some visitors, one of the main reasons to come to Gdańsk is to source jewellery made of Baltic gold – fossilised tree resin found on the Baltic shores of Poland and Russia, commonly known as amber.

But beware: at some smaller, less-reputable stalls, you may not be getting the real deal, with some pieces containing well-crafted chunks of Russian or Chinese plastic.

Here are three ways locals recommend you can tell if the amber you are being offered is bona fide prehistoric sap. Not all shopkeepers will be happy to see you testing their wares in these ways, for obvious reasons.

○ Take a lighter and put the amber into the heat – it should give off a characteristic smell, like incense.

○ Amber floats in 20% salt water, while plastic or synthetic amber won't.

○ Rub amber against cloth and the static electricity produced attracts tiny pieces of paper.

National Museum's Department of Early Art is housed in the vaulted interiors of a former Franciscan monastery. It covers the broad spectrum of Polish and international art and crafts, boasting extensive collections of paintings, woodcarvings, gold and silverware, embroidery, fabrics, porcelain, faience, wrought iron and furniture.

Some of the highlights include the original figure of St George from the spire of the defunct Court of the Fraternity of St George, an assortment of huge, elaborately carved Danzig-style wardrobes (typical of the city, from where they were sent all over the country), and several beautiful ceramic tiled stoves.

The 1st floor is given over to paintings, with a section devoted to Dutch and Flemish work. The jewel of the collection is Hans Memling's (1435–94) triptych of *The*

Last Judgment, one of the earlier works of the artist, dating from 1472 to 1473. You'll also find works by the younger Brueghel and Van Dyck, and the beautifully macabre *Hell* by Jacob Swanenburgh, who was the master of the young Rembrandt.

Oliwa Cathedral Church

(ul Nowickiego 5; ☺9am-5pm) The first surprise as you approach the cathedral is the facade, a striking composition of two slim octagonal Gothic towers with a central baroque portion wedged between them. The interior looks extraordinarily long, mainly because of the unusual proportions of the building – the nave and chancel together are 90m long but only 8.3m wide. At the far end of this 'tunnel' is a baroque high altar (1688); the marble tombstone of the Pomeranian dukes (1613) is in the right transept.

🅐 SHOPPING

Gdańsk shopping isn't all about amber – Goldwasser makes an unusual take-home item and pretty Kashubian handicrafts are also worth considering.

Galeria SAS Art

(www.galeriab.pl; ul Szeroka 18/19; ☺10.30am-5pm Mon-Fri, to 4pm Sat) The quality oil paintings at this commercial gallery make unique and interesting souvenirs. All are by local artists and the owner is very knowledgeable about her collection.

Galeria Sztuki Kaszubskiej Arts & Crafts

(ul Św Ducha; ☺11am-6pm Mon-Sat Jul-Aug, shorter hours Sep-Jun) For genuine handmade Kashubian handicrafts, look no further than this small shop near St Mary's Church. Porcelain and embroidery dominate the range, much of which is designed and produced by the owner.

🅧 EATING

Bar Mleczny Neptun Cafeteria $

(☏58 301 4988; www.barneptun.pl; ul Długa 33/34; mains 4-9zł; ☺7.30am-7pm Mon-Fri,

Oliwa Cathedral's great organ

10am-6pm Sat & Sun, 1hr later Jul & Aug; 🛜)
It's surprising just where some of Poland's
communist-era milk bars have survived
and this one, right on the tourist drag, is
no exception. However, the Neptun is a cut
above your run-of-the-mill *bar mleczny*,
with potted plants, decorative tiling and
free wi-fi. Popular with foreigners on a
budget, it even has an English menu of
Polish favourites such as *naleśniki* (crêpes)
and *gołąbki* (cabbage rolls).

Tawerna Mestwin   Polish $$

(📞58 301 7882; ul Straganiarska 20/23; mains 20-
40zł; ⏺11am-10pm Tue-Sun, to 6pm Mon; 🛜) The
speciality here is Kashubian regional cooking from the northwest of Poland, and dishes
like potato dumplings and stuffed cabbage
rolls have a pronounced homemade quality.
There's usually a fish soup and fried fish as
well. The interior is done out like a traditional
cottage and the exposed beams and dark-
green walls create a cosy atmosphere.

Velevetka   Polish $$

(www.velevetka.pl; ul Długa 45; mains 26-49zł;
⏺noon-11pm daily; 🖋) Go Kashubian at this
delightful eatery opposite the Town Hall,
which manages to evoke a rural theme
without a single ancient agricultural knick-
knack or trussed waitress in sight. Admire
the crisp interior of heavy wooden furniture
decorated with stylised Kashubian motifs
and soothing scenes of the countryside,
while sampling finely prepared regional
dishes.

Kresowa   Eastern European $$

(ul Ogarna 12; mains 19-45zł; ⏺noon-10pm) Take
your taste buds to Poland's long-lost east
and beyond at this two-level, 19th-century
period restaurant with the mood of an
imperial-era Chekhovian parlour. Start with
Ukrainian borsch (beetroot soup), order
a main of Hutsul lamb and finish with a
piece of Polish cheesecake while sipping
homemade *kvas* (partially fermented bread
and water). There's even bison goulash for
those who dare to ask.

Przystań Gdańska   Polish $$

(📞58 301 1922; ul Wartka 5; mains 17-43zł;
⏺11am-10pm) An atmospheric place to enjoy
outdoor dining, with a view along the river

 **Understand**

The Hanseatic League

It wasn't easy being a merchant in the Middle Ages. There were no chambers of commerce or Rotary Clubs, and traders received very little respect from the ruling classes. Local lords saw travelling salesmen as easy pickings, requiring them to pay heavy tolls as they moved from province to province in Central Europe. Taking to the sea wasn't much better, as pirates preyed upon merchants' slow-moving boats.

The answer to their problems was to band together in the Hanseatic League, a group of trading ports that formed in the late 13th century and wielded unprecedented economic power. The Hansa (from the German for 'association') was based in Germany, making good use of its central location, with members also scattered throughout Scandinavia, across the Baltic to Russia and west to the Netherlands. The league also had trading posts in cities like London and Venice. As a result, it could trade wax from Russia with items from English or Dutch manufacturers, or Swedish minerals with fruit from the Mediterranean.

The league took a far more muscular approach than that of today's business councils. It bribed rulers, built lighthouses and led expeditions against pirates, and on one memorable occasion raised an armed force that defeated the Danish military in 1368.

At its height the league had almost 200 members, including major cities such as Danzig (Gdańsk), Lübeck, Rīga and Bergen.

But it was all downhill from there. With no standing army and no government beyond irregular assemblies of city representatives, the league was unable to withstand the rise of the new nation-states of the 15th century and the shift of trade to Atlantic ports after the discovery of the New World. The assembly met for the last time in 1669, and by the time of its eventual disintegration in 1863 its membership had been reduced to the core cities of Hamburg, Bremen and Lübeck.

The memory of the Hanseatic League lives on, however, in the New Hanse (www.hanse.org), founded in 1980 and bringing together the former Hansa member cities in a body promoting cultural cooperation and tourism.

to the Gdańsk crane. Serves Polish classics and a range of fish dishes, plus a few pizzas tossed in. The food's above average and the view from the terrace is arguably the best in the Old Town.

Metamorfoza   Polish $$$

(☏725 005 006; www.restauracjametamorfoza.pl; ul Szeroka 22/23; set menu 90-270zł; ◷1pm-last customer) Pomeranian fare is hardly ever given the gourmet treatment, but if refined seasonal dishes are what you seek, Metamorfoza is the place. Enjoy dishes prepared with only the finest local ingredients from the region's farms, forests, rivers and offshore waters in an interior that blends crystal chandeliers

and Chesterfield sofas with ultra-modern display cases and the odd antique.

Restauracja
Pod Łososiem   Polish $$$

(☏58 301 7652; www.podlososiem.com.pl; ul Szeroka 52/54; mains 40-110zł; ◷noon-11pm) Founded in 1598 and famous for salmon, this is one of Gdańsk's most highly regarded restaurants. Red leather seats, brass chandeliers and a gathering of gas lamps fill out the rather sober interior, illuminated by the speciality drink – Goldwasser. This gooey, sweet liqueur with flakes of gold was produced in its cellars from the 16th century until WWII.

🍸 DRINKING & NIGHTLIFE

Józef K   Bar

(📞58 550 4935; ul Piwna 1/2; 🕙10am-last customer; 🛜) Is it a bar or a junk shop? You decide as you relax with a cocktail or a glass of excellent Polish perry on one of the battered sofas, illuminated by an old theatre spotlight. Downstairs is an open area where the party kicks off at weekends; upstairs is more intimate with lots of soft seating and well-stocked bookcases.

Brovarnia   Microbrewery

(www.brovarnia.pl; ul Szafarnia 9; 🕙1-11pm) Northern Poland's best microbrewery cooks up award-winning dark, wheat and lager beers in polished copper vats amid sepia photos of old Gdańsk. Tables are tightly packed but this place lacks a beer-hall feel, possibly as it's squeezed into vacant granary space in the posh Hotel Gdańsk.

Goldwasser   Cafe

(Długie Pobrzeże 22; 🕙10am-8pm) Experience the spirit of the interwar Free City of Danzig at the home of three tasty local tipples – Goldwasser, Kurfüsten and locally produced Machandel vodka. A quiet oasis with a leathery upmarket feel. Enter from Długi Targ.

Cafe Ferber   Bar

(📞791 010 005; www.ferber.pl; ul Długa 77/78; 🕙9am-late; 🛜) It's startling to step straight from Gdańsk's historic main street into this very modern cafe-bar, dominated by bright red panels, a suspended ceiling and boxy lighting. The scarlet decor contrasts with its comfy armchairs, from which you can sip coffee and cocktail creations such as the

szary kot (grey cat). On weekends, DJs spin tunes into the wee small hours.

Literacka   Wine Bar

(www.literacka.gda.pl; ul Mariacka 52; 🕙noon-last customer) This intimate, two-level wine bar stocks reds and whites from all over the world, including – wait for it – Poland! Staff know their Dornfelder from their Douce noir and there are inexpensive pasta dishes, sandwiches and soups to accompany your wine of choice.

ℹ️ INFORMATION

Tourist Office Train station (📞58 721 3277; www.gdansk4u.pl; ul Podwale Grodzkie 8; 🕙9am-7pm May-Sep, to 5pm Oct-Apr); **Main Town** (📞58 301 4355; Długi Targ 28/29; 🕙9am-7pm May-Sep, to 5pm Oct-Apr) Relatively efficient but occasionally visitor-weary info points. The train station branch is hidden in the underpass leading to the city centre.

ℹ️ GETTING AROUND

A commuter train, known as the SKM (Szybka Kolej Miejska; Fast City Train), runs constantly between Gdańsk Główny and Gdynia Główna (35 minutes). The trains run every five to 10 minutes at peak times. You buy tickets at the stations and validate them in the machines at the platform entrance (not in the train itself), or purchase them prevalidated from vending machines on the platform.

Trams and buses cover the city. Tickets cost 3zł for any one way journey and 3.60zł for one hour's travel. A day ticket valid for a 24-hour period costs 12zł. Remember to validate your ticket in the vehicle, so it is stamped with the date and time.

Lerwick Town Hall

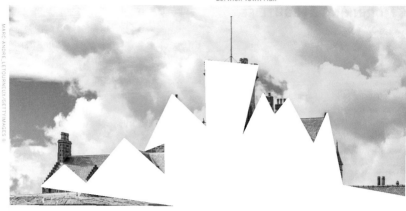

Shetland Islands

Close enough to Norway geographically and historically to make nationality an ambiguous concept, the Shetland Islands are Britain's most northerly outpost. The stirringly bleak setting – a Unesco geopark – feels uniquely Scottish.

Great For...

☑ **Don't Miss**

The seabird cliffs at Sumburgh Head.

Shetland Museum

This **museum** (☏01595-695057; www.shetlandmuseumandarchives.org.uk; Hay's Dock; ◷10am-5pm Mon-Sat, noon-5pm Sun May-Aug, 10am-4pm Mon-Sat, noon-5pm Sun Sep-Apr) **FREE** in Lerwick is an impressive recollection of 5000 years' worth of culture, people and their interaction with this ancient landscape. Comprehensive but never dull, the display covers everything from the archipelago's geology to its fishing industry, via local mythology – find out about scary *nyuggles* (ghostly horses), or detect *trows* (fairies). Pictish carvings and replica jewellery are among the finest pieces.

Bressay & Noss

These islands lie across Bressay Sound just east of Lerwick. Bressay (bress-ah) has interesting walks, especially along the cliffs

Guillemot, Sumburgh Head

MICHAEL NOLAN/GETTYIMAGES ©

Explore Ashore

The best way to explore with limited time is to take a tour or hire a car. In a day, you could see Lerwick, the main town, and some of the highlights of the southern portion of Mainland, the principal island. You can also reach the Sumburgh cliffs and Jarlshof by bus from Lerwick.

❶ Need to Know

Discover Shetland (☎07867-434354; www.discovershetland.net) offer customisable tours with a knowledgeable guide.

and up **Ward Hill** (226m), which has good views of the islands. Much smaller **Noss** (www.nnr-scotland.org.uk/noss; boat adult/child £3/1.50; ⊙10am-5pm Tue-Wed & Fri-Sun mid-Apr–Aug) is a nature reserve. As well as the crossing to Noss from Bressay, there are boat trips around the island from Lerwick.

Jarlshof

Old and new collide here, with Sumburgh airport right by this picturesque, instructive archaeological **site** (HES; ☎01950-460112; www.historicenvironment.scot; adult/child £5.50/3.30; ⊙9.30am-5.30pm Apr-Sep, 9.30am-dusk Oct-Mar). Various periods of occupation from 2500 BC to AD 1500 can be seen; the complete change upon the Vikings' arrival is obvious: their rectangular longhouses present a marked contrast to the preceding brochs, roundhouses and wheelhouses.

Atop the site is 16th-century Old House, named 'Jarlshof' in a novel by Sir Walter Scott.

Sumburgh Head

At Mainland's southern tip, these spectacular **cliffs** (www.rspb.org.uk) offer a good chance to get up close to puffins, and huge nesting colonies of fulmars, guillemots and razorbills. If you're lucky, you might spot dolphins, minke whales or orcas. Also here is an excellent **visitor centre** (☎01595-694688; www.sumburghhead.com; adult/child £6/2; ⊙11am-5.30pm Apr-Sep), in the lighthouse buildings. Displays explain about the lighthouse, foghorn and radar station that operated here, and there's a good exhibition on the local marine creatures and birds.

St Ninian's Isle

This is the largest shell-and-sand tombolo (sand or gravel isthmus) in Britain. Walk across to beautiful, emerald-capped St Ninian's Isle. Here you'll find the ruins of a 12th-century church where a famous hoard of silver Pictish treasure was found; there are replicas in Lerwick's Shetland Museum.

Orkney Islands

There's a real magic to this storied archipelago of mostly flat, green-topped islands famed for its wonderful neolithic archaeological sites, sublime sandy beaches and spectacular coastal scenery.

Great For...

☑ Don't Miss

Orkney's utterly extraordinary assemblage of neolithic sites.

Skara Brae

Idyllically situated by a sandy bay eight miles north of Stromness, and predating Stonehenge and the pyramids of Giza, extraordinary **Skara Brae** (HES; www.historic environment.scot; adult/child £6.10/3.70, incl Skaill House adult/child £7.10/4.30; ⏱9.30am-5.30pm Apr-Sep, 10am-4pm Oct-Mar) is Northern Europe's best-preserved prehistoric village. Even the stone furniture has survived the 5000 years since a community lived and breathed here. It was hidden until 1850, when waves whipped up by a severe storm eroded the sand and grass above the beach, exposing the houses underneath.

Maeshowe

Egypt has pyramids, Scotland has **Maeshowe** (HES; ☎01856-761606; www.historic environment.scot; adult/child £5.50/3.30;

Excavations at Ness of Brodgar

WOZZIE/SHUTTERSTOCK ©

Explore Ashore

To make the most of a day ashore, we recommend booking a private tour. An unhurried but comprehensive day could see you explore the principal neolithic archaeological sights, as well as the capital Kirkwall.

❶ Need to Know

Orkney Uncovered (☏01856-878822; www.orkneyuncovered.co.uk), **Great Orkney Tours** (☏01856-861443; www.great orkneytours.co.uk) and **Orkney Aspects** (☏01856-741433; www.orkneyaspects.co.uk) are recommended tour operators.

Evidence of a major settlement centred on a monumental building has been revealed, dating from the 4th and 3rd millennia BC. During the summer dig season, students offer free guided tours daily, though you'll only see archaeologists at work from Monday to Friday.

St Magnus Cathedral

Constructed from local red sandstone, Kirkwall's **centrepiece** (www.stmagnus. org; Broad St; ⊙9am-6pm Mon-Sat, 1-6pm Sun Apr-Sep, 9am-1pm & 2-5pm Mon-Sat Oct-Mar) **FREE**, is among Scotland's most interesting cathedrals. The powerful atmosphere of an ancient faith pervades the impressive interior.

Highland Park

South of the centre, this **distillery** (www. highlandpark.co.uk; Holm Rd; tour adult/child £7.50/free; ⊙10am-5pm Mon-Sat & noon-5pm Sun May-Aug, 10am-5pm Mon-Fri Apr & Sep, 1-5pm Mon-Fri Oct-Mar) is great to visit. They malt their own barley; you can see it and the peat kiln used to dry it on the excellent, well-informed hour-long tour.

⊙9.30am-5pm Apr-Sep, 10am-4pm Oct-Mar, tours hourly 10am-4pm, plus 6pm & 7pm Jul & Aug.). Constructed about 5000 years ago, it's an extraordinary place, a Stone Age tomb built from enormous sandstone blocks. Creeping down the long stone passageway to the central chamber, you feel the indescribable gulf of years that separate us from the architects of this mysterious place. Entry is by 45-minute guided tours on the hour: you must reserve your tour slot ahead by phone.

Ness of Brodgar

The spectacular finds from ongoing excavations at this archaeological site between the imposing stone circle of the **Ring of Brodgar** and the four mighty **Standing Stones of Stenness** have revolutionised understanding of the neolithic in Britain.

REYKJAVÍK, ICELAND

Reykjavík at a Glance...

Reykjavík is loaded with captivating art, rich cuisine and quirky, creative people. The music scene is epic, with excellent festivals, creative DJs gigging and any number of home-grown bands.

Even if you come for a short visit, be sure to take a trip to the countryside. Tours and services abound, and understanding Reykjavík and its people is helped by understanding the vast, raw and gorgeous land they anchor. The majority of Icelanders live in the capital, but you can guarantee their spirits also roam free across the land. Absorb what you see, hear, taste, smell – it's all part of Iceland's rich heritage.

With One Day in Port

Explore the historic Old Reykjavík quarter, taking in the **Ráðhús** (town hall; p271) and **Alþingi** (Parliament; p270), then peruse the city's best museums, such as the impressive **National Museum** (p265), **Reykjavík Art Museum** (p271) or the **Settlement Exhibition** (p270), built around a Viking longhouse. Wander up arty Skólavörðustígur and photograph the immense church, **Hallgrímskirkja** (p271). For a perfect view, zip up the tower.

Best Places for...

Cafe Stofan Kaffihús (p279)

Seafood Messinn (p279)

New Nordic Dill (p280)

Brewpub Bryggjan Brugghús (p281)

Bar Kaffibarinn (p282)

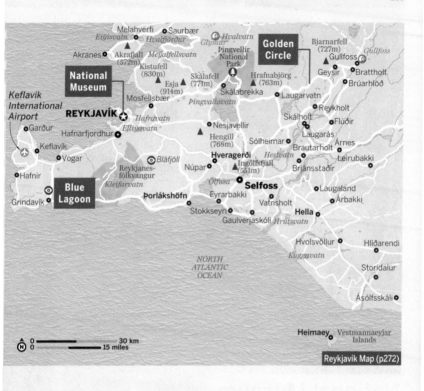

Reykjavík Map (p272)

Getting from the Port

Some smaller ships dock right in the centre at the Miðbakki berth in the Old Harbour. Most, however, use Skarfabakki, 4km east of the centre. Bus 16 runs from outside the terminal to downtown (kr420, 10 minutes) and there are usually shuttles available. A taxi will cost around kr3000.

Fast Facts

Currency Icelandic króna (kr)

Language Icelandic

Free wi-fi Many cafes have free wi-fi.

Tourist information The friendly main tourist office can book tours and activities.

Transport Excellent bus coverage; see www.straeto.is for timetables.

Reconstructed traditional driftwood house

National Museum

Iceland's premier museum is packed with artefacts and interesting displays. Exhibits give an excellent overview of the country's history and culture, and the museum's rotating photographic exhibitions are well worth a visit.

The superb National Museum beautifully displays Icelandic artefacts from settlement to the modern age, providing a meaningful overview of Iceland's history and culture. Brilliantly curated exhibits lead you through the struggle to settle and organise the forbidding island, the radical changes wrought by the advent of Christianity, the lean times of domination by foreign powers and Iceland's eventual independence.

Settlement Era Finds

The premier section of the museum describes the Settlement Era – including how the chieftains ruled and the introduction of Christianity – and features swords, meticulously carved drinking horns, and silver hoards. A powerful bronze figure of Thor is thought to date to about 1000. The priceless 13th-century Valþjófsstaðir church

Great For...

☑ Don't Miss

The gaming pieces made from cod ear bones, and the wooden doll that doubled as a kitchen utensil.

⚓

Explore Ashore

Allow half an hour for the trip from the cruise terminal to the museum. Catch bus 16 to its Hlemmur terminus, then change to bus 15. You'll need to get a *skiptimiði* (transfer ticket) from the driver. Plan on at least two hours here.

❶ Need to Know

Þjóðminjasafn Íslands; ☎530 2200; www. nationalmuseum.is; Suðurgata 41; adult/child kr2000/free; ☑10am–5pm May–mid-Sep, closed Mon mid-Sep–Apr; 🚍1, 3, 6, 12, 14

door is carved with the story of a knight, his faithful lion and a passel of dragons.

Domestic Life

Exhibits explain how the chieftains ruled and how people survived on little, lighting their dark homes and fashioning bog iron. There's everything from the remains of early *skyr* (yoghurt-like dessert) production to intricate pendants and brooches. Look for the Viking-era *hnefatafl* game set (like chess); this artefact's discovery in a grave in Baldursheimar led to the founding of the museum.

Viking Graves

Encased in the floor, you'll find Viking-era graves,with their precious burial goods: horse bones, a sword, pins, a ladle, a comb. One of the tombs containing an eight-month-old infant is the only one of its kind ever found.

Ecclesiastical Artefacts

The section of the museum that details the introduction of Christianity is chock-a-block with rare art and artefacts such as the priceless 13th-century Valþjófsstaðir church door.

The Modern Era

Upstairs, collections span four centuries, from 1600 to the present, and give a clear sense of how Iceland struggled under foreign rule, finally gained independence and went on to modernise. Look for the papers and belongings of Jón Sigurðsson, the architect of Iceland's independence.

Museum Guides

The excellent audio guide (kr300) adds loads of useful detail. The one for kids is in Icelandic or English only.

Free English tours run at 11am on Wednesday, Saturday and Sunday from May to mid-September.

Blue Lagoon

In a magnificent black-lava field, this milky-teal spa is fed water from the futuristic Svartsengi geothermal plant. With its silver towers, roiling clouds of steam and people daubed in white silica mud, it's an other-worldly place.

Great For...

☑ Don't Miss

A bike or quad-bike tour in the lava fields.

A Good Soak

Before your dip, don't forget to practise standard Iceland pool etiquette: a thorough naked pre-pool showering.

The super-heated spa water (70% sea water, 30% fresh water) is rich in blue-green algae, mineral salts and fine silica mud, which condition and exfoliate the skin – sounds like advertising speak, but you really do come out as soft as a baby's bum. The water is hottest near the vents where it emerges, and the surface is several degrees warmer than the bottom.

Explore the Complex

The lagoon has been developed for visitors, with an enormous, modern complex of changing rooms, restaurants, a rooftop view-point and a gift shop, and landscaped with hot-pots, steam rooms, a sauna, a bar and a

Explore Ashore

Most cruise passengers visit on an organised tour, but transport to the Blue Lagoon runs from Reykjavík (www.re.is, 4500kr return, hourly, 50 minutes). You must prebook both transport and admission; combined deals can save you money. Allow five to six hours in total from Reykjavík.

🛈 Need to Know

Bláa Lónið; 📞 420 8800; www.bluelagoon.com; adult/child from kr6990/free; ⊘7am-midnight Jul–mid-Aug, 7am-11pm mid-May–Jun, 8am-10pm Jan–mid-May & mid-Aug–Sep, 8am-9pm Oct-Dec

piping-hot waterfall that delivers a powerful hydraulic massage – like being pummelled by a troll. A VIP section has its own interior wading space, lounge and viewing platform.

Massage

For extra relaxation, you can lie on a floating mattress and have a massage therapist knead your knots (30/60 minutes kr10,200/31,200). You must book spa treatments well in advance. Towel or bathing-suit hire is kr700.

Guided Tours

In addition to the spa opportunities at the Blue Lagoon, you can combine your visit with package tours, or hook up with nearby **ATV Adventures** (📞857 3001; www.atv4x4.is) for quad-bike or cycling tours (kr9900 from the Blue Lagoon through the lava fields) or

bicycle rental. The company can pick you up and drop you off at the lagoon.

Cycling & Quad Bikes

Combine your Blue Lagoon visit with myriad package tours, or hook up with nearby ATV Adventures for cycling or quad-bike tours or bicycle rental. It picks up and drops off at the lagoon.

When booking tours, verify whether your ticket for the lagoon is included or if you need to book it separately.

Booking Your Ticket

○ There is an hourly cap on admissions; book ahead or you will be turned away. The lagoon is often sold out days in advance.

○ Cut long lines and get e-ticket deals from the website or tour company vouchers (eg Reykjavík Excursions).

Gulfoss, Hvitau River

Golden Circle

*The Golden Circle is a beloved
tourist circuit that takes in three
popular attractions all within
100km of the capital: Þingvellir,
Geysir and Gullfoss.*

The Golden Circle offers the opportunity
to see a meeting point of the continental
plates and the site of the ancient Icelandic
parliament (Þingvellir), a spouting hot
spring (Geysir) and a roaring waterfall
(Gullfoss), all in one doable-in-a-day loop.

Almost every tour company in the Reykjavík area offers a Golden Circle excursion,
often combinable with virtually any activity
from quad-biking to caving and rafting.

If you're planning to spend the night in
the relatively small region, Laugarvatn is a
good base with excellent dining options.

Þingvellir National Park

Þingvellir National Park (www.thingvellir.
is), 40km northeast of central Reykjavík,
is Iceland's most important historical site
and a place of vivid beauty. The Vikings
established the world's first democratic

Great For...

☑ **Don't Miss**

The Sigríður memorial near the foot
of the stairs from the Gullfoss tourist
information centre.

Geysir

Explore Ashore

The easiest way to visit for cruise passengers is on an organised tour. There are numerous operators. The Golden Circle is best done as a full-day trip.

ℹ Need to Know

Tours generally go from 8.30am to 6pm or from noon to 7pm. In summer there are evening trips from 7pm to midnight.

parliament, the **Alþingi**, here in AD 930. The meetings were conducted outdoors and, as with many Saga sites, there are only the stone foundations of ancient **encampments**. The site has a superb natural setting with rivers and waterfalls in an immense, fissured rift valley, caused by the meeting of the North American and Eurasian **tectonic plates**.

Geysir

One of Iceland's most famous tourist attractions, **Geysir** FREE (*gay*-zeer; literally 'gusher') is the original hot-water spout after which all other geysers are named. Earthquakes can stimulate activity, though eruptions are rare. Luckily for visitors, the very reliable **Strokkur** geyser sits alongside. You rarely have to wait more than five to 10 minutes for the hot spring to shoot

an impressive 15m to 30m plume before vanishing down its enormous hole. Stand downwind only if you want a shower.

The geothermal area containing Geysir and Strokkur was free to enter at the time of writing, though there is discussion of instituting a fee.

Gullfoss

Iceland's most famous waterfall, **Gullfoss** (Golden Falls; www.gullfoss.is) FREE is a spectacular double cascade. It drops 32m, kicking up tiered walls of spray before thundering away down a narrow ravine. On sunny days the mist creates shimmering rainbows, and it's also magical in winter when the falls glitter with ice.

A tarmac path suitable for wheelchairs leads from the tourist information centre to a lookout over the falls, and stairs continue down to the edge. There is also an access road down to the falls.

⊙ SIGHTS

◎ Old Reykjavík

With a series of sights and interesting historic buildings, Old Reykjavík forms the heart of the capital, and the focal point of many historic walking tours. It's a top area for a stroll, from scenic lake Tjörnin to the old-fashioned houses surrounding Austurvöllur and Ingólfstorg squares.

Settlement Exhibition   Museum

(Landnámssýningin; 📞411 6370; www.reykjavik museum.is; Aðalstræti 16; adult/child kr1600/ free; ⊙9am-6pm) This fascinating archaeological ruin/museum is based around a 10th-century **Viking longhouse** unearthed here from 2001 to 2002, and other Settlement Era finds from central Reykjavík. It imaginatively combines technological wizardry and archaeology to give a glimpse into early Icelandic life. Don't miss the fragment of **boundary wall** at the back of the museum that is older still (and the oldest human-made structure in Reykjavík). Among the captivating high-tech displays, a wraparound panorama shows how things would have looked at the time of the longhouse.

Tjörnin   Lake

This placid lake at the centre of the city is sometimes locally called the Pond. It echoes with the honks and squawks of over 40 species of visiting birds, including swans, geese and Arctic terns; feeding the ducks is a popular pastime for under-fives. Pretty sculpture-dotted parks like **Hljómskálagarður** FREE line the southern shores, and their paths are much used by cyclists and joggers. In winter, hardy souls strap on ice skates and turn the lake into an **outdoor rink**.

i8   Gallery

(📞551 3666; www.i8.is; Tryggvagata 16; ⊙11am-6pm Tue-Fri, 1-5pm Sat) FREE This gallery represents some of the country's top modern artists, many of whom show overseas as well.

Alþingi   Historic Building

(Parliament; 📞563 0500; www.althingi.is; Kirkjustraeti) FREE Iceland's first parliament, the

Hallgrímskirkja

Alþingi, was created at Þingvellir in AD 930. After losing its independence in the 13th century, the country gradually won back its autonomy, and the modern Alþingi moved into this current basalt building in 1881; a stylish glass-and-stone annexe was completed in 2002. Visitors can attend sessions (four times weekly mid-September to early June; see the website for details) when parliament is sitting.

Ráðhús
Notable Building

(Vonarstræti; ⊙8am-4pm Mon-Fri) **FREE** Reykjavík's waterside Ráðhús is a beautifully positioned postmodern construction of concrete stilts, tinted windows and mossy walls rising from Tjörnin. Inside there's an interesting 3D topographical map of Iceland.

◉ Laugavegur & Skólavörðustígur

This district is Reykjavík's liveliest. While it's justifiably well known for its shops and pubs, it's also home to some of the city's top restaurants, local music venues and the city's top art-house cinema.

Hallgrímskirkja
Church

(☑510 1000; www.hallgrimskirkja.is; Skólavörðustígur; tower adult/child kr900/100; ⊙9am-9pm Jun-Sep, to 5pm Oct-May) Reykjavík's immense white-concrete church (1945–86), star of a thousand postcards, dominates the skyline, and is visible from up to 20km away. Get an unmissable view of the city by taking an elevator trip up the 74.5m-high **tower**. In contrast to the high drama outside, the Lutheran church's interior is quite plain. The most eye-catching feature is the vast 5275-pipe **organ** installed in 1992. The church's size and radical design caused controversy, and its architect, Guðjón Samúelsson (1887–1950), never saw its completion.

Harpa
Arts Centre

(☑box office 528 5050; www.harpa.is; Austurbakki 2; ⊙8am-midnight, box office 10am-6pm) With its ever-changing facets glistening on the water's edge, Reykjavík's sparkling

Reykjavík Art Museum

The excellent **Reykjavík Art Museum** (Listasafn Reykjavíkur; www.artmuseum.is; adult/child kr1600/free) is split over three well-done sites: the large, modern downtown **Hafnarhús** (☑411 6400; Tryggvagata 17; ⊙10am-5pm Fri-Wed, to 10pm Thu) focusing on contemporary art; **Kjarvalsstaðir** (☑411 6420; Flókagata 24, Miklatún Park; ⊙10am-5pm), in a park just east of Snorrabraut, and displaying rotating exhibits of modern art; and **Ásmundarsafn** (Ásmundur Sveinsson Museum; ☑411 6430; Sigtún; ⊙10am-5pm May-Sep, 1-5pm Oct-Apr; ☐2, 4, 14, 15, 17, 19), a peaceful haven near Laugardalur for viewing sculptures by Ásmundur Sveinsson.

One ticket is good at all three sites, and if you buy after 3pm you get a 50% discount should you want a ticket the next day.

Reykjavík Art Museum at Hafnarhús
GODDARD_PHOTOGRAPHY/GETTY IMAGES ©

Harpa concert hall and cultural centre is a beauty to behold. In addition to a season of top-notch shows (some free), it's worth stopping by to explore the shimmering interior with harbour vistas, or take a 30-minute guided **tour** (kr1500; ⊙1pm, 3.30pm, 4.30pm Mon-Fri, 11am, 1pm and 3.30pm Sat-Sun).

Culture House
Gallery

(Þjóðmenningarhúsið; ☑530 2210; www.culture house.is; Hverfisgata 15; adult/child incl National Museum kr2000/free; ⊙10am-5pm May–mid-Sep, closed Mon mid-Sep–Apr) This fantastic collaboration between the National

Reykjavík

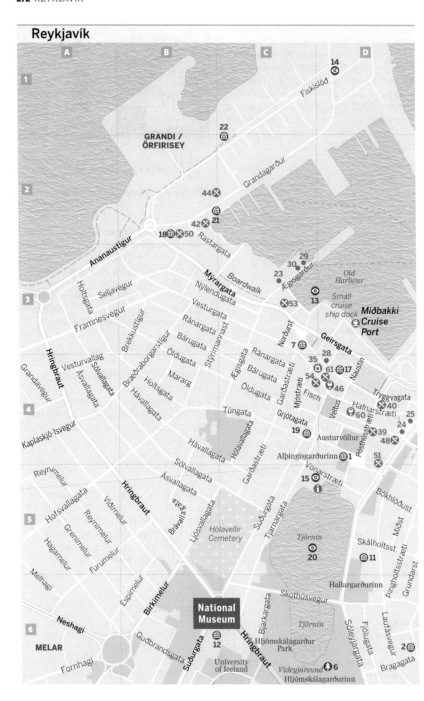

Fiskislóð

14

22

GRANDI /
ÖRFIRISEY

Grandagarður

44

42 **21**

18 **50** Rastargata

Ananaustigur

Mýrargata

Boardwalk

Nýlendugata

Seljavegur

Holtsgata

Vesturgata

29

30 **23** Ægisgarður

Old
Harbour

13 Small
cruise
ship dock

Miðbakki
Cruise
Port

53

Framnesvegur

Brekkustígur

Ránargata

Bárugata

Öldugata

Mararg

Holtsgata

Styrimannast

Norðurst

7 Geirsgata

Hringbraut

Vesturvallag

Sólvallagata

Ásvallagata

Bræðraborgarstígur

Hávallagata

Ránargata

Bárugata

Öldugata

Ægisgata

Garðastræti

Miðstræti

Fisch

35 **28**

54 **61** **17**
46

Nýlstin

Tryggvagata

Grandavegur

Túngata

40

Hafnarstræti **60**

25

24

Veltus

Kaplaskjó-Ísvegur

HáVallagata

HólaVallagata

Garðastræti

19 Austurvöllur

39

48

Reynimelur

Sólvallagata

Ásvallagata

Alþingisgarðurinn **1**

Pósthússtræti

51

Hringbraut

Bráva

Ljósvallagata

Hólavellir
Cemetery

Suðurgata

Tjarnargata

Vonarstræti

15

Bókhlöðust

Hofsvallagata

Viðimelur

Reynimelur

Grenimelur

Furumelur

Hagamelur

Tjörnin

20

Skálholtsst

Miðst

11

Þingholtsstræti

Grundarst

Melhagi

Espimelur

Birkimelur

Hringbraut

Hallargarðurinn

Skothúsvegur

National
Museum

Bjarkargata

Tjörnin

Laufásvegur

Sóleyjargata

Fjólugata

Neshagi

MELAR

Guðbrandsgata

Suðurgata

Hringbraut

Hljómskálagarðður
Park

2

Bragagata

Fornhagi

12

University
of Iceland

Videyjarsund

6

Hljómskálagarðurinn

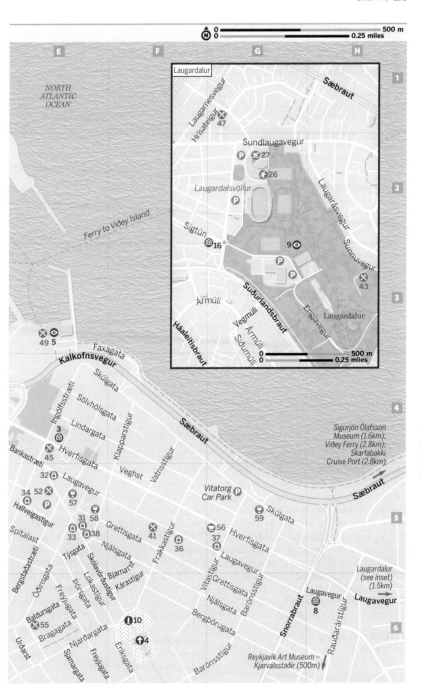

Reykjavík

Museum, National Gallery and four other organisations creates a superbly curated exhibition covering the artistic and cultural heritage of Iceland from settlement to today. Priceless artefacts are arranged by theme, and highlights include 14th-century manuscripts, contemporary art and items including the skeleton of a great auk (now extinct). The renovated 1908 building is beautiful, with great views of the harbour, and a cafe on the ground floor. Check the website for free guided tours.

National Gallery of Iceland
Museum

(Listasafn Íslands; ☑515 9600; www.listasafn. is; Fríkirkjuvegur 7; adult/child kr1500/free;

☺10am-5pm daily mid-May–mid-Sep, 11am-5pm Tue-Sun mid-Sep–mid-May) This pretty stack of marble atriums and spacious galleries overlooking Tjörnin offers ever-changing exhibits drawn from the 10,000-piece collection. The museum can only exhibit a small sample at any time; shows range from 19th- and 20th-century paintings by Iceland's favourite sons and daughters (including Jóhannes Kjarval and Nína Sæmundsson) to sculptures by Sigurjón Ólafsson and others. The museum ticket also covers entry to the **Ásgrímur Jónsson Collection** (☑515 9625; www.listasafn.is; Bergstaðastræti 74; adult/child kr1000/free; ☺2-5pm Tue, Thu, Sat & Sun mid-May–mid-Sep, 2-5pm Sat & Sun mid-Sep–Nov & Feb–mid-May) and **Sigurjón Ólafsson Museum** (Listasafn Sigurjóns Ólafssonar; ☑553 2906; www.lso.is; Laugarnestanga 70; adult/child kr1000/free; ⊗2-5pm Tue-Sun Jun-Aug, 2-5pm Sat & Sun Sep-Nov & Feb-May; ☑12, 16).

Icelandic Phallological Museum
Museum

(Hið Íslenzka Reðasafn; ☑561 6663; www.phallus. is; Laugavegur 116; adult/child kr1500/free; ⊗10am-6pm) Oh, the jokes are endless here, but although this unique museum houses a huge collection of penises, it's actually very well done. From pickled pickles to petrified wood, there are 286 different members on display, representing all Icelandic mammals and beyond. Featured items include contributions from sperm whales and a polar bear, minuscule mouse bits, silver castings of each member of the Icelandic handball team and a single human sample – from deceased mountaineer Páll Arason.

◉ Old Harbour

Largely a service harbour until recently, the **Old Harbour** (Geirsgata; ☑1, 3, 6, 11, 12, 13, 14) has blossomed into a hot spot for tourists, with several museums, volcano and Northern Lights films, and excellent restaurants. Whale-watching and puffin-viewing trips depart from the pier.

Omnom Chocolate
Factory

(☑519 5959; www.omnomchocolate.com; Hólmaslóð 4, Grandi; adult/child kr3000/1500; ⊗11am-6pm Mon-Fri, from noon Sat) Reserve ahead for a tour at this full-service chocolate factory where you'll see how cocoa beans are transformed into high-end scrumptious delights. The shop sells its bonbons and stylish bars, with specially designed labels and myriad sophisticated flavours. You'll find the bars in shops throughout Iceland.

Víkin Maritime Museum
Museum

(Víkin Sjóminjasafnið; ☑411 6300; www. maritimemuseum.is; Grandagarður 8; adult/child kr1600/free; ⊗10am-5pm; ☑14) Based appropriately in a former fish-freezing plant, this museum celebrates the country's seafaring heritage, focusing on the trawlers that transformed Iceland's economy. Guided tours go aboard coastguard ship *Óðinn* (kr1300, or joint ticket with museum kr2400; check website for times). The boat is a veteran of the 1970s Cod Wars, when British and Icelandic fishers came to blows over fishing rights in the North Atlantic.

Saga Museum
Museum

(☑511 1517; www.sagamuseum.is; Grandagarður 2; adult/child kr2100/800; ⊗10am-6pm; ☑14) The endearingly bloodthirsty Saga Museum is where Icelandic history is brought to life by eerie silicon models and a multi-language soundtrack with thudding axes and hair-raising screams. Don't be surprised if you see some of the characters wandering around town, as moulds were taken from Reykjavík residents (the owner's daughters are the Irish princess and the little slave gnawing a fish!).

There's also a room for posing in Viking dress, a documentary about the making of the museum (look for *Icelandic Idol*–winner Kalli Bjarni in the audience) and restaurant Matur og Drykkur.

Whales of Iceland
Museum

(☑571 0077; www.whalesoficeland.is; Fiskislóð 23-25; adult/child kr2900/1500; ⊗10am-5pm; ☑14) Ever stroll beneath a blue whale? This museum houses full-sized models of the 23 whales found off Iceland's coast. The largest museum of this type in Europe, it also displays models of whale skeletons, and has good audio guides and multimedia screens to explain what you're seeing. It has a cafe and gift shop, online ticket discounts and family tickets (kr5800).

✈ ACTIVITIES
Atlantsflug
Flight Tour

(☑854 4105; www.flightseeing.is; Reykjavík Domestic Airport; from adult/child kr20,000/10,000) Offers flightseeing tours from Reykjavík, Bakki Airport and Skaftafell. From Reykjavík Domestic Airport you can fly over Eyjafjallajökull crater or Reykjanes Peninsula, or take a day trip with

🩴 Laugardalur: Hot-Springs Valley

Encompassing a verdant stretch of land 4km east of the city centre, **Laugardalur** (🗺 2, 5, 14, 15, 17) was once the main source of Reykjavík's hot-water supply: it translates as 'Hot-Springs Valley', and in the park's centre you'll find relics from the old wash house. The park is a favourite with locals for its huge **swimming complex** (📞 411 5100; www.reykjavik. is/stadir/laugardalslaug; Sundlaugavegur 30a; adult/child kr950/150, suit/towel rental kr850/570; ⏱6.30am-10pm Mon-Fri, 8am-10pm Sat & Sun; 🚻), fed by the geothermal spring, alongside a **spa** (📞 553 0000; www. laugarspa.com; Sundlaugavegur 30a; day pass kr5500; ⏱6am-11pm Mon-Fri, 8am-9.30pm Sat & Sun), a skating rink, botanical gardens, sporting and concert arenas, and a kids' zoo and entertainment park.

Stop by the sun-dappled tables of **Café Flóra** (Flóran; 📞 553 8872; www. floran.is; Botanic Gardens; cakes kr10,000, mains kr1500-3100; ⏱10am-10pm May-Sep; 🍴) 🦵 for lovely food made from wholesome local ingredients – some grown in the park's gardens! Soups come with fantastic sourdough bread, and snacks range from cheese platters with nuts and honey to pulled-pork sandwiches. Weekend brunch, good coffee and homemade cakes round it all out.

In the surrounding streets you'll find **Frú Lauga farmers market** (📞 534 7165; www.frulauga.is; Laugalækur 6; ⏱11am-6pm Mon-Fri, to 4pm Sat; 🍴) 🦵 and **Reykjavík Art Museum – Ásmundarsafn** (p271).

Laugardalur's outdoor swimming pool
JEREMY HOARE/ALAMY STOCK PHOTO ©

tours around Skaftafell and Jökulsárlón glacial lagoon. Also runs scheduled flights to Vestmannaeyjar.

Literary Reykjavík   Walking
(www.bokmenntaborgin.is; Tryggvagata 15; ⏱3pm Thu Jun-Aug) **FREE** Part of the Unesco City of Literature initiative, free literary walking tours of the city centre start at the main library and include the Dark Deeds tour focusing on crime fiction. There is also a downloadable *Culture Walks* app with several themes.

Elding Adventures at Sea   Wildlife
(📞 519 5000; www.whalewatching.is; Ægisgarður 5; adult/child kr11,000/5500; ⏱harbour kiosk 8am-9pm; 🚌14) 🦵 The city's most established and ecofriendly outfit, with an included whale exhibition and refreshments served on board. Elding also offers angling (adult/child kr14,200/7100) and puffin-watching (adult/child from kr6500/3250) trips and combo tours, and runs the ferry to Viðey. Offers pick-up.

Reykjavík Bike Tours   Cycling
(Reykjavík Segway Tours; 📞 bikes 694 8956, segways 897 2790; www.icelandbike.com; Ægisgarður 7, Old Harbour; bike rental per 4hr from kr3500, tours from kr7500; ⏱9am-5pm Jun-Aug, reduced hours Sep-May; 🚌14) This outfitter rents bikes and offers tours of Reykjavík and the countryside, eg Classic Reykjavík (2½ hours, 7km); Coast of Reykjavík (2½ hours, 18km); and Golden Circle and Bike (eight hours, 25km of cycling in 1½ hours). It also offers Reykjavík Segway (kr15,000) and walking (from kr20,000) tours.

Free Walking Tour Reykjavik   Walking
(www.freewalkingtour.is; ⏱noon & 2pm Jun-Aug, 1pm Sep-May) One-hour, 1.5km walking tour of the city centre, starting at the little clock tower on Lækjartorg Sq.

Iceland Excursions   Bus
(Gray Line Iceland; 📞 540 1313; www.grayline. is; Hafnarstræti 20) Bus-tour operator with comprehensive day trips (Golden Circle kr8700) that often combine destinations

and activities such as white-water rafting and horse riding. Book online for the best prices; expect large groups.

Special Tours
Wildlife

(☎560 8800; www.specialtours.is; Ægisgarður 13; adult/child kr9900/4950; ☺harbour kiosk 8am-8pm; ☐14) One of the smallest, fastest boats in the fleet of operators, used for sea angling and whale watching (20 minutes to reach the prime viewing spot). It uses a smaller vessel for puffin tours (adult/child kr5500/2250), and offers multiple combo tours.

🔒 SHOPPING

Laugavegur and Skólavörðustígur are the central streets of Reykjavík's shopping scene. You'll find them densely lined with everything from stereotypical souvenir shops (derisively called 'Puffin Shops' by Reykjavíkers) to design shops and galleries selling beautiful handmade Icelandic arts and crafts, couture clothing lines and cool outdoorwear.

Puffins

Álafoss
Clothing

(☎566 6303; www.alafoss.is; Álafossvegur 23, Mosfellsbær; ☺8am-8pm Mon-Fri, 9am-8pm Sat & Sun; ☐15) One of the best places in Iceland for hand- or machine-made *lopapeysur* (Icelandic woollen sweaters) and other wool products, this factory-outlet in Mosfellsbær, one of Reykjavík's outer suburbs, can be an add-on to your Golden Circle adventure. Prices are somewhat lower than most tourist shops. Reykjavík bus 15 stops nearby (Háholt stop). Álafoss also has a Reykjavík **boutique** (☎562 6303; Laugavegur 8; ☺10am-6pm).

Geysir
Clothing

(☎519 6000; www.geysir.com; Skólavörðustígur 16; ☺10am-7pm Mon-Sat, 11am-6pm Sun) For traditional Icelandic clothing and unique modern designs, Geysir boasts an elegant selection of sweaters, blankets, and men's and women's clothes, shoes and bags. There's also a branch down the street at

Whale-watching and puffin-viewing trips depart from the pier (Old Harbour)

From left: lunch by the marina; Stofan Kaffihús; KronKron

Skólavörðustígur 7 with the same opening hours.

Orrifinn
Jewellery

(📞789 7616; www.orrifinn.com; Skólavörðustígur 17a; ⊙10am-6pm Mon-Fri, 11am-4pm Sat) Subtle, beautiful jewellery captures the natural wonder of Iceland and its Viking history. Delicate anchors, axes and pen nibs dangle from understated matte chains.

KronKron
Clothing

(📞561 9388; www.kronkron.com; Laugavegur 63b; ⊙10am-6pm Mon-Thu, to 6.30pm Fri, to 5pm Sat) This is where Reykjavík goes high fashion, with labels such as Marc Jacobs and Vivienne Westwood. But we really enjoy its Scandinavian designers (including Kron by KronKron) and their offerings of silk dresses, knit capes, scarves and even woollen underwear. The handmade shoes are off the charts, and are also sold down the street at **Kron** (📞551 8388; www.kron.is; Laugavegur 48; ⊙10am-6pm Mon-Fri, to 5pm Sat).

Kiosk
Clothing

(📞571 3636.; www.kioskreykjavik.com; Ingólfsstræti 6; ⊙11am-7pm Mon-Fri, to 5pm

Sat) This wonderful designers' cooperative is lined with creative women's fashion in a glass-fronted boutique. Designers take turns staffing the store.

Kirsuberjatréð
Arts & Crafts

(Cherry Tree; 📞562 8990; www.kirs.is; Vesturgata 4; ⊙10am-6pm Mon-Fri, to 5pm Sat & Sun) This women's art-and-design collective in an interesting 1882 former bookshop sells weird and wonderful fish-skin handbags, music boxes made from string, and, our favourite, beautiful coloured bowls made from radish slices. It's been around for 25 years and now has 11 designers.

🍴 EATING
🍽 Old Reykjavík

You'll find some of the city's highest-end restaurants in the Old Reykjavík area, where you should book ahead in high season to guarantee a table. On the other hand, you'll also encounter Reykjavík's famed hot-dog stand, **Bæjarins Beztu** (www.bbp.is; Tryggvagata; hot dogs kr420; ⊙10am-1am Sun-Thu, to 4.30am Fri & Sat;), and other food trucks

set up in Lækjartorg Sq – everything from lobster soup to fish and chips or doughnuts.

Stofan Kaffihús Cafe **$**
(📞546 1842; www.facebook.com/stofan.cafe; Vesturgata 3; dishes kr1500-1700; ⏰9am-11pm Mon-Wed, to midnight Thu-Sat, 10am-10pm Sun; 📶) This laid-back cafe in an historic brick building has a warm feel with its worn wooden floors, plump couches and spacious main room. Settle in for coffee, cake or soup, and watch the world go by.

Messinn Seafood **$$**
(📞546 0095; www.messinn.com; Lækjargata 6b; lunch mains kr1850-2100, dinner mains kr2700-4100; ⏰11.30am-3pm & 5-10pm; 📶) Make a beeline to Messinn for the best seafood that Reykjavík has to offer. The speciality is amazing pan-fries where your pick of fish is served up in a sizzling cast-iron skillet accompanied by buttery potatoes and salad. The mood is upbeat and comfortable, and the staff friendly.

Grillmarkaðurinn Fusion **$$$**
(Grill Market; 📞571 7777; www.grillmarka-durinn.is; Lækargata 2a; mains kr4600-9900;

⏰11.30am-2pm Mon-Fri, 6-10.30pm Sun-Thu, to 11.30pm Fri & Sat) Tippety-top dining is the order of the day here, from the moment you enter the glass atrium with the golden-globe lights to your first snazzy cocktail, and on through the meal. Service is impeccable, and locals and visitors alike rave about the food: locally sourced Icelandic ingredients prepared with culinary imagination by master chefs.

Fiskfélagið Seafood **$$$**
(📞552 5300; www.fishcompany.is; Vesturgata 2a; mains lunch kr2400-3000, dinner kr4900-6000; ⏰11.30am-2.30pm Mon-Sat, 5.30-11pm Sun-Thu, to 11.30pm Fri & Sat) The 'Fish Company' takes Icelandic seafood recipes and spins them through a variety of far-flung inspirations from Fiji coconut to Spanish chorizo. Dine in an intimate-feeling stone-and-timber room with copper light fittings and quirky furnishings or out on the terrace.

Apotek Fusion **$$$**
(📞551 0011; www.apotekrestaurant.is; Austurstræti 16; mains kr2500-6000; ⏰11.30am-11pm Sun-Thu, to midnight Fri & Sat) This beautiful

restaurant and bar with shining glass fixtures and a cool ambience is equally known for its delicious menu of small plates that are perfect for sharing and its top-flight cocktails. It's on the ground floor of the hotel of the same name.

⊗ Laugavegur & Skólavörðustígur

Bakarí Sandholt   Bakery $

(☏551 3524; www.sandholt.is; Laugavegur 36; snacks kr600-1200; ⊗7am-9pm; 🛜) Reykjavík's favourite bakery is usually crammed with folks hoovering up the generous assortment of fresh baguettes, croissants, pastries and sandwiches. The soup of the day (kr1600) comes with delicious sourdough bread.

Ostabúðin   Deli $$

(Cheese Shop; ☏562 2772; www.ostabudin.is; Skólavörðustígur 8; mains kr3750-5000; ⊗restaurant noon-10pm, deli 10am-6pm Mon-Thu, to 7pm Fri, 11am-4pm Sat) Head to this gourmet cheese shop and deli, with a large dining room for the friendly owner's cheese and meat platters (from kr1900 to kr4000), or the catch of the

day, accompanied by homemade bread. You can pick up other local goods, like terrines and duck confit, on the way out.

Dill   Icelandic $$$

(☏552 1522; www.dillrestaurant.is; Hverfisgata 12; 5-course meals from kr12,000; ⊗6-10pm Wed-Sat) Top 'New Nordic' cuisine is the major drawcard at this elegant yet simple bistro. The focus is very much on the food – locally sourced produce served as a parade of courses. The owners are friends with Copenhagen's famous Noma clan, and take Icelandic cuisine to similarly heady heights. Popular with locals and visitors alike, a reservation is a must.

Þrír Frakkar   Icelandic, Seafood $$$

(☏552 3939; www.3frakkar.com; Baldursgata 14; mains kr4000-6000; ⊗11.30am-2.30pm & 6-10pm Mon-Fri, 6-11pm Sat & Sun) Owner-chef Úlfar Eysteinsson has built up a consistently excellent reputation at this snug little restaurant – apparently a favourite of Jamie Oliver's. Specialities range throughout the aquatic world from salt cod and halibut to *plokkfiskur* (fish stew) with black

Lobster soup at Sægreifinn

bread. Nonfish items run towards guillemot, horse, lamb and whale.

Old Harbour

Sægreifinn Seafood $

(Seabaron; ☎553 1500; www.saegreifinn.is; Geirsgata 8; mains kr1350-1900; ⏰11.30am-11pm mid-May–Aug, to 10pm Sep–mid-May) Sidle into this green harbourside shack for the most famous lobster soup (kr1400) in the capital, or to choose from a fridge full of fresh fish skewers to be grilled on the spot. Though the original sea baron sold the restaurant some years ago, the place retains a homey, laid-back feel.

Coocoo's Nest Cafe $$

(☎552 5454; www.coocoosnest.is; Grandagarður 23; mains kr1700-4500; ⏰11am-10pm Tue-Sat, to 4pm Sun; 📶) Pop into this cool eatery tucked behind the Old Harbour for popular weekend brunches (dishes kr1700 to kr2500; 11am to 4pm Friday to Sunday) paired with decadent cocktails (kr1800). Casual, small and groovy, with mosaic plywood tables; the menu changes and there are nightly themes, but it's always scrumptious.

Matur og Drykkur Icelandic $$

(☎571 8877; www.maturogdrykkur.is; Grandagarður 2; lunch mains kr1900-2700, dinner mains/tasting menus kr3700/10,000; ⏰11.30am-3pm & 6-10pm Mon-Sat, 6-10pm Sun; 🚌14) One of Reykjavík's top high-concept restaurants, Matur og Drykkur means 'Food and Drink', and you surely will be plied with the best of both. This brainchild of brilliant chef Gísli Matthías Auðunsson, who also owns excellent **Slippurinn** (☎481 1515; www.slippurinn.com; Strandvegur 76; lunch kr2200-3000, dinner mains kr3490-6990, set menu kr7990-11,990; ⏰noon-2.30pm & 5-10pm early May–mid-Sep; 📶) in the Vestmannaeyjar, creates inventive versions of traditional Icelandic fare. Book ahead in high season and for dinner.

Bryggjan Brugghús Pub Food $$

(☎456 4040; www.bryggjanbrugghus.is; Grandagarður 8; mains kr2300-5000; ⏰11am-midnight Sun-Thu, to 1am Sat & Sun; 📶) This enormous, golden-lit microbrewery and bistro is a welcome respite for one of its home-brewed beers (start with IPA, lager and seasonal beers, from 12 taps) or for an extensive menu of seafood and meat dishes, and occasional DJs. There are also

Take a Day Trip to Viðey

On fine-weather days, the tiny uninhabited island of Viðey (www.reykjavikmuseum.is) makes a wonderful day trip. Just 1km north of Reykjavík's Sundahöfn Harbour, where most cruise ships dock, it feels a world away, with well-preserved historic buildings, surprising modern art, an abandoned village and great birdwatching.

Iceland's oldest stone house, **Viðeyarstofa**, is just above the harbour. Icelandic treasurer Skúli Magnússon was given the island in 1751 and he built the house as his residence. There's also an interesting 18th-century wooden **church**, the second oldest in Iceland, with some original decor and Skúli's tomb (he died here in 1794). Excavations of the old **monastery foundations** unearthed 15th-century wax tablets and a runic love letter, now in the National Museum.

Just northwest along the coast, Yoko Ono's **Imagine Peace Tower** (2007) is a 'wishing well' blasting a dazzling column of light into the sky every night between 9 October (John Lennon's birthday) and 8 December (the date he died). Further along, **Viðeyjarnaust day-hut** has a barbecue (bring supplies). Check online for free guided walks in summer.

Viðey Ferry (☎533 5055; www.videy.com; return adult/child kr1500/750; ⏰from Skarfabakki hourly 10.15am-5.15pm mid-May–Sep, weekends only Oct–mid-May) takes five minutes from Skarfabakki, 4.5km east of the city centre and where most cruise ships berth. During summer, two boats a day start from Elding at the Old Harbour and the Harpa concert hall.

Understand

Exploring Icelandic Pop

Iceland's pop music scene is one of its great gifts to the world. Internationally famous Icelandic musicians include (of course) Björk and her former band, the Sugarcubes. Sigur Rós followed Björk to stardom; their concert movie *Heima* (2007) is a must-see. Indie-folk Of Monsters and Men stormed the US charts in 2011 with *My Head Is an Animal;* their latest album is *Beneath the Skin* (2015). Ásgeir had a break-out hit with *In the Silence* (2014).

Reykjavík's flourishing music landscape is constantly changing – visit www.icelandmusic.is and www.grapevine.is for news and listings. Just a few examples of local groups include Seabear, an indie-folk band, which spawned top acts like Sin Fang (*Flowers;* 2013) and Sóley (*We Sink;* 2012). Árstíðir record minimalist indie-folk, and released *Verloren Verleden* with Anneke van Giersbergen in 2016.

Other local bands include GusGus, a pop-electronica act, FM Belfast (electronica) and múm (experimental electronica mixed with traditional instruments). Or check out Singapore Sling for straight-up rock and roll. If your visit coincides with one of Iceland's many music festivals, go!

If you can't get enough, check out **12 Tónar** (☏511 5656; www.12tonar.is; Skolavörðustígur 15; ◷10am-6pm Mon-Sat, from noon Sun), a very cool place to hang out in, and responsible for launching some of Iceland's favourite bands. Drop by to listen to CDs, drink coffee and sometimes catch a live performance.

Sigur Rós MELIS/SHUTTERSTOCK ©

great harbour views out the back windows. Settle in for a while.

DRINKING & NIGHTLIFE

Kaffibarinn
Bar

(☏551 1588; www.kaffibarinn.is; Bergstaðastræti 1; ◷3pm-1am Sun-Thu, to 4.30am Fri & Sat; ☏) This old house with the London Underground symbol over the door contains one of Reykjavík's coolest bars; it even had a starring role in the cult movie *101 Reykjavík* (2000). At weekends you'll feel like you need a famous face or a battering ram to get in. At other times it's a place for artistic types to chill with their Macs.

Kaldi
Bar

(☏581 2200; www.kaldibar.is; Laugavegur 20b; ◷noon-1am Sun-Thu, to 3am Fri & Sat) Effortlessly cool with mismatched seats and teal banquettes, plus a popular smoking court-yard, Kaldi is awesome for its full range of Kaldi microbrews, not available elsewhere. Happy hour (4pm to 7pm) gets you one for kr700. Anyone can play the in-house piano.

Kaffi Vínyl   Cafe
(⌕537 1332; www.facebook.com/vinilrvk; Hver-fisgata 76; ☺8am-11pm; ☎) This bright light in the Reykjavík coffee, restaurant and music scene is popular for its chilled vibe, great music, and delicious vegan and vegetarian food.

Micro Bar   Bar
(⌕865 8389; www.facebook.com/MicroBar Iceland; Vesturgata 2; ☺4pm-12.30am Sun-Thu, to 1.30am Fri & Sat) Boutique brews are the name of the game at this low-key spot in the heart of the action. Bottles of beer represent a slew of brands and countries, but more importantly you'll discover 10 local draughts on tap from the island's top microbreweries: one of the best selections in Reykjavík. Happy hour (4pm to 7pm) offers kr870 beers.

Loftið   Cocktail Bar
(Jacobsen Loftið; ⌕551 9400; www.face-book.com/loftidbar; 2nd fl, Austurstræti 9; ☺4pm-1am Sun-Thu, to 4am Fri & Sat) Loftið is all about high-end cocktails and good living. Dress up to join the fray at this airy upstairs lounge with a zinc bar, retro tailor-shop-inspired decor, vintage tiles and a swank, older crowd. The basic booze here is the top-shelf liquor elsewhere, and jazzy bands play from time to time.

KEX Bar   Bar
(www.kexhostel.is; Skúlagata 28; ☺11.30am-11pm; ☎) Locals like this hostel bar-restaurant (mains kr1800 to kr2600) in

an old cookie factory (*kex* means 'cookie') for its broad windows facing the sea, an inner courtyard and kids' play area. Happy hipsters soak up the 1920s Vegas vibe: saloon doors, old-school barber station, scuffed floors and happy chatter.

ℹ INFORMATION

DISCOUNT CARDS
Reykjavík Loves the City Card (⌕411 6040; www.visitreykjavik.is) This popular travel-pass gives access to all public museums, swimming pools and transportation in Reykjavík, including the ferry to Viðey Island (p281). The three du-ration forms available are 24 hours (adult/child kr3700/1500), 48 hours (kr4900/2500) and 72 hours (kr5900/3300). For sale at the Main Tourist Office and elsewhere downtown.

TOURIST INFORMATION
Main Tourist Office (Upplýsingamiðstöð Ferðamanna; ⌕411 6040; www.visitreykjavik. is; Ráðhús City Hall, Tjarnargata 11; ☺8am-8pm) Friendly staff and mountains of free brochures, plus maps, Reykjavík City Card and Strætó city bus tickets. Books accommodation, tours and activities.

ℹ GETTING AROUND

The best way to see compact central Reykjavík is by foot. **Strætó** (www.bus.is) operates regular, easy buses in the city centre and environs, running 7am until 11pm or midnight daily (from 11am on Sunday). The fare is kr420; you can buy tickets at the cruise terminal, pay on board (though no change is given) or by using its app. Buy one-/three-day passes (kr1500/3500) at the Main Tourist Office, and 10-11 convenience stores.

Nyhavn (p100), Copenhagen, Denmark

In Focus

Gamla Stan (p150), Stockholm, Sweden

SCANRAIL/SHUTTERSTOCK ©

Scandinavia Today

The Nordic nations tend to be table-toppers in global measures of equality, development, sustainability and liveability and, in spite of the global financial crisis, they remain at the forefront of all that is forward-thinking and progressive. Despite the region's isolation, the world has come knocking at its door with immigration and climate change, impacting the political order and posing serious questions for its present and future.

Environment

Scandinavia is a model of sustainability, with high – 100% in the cases of Norway and Iceland – renewable electricity output, a firm and long-standing commitment to recycling, stringent environmental certifications and lots of investment in green technology. Winter heating bills add to the overall carbon footprint, but in general the region is an example for the world. Firm government commitments have pledged to make most of the Nordic nations carbon neutral within a few years.

Nevertheless, the rest of the world hasn't done Scandinavia any favours. Dramatically changed weather patterns have already affected the region, which is experiencing much milder winters and a corresponding decrease in snow cover. The rapid warming of the polar region will have huge and potentially devastating effects on the Scandinavian ecosys-

belief systems
(% of population)

65 Lutheran   26 unaffiliated   4 other   3 Muslim   2 Catholic

if Scandinavia were 100 people

38 live in Sweden
21 live in Denmark
20 live in Finland
19 live in Norway
1 live in Tallinn
1 live in Iceland

population per sq km

♟ ≈ 30 people

Scandinavia   UK   USA

tem, impacting everything from fisheries to indigenous rights.

As members of the Arctic Council (www.arctic-council.org), which strives to protect the northern environment, the Nordic countries are intimately engaged in trying to find solutions. However, questions about the management of resources under the ice cap in Russian and Canadian territories remain unanswered, which threatens to delay serious action until it is too late.

Immigration

Exacerbated by the financial crisis, when bailouts of several European nations raised questions in the media and parliament about whether Scandinavians were being made to pay for the sins of others, the relatively rapid influx of immigrants to formerly rather homogeneous Nordic societies has raised tensions in recent years.

Anti-immigration and far-right political parties have gained substantial portions of the popular vote and a polarisation of local opinion raises the question of whether the region's famed tolerance was just a veneer. Much of the debate has been focused on the 2017 terrorist attack in Stockholm by a failed asylum seeker cited by politicians across the region as evidence of the need for tighter controls. On the other side, Anders Breivik's 2011 massacre of Norwegian teenagers or Finland's troubled history with guns could be seen as powerful evidence that local extremism is a bigger problem.

There has always been a divide between Scandinavia's liberal cities and its more conservative countryside and settlement of refugees in largely rural areas has brought global issues to remote doorsteps. For some, particularly older generations, the perception of overwhelming immigration, combined with the sharp decline of churchgoing in recent decades and the technological development of modern society, has led to worries about the loss of traditional values and culture. How the Scandinavian countries manage these perceptions and this transition will be key in coming years.

EU

If the European Union (EU) is a house party, then festivities were badly soured by the economic crisis and immigration issue. Finns grumbled that they were paying for everyone else to get drunk, while Danes and Swedes wanted to tighten up their formerly liberal policies on those perceived by some as gate-crashers. Then Britain left in a huff and those remaining have begun to feel that maybe the party isn't so bad after all – it's cold outside and there's a big bear lurking. Meanwhile, friendly neighbour Norway isn't a party person but now wonders if its standing invitation to share the food and beer might be re-evaluated after the commotion of Britain's exit. And Iceland? Still dithering by the doorbell, wondering if the party is worthwhile.

Replica of a traditional Viking home

DAVID ACHIRA/SHUTTERSTOCK ©

History

From Vikings to social democrats, through wars, treaties and peace, Scandinavia has had an interesting ride. Innovation has been a constant, from longships ploughing furrows across the known world and beyond to wholesale religious change, from struggles for independence to postwar democracy that changed the very idea of what it meant to be a nation-state citizen. The sparsely populated Nordic lands have punched well above their weight.

12,000–9000 BC
In the wake of the receding glaciers of the last ice age, the reinhabiting of Scandinavia begins.

4000 BC
Agriculture begins in Denmark and southern Sweden.

1800 BC
Bronze is introduced to Denmark, giving rise to skilled artisans who fashion weapons, tools, jewellery and works of art.

Guksi (drinking cups) made by Sámi people

VELVETEYE/SHUTTERSTOCK ©

Prehistory

What are now the Nordic nations were inhabited way back: pre-ice-age remains have been found dating from some 120,000 years ago. But the big chill erased most traces and sent folk scurrying south to warmer climes. Only at the retreat of the formidable glaciers, which had blanketed the region 3km deep in parts, was human presence re-established.

Retreating glaciers let lichen and mosses grow, attracting herds of reindeer. The people used stone tools and hunted them, as well as elk and beaver. The first post-thaw inhabitants had spread over most of the region by about 9000 BC.

Pottery in the archaeological record shows that a new influence arrived from the east to southern Finland about 5000 years ago. Because Finland was the furthest point west that this culture reached, it's suggested that these new people brought a Finnic language with them from Russia. If so, those who lived in Finland at this time were the ancestors of the Finns and the Sámi.

AD 100
The Roman historian Tacitus refers to the Suinoes in Sweden and the 'Fenni', most likely the Sámi.

500
The Danes, thought to have migrated south from Sweden, arrive in Denmark.

600–700
Irish monks voyage to uninhabited Iceland, becoming the first (temporary) settlers.

It seems the Sámi gradually migrated northwards, probably displaced by various southern arrivals and the advance of agriculture into former hunting lands.

Stone Age culture relied primarily on hunting, but as the climate gradually warmed, some hunting groups resettled near the sea, subsisting on fish, seabirds and seals. Small-scale agriculture followed and villages developed around the fields.

Around 1800 BC the first artisans began fashioning weapons, tools, jewellery and finely crafted works of art in the new metal, bronze, traded from as far away as Crete and Mycenae. Locally available iron led to superior ploughs, permitting larger-scale agricultural communities.

Vikings

Few historical people have captured the imagination quite like the Vikings. Immortalised in modern culture and considered to be the most feared predators of ancient Europe, the Vikings may have disappeared from history, but as a seafaring nation with its face turned towards distant lands, they remain very much the forerunners of modern Scandinavia. But who were these ancient warriors who took to their longboats and dominated Europe for five centuries?

Beginnings

Under pressure from shrinking agricultural land caused by a growing population, settlers from Norway began arriving along the coast of the British Isles in the 780s. When the boats returned home to Norway with enticing trade goods and tales of poorly defended coastlines, the Vikings began laying plans to conquer the world. The first Viking raid took place on St Cuthbert's monastery on the island of Lindisfarne in 793. Soon the Vikings were spreading across Britain, Ireland and the rest of Europe with war on their minds and returning home with slaves *(thrall)* in their formidable, low Norse longboats.

The Vikings sailed a new type of boat that was fast and highly manoeuvrable but sturdy enough for ocean crossings. Initial hit-and-run raids along the European coast were followed by major military expeditions, settlement and trade. The well-travelled Vikings settled part of the Slavic heartland, giving it the name 'Rus,' and ventured as far as Newfoundland, Constantinople (modern-day Istanbul) and Baghdad, setting up trade with the Byzantine Empire.

Coastal regions of Britain, Ireland, France (Normandy was named for these 'Northmen'), Russia (as far east as the river Volga), Moorish Spain (Seville was raided in 844) and the Middle East all came under the Viking sway. Well-defended Constantinople proved a bridge too far – the Vikings attacked six times but never took the city. Such rare setbacks notwithstanding, the Viking raids transformed Scandinavia from an obscure backwater on Europe's northern fringe to an all-powerful empire.

For all of their destruction elsewhere, Vikings belonged very much to the shores from which they set out or sheltered on their raids. Viking raids increased standards of living at

793	**850**	**872**
The first recorded sacking of an English monastery marks the beginning of the Age of the Vikings.	Norse settlers begin to take up residence in Iceland.	Harald Hårfagre (Harald Fair-Hair) fights his fellow Viking chieftains in the Battle of Hafrsfjord and unites Norway for the first time.

home. Emigration freed up farmland and fostered the emergence of a new merchant class, while captured slaves provided farm labour. Norwegian farmers also crossed the Atlantic to settle the Faroes, Iceland and Greenland during the 9th and 10th centuries and Viking ships reached Newfoundland and possibly beyond.

The Coming of Christianity

The Vikings gave the northern lands their love of the sea and it was during the late Viking period that they bequeathed to them another of their most enduring national traits – strong roots in Christianity. However, this overturning of the Viking pantheon of gods did not come without a struggle.

King Håkon the Good, who had been baptised a Christian during his English upbringing, brought the new faith (as well as missionaries and a bishop) with him upon his return to Norway. Despite some early success, most Vikings remained loyal to their gods Thor, Odin and Freyr. Although the missionaries were eventually able to replace the names of the gods with those of Catholic saints, the pagan practice of blood sacrifice continued unabated. When Håkon the Good was defeated and killed in 960, Norwegian Christianity all but disappeared.

Christianity in Norway was revived during the reign of King Olav Tryggvason (Olav I). Like any good Viking, Olav decided that only force would work to convert his countrymen to the 'truth'. Unfortunately for the king, his intended wife, Queen Sigrid of Sweden, refused to convert. Olav cancelled the marriage contract and Sigrid married the pagan King Svein Forkbeard of Denmark. Together they orchestrated Olav's death in a great Baltic sea battle, then took Norway as their own.

Christianity was finally cemented in Norway by King Olav Haraldsson, Olav II, who was also converted in England. Olav II and his Viking hordes allied themselves with King Ethelred and managed to save London from a Danish attack under King Svein Forkbeard by destroying London Bridge (from whence we derive the song 'London Bridge Is Falling Down'). Succeeding where his namesake had failed, Olav II spread Christianity with considerable success. In 1023 Olav built a cross in Voss, where it still stands, and in 1024 he founded the Church of Norway. After an invasion by King Canute (Knut) of Denmark in 1028, Olav II died during the Battle of Stiklestad in 1030. For Christians, this amounted to martyrdom and the king was canonised as a saint; the great Nidaros Cathedral in Trondheim stands as a memorial to St Olav and, until the Protestant Reformation, the cathedral served as a destination for pilgrims from all over Europe. His most lasting legacy, however, was having forged an enduring identity for Norway as an independent kingdom.

As belief in Valhalla's free bar and the end-of-days vision of Ragnarök were slowly superseded by heavenly harps and the Last Judgment, so the Vikings blended gradually into what came afterwards. The best example is the defeat of Harald Hardråde, king of Norway, in England in 1066. It's often cited as the end of the Viking Age, yet victorious King Harold's forebears were Viking royalty, and the Norman conquerors who defeated him at Hastings shortly thereafter took their name from 'Norsemen' and were descended from Vikings who had settled in northwest France.

930	**986**	**1000**
The world's oldest existing parliament, the Alþingi, is founded in Iceland.	Eiríkur Rauðe (Eric the Red) founds the first permanent European colony in Greenland.	Almost five centuries before Columbus, Eric's son Leifur Eiríksson lands on Newfoundland and explores the North American coast.

Iceland's Sagas

Iceland's medieval prose sagas are some of the most imaginative and enduring works of early literature – epic, brutal tales that flower repeatedly with wisdom, magic, elegiac poetry and love.

Written down during the 12th to early 14th centuries, these sagas look back on the disputes, families, doomed romances and larger-than-life characters (from warrior and poet to outlaw) who lived during the Settlement Era. Most were written anonymously, though *Egil's Saga* has been attributed to Snorri Sturluson.

The sagas are very much alive today. Icelanders of all ages can (and do) read them in Old Norse, the language in which they were written 800 years ago. Most people can quote chunks from them, know the farms where the characters lived and died, and flock to cinemas to see film versions of these eternal tales.

The Hanseatic League

Many of the towns and cities around the Baltic and beyond were significantly influenced by the Hanseatic League, whose origins go back to various guilds and associations established from about the mid-12th century by out-of-town merchants to protect their interests. After Hamburg and Lübeck signed an agreement in 1241 to protect their ships and trading routes, they were joined in their league by Lüneburg, Kiel and a string of Baltic Sea cities stretching east to Greifswald. By 1356 this had grown into the Hanseatic League, encompassing half a dozen other large alliances of cities, with Lübeck playing the lead role.

At its zenith, the league had about 200 member cities. It earned a say in the choice of Danish kings after fighting two wars against the Danes between 1361 and 1369. The resulting Treaty of Stralsund in 1370 turned it into Northern Europe's most powerful economic and political entity.

Some 70 inland and coastal cities – mostly German – formed the core of the Hanseatic League, but another 130 beyond the Reich maintained a loose association, making it truly international. During a period of endless feudal squabbles in Germany, it was a bastion of political and social stability.

By the 15th century, however, competition from Dutch and English shipping companies, internal disputes and a shift in the centre of world trade (from the North and Baltic Seas to the Atlantic) had caused decline. The ruin and chaos of the Thirty Years' War in the 17th century delivered the final blow, although Hamburg, Bremen and Lübeck retained the 'Hanse City' title.

Union...for a Time

Margrethe, who had assumed de facto control of the Danish Crown after her young son Oluf died in 1387, became the official head of state and Denmark's first ruling queen. The next year Swedish nobles sought Margrethe's assistance in a rebellion against their unpopular German-born king. The Swedes hailed Margrethe as their regent, and in turn she sent Danish troops to Sweden, securing victory over the king's forces.

1066	1319	1397
The defeat of Norwegian Vikings by Harold II of England heralds the end of the Viking era.	Magnus becomes King of Sweden and unites Sweden and Norway. This ends Norwegian independence.	The Kalmar Union joins much of Scandinavia together under the direction of a common monarch.

A decade later Margrethe established a formal alliance between Denmark, Norway and Sweden known as the Kalmar Union, to counter the powerful German-based Hanseatic League that had come to dominate regional trade.

In 1410 King Erik of Pomerania, Margrethe's grandson, staged an unsuccessful attack on the Hanseatic League, which sapped the Kalmar Union's vitality. This, together with Erik's penchant for appointing Danes to public office in Sweden and Norway, soured relations with aristocrats in those countries. In 1438 the Swedish council withdrew from the union, whereupon the Danish nobility deposed Erik in 1439.

Out of the chaos following Erik's deposition, Sten Sture the Elder (1440–1503) eventually emerged as 'Guardian of Sweden' in 1470, going on to fight and defeat an army of unionist Danes at the Battle of Brunkeberg (1471) in Stockholm. In a move of retaliation that sounded the union's death knell, Christian II of Denmark invaded Sweden and killed the regent Sten Sture the Younger (1493–1520), adding a massacre in Stockholm's Gamla Stan to his list of accomplishments.

In 1523 the Swedes elected their own king, Gustav Vasa. The Kalmar Union was permanently dissolved, but Norway would remain under Danish rule for another three centuries.

The Reformation

During the second quarter of the 16th century, the Reformation swept through Scandinavia and Lutheran Protestantism was adopted by royal decrees and force. Catholicism, which had taken over from the Norse gods some five centuries earlier, almost ceased to exist in the region.

The Reformation played out its most dramatic chapters in Denmark as the monarchy and the Catholic Church engaged in a pivotal power struggle. Caught in the middle of this religious and political foment was King Frederik I, who over the course of 10 years went from promising to fight heresy against Catholicism to inviting Lutheran preachers to Denmark.

When Frederik died, the lack of a clear successor left the country in civil war. The following year (1534) Hanseatic mercenaries from Lübeck (now in Germany) invaded southern Jutland and Zealand. By and large, the Lübeckers were welcomed as liberators by peasants and members of the middle class, who were in revolt against the nobility.

Alarmed by the revolt, a coalition of aristocrats and Catholic bishops crowned the Lutheran Christian III as king. Still, the rebellion raged on. In Jutland, manor houses were set ablaze and the peasants made advances against the armies of the aristocracy.

Christian's general, Rantzau, took control, cutting Lübeck off from the sea and marching northward through Jutland, brutally smashing peasant bands. Rantzau's troops besieged Copenhagen, where merchants supported the uprising and welcomed the prospect of becoming a Hanseatic stronghold. Cut off from the outside world, Copenhagen's citizens suffered starvation and epidemics before surrendering after a year in 1536.

Christian III quickly consolidated his power, offering leniency to the merchants and Copenhagen burghers who had revolted in exchange for their allegiance. Catholic bishops, on

1469	**1517–50**	**1630**
The Orkney and Shetland Islands are sold by Norway to the Scots.	The Reformation sweeps across Scandinavia, establishing Lutheran Protestantism as the totally dominant religion.	Sweden's intervention in the Thirty Years' War ignites a pan-European conflagration.

the other hand, were arrested, and monasteries, churches and other ecclesiastical estates became the property of the Crown.

Thus the Danish Lutheran Church became the only state-sanctioned denomination and was placed under the direct control of the king. Buoyed by a treasury enriched by confiscated Church properties, the monarchy emerged from the civil war stronger than ever.

Meanwhile, in Sweden, King Gustav Vasa adopted the Lutheran faith in 1527 and confiscated much of the property of the Catholic Church. Norway did the same in 1537 and the Finnish Reformation was ushered in by Mikael Agricola, who studied with Luther in Germany and returned to Finland in 1539 to translate parts of the Bible into Finnish. Hardline Protestant attitudes brought in unadorned, severe churches and a final break with the pagan past.

Sweden versus Denmark

For around 600 years from the early 13th to the early 19th centuries, Scandinavia was dominated by the kingdoms of Sweden and Denmark, which signed treaties, broke them, fought as allies and enemies, conquered territory across Northern Europe and lost it again. Finland basically became a Swedish possession and was a frequent venue for Sweden's territorial squabbles with Novgorod (Russia), which ended up taking control of Finland after heavily defeating Sweden in 1809. Norway was a junior partner to Sweden, then Denmark, then Sweden again. Iceland fell under Danish control, with Danish merchants establishing a legal monopoly on Iceland's resources that lasted nearly 200 years.

Danish Miscalculations

A period of peace marked the early reign of Danish king Christian IV, who then spoiled it by embarking on what would become the ruinous Thirty Years' War. The aim of the war was to neutralise Swedish expansion; its outcome for Denmark was morale- and coffer-sapping losses.

Seeing a chance for revenge against Sweden, following its troubled occupation of Poland, Christian IV's successor, Frederik III, once again declared war in 1657. For the Danes, ill-prepared for battle, it was a tremendous miscalculation.

Sweden's King Gustave led his troops back from Poland through Germany and into Jutland, plundering his way north. During 1657–58 – the most severe winter in Danish history – King Gustave marched his soldiers across the frozen seas of the Lille Bælt between Fredericia and the island of Funen. King Gustave's uncanny success unnerved the Danes and he proceeded without serious resistance across the Store Bælt to Lolland and then on to Falster.

The Swedish king had barely made it across the frozen waters of the Storstrømmen to Zealand when the thawing ice broke away behind him, precariously separating him and his advance detachment from the rest of his forces. However, the Danes failed to recognise

1658	1700	1800–01
Denmark signs the Treaty of Roskilde, the most lamented humiliation in its history, losing a third of its territory.	Karl XII of Sweden is drawn into the Great Northern War, the beginning of the end for the Swedish empire.	Denmark signs a pact of armed neutrality with Sweden, Prussia and Russia. In response, Britain's navy attacks Copenhagen.

their sudden advantage; instead of capturing the Swedish king, they sued for peace and agreed to yet another disastrous treaty.

In 1658 Denmark signed the humiliating Treaty of Roskilde, ceding a third of its territory, including the island of Bornholm and all territories on the Swedish mainland. Only Bornholm, which eventually staged a bloody revolt against the Swedes, would again fly the Danish flag.

Absolute monarchy returned in 1660, when King Frederik III cunningly convened a gathering of nobles, placed them under siege, and forced them to nullify their powers of council. Frederik declared his right of absolute rule, proclaiming the king the highest head on earth, above all human laws and inferior to God alone.

In the following decades the now all-powerful monarchy rebuilt the military and

Sweden (Not) at War

Sweden declared itself neutral in 1912, and remained so throughout the bloodshed of WWI. Swedish neutrality during WWII was ambiguous: letting German troops march through to occupy Norway and selling iron ore to both warring sides certainly tarnished Sweden's image, leading to a crisis of conscience at home as well as international criticism.

On the other hand, Sweden was a haven for refugees from Finland, Norway, Denmark and the Baltic states; downed Allied air crew who escaped the Gestapo; and many thousands of Jews who escaped persecution and death.

continued to pick fruitless fights with Sweden. Peace of a sort eventually descended as Sweden's power waned, and for much of the 18th century the Danes and Swedes managed to coexist without serious hostilities.

Sweden's Rise, Fall & Rise

The zenith and collapse of the Swedish empire happened remarkably quickly. During Karl XI's reign, successful battles were waged against Denmark and Norway, the latter resulting in the seizure of Bohuslän, Härjedalen and Jämtland, and the empire reached its maximum size when Sweden established a short-lived American colony in what is now Delaware.

Inheritor of this huge and increasingly sophisticated country was 15-year-old King Karl XII (1681–1718), an overenthusiastic military adventurer who spent almost all of his reign at war. Karl XII cost Sweden its Latvian, Estonian and Polish territory, with the Swedish coast sustaining damaging attacks from Russia, and he perished by a mystery sniper's hand in 1718.

Gustav III (1746–92) was a popular and sophisticated king who granted freedom of worship and was surprisingly successful in the maritime battle in the Gulf of Finland against Russia in 1790. Still, his costly foreign policy earned him enemies in the aristocracy and led to his assassination.

The rule of his son Gustav IV Adolf (1778–1837), forced to abdicate after getting drawn into the Napoleonic Wars and permanently losing Finland (one-third of Sweden's territory) to Russia, ended unrestricted royal power with the 1809 constitution.

1808–9	**1895**	**1905**
Finland is invaded and occupied by Russia, becoming a grand duchy of the Russian Empire.	Alfred Nobel's will establishes the Nobel prizes from the interest to his vast fortune.	Norway finally regains independence, followed by Finland (1917) and Iceland (1918, 1944).

Tracing Your Swedish Ancestry

Around a million people emigrated from Sweden to the USA and Canada between 1850 and 1930. Many of their 12 million descendants are now returning in search of their roots.

Luckily, detailed parish records of births, deaths and marriages have been kept since 1686 and there are *landsarkivet* (regional archives) around the country. The national archive is Riksarkivet (www.riksarkivet.se), in Stockholm; its newly digitised system allows you to search the National Archives Database and to use SVAR, the Digital Research Room.

Utvandrarnas Hus (House of Emigrants; ☏0470-70 42 00; www.utvandrarnashus.se; Vilhelm Mobergs gata 4; adult/child 90kr/free; ⌚10am-5pm Tue-Fri, to 4pm Sat & Sun) in Växjö is a particularly good museum dedicated to the mass departure.

Also worth a look is *Tracing Your Swedish Ancestry,* by Nils William Olsson, a free do-it-yourself genealogical guide. Download the latest version from the New York Consulate-General of Sweden's website: www.swedenabroad. com/SelectImage/15063/tracingyourswedishancestry.pdf, or get it free from Amazon.com.

More or less out of the blue, Napoleon's marshal Jean-Baptiste Bernadotte (1763–1844) was invited by a nobleman, Baron Mörner, to take the Swedish throne – which he did, along with the name Karl Johan. Judiciously changing sides, he led Sweden, allied with Britain, Prussia and Russia, against France and...no surprises here...Denmark.

He defeated Denmark, taking Norway from it as part of the peace treaty. When Norway demurred and elected its own king, Karl Johan enforced his rule by invading. Norway would be a subordinate partner to Sweden until 1905.

Independence

By the end of the 19th century, independence movements in Finland, Norway and Iceland were strong and by 1920 all three were autonomous. The Nordic nations as we know them today were in place.

WWII

The Nordic nations all had a different experience of WWII. The first to be attacked was Finland, whose heroic but ultimately unsuccessful harsh winter struggle against Soviet invasion began in November 1939. A few months later, in April 1940, Germany occupied Denmark without a struggle and simultaneously invaded Norway, which finally succumbed after bitter fighting from Norwegian and other Allied troops.

Iceland, in a royal union with Denmark, remained free but army-less and soon accepted British, then American troops to prevent the strategically placed North Atlantic island from falling under German control. Meanwhile, Sweden had declared itself neutral and remained so – more or less – throughout the war.

1939–40	1974	1989
Finland is invaded by the Soviet Union, and Denmark and Norway by Germany.	ABBA triumphs in the Eurovision Song Contest, kick-starting a hugely successful career.	Beer is legalised in Iceland, same-sex unions in Denmark.

Finland, forced to cede territory to the Soviets and ignored by the other Allies, now looked to Germany for help and soon was at war with Russia again as the Germans launched their doomed invasion. They reclaimed their lands but Russia bounced back in 1944. Finland had to cede them more territory and then drive the Germans out. As the Wehrmacht retreated across northern Finland and Norway, they destroyed everything in their path, leaving large parts of Lapland devastated. When peace came, the Danes and Norwegians – whose resistance throughout the war had cost them many lives – celebrated the end of occupation with gusto, Sweden dusted itself down slightly sheepishly, Iceland grabbed full independence and the luckless Finns were left without a big chunk of territory and forced to pay reparations to the Allies.

Denmark's Finest Hour

Soon after taking full control of the country in August 1943, Denmark's Nazi occupiers planned, as they did in the other parts of Europe they occupied, to round up Jewish Danes and deport them to their deaths in concentration camps. The Danish resistance had other ideas and in an extraordinarily well-coordinated operation smuggled some 7200 Jews – about 90% of those left in Denmark – into neutral Sweden. In recognition of its actions in saving its Jewish population, Denmark is remembered as one of the Righteous Among the Nations at the Yad Vashem Holocaust Memorial in Jerusalem.

Social Democracy

After the war it was time to rebuild and there was a chance for the Nordic countries to ask themselves what sort of country they wanted to construct. Governments across the region began laying the foundations for social democratic states in which high taxes and a socially responsible citizenry would be recompensed with lifelong medical care, free education, fair working conditions, excellent infrastructure, comfortable pensions and generous welfare payments for parents and the unemployed.

These nations became standard-bearers for equality and tolerance and overall wealth increased rapidly, leaving the privations of the war years to memory. Women achieved significant representation at all levels of society and forward-thinking in policy was much in evidence.

Though the political consensus for the social democratic model of government has waned in recent decades – taxes have fallen and some benefits have been sheared away – in general Scandinavians are still very well looked after by the state and inequality is low.

Despite all this social democracy, Norway, Sweden and Denmark all have monarchs. Their royal families are, however, generally known for their grounded attitudes.

1995	2000	2008
Finland and Sweden join what is now the EU. Denmark had already joined in 1973. Norway says no.	The Øresund Bridge is completed, physically linking Sweden (and hence Norway and Finland) to Denmark and the rest of northern Europe.	The worldwide financial downturn hits Iceland particularly hard; all three of the country's major banks collapse.

Geirangerfjord (p135), Norway

Landscapes

Scandinavia's buzzy cities are enticing, but the real soul of the region can be found in its glorious natural landscapes. Some of Europe's real wild places are here. From soaring fjord walls in Norway to the volcanic brutality of Iceland, from the awe-inspiring colours of autumn's forest palette to charming Baltic islands, from sparkling summer lakes to Arctic snowscapes, there's a feast of distinct beauties.

Scandinavia

Scandinavia's diverse scenery encompasses gentle pastoral landscapes in the south to untamed canvases wrought by nature's forces in the north. Wild, rugged coasts and mountains, hundreds of kilometres of forest broken only by lakes and the odd cottage, and unspoilt Baltic archipelagos make up a varied menu of uplifting visual treats.

Flat Denmark in the south doesn't have the mountainous magnificence of Norway or the volcanoes of Iceland but has a charming coastal landscape across its hundreds of islands. Offshore Bornholm, as well as the Baltic archipelagos of Sweden and Finland, present a fascinating patchwork where charmingly rural farms alternate with low rock polished smooth by the glaciers of the last ice age.

Norway's phenomenal coastline is famous for a reason; the fjords here take your breath away, while the northern mountains are heart-achingly beautiful. Inland, much of mainland Scandinavia is taken up with forests. The region has some of the world's highest tree cover and the woods – largely managed for forestry, some wild – stretch for hundreds of kilometres. Mainly composed of spruce, pine and birch, these forests are responsible for the crisp, clean, aromatic northern air and are dotted with lakes.

Volatile Iceland

It's difficult to remain unmoved by the amazing diversity of the Icelandic landscape. Prepare to explore everything from lunar-like landscapes of ornate lava flows and towering volcanoes with misty ice caps to steep-sided glistening fjords, lush emerald-green hills, glacier-carved valleys, bubbling mudpots and vast, desert-like expanses. It is this rich mix of extraordinary scenery and the possibility of experiencing such extremes, so close together, that attracts and then dazzles visitors.

Situated on the Mid-Atlantic Ridge, a massive 18,000km-long rift between two of the earth's major tectonic plates, Iceland is a shifting, steaming lesson in schoolroom geology. Suddenly, you'll be racking your brains to remember long-forgotten homework on how volcanoes work, what a solfatara is (spoiler: it's a volcanic vent emitting hot gases), and why lava and magma aren't quite the same thing.

Iceland is one of the youngest landmasses on the planet, formed by underwater volcanic eruptions along the joint of the North American and Eurasian plates around 20 million years ago. The earth's crust in Iceland is only a third of its normal thickness, and magma (molten rock) continues to rise from deep within, forcing the two plates apart. The result is clearly visible at Þingvellir, where the great rift Almannagjá broadens by between 1mm and 18mm per year, and at Námafjall (near Mývatn), where a series of steaming vents mark the ridge.

The Southern Baltic

Where Germany meets Holland in the northwest and Denmark in the north, the land is flat; the westerly North Sea coast consists partly of drained land and dykes. To the east, the Baltic coast is riddled with bays and fjords in Schleswig-Holstein but gives way to sandy inlets and beaches. At the northeastern tip is Germany's largest island, Rügen, renowned for its chalk cliffs.

Poland's bumps and flat bits were largely forged during the last ice age, when the Scandinavian ice sheet crept south across the plains and receded some 10,000 years later. The sand-fringed Baltic coast stretches across northern Poland from Germany to Russia's Kaliningrad enclave. The coastal plain that fringes the Baltic Sea was shaped by the rising water levels after the retreat of the Scandinavian ice sheet and is now characterised by swamps and sand dunes. These sand and gravel deposits form not only the beaches of Poland's seaside resorts but also the shifting dunes of Słowiński National Park, the sand bars and gravel spits of Hel, and the Vistula Lagoon.

Beyond Rīga's clutch of twisting spires and towering housing blocks you'll find miles and miles of quiet forests, intimate lakelands and flaxen shores that beckon the crashing Baltic tides. Meanwhile, Estonia's countryside may be flat and unassuming compared with craggier parts of Europe, but its low population density and extensive forests, bogs and wetlands make it an important habitat for a multitude of mammals large and small, as well as a biannual seasonal influx of feathered visitors. Similarly, the Baltic coast, the dunes of Curonian Spit and the large forests broken up by meadows and lakes make Lithuania's landscape blissfully unspoiled.

National Parks

It is an indication of how the Nordic nations value their natural environments that the region has well over a hundred national parks, conserving everything from jewel-like Baltic archipelagos to glaciers and snowy wastes. As well as being crucial drivers of conservation, many of these parks also offer the best chance to appreciate Scandinavia's deep nature.

Arctic Phenomena

The Northern Lights

The aurora borealis (Northern Lights), an utterly haunting and exhilarating sight, is often visible to observers in the far north. The phenomenon is particularly striking during the dark winter; in summer the sun more or less renders it invisible.

The aurora appears in many forms – pillars, streaks, wisps and haloes of vibrating light – but they're most memorable when they take the form of pale curtains, apparently wafting on a gentle breeze. Most often, the Arctic aurora is faint green, light yellow or rose-coloured, but in periods of extreme activity it can change to bright yellow or crimson. Hues of blue and violet can also be seen. The lights seem to dance and swirl in the night sky.

These auroral storms, however eerie, are quite natural. They're created when charged particles (protons and electrons) from the sun bombard the earth. These are deflected towards the North and South Poles by the earth's magnetic field. There they hit the earth's outer atmosphere, 100km to 1000km above ground, causing highly charged electrons to collide with molecules of nitrogen and oxygen. The excess energy from these collisions creates the colourful lights.

The ancient inhabitants of Lapland believed the aurora borealis was caused by a giant fox swishing its tail above the Arctic tundra. One of the Finnish words for the aurora is *revontulet* (fires of the fox).

To see the lights, you'd best have a dark, clear night with high auroral activity. October, November and March are often optimal for this. Then it's a question of waiting patiently, preferably between the hours of 9pm and 2am, and seeing if things kick off. There are several useful websites for predicting auroral activity:

Geophysical Institute (www.gi.alaska.edu/AuroraForecast) Change the map view to Europe to view activity levels.

Service Aurora (www.aurora-service.eu) Daily and hourly forecasts and text-message notification service.

University of Oulu (http://cc.oulu.fi/~thu/Aurora/forecast.html) Finland-based page with links so you can make your own prediction.

Midnight Sun & Polar Night

Because the Earth is tilted on its axis, the polar regions are constantly facing the sun at their respective summer solstices, and are tilted away from it in winter. The Arctic and Antarctic Circles, at latitudes 66°32'N and 66°32'S respectively, are the southern and northern limits of constant daylight on the longest day of the year.

The northern parts of Scandinavia lie north of the Arctic Circle, but even in central Sweden, Norway and Finland the summer sun is never far below the horizon. Between late May and mid-July, nowhere north of Stockholm experiences true darkness. Although many visitors initially find it difficult to sleep while the sun is shining brightly outside, most people get used to it.

Conversely, winters (especially in the far north) can be dark and bitterly cold, with only a few hours of twilight to break the long polar nights. Nevertheless, there's a haunting magic to the light and landscape at this time.

Bull elk

ONDREJ PROSICKY/SHUTTERSTOCK ©

Wildlife

Vast tracts of barely populated land away from the bustle of Central Europe and wide, remote nutrient-rich seas make Scandinavia and Northern Europe an important refuge for numerous species. Seabirds clamour in the Atlantic air while whales roll beneath the waves. Elk are widespread, forests harbour serious carnivores, domesticated reindeer roam the north and mighty polar bears still lord it – for now – over Svalbard.

Mammals

The region is stocked with a very wide range of land mammals: reindeer, herded by the indigenous Sámi, roam in Lapland, while elk (moose) are common in the mainland forests and occasionally blunder into towns. Brown bears, lynx and wolves are the apex predators – humans excepted – pacing the Finnish, Swedish and Norwegian forests, while the lonely wolverine prowls the northern wastes and the mighty reintroduced musk ox ruminates in Norwegian highlands.

On a smaller scale, lemmings are famous for their extraordinary reproductive capacity. Every 10 years or so the population explodes, resulting in denuded landscapes and thousands of dead lemmings in rivers and lakes and on roads.

In the sea, several types of whale roam the North Sea and Atlantic, and are easily seen on boat trips out of Norway or Iceland. Seals and dolphins are aplenty and the weighty walrus hangs out way up north in Svalbard. Up here, too, you'll find the polar bear, in charge of its domain to the extent that by law you need to carry a gun, to be used as a last resort only, to leave town.

Whales

The seas around Norway and Iceland are rich fishing grounds, due to the ideal summer conditions for the growth of plankton. This wealth of nutrients also attracts fish and baleen whales, which feed on the plankton, as well as other marine creatures that feed on the fish. Sadly, centuries of whaling in the North Atlantic and Arctic Oceans have reduced several whale species to perilously small populations. Apart from the minke whale, there's no sign that the numbers will ever recover in this area. Given this history, the variety of whale species in these waters is astonishing. You're very likely to see some from your cruise ship.

Minke whales, one of the few whale species that is not endangered, measure around 7m to 10m long and weigh between 5 and 10 tonnes. They're baleen whales, which means that they have plates of whalebone baleen rather than teeth, and migrate between the Azores area and the Arctic.

Humpback whales are baleen whales that measure up to 15m and weigh up to 30 tonnes. These are among the most acrobatic and vocal of whales, producing deep songs that can be heard and recorded hundreds of kilometres away.

Killer whales, or orcas, are the top sea predators and measure up to 7m and weigh around 5 tonnes. They patrol the coasts, swimming in pods of two or three. They eat fish, seals, dolphins, porpoises and other whales (such as minke), which may be larger than themselves.

The long-finned pilot whales, about 6m long, may swim in pods of up to several hundred and range as far north as Nordkapp.

White, finless belugas, which are up to 4m long, are found mainly in the Arctic Ocean.

The grey and white narwhal, which grow up to 3.5m long, are best recognised by the peculiar 2.7m spiral ivory tusk that projects from the upper lip of the males. This tusk is in fact one of the whale's two teeth and was prized in medieval times. Narwhal live mainly in the Arctic Ocean and occasionally head upstream into freshwater.

The endangered sei whale, a baleen whale, swims off the coast of Finnmark and is named because its arrival corresponds with that of the *sei* (pollacks), which come to feast on the seasonal plankton. It can measure 18m and weigh up to 30 tonnes (calves measure 5m at birth). The annual migration takes the sei from the seas off northwest Africa and Portugal (winter) up to the Norwegian Sea and southern Barents Sea in summer.

Fin whales measure 24m and can weigh 80 tonnes. These whales were a prime target after the Norwegian Svend Føyn developed the exploding harpoon in 1864 and unregulated whaling left only a few thousand in the North Atlantic. Fin whales are also migratory, wintering between Spain and southern Norway and spending summer in northern Norway.

Toothed sperm whales, which can measure 19m and weigh up to 50 tonnes, are characterised by their odd squarish profile. They subsist mainly on fish and squid and usually live in pods of 15 to 20. Their numbers were depleted by whalers seeking whale oil and the valuable spermaceti wax from their heads. The fish-rich shoals off Vesterålen in Norway attract quite a few sperm whales and they're often observed on boat tours.

The largest animal on earth, blue whales measure around 28m and weigh in at a staggering 110 tonnes. Although they can live to 80 years of age, 50 is more common. Heavily hunted for its oil, the species finally received protection, far too late, from the International Whaling Commission in 1967. The blue whale is listed as Endangered by the International Union for the Conservation of Nature (IUCN), which estimates blue whale numbers worldwide to be somewhere between 10,000 and 25,000; 341,830 blue whales were recorded as killed in the Antarctic and sub-Antarctic in the 20th century. Recent evidence suggests that a few hardy blue whales are making a comeback in the northeast Atlantic and blue whales are occasionally sighted in the waters surrounding Iceland and Svalbard.

Bowhead whales, or Greenland right whales, were virtually annihilated by the end of the 19th century for their baleen, which was used in corsets, fans and whips, and because they are slow swimmers and float when dead. In 1679 Svalbard had around 25,000 bowheads, but only a handful remains and worldwide numbers are critically low. These whales can live for over 200 years.

Birds

Birdlife is fabulous, with a wonderful array of seabirds breeding in salty clamour in Iceland, Shetland and the Faroes. Coastal species include common, little and Arctic terns, puffins, gannets, various gulls, oystercatchers, cormorants, guillemots and razorbills. Territorial Arctic skuas can be seen in a few places.

Other notable bird species seen in various parts of Scandinavia include white-tailed eagles, ospreys, ptarmigans, whooper swans and capercaillie. The impressive golden eagle is an endangered species. Found in the mountains and deep Finnish wilderness, it's easily identified by its immense wingspan.

The Netherlands is a paradise for birds and those who love to follow them around. The wetlands are a major migration stop for European birds, particularly Texel's Duinen van Texel National Park, Flevoland's Oostvaardersplassen Nature Reserve and the Delta. Just take geese: a dozen varieties, from white-fronted to pink-footed, break their V-formations to winter here. Along urban canals you'll see plenty of mallards, coots and swans as well as the lovely grebe with its regal head plumage. The large and graceful blue heron spears frogs and tiny fish in the ditches of the polder lands, but also loiters on canal boats in and out of town. The black cormorant, an accomplished diver with a wingspan of nearly 1m, is another regal bird.

Polar Bears

Polar bears, the world's largest land carnivore, are found in Svalbard, spending much of their time on pack or drift ice. Since protection in 1973, their numbers have increased to around 3500. A cruise is your main chance to see one. Despite weighing up to 720kg and measuring up to 2.5m long, polar bears are swift and manoeuvrable, thanks to the hair on the soles of their feet, which facilitates movement over ice and snow and provides additional insulation.

A polar bear's diet consists mostly of seals, beached whales, fish and birds, and only rarely do they eat reindeer or other land mammals (including humans). Polar-bear milk contains 30% fat (the richest of any carnivorous land mammal), which allows newborn cubs to grow quickly and survive extremely cold temperatures.

Birdwatching in Iceland

On coastal cliffs right around the country you can see huge numbers of seabirds, often in massive colonies. The best time for birdwatching is between June and mid-August, when puffins, gannets, guillemots, razorbills, kittiwakes and fulmars get twitchers excited. The best bird cliffs and colonies to look out for on your circumnavigation of the island:

Vestmannaeyjar Puffins swarm like frantic bees on this volcanic archipelago.

Hornstrandir This preserve offers an endless wall of stone housing numerous nesters.

Látrabjarg Famous in the Westfjords for the eponymous bird cliffs.

Langanes Remote windswept cliffs are home to prolific birdlife.

Ingólfshöfði This dramatic promontory has swooping skuas and posing puffins.

Grímsey On the Arctic Circle, with countless puffins and Arctic terns.

Drangey This storied Skagafjörður islet is festooned with puffins, guillemots, gannets and more.

Seafood is a staple of the Scandinavian diet

MARTINA LANOTTE/SHUTTERSTOCK ©

Food & Drink

Scandinavian cooking, once viewed as meatballs, herring and little else, has wowed the world in recent years. While the crest of the New Nordic wave has now passed, the 'foraging' ethos it championed has made a permanent mark. Its focus is on showcasing local produce prepared using traditional techniques and contemporary experimentation, and focused on clean, natural flavours.

New Nordic

Despite some claims of overexposure, New Nordic cuisine continues to garner lots of media attention and praise from food critics, bloggers and general gluttons across the globe. It is evolving, too, which all good trends should do.

The movement stems from 2004, when Nordic chefs attending a food symposium in Copenhagen created a 10-point manifesto defining the cuisine's aims. According to the manifesto, New Nordic is defined by seasonality, sustainability, local ingredients and produce, and the use of Nordic cooking methods to create food that originally and distinctly reflects Scandinavian culture, geography and history.

The movement threw the spotlight on Scandinavia's fantastic raw ingredients, from excellent pork products, beef, game and seafood, to root vegetables, wild berries and herbs.

It also serves as a showcase for rarer ingredients from the wider Nordic region, among them Greenlandic musk ox, horse mussels from the Faroe Islands, obscure berries from Finland, and truffles from the Swedish island of Gotland.

With this ethos at heart, numerous upmarket restaurants opened and have flourished across the region's capitals, which are all now a foodie's delight. The world's most famous New Nordic restaurant was Noma, four times topping the list of the World's 50 Best Restaurants. In its heyday, owner-chef René Redzepi eschewed all nonindigenous produce in his creations, including olive oil and tomatoes. Redzepi is renowned for playing with modest, often-overlooked ingredients and consulting food historians, digging up long-lost traditions. Famously, he also forages in the wilderness for herbs and plants. At Noma, the ingredients were then skilfully prepared using traditional techniques (curing, smoking, pickling and preserving) alongside contemporary experiments that included, among other things, ants.

From 2014 to 2017, Noma took to the road and set up in new homes (in Tokyo, Sydney and Tulum in Mexico) for a short spell, embracing indigenous ingredients and methods in each location. At the end of 2016, Noma's Copenhagen restaurant closed. There are plans to reopen in a different format, in a different location in the capital – stay tuned.

In the meantime, a newer wave of chefs (many of whom are Noma alumni) seem to be taking a less dogmatic approach, with their own seasonal, Nordic menus splashed with the odd foreign ingredient. Some are creating more casual restaurants, making New Nordic relatively affordable and more accessible.

A newer trend is super high-quality, contemporary 'non-Scandinavian' food made with the same precision and design savvy that defines New Nordic. While some may argue that this compromises the very concept of New Nordic, others see it as the next step in the evolution of contemporary Nordic cooking.

Old Nordic

Despite all the contemporary brilliance, traditional eateries still abound, and are focused on old-school staples like herring, salmon, pork and beef, accompanied by root vegetables, berries and mushrooms. The pleasures of wandering a Scandinavian food market are memorable, particularly in summer when the short but intense season festoons the land with nature's bounty.

Similarly, across the water in the southern Baltic, gastronomy has its roots planted firmly in the land, with livestock and game forming the basis of a hearty diet. Many national diets relied traditionally on pork, chicken, sausage, cabbage and potatoes, with smoked or pickled fish as an extra.

Weird & Wonderful Iceland

Eyeball a plate of old-fashioned Icelandic food, and chances are it will eyeball you back. In the past nothing was wasted, and some traditional specialities look more like horror-film props than food.

Svið Singed sheep's head (complete with eyes) sawn in two, boiled and eaten fresh or pickled.

Sviðasulta (head cheese) Made from bits of *svið* pressed into gelatinous loaves and pickled in whey.

Slátur (the word means 'slaughter') Comes in two forms: *lifrarpylsa* is liver sausage, made from a mishmash of sheep intestines, liver and lard tied up in a sheep's stomach and cooked (kind of like Scottish haggis). *Blóðmör* has added sheep's blood (and equates to blood pudding).

Best Shots

Denmark Akvavit, usually made from potatoes and caraway seeds, is swallowed straight with a chaser of beer.

Finland *Salmiakkikossu*, which combines dissolved liquorice sweets with the iconic Koskenkorva vodka or *fisu*, which does the same but with Fisherman's Friend pastilles.

Iceland The local schnapps is potent *brennivín*, which has the foreboding nickname *svarti dauði* (black death).

Norway The best Norwegian shot, *linje aquavit*, has spent time at sea, crossing the equator and back.

Sweden Fiery *snaps* is a potato-based, herb-infused shot.

Estonia Vana Tallinn is a sweet, strong syrupy liqueur that's a local favourite.

Latvia Not to be missed is Latvia's famous Black Balzām, which Goethe called 'the elixir of life'. This insidious jet-black, 45% proof concoction is a secret 18th-century recipe.

Poland *Wódka* (vodka) is the staple but look out for Goldwasser in Gdańsk; this liqueur dates back over 400 years and has flakes of gold suspended in it.

Russia Vodka, distilled from wheat, rye or, occasionally, potatoes, is the quintessential Russian alcohol.

Netherlands *Jenever* (ya-nay-ver; Dutch gin) is made from juniper berries and drunk chilled from a tiny glass filled to the brim.

Orkney A dram of local Highland Park or Scapa single malt whisky goes down a treat.

Súrsaðir hrútspungar Rams' testicles pickled in whey and pressed into a cake.

Hákarl Iceland's most famous stomach churner, *hákarl* is Greenland shark, an animal so inedible it has to rot away underground for six months before humans can even digest it. Most foreigners find the stench (a cross between ammonia and week-old roadkill) too much to bear, but it tastes better than it smells... It's the aftertaste that really hurts. A shot of *brennivín* is traditionally administered as an antidote.

Northern Foraging

The forage ethos is one of the principal drivers of New Nordic cuisine, but it's not a new concept. Scandinavians head out gleefully all summer to pick berries and mushrooms: blueberries, jewel-like wild strawberries, peppery chanterelles and the north's gloriously tart, creamy cloudberries, so esteemed that they feature on Finland's €2 coin. People here are enthusiastic kitchen gardeners too, with tender new potatoes and fresh dill featuring heavily. The variety and quality of fresh produce means that summer is by far the best time to eat in Scandinavia.

Drinking

Many Scandinavians are fond of a drink, but what gets knocked back in really alarming quantities is coffee. Finns slurp an incredible 12kg of coffee each year, more than twice as much per capita as Italians. Norway, Iceland, Denmark and Sweden aren't far behind. The daily ritual of a cup of percolated coffee (though espresso-style machines are slowly taking over) with a cake or pastry is sacred.

Beer is a staple, with generic lagers now facing stiff competition from the range of excellent microbreweries that have sprung up across the region, led by a name revered by beerhounds worldwide, Denmark's Mikkeller.

There's a good range of imported wine, though restaurants usually extract quite a premium for it.

Every country has its own favourite spirit. Spirits, wine and normal-strength beer can only be bought from government-run alcohol stores in Norway, Sweden, Finland and Iceland.

Fløibanen Funicular (p139), Bergen, Norway

Survival Guide

Directory A–Z

Customs Regulations

From non-EU to EU countries
For EU countries (ie Denmark, Sweden, Finland and Estonia), travellers arriving from outside the EU can bring duty-free goods up to the value of €430 without declaration. You can also bring in up to 16L of beer, 4L of wine, 2L of liquors not exceeding 22% vol or 1L of spirits, 200 cigarettes or 250g of tobacco.

Within the EU If you're coming from another EU country, there is no restriction on the value of purchases for your own use.

Other Nordic countries
Norway, Iceland and the Faroe Islands have lower limits.

Dangers & Annoyances

Scandinavia and Northern Europe are very safe places to travel, with very low crime rates, but you should always employ common sense.

o Pickpockets and purse-snatchers operate in crowded places. Keep your valuables close.

o Extreme winter temperatures must be taken seriously: wear proper protective clothing when outdoors.

Climate

Berlin

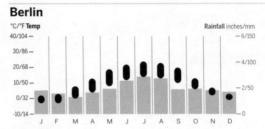

Reykjavík

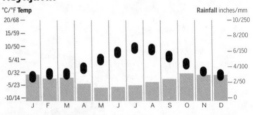

St Petersburg

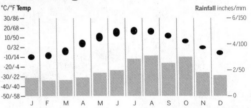

o In northern Scandinavia, biting insects, such as mosquitoes, can be a major annoyance in summer.

Etiquette

Greetings Shake hands with men, women and children when meeting them for the first time.
Shoes Take them off when entering someone's home.
Saunas Shower before entering a sauna. Naked is normally the way to go.

Gifts Bring flowers, pastries, wine or chocolate when invited to someone's house.

Electricity

In the Netherlands, Germany, Denmark, Norway, Finland, Iceland, Russia, Estonia, Latvia and Poland access electricity (230V, 50Hz AC) with a European plug with two round pins (type C and F). In Denmark plug type K is also used. Scotland uses 230V, 50Hz; UK-type plug with three flat pins.

Type C
220V/50Hz

Type G
230V/50Hz

Type F
230V/50Hz

Type K
230V/50Hz

Gay & Lesbian Travellers

Northern European nations are very tolerant, although public displays of affection are less common in rural areas, particularly Lapland. In general, Eastern European nations are a little less tolerant, and homophobia is a problem in Russia.

Health

Travel in Scandinavia and Northern Europe presents very few health problems.

The level of hygiene is high and there are no endemic diseases.

The extreme winter climate poses a risk; you must be aware of the risk of hypothermia and frostbite.

The standard of health care is extremely high and English is widely spoken by doctors and medical-clinic staff. Even if you are covered for health care here, you may be required to pay a per-visit fee as a local would. This is likely to be around €30 to €100 for a doctor or hospital visit.

Insurance

Citizens of the European Economic Area (EEA) are covered for emergency medical treatment in other EEA countries (including Denmark, Finland, Iceland, Norway and Sweden) on presentation of a European Health Insurance Card (EHIC), though they may be liable to pay a daily or per-appointment fee as a local would. Enquire about EHICs at your health centre, travel agency or (in some countries) post office well in advance of travel.

Citizens from countries outside the EEA should find out if there is a reciprocal arrangement for free medical care between their country and the country visited. If not, travel health insurance is recommended.

Comprehensive travel insurance to cover theft, loss and medical problems is highly recommended.

Internet Access

○ Wireless (wi-fi) hot spots are rife. Numerous cafes and bars offer the service for free. Some cities have free public wi-fi across the centre.

○ Data is cheap. Buy a local SIM card, pop it in an unlocked phone, laptop or USB modem, and away you go.

○ Internet cafes are increasingly uncommon, but libraries provide free or very cheap internet service.

Money

ATMs Widespread, even in small places. This is the best way to access cash. Find out what your home bank will charge you per withdrawal before you go as you may be better off taking out larger sums.

Cash cards Much like debit or credit cards but are loaded with a set amount of money. They also have the advantage of lower withdrawal fees than your bank might otherwise charge you.

Charge cards Includes cards like American Express and Diners Club. Less widely accepted than credit cards because they charge merchants high commissions.

Debit and credit cards Scandinavians love using plastic, even for small transactions, and you'll find that debit and credit cards are the way to go here. In Northern Europe credit cards are becoming more widely accepted, but it's best not to assume that you'll be able to use one.

Foreign currencies Easily exchanged, with rates usually slightly better at exchange offices rather than banks. Avoid exchanging at airports if possible; you'll get better rates elsewhere. Always ask about the rate and commission before handing over your cash.

Tax A value-added tax (VAT) applies to most goods and services throughout the region. International visitors from outside the EEA can claim back the VAT above a set minimum amount on purchases that are being taken out of the country. The procedure for making the claim is usually pretty straightforward.

Tipping Isn't required in Scandinavia. But if you round up the bill or leave a little something in recognition of good service, it won't be refused. In Northern Europe 'service charges' are increasingly added to bills. In theory this means you're not obliged to tip. In practice that money often doesn't go to the server. Don't pay twice. If the service charge is optional,

Exchange Rates

	Australia A$1	Canada C$1	Eurozone €1	Japan ¥100	New Zealand NZ$1	UK£1	US$1
Danish krone (kr; DKK)	4.99	5.11	7.45	5.63	4.55	8.47	6.24
Euro (€; EUR)	0.67	0.69	-	0.76	0.61	1.14	0.84
Icelandic króna (kr; ISK)	85.10	87.19	126.98	95.94	77.53	144.46	106.30
Norwegian krone (kr; NOK)	6.28	6.44	6.37	7.08	5.72	10.67	7.85
Polandish złoty (zł)	2.73	2.88	4.12	3.02	2.50	5.82	3.73
Swedish krona (kr; SEK)	6.37	6.53	6.51	7.19	5.81	10.82	7.96
Russian rouble (R)	R48	R48	R70	R54	R45	R78	R60
British pounds sterling (£)	0.57	0.59	0.84	0.72	0.55	-	0.75

For current exchange rates, see www.xe.com.

remove it and pay a tip. If it's not optional, don't tip. If you tip, 5% to 10% will usually suffice.

Travellers cheques Rapidly disappearing but still accepted in big hotels and exchange offices.

Public Holidays

Major Christian holidays are generally taken across the region, with specific national public holidays added to them.

New Year's Day 1 January
Good Friday March or April
May Day 1 May
Pentecost/Whitsun May/June
Christmas Day 25 December
Boxing Day 26 December

Telephone

To call abroad dial 00 (the IAC, or international access code from Scandinavia and Northern Europe), the country code (CC) for the country you are calling, the local area code (usually dropping the leading zero if there is one) and then the number. In Russia dial 8, wait for a second dial tone, then dial 10, then the country code etc.

Emergencies The emergency number is the same throughout Scandinavia and Northern Europe: 112. In Russia it is 01 (fire), 02 (police) and 03 (ambulance).

Internet Calling via the internet is a practical and cheap solution

Time Zones

City	Time in Winter	Time in Summer
New York	11am (UTC -5)	noon (UTC -4)
Reykjavík	4pm (UTC)	4pm (UTC; no summer time)
London	4pm (UTC)	5pm (UTC +1)
Oslo, Copenhagen, Stockholm, Berlin, Gdańsk, Amsterdam	5pm (UTC +1)	6pm (UTC +2)
Helsinki, Tallinn, Rīga	6pm (UTC +2)	7pm (UTC +3)
St Petersburg	7pm (UTC +3)	7pm (UTC +3; no summer time)

for making international calls, whether from a laptop, tablet or smartphone.

Mobile phones Bring a mobile that's not tied to a specific network (unlocked) and buy local SIM cards.

Phone boxes Almost nonexistent in most areas.

Phonecards Easily bought for cheaper international calls.

Reverse-charge (collect) calls Usually possible, and communicating with the local operator in English should not be much of a problem.

Roaming Roaming charges for EU phones within the EU have been abolished and are low for other EEA countries.

Time

Scandinavia and Northern Europe sprawl across several time zones. The 24-hour clock is widely used. Note that Europe and the US move clocks forward

and back at slightly different times.

Toilets

Public toilets are usually good, but often expensive; they can cost €1 or €2 or equivalent to enter.

Tourist Information

Facilities Generally excellent, with piles of regional and national brochures, helpful free maps and friendly employees. Staff are often multilingual, speaking English and perhaps other major European languages.

Locations Offices at train stations or centrally (often in the town hall or central square) in most towns.

Opening hours Longer office hours over summer, reduced

hours over winter; smaller offices may open only during peak summer months.

Services Will book transport reservations and tours; a small charge may apply.

Websites Most towns have a tourist information portal, with good information about sights and more.

Travellers with Disabilities

○ Scandinavia leads the world as the best-equipped region for travellers with disabilities. By law, most institutions must provide ramps, lifts and special toilets for people with disabilities; all new restaurants must install disabled facilities. Most trains and city buses are also accessible by wheelchair.

○ Some national parks offer accessible nature trails, and cities have ongoing projects in place designed to maximise disabled access in all aspects of urban life.

○ Iceland is a little further behind the rest of the region

Practicalities

Smoking Widely forbidden, but some countries have dedicated smoking rooms in hotels and smoking areas in bars. Vaping laws depend on the country.

Weights & Measures The metric system is used across the region.

so check access issues before you travel. Scandinavian tourist office websites generally contain good information on disabled access.

○ Before leaving home, get in touch with your national support organisation – preferably the 'travel officer' if there is one. They often have complete libraries devoted to travel and can put you in touch with agencies that specialise in tours for the disabled. One such agency in the UK is Can Be Done (www.canbedone.co.uk).

○ Download Lonely Planet's free Accessible Travel guide from http://lptravel.to/AccessibleTravel.

Visas

○ Denmark, Estonia, Finland, Iceland, Norway, Sweden Germany, the Netherlands and Poland are all part of the Schengen area. A valid passport or EU identity card is required to enter the region. A Schengen visa can be obtained by applying to an embassy or consulate of any country in the Schengen area.

○ Most Western nationals don't need a tourist visa for stays of less than three months. South Africans, Indians and Chinese, however, are among those who need a Schengen visa.

○ All nationalities require a visa to enter Russia. Apply at least a month in advance of your trip.

Transport

Getting There & Away

Scandinavia is easily accessed from the rest of Europe and beyond. There are direct flights from numerous destinations into Sweden, Norway, Denmark and Finland. There is less choice to Iceland.

Flights, cars and tours can be booked online at lonelyplanet.com/bookings.

Air

As well as the many national carriers that fly directly into Scandinavia's airports, there are several budget options. These routes change frequently and are best investigated online.

Airports & Airlines

The following are major hubs:

Berlin-Schönefeld (www.berlin-airport.de) Berlin.

Berlin-Tegel (www.berlin-airport.de) Berlin.

Copenhagen Kastrup Airport (www.cph.dk) Denmark.

Helsinki Vantaa Airport (www.helsinki-vantaa.fi) Finland.

Oslo Gardermoen Airport (www.osl.no) Norway.

Pulkovo International Airport (www.pulkovoairport.ru) St Petersburg.

Reykjavík Keflavík Airport
(www.kefairport.is) Iceland.

Schiphol Airport (www.
schiphol.nl) Amsterdam.

Stockholm Arlanda Airport
(www.swedavia.com/arlanda)
Sweden.

SAS (www.flysas.com) is the
national carrier for Sweden,
Norway and Denmark, **Fin-
nair** (www.finnair.com) for
Finland, **Icelandair** (www.
icelandair.com) for Iceland
and **Lufthansa** (www.
lufthansa.com) for Germany.
Other important regional
airlines include **Norwegian**
(www.norwegian.com), **LOT**
(www.lot.com) and **EasyJet**
(www.easyjet.com).

Train

○ Apart from trains into
Finland from Russia, the
rail route into Scandina-
via goes from Germany
into Denmark, then on to
Sweden and then Norway
via the Copenhagen–Malmö
bridge-tunnel connection.
Hamburg and Cologne are
the main gateways in Ger-
many for this route.

○ See the exceptional Man
in Seat 61 website (www.
seat61.com) for details of all
train routes.

○ Contact Deutsche Bahn
(www.bahn.com) for details
of frequent special offers
and for reservations and
tickets.

○ For more information on
international rail travel check
out www.voyages-sncf.com.

Sea

Ferry services are year-
round between major cities:

book ahead in summer, at
weekends and if travelling
with a vehicle. Many boats
are amazingly cheap if you
travel deck class (without a
cabin). Many ferry lines offer
50% discounts for holders of
Eurail, Scanrail and InterRail
passes. Ferry companies
have detailed timetables and
fares on their websites. Fares
vary according to season.

Getting Around

Getting around populated
areas is generally a breeze,
with efficient public transport and snappy connec-
tions. Most travellers will
find that areas of interest
in cities can be easily
traversed by foot or bicycle.

Bicycle

Scandinavia and Northern
Europe are exceptionally
bike friendly, with loads
of cycle paths, courteous
motorists, easy public

transport options and lots of
flattish, picturesque terrain.

Hire bikes from train
station bike-rental counters
and tourist offices; several
cities have bike-sharing
schemes accessible for a
small fee.

Local Transport

Cities often have an excellent integrated transport
networks of buses, trains
and trams. Buying tickets
or a travel pass is usually
possible at cruise terminals
or on board.

Taxi

Taxis in Europe are metered
and rates are usually high.
There might also be sup-
plements for things such as
time of day, location of pick-
up and extra passengers.

Good bus, rail and under-
ground railway networks
often render taxis unneces-
sary, but if you need one in
a hurry, they can be found
idling near train stations or
outside big hotels.

Climate Change & Travel

Every form of transport that relies on carbon-based
fuel generates CO_2, the main cause of human-induced
climate change. Modern travel is dependent on aero-
planes, which might use less fuel per kilometre per person than most cars but travel much greater distances.
The altitude at which aircraft emit gases (including CO_2)
and particles also contributes to their climate change
impact. Many websites offer 'carbon calculators' that
allow people to estimate the carbon emissions generat-
ed by their journey and, for those who wish to do so, to
offset the impact of the greenhouse gases emitted with
contributions to portfolios of climate-friendly initiatives
throughout the world. Lonely Planet offsets the carbon
footprint of all staff and author travel.

Behind the Scenes

Acknowledgements

Climate map data adapted from Peel MC, Finlayson BL & McMahon TA (2007) 'Updated World Map of the Köppen-Geiger Climate Classification', Hydrology and Earth System Sciences, 11, 163344.

Illustrations p188–9 by Javier Zarracina.

This Book

This first edition of Lonely Planet's *Cruise Ports Scandinavia & Northern Europe* guidebook was researched and written by Andy Symington, Alexis Averbuck, Oliver Berry, Abigail Blasi, Cristian Bonetto, Marc Di Duca, Catherine Le Nevez, Hugh McNaughtan, Becky Ohlsen, Leonid Ragozin, Simon Richmond, Andrea Schulte-Peevers, Regis St Louis and Donna Wheeler. This guidebook was produced by the following:

Destination Editors Daniel Fahey, Gemma Graham, Niamh O'Brien, Clifton Wilkinson, Branislava Vladisavljevic

Product Editors Kathryn Rowan, Kate Mathews

Senior Cartographer Valentina Kremenchutskaya

Book Designer Clara Monitto

Assisting Editors Andrea Dobbin, Paul Harding, Victoria Harrison, Anne Mulvaney, Ross Taylor, Kira Tverskaya

Assisting Book Designers Nicholas Colicchia, Virginia Moreno, Michael Weldon

Cover Researcher Campbell McKenzie

Thanks to Ronan Abayawickrema, Liz Heynes, Alison Ridgway, Tony Wheeler

Send Us Your Feedback

We love to hear from travellers – your comments keep us on our toes and help make our books better. Our well-travelled team reads every word on what you loved or loathed about this book. Although we cannot reply individually to postal submissions, we always guarantee that your feedback goes straight to the appropriate authors, in time for the next edition. Each person who sends us information is thanked in the next edition, the most useful submissions are rewarded with a selection of digital PDF chapters.

Visit lonelyplanet.com/contact to submit your updates and suggestions or to ask for help. Our award-winning website also features inspirational travel stories, news and discussions.

Note: We may edit, reproduce and incorporate your comments in Lonely Planet products such as guidebooks, websites and digital products, so let us know if you don't want your comments reproduced or your name acknowledged. For a copy of our privacy policy visit lonelyplanet.com/privacy.

A – Z
Index

Symbols & Map Key

Look for these symbols to quickly identify listings:

- ◉ Sights
- ✚ Activities
- ◉ Courses
- ◉ Tours
- ✸ Festivals & Events
- ✕ Eating
- ◉ Drinking
- ✦ Entertainment
- ◉ Shopping
- ◉ Information & Transport

These symbols and abbreviations give vital information for each listing:

- ⬤ Sustainable or green recommendation
- **FREE** No payment required

- ☏ Telephone number
- ☺ Opening hours
- P Parking
- ⊖ Nonsmoking
- ❋ Air-conditioning
- @ Internet access
- ☎ Wi-fi access
- ☷ Swimming pool

- ☐ Bus
- ⊛ Ferry
- ▣ Tram
- ▣ Train
- ▣ English-language menu
- ▸ Vegetarian selection
- ♦ Family-friendly

Find your best experiences with these Great For... icons.

- Art & Culture
- Beaches
- Budget
- Cafe/Coffee
- Cycling
- Detour
- Drinking
- Entertainment
- Events
- Family Travel
- Food & Drink
- History
- Local Life
- Nature & Wildlife
- Photo Op
- Scenery
- Shopping
- Short Trip
- Sport
- Walking
- Winter Travel

Sights

- Beach
- Bird Sanctuary
- Buddhist
- Castle/Palace
- Christian
- Confucian
- Hindu
- Islamic
- Jain
- Jewish
- Monument
- Museum/Gallery/ Historic Building
- Ruin
- Shinto
- Sikh
- Taoist
- Winery/Vineyard
- Zoo/Wildlife Sanctuary
- Other Sight

Points of Interest

- Bodysurfing
- Camping
- Cafe
- Canoeing/Kayaking
- Course/Tour
- Diving
- Drinking & Nightlife
- Eating
- Entertainment
- Sento Hot Baths/ Onsen
- Shopping
- Skiing
- Sleeping
- Snorkelling
- Surfing
- Swimming/Pool
- Walking
- Windsurfing
- Other Activity

Information

- Bank
- Embassy/Consulate
- Hospital/Medical
- Internet
- Police
- Post Office
- Telephone
- Toilet
- Tourist Information
- Other Information

Geographic

- Beach
- Gate
- Hut/Shelter
- Lighthouse
- Lookout
- Mountain/Volcano
- Oasis
- Park
- Pass
- Picnic Area
- Waterfall

Transport

- Airport
- BART station
- Border crossing
- Boston T station
- Bus
- Cable car/Funicular
- Cycling
- Ferry
- Metro/MRT station
- Monorail
- Parking
- Petrol station
- Subway/S-Bahn/ Skytrain station
- Taxi
- Train station/Railway
- Tram
- Tube Station
- Underground/ U-Bahn station
- Other Transport

Andrea Schulte-Peevers

Born and raised in Germany and educated in London and at UCLA, Andrea has travelled the distance to the moon and back in her visits to some 75 countries. She has earned her living as a professional travel writer for over two decades and authored or contributed to nearly 100 Lonely Planet titles as well as to newspapers, magazines and websites around the world. She also works as a travel consultant, translator and editor. Andrea's destination expertise is especially strong when it comes to Germany, Dubai and the UAE, Crete and the Caribbean Islands. Despite a passion for her home town, she packed her bags right after school, decamping first to London, then to Los Angeles, where she haunted the hallowed halls of UCLA in pursuit of a degree in English literature. Equipped with such highly sought-after credentials, she fearlessly embarked on a career in journalism, soon getting tapped by Lonely Planet for her Germany expertise.

Regis St Louis

Regis grew up in a small town in the American Midwest – the kind of place that fuels big dreams of travel – and he developed an early fascination with foreign dialects and world cultures. He spent his formative years learning Russian and a handful of Romance languages, which served him well on journeys across much of the globe. Regis has contributed to more than 50 Lonely Planet titles, covering destinations across six continents. His travels have taken him from the mountains of Kamchatka to remote island villages in Melanesia, and to many grand urban landscapes. When not on the road, he lives in New Orleans. Follow him on www.instagram.com/regisstlouis.

Donna Wheeler

Donna has written guidebooks for Lonely Planet for over ten years, including the Italy, Norway, Belgium, Africa, Tunisia, Algeria, France, Austria and Australia titles. She is the author of *Paris Precincts,* and is reporter for Italian contemporary art publisher My Art Guides. She became a travel writer after various careers as a commissioning editor, creative director, digital producer and content strategist. Born and bred in Sydney, Australia, Donna fell in love with Melbourne's moody bluestone streets as a teenage art student. She has divided her time between there and her beloved home town for over two decades, along with residential stints in Turin, Paris, Bordeaux, New York, London and rural Ireland. Donna travels widely (and deeply) in Europe, North Africa, the US and Asia.

Abigail Blasi

A freelance travel writer, Abigail has lived and worked in London, Rome, Hong Kong and Copenhagen. Lonely Planet have sent her to India, Egypt, Tunisia, Mauritania, Mali, Italy, Portugal, Malta and round Britain. She writes regularly for newspapers and magazines, such as the *Independent*, the *Telegraph*, and *Lonely Planet Traveller*. She has three children and they often come along for the ride. Twitter/Instagram: @abiwhere

Cristian Bonetto

Cristian has contributed to over 30 Lonely Planet guides to date, including New York City, Italy, Venice & the Veneto, Naples & the Amalfi Coast, Denmark, Copenhagen, Sweden and Singapore. Lonely Planet work aside, his musings on travel, food, culture and design appear in numerous publications around the world, including *The Telegraph* (UK) and *Corriere del Mezzogiorno* (Italy). When not on the road, you'll find the reformed playwright and TV scriptwriter slurping espresso in his beloved hometown, Melbourne. Instagram: rexcat75.

Marc Di Duca

A travel author for the last decade, Marc has worked for Lonely Planet in Siberia, Slovakia, Bavaria, England, Ukraine, Austria, Poland, Croatia, Portugal, Madeira and on the Trans-Siberian Railway, as well as writing and updating tens of other guides for other publishers. When not on the road, Marc lives between Sandwich, Kent and Mariánské Lázně in the Czech Republic with his wife and two sons.

Catherine Le Nevez

Catherine's wanderlust kicked in when she roadtripped across Europe from her Parisian base aged four, and she's been hitting the road at every opportunity since, travelling to around 60 countries and completing her Doctorate of Creative Arts in Writing, Masters in Professional Writing, and postgrad qualifications in Editing and Publishing along the way. Over the past dozen-plus years she's written scores of Lonely Planet guides and articles covering Paris, France, Europe and far beyond. Her work has also appeared in numerous online and print publications. Topping Catherine's list of travel tips is to travel without any expectations.

Hugh McNaughtan

A former English lecturer, Hugh swapped grant applications for visa applications, and turned his love of travel into a full-time thing. Having done a bit of restaurant-reviewing in his home town (Melbourne)

he's now eaten his way across four continents. He's never happier than when on the road with his two daughters. Except perhaps on the cricket field.

Becky Ohlsen

Becky is a freelance writer, editor and critic based in Portland, Oregon. She writes guidebooks and travel stories about Scandinavia, Portland and elsewhere for Lonely Planet. Becky grew up with a thick book of Swedish fairy tales illustrated by John Bauer, so the deep black forests of Norrland hold particular fascination for her. Hiking through them, she's alert for trolls and tomtes (which, to the untrained eye, look just like big rocks). Though raised in the mountains of Colorado, Becky has been exploring Sweden since childhood, while visiting her grandparents and other relatives in Stockholm and parts north. She's thoroughly hooked on pickled herring and saffron ice cream but has nothing good to say about Swedish beer. When she's not covering ground for LP, Becky is working on a book about motorcycles and the paradoxical appeal of risk.

Leonid Ragozin

Leonid Ragozin studied beach dynamics at the Moscow State University, but for want of decent beaches in Russia, he switched to journalism and spent 12 years voyaging through different parts of the BBC, with a break for a four-year stint as a foreign correspondent for the Russian *Newsweek*. Leonid is currently a freelance journalist focusing largely on the conflict between Russia and Ukraine (both his Lonely Planet destinations), which prompted him to leave Moscow and find a new home in Rīga.

Simon Richmond

Journalist and photographer Simon Richmond has specialised as a travel writer since the early 1990s and first worked for Lonely Planet in 1999 on their Central Asia guide. He's long since stopped counting the number of guidebooks he's researched and written for the company, but countries covered include Australia, China, India, Iran, Japan, Korea, Malaysia, Mongolia, Myanmar (Burma), Russia, Singapore, South Africa and Turkey. For Lonely Planet's website he's penned features on topics from the world's best swimming pools to the joys of Urban Sketching – follow him on Instagram to see some of his photos and sketches. His travel features have been published in newspapers and magazines around the world, including in the UK's *Independent, Guardian, Times, Daily Telegraph* and *Royal Geographical Society Magazine;* and Australia's *Sydney Morning Herald* and *Australian Financial Review Magazine.*

Our Story

A beat-up old car, a few dollars in the pocket and a sense of adventure. In 1972 that's all Tony and Maureen Wheeler needed for the trip of a lifetime – across Europe and Asia overland to Australia. It took several months, and at the end – broke but inspired – they sat at their kitchen table writing and stapling together their first travel guide, *Across Asia on the Cheap*. Within a week they'd sold 1500 copies. Lonely Planet was born.

Today, Lonely Planet has offices in Franklin, London, Melbourne, Oakland, Dublin, Beijing and Delhi, with more than 600 staff and writers. We share Tony's belief that 'a great guidebook should do three things: inform, educate and amuse'.

Our Writers

Andy Symington

Andy has written or worked on over a hundred books and other updates for Lonely Planet (especially in Europe and Latin America) and other publishing companies, and has published articles on numerous subjects for a variety of newspapers, magazines and websites. He part-owns and operates a rock bar, has written a novel and is currently working on several fiction and non-fiction writing projects. Andy, from Australia, moved to Northern Spain many years ago. When he's not off with a backpack in some far-flung corner of the world, he can probably be found watching the tragically poor local football team or tasting local wines after a long walk in the nearby mountains.

Alexis Averbuck

Alexis Averbuck has travelled and lived all over the world, from Sri Lanka to Ecuador, Zanzibar and Antarctica. In recent years she's been living on the Greek island of Hydra and exploring her adopted homeland and adventuring along Iceland's surreal lava fields, sparkling fjords and glacier tongues. A travel writer for over two decades, Alexis has lived in Antarctica for a year, crossed the Pacific by sailboat and written books on her journeys through Asia, Europe and the Americas. She's also a painter – visit www. alexisaverbuck.com – and promotes travel and adventure on video and television.

Oliver Berry

Oliver Berry is a writer and photographer from Cornwall. He has worked for Lonely Planet for more than a decade, covering destinations from Cornwall to the Cook Islands, and has worked on more than 30 guidebooks. He is also a regular contributor to many newspapers and magazines, including *Lonely Planet Traveller*. His writing has won several awards, including The Guardian Young Travel Writer of the Year and the TNT Magazine People's Choice Award. His first trip abroad was to the south of France at the tender age of two, and since then his travels have carried him several times round the globe.

→ More Writers ←

STAY IN TOUCH LONELYPLANET.COM/CONTACT

AUSTRALIA The Malt Store, Level 3, 551 Swanston St, Carlton, Victoria 3053
☏ 03 8379 8000,
fax 03 8379 8111

IRELAND Digital Depot, Roe Lane (off Thomas St), Digital Hub, Dublin 8, D08 TCV4

USA 124 Linden Street, Oakland, CA 94607
☏ 510 250 6400,
toll free 800 275 8555,
fax 510 893 8572

UK 240 Blackfriars Road, London SE1 8NW
☏ 020 3771 5100,
fax 020 3771 5101

 twitter.com/ lonelyplanet   facebook.com/ lonelyplanet   instagram.com/ lonelyplanet   youtube.com/ lonelyplanet   lonelyplanet.com/ newsletter